My Life--It's Nothing Personal, and Neither is Yours

A Spiritual Mystery

By Marie Yvette Simmons
Juliana Whitten, Ghostwriter
Presented By La Wanda Marrero

Copyright © 2022
All rights reserved. Published and printed in the United States of America.
No part of this book may be reproduced or transmitted in any form or by any means without the written permission of author.
Edited by Juliana Whitten and La Wanda Marrero
Published by Unstoppable Publishing Company
ISBN 978-1-7358181-2-2

TABLE OF CONTENTS

Author's Biography
Dedication
Acknowledgements
Forward

Chapter 1: *Childhood ~~The Journey Begins*............Page...12

Chapter 2: *Adolescence ~~ The Search For Identity*.....Page....31

Chapter 3: *Young Adult ~~ Self Definition*................Page...51

Chapter 4: *Four Midlife ~~ Self Expression*................Page...75

Chapter 5: *Landmines ~~ Exploration of Family Codependencies, Addictions and Triangles*..................................Page..140

Chapter 6: *Landmarks ~~Confrontation of Shadows*.....Page..247

Chapter 7: *Maturity ~~ Self Acceptance* ....Page..353

Chapter 8: *Old Age ~~ The Harvest and Passing It On*..Page..505

Chapter 9: *The Mystery ~~Who Murdered Marie?*....... Page..560

Reflections of Family and Friends........................Page..594

My Life--It's Nothing Personal, and Neither is Yours

A Spiritual Mystery

~AUTHOR'S BIOGRAPHY~

Marie Simmons was born in 1936 in St. Louis, Missouri, where her African American family struggled with many of the problems resulting from racism, poverty, and inadequate education. Marie is the youngest of thirteen children and the first in her family to graduate from college. She earned a master's degree in social work from Washington University. She has held a variety of professional positions, including the Director of Social Services at UCSF for twelve years, where she was also an assistant professor in the Department of Pediatrics. During a two-year sabbatical from her directorship, she developed and facilitated a Cultural Awareness and Race Relations Education program for the UCSF campus: faculty, staff, and students. She has more than forty years' experience working as a psychotherapist, family counselor, administrator, consultant, teacher, and researcher. She has written a number of professional papers and lectures.

Ms. Simmons was married briefly and raised many children for many years. She assisted many adult children to grow up by teaching them the art of gentle self-discipline. She was raised

Baptist but always believed that the Spirit is universal. She has been a seeker all of her life and has studied many religions ranging from Christianity to Hinduism to Buddhism and everything in between. She was surprised to discover that in truth all these disciplines are saying the same thing: We are all one, and we should love one another as Ourself. She is convinced beyond any doubt that there are many roads to the mountain, but only one top, and the top is Love. She asked God to teach her to love indiscriminately and unconditionally. The first lesson love taught her was that it is not personal. For the past ten years she has been involved in an intense physical and mental experience of a spiritual transformation which has led to the writing of this book.

DEDICATION

I dedicate this book in loving memory of my mother, who continues to light my journey with her wisdom, courage, strength, and love, and that feels very personal!

ACKNOWLEDGEMENTS

To my good friend Julie Whitten, without whose help this book may never have been written and certainly would not have happened when it did. Julie's enthusiasm, encouragement, availability, and unconditional love and acceptance accompanied me on the journey of writing this book. She is especially suited to the task because she knows me so well and has an excellent command of the English language. She has shared and/or witnessed many of my life experiences. Our common values, long term commitment, and work ethic provided a solid foundation; and our similar life views and untamed sense of humor made it fun.

To my daughter Benita Turner, for her unconditional love, acceptance, validation, and concrete support. I am continually amazed and humbled by her steadfast devotion. She is a living example of the Bible's teaching to honor our fathers and mothers.

To my daughter La Wanda Marrero, for her love, support, and helpfulness. I am inspired by her strength, courage and devotion to her walk in the Spirit. She is willing to meet life on its own terms and to grow with it. I appreciate her positive attitude and ability to see the humor in any situation, while experiencing the pain. She is a true witness to God's power to heal and transform.

FOREWORD

The book is a lighthearted, contemporary, funny application of ancient wisdom which illuminates the mysteries and majesty of everyday life experiences. It demonstrates one guaranteed path to self-realization while acknowledging that there are many others. It tells how one person was able to gradually let go of fear thoughts and to become present in the moment of Now, where love is available and all there is. It touches the paths of some of the better-known religions and philosophies, and delights in the fact that they all agree: 1. That there is only one source of life, and 2. That the highest form of self-realization is love. The book acknowledges the oneness of all things and celebrates universal kinship. Imagery and stories are used as a bridge between writer and reader, joining them in feelings and emotions which are universal and timeless. Everyday life experiences come alive with the demonstration of the writer's dramatic shifts in consciousness, allowing the reader to witness the impersonal nature of experiences. The author dances playfully and artistically with life's major challenges. Stages and tasks of psycho-social development provide the background.

The book spotlights the ways and rewards of meeting life on life's terms and taking responsibility for our choices. Our life is a collection of the results of the choices we have made. Readers of all persuasions, positions, and beliefs will find themselves reflected in the human struggles of wanting to be first, right, better, more important, etc., and at the same time wanting to be loved.

Change in conventional thinking is encouraged with the offer of the opportunity to experience everyday life in a new way. Response to this invitation liberates the readers' awareness to their personal power to choose, inspiring self-mastery, self-love, and the love of life. The good news is we were born free with the power to choose our thoughts. When we change our thinking, we change our world. We can choose to allow the gentle paddles of love to teach us to be at peace in the eye of the storm and row, row, row our boats gently down life's many streams.

On one level of awareness, I felt I was complete with the various roles I had played on life's stage. As satisfying as some of them were, I had no desire to "become the role," and I knew I would have to let it go when the time came, or become stuck in it.

I had raised five girls most of their lives and contributed to the rearing of ten other children and many adults.

I had taken care of my mother who was a quadriplegic for three years, creating a hospital room with all the accoutrements in my living room. On one occasion when my mother had hit her tolerance wall she asked me why I thought she had to suffer so much. I said, "I don't know, but if there is any meaning to suffering, I promise I will find out what it is." This was a pivotal moment in my life. Subsequently I learned that pain is inevitable but suffering is optional.

I had achieved what was for me the top of the line in my profession.

I owned a beautiful home in one of the most desirable cities in the world. I wore designer clothes and drove a fancy sports car.

Although marriage was never a goal, I was married briefly. I have had several romantic relationships, some better than others, but I knew there had to be something more in life.

I realized that the first fifty years I was trying to conform to society's rules and expectations, yet I felt unfulfilled. I vowed that my next fifty years would be directed toward exploring my own truth. I asked God to teach me how to love unconditionally.

I am a free spirit as we all are. I am also a true seeker. I wanted to understand who I am really and why I'm here. I truly believe "When the student is ready, the teacher will appear, in the form best suited for the student's learning." My body emerged as the master teacher to teach me love and lead me to wholeness.

(Taoist scripture, written 500 BC, translated as "The Way of Life.")

There is a thing, confusedly formed

Born before Heaven and Earth

Silent and Void

It stands alone and does not change,

Goes round and round and does not weary.

It is capable of being the Mother of the World.

I do not know its true name,

So I call it 'The Way' (the Tao).

As a thing, the way is shadowy and indistinct

Indistinct and shadowy,

Yet within it is an image,

Shadowy and indistinct.

Yet, within it is a substance,

Dim and dark.

Yet within it is an Essence.

You are a part of this essence.

(Your life is Real--but it is not personal.)

CHAPTER ONE

CHILDHOOD~~ THE JOURNEY BEGINS

"Every baby comes with the message that God is not yet discouraged of man."   R. Tagore

Although I have no memory of my life in the womb, it's probably safe to say it must have been turbulent. My mother, Hattie Ann Ford, had already given birth to twelve children, and was experiencing menopause at thirty-seven when I was conceived. She and my father were not getting along, and she shouldered most of the responsibilities for keeping the family going. Needless to say, I was not planned and by her own admission she was not looking forward to a thirteenth child. However, later in life she told me that I was a blessing and her gift from God.

To add insult to injury, my birth was very difficult and life threatening. I am told that my mother was in labor for fifteen hours while I simply refused to come out. I was born at home and delivered country style by a very obese white general practitioner who drank gallons of water during my delivery. I'm told that my siblings kept anxious watch outside the door, fearing for my mother's life. When the doctor was finally able to extricate me from the womb, he apparently had to beat me mercilessly before I would cry. I think I must have changed my mind about coming here.

According to my oldest sister, she and all of the family were angry at me for almost killing my mother. My sister often told me that I was very black and ugly, and she would pinch me on various parts of my body whenever she got the opportunity. She even said that she had planned to drown me when my mother went to work in the cotton fields. Fortunately the plan never materialized. I was lucky enough to be breastfed, probably for financial reasons. I was told that I toilet trained myself at six months old--I would slide out of bed and urinate on the floor. Although I had never crawled, the story goes that I walked at ten months when a woman offered me peanuts.

I grew up in the late thirties and forties in a working-class black ghetto in the inner city of St. Louis, Missouri. Segregation and racial discrimination were alive and well, and we seldom left the little cocoon of our neighborhood. We did not encounter white America very often, just on occasional visits downtown or to Grand Avenue where we strolled and looked in restaurants and watched white people dining in splendor and wearing expensive clothes.

At home we played freely in each other's yards and houses. One of our favorite locations for an imaginary theater was the parking lot of an abandoned filling station, where we displayed our talents entertaining each other with impersonations of Pearl Bailey, Etta James, Dinah Washington, and other favorite black stars. My niece still recalls our gyrations and fascination with the song "Put the Blame on Me, Boy." What an image! Little did we know that we were preparing for our future victimhood at the hands of men.

I remember discussions on the radio and in my home about the "Japs" and World War II. I stood with my mother in long lines to receive rationed sugar and butter. One of my oldest brothers was drafted in the Army and I remember being very proud of how good he looked in his uniform. He may have looked good going in, but he suffered from post-traumatic stress when he came out with a medical discharge. He was mentally affected for the rest of his life. He developed paranoia and a tremor in his hands that was similar to Parkinson's.

I loved my family, especially my mother, very intensely. My maternal grandmother died when my mother was around four years old. My mother was raised by her father and an evil stepmother on a farm near Tupulo, Mississippi. She talked freely with me about the severe deprivations and difficulties of her childhood. She told me that her dress was so badly tattered that she would stand sideways on dates to hide the holes. She married at thirteen to my father, twenty years her senior, in order to get away from home. She had dreams of having two children and saw them very dressed up in her mind. In reality she had thirteen, twelve of whom survived. Due to a lack of education, racism, and poverty, the older children were as raggedy in reality as the fantasy children were well dressed in her mind. Although she married to escape the frying pan, she told me her marriage turned out to be a jump into the fire.

My father was described as a drinking man with little or no knowledge about how to be a husband or father. My mother said he treated her like a child and physically abused her to express his authority. She was much wiser and more capable than he, and when she matured, he failed to notice. I didn't learn until I was an adult that he was also illiterate, and my mother taught him to read. As the story goes, on a warm, rainy evening in the backwoods of Mississippi, he was sitting on the porch with his moonshine, and was struck by lightning. Only the buckles and straps on his overalls were burnt; he was unharmed. This "epiphany" made a believer out of him, and he stopped drinking and smoking and became an itinerant preacher.

My parents and older siblings moved to Little Rock, Arkansas in 1930. My mother told me that she worked extremely hard sharecropping on a farm. She planted, harvested, and marketed the cotton and other crops by herself, while my father was off preaching the gospel and neglecting his family responsibilities. The family then moved to St. Louis, facilitated by my oldest brother, who had escaped earlier to the city. There my mother worked two jobs, domestic service by day, and brickyard worker by night, moving bricks with a wheelbarrow. My father remained unemployed except for an occasional odd job here and there. My mother came home for a few hours between jobs and managed to spend a few minutes of quality time with her many children. I remember her falling asleep in a chair whenever she sat down. Her arrival home was the brightest time of my day.

Being the youngest, I got the lion's share of her limited time. My mother always got up at five o'clock in the morning to start breakfast. One of my favorite childhood memories was waking up to the smell of bacon and coffee. In her "spare time" she canned fresh fruits and preserves, churned butter from cream, and even made lard. She spent all day on Saturday making her famous Sunday dinners. According to her, everything tastes better when cooked with love. I have fond memories of the times my sisters and I spent in the kitchen, either watching or helping my mother prepare meals. Seeing her spend so much of her precious free time in the kitchen, I was determined that this would not be my fate. Although I avoided learning to cook for years, I now appreciate the power of the role of nurturing others, especially with food.

Going to church on Sunday mornings and evenings with my mother and family was a very special time for me. Whenever I saw her putting on her hat, I knew it was time for church. After an hour or so of good gospel music and the shouting sisters running up and down the aisle, I was usually exhausted and would fall asleep leaning on my mother's arms which were as soft as a feather bed. This was heaven to me. My mother somehow also found time to take me to the clinic for medical appointments. I never minded them, because it was an opportunity to hold her hand, and she rewarded me with an Eskimo Pie afterwards.

I remember one day around age five on a visit to the clinic, we passed an orphanage where the kids were outside playing and I asked her what it was. She explained that it was a place where they put children who didn't have parents. My heart opened with sadness at the terrible thought. I said when I grew up I was going to take care of all the children who didn't have mothers to take care of them. When I went to the hospital for a tonsillectomy, the social worker from this orphanage came to the hospital on Saturday mornings to read books to us. I believe this experience sowed the seeds of my choice of careers. Years later, when I became a social worker myself, my first client was a girl named Alberta from this same orphanage. She was extremely overweight, with many emotional problems, and it was she who inspired me to specialize in mental health and child welfare.

The older girls in my family took responsibility for the younger children and for managing the home while my mother was at work. My sister Elizabeth who disliked me from babyhood was usually left in charge. She referred to me as "fast," and predicted

I'd have many babies before I was fifteen. (She now has selective amnesia and claims that she has always loved me and held me in high regard.) There was little order in the home and much chaos. People were yelling at each other, looking for lost or misplaced belongings which they accused each other of taking, several conversations going on simultaneously, radios blasting, etc. I often retreated to the bathroom for peace and solitude, but I couldn't remain too long because we had only one bathroom for fifteen people.

With a fourth grade education, my mother showed amazing ability to stretch a dollar as if it were elastic. She often walked long distances to avoid paying for a bus ride, and she went without stockings to provide lunch money for her children. She was self sacrificing, ambitious, resourceful, and courageous. She bought a two-family flat in a white neighborhood in decline before most blacks dared to even imagine doing such a thing. She opened her own laundry and two restaurants called Simmons Dinette 1 and Simmons Dinette 2. She was also very wise, and could quote from every book in the Bible. I will always remember the story of Solomon. She told me that God offered Solomon his choice of gifts and he chose wisdom, and because he chose wisdom God said he could have everything else. This touched me deeply and I vowed when I grew up I would be like Solomon.

Having been devalued and disregarded herself, my mother

valued and respected all children. She was a very loving woman who gave of herself unselfishly not only to her own children but to their friends and her many grandchildren. For years one of my brother's friends lived with us after the death of his parents. Several of my childhood friends continue to talk about things my mother did and told them. She is still remembered for the Sunday feasts she prepared for the multitudes. Her wise sayings are still repeated (if not followed) by her grandchildren and great grandchildren.

I had always been close to my mother and felt very dependent on her, as if she were my reason for living. As a young child, I recall being in the bathroom praying to God to please let me die before my mother. I could not imagine life without her. I had a difficult time leaving my mother when it was time to go to kindergarten, and I experienced intense separation anxiety.

As a child I didn't know that my family was and continues to be dysfunctional; I felt, however, somebody needed to take responsibility for their well being, and I silently volunteered for the job. In spite of having survival issues of my own, in many ways I set myself up as the conscience among my siblings. I assumed the role of pointing out to them the errors and pitfalls of their ways and encouraged them to make different choices. For the most part they accepted my advice in good humor, and then they did exactly what they wanted. Sometimes they just downright didn't want to hear it. Despite their recalcitrant attitudes, I loved them so much that I asked God not to give me anything that would separate me from my family, and I was unhappy when away from them. Even as a college professor, many years later, I remember feeling not fully present on the first day of school because I was wishing my family could be there. I would have preferred to be educating them. I was often lost in the nostalgia for my former cocoon within my family.

My father, Ezekial Simmons, was a Baptist minister whose many insecurities bound him to tradition and external controls. According to my mother, the insanity in our family came from his side. He was said to have had a brother who was a full-blown schizophrenic, who rode a horse up and down the road, eating lard as if it was candy. His youngest brother, Uncle Boston, also had a nervous breakdown after he was an adult and was hospitalized for several years. I remember him well; he was a gentle, soft spoken man who provided well for his family doing whatever work he could find. After his illness, he would sit in an overstuffed armchair for long hours without moving or talking.

My father was a tall, thin, dark-skinned man who didn't talk much and spent a lot of time away from home. My parents separated when I was twelve and divorced a year later. I don't remember their separation being very traumatic because I still had my mother, and only a vague experience of my father. Most of the information I had about him was provided by my mother. In retrospect, I realize my memory of my father was drawn from my mother's perspective, rather than my own experience.

I remember him taking me to school on my first day, and then taking me back home when I wouldn't stop crying and clinging to him. He told me sternly that I was going to have to go to school. Another memory of him is his coming out of the bedroom with tears in his eyes. When I asked him why he was crying, he said because he was happy. I was bewildered by this explanation, although now I think he must have been praying. He was of the belief that children should be seen and not heard. He was from the old school which believed if you spared the rod you spoiled the child. I only remember getting whupped once by him, when my brother talked my sister and me into taking a detour to a friend's house which made us late to our father's house.

My mother was the primary disciplinarian who also used physical punishment, with ironing cords, tree switches, and sometimes her bare hands, probably out of frustration, being overwhelmed, and not knowing what else to do. While she was beating us, her favorite saying was "This is hurting me more than it's hurting you." The logic of this reasoning escaped me, but I didn't hold it against her. I think this indiscriminate conflicting combination of love and abuse was the landscape and architectural design for my subsequent confusion about men who abused me in the name of love.

As a child I was powerless to change my mother, and leaving home was not an option, so I had to find some way to accept the bad with the good. As an adult, I now know I always have a choice. If I can't change the situation, I'm free to leave it.

My father was a guest minister who often traveled to revivals. This brought a lot of criticism from my mother who thought he should be working a regular paying job to support his family. After he and my mother separated, I remember going to his house complaining loudly that he had failed to provide for us. I had asked him for money for pedal pushers, the newest fashion in pants, and I wanted them badly. He said he couldn't afford it, which made me angry. I went upstairs and complained bitterly to my aunt. From downstairs he overheard me complaining, silently came up the stairs and into the room where I was yelling, and quietly told me that I really didn't know what I was talking about, so I should *shut up*! I was shocked. And I shut up.

My mother was a spiritual woman who was more grounded in truth than tradition (she was my first unidentified guru). One of the many things she taught me is that it is a wise person who profits from others' mistakes. Very early I realized that if certain behavior didn't work for other people, it probably wouldn't work for me either. I tried to avoid making choices that would have lifetime consequences and determine my future before I knew what was good for me.

For years I pleaded with my sisters to stop having babies, especially until they had some idea of what they were doing and had the resources to do it well. Many of my friends also became pregnant early without the benefit of marriage. As young mothers they had had little preparation, information, or clear intention about raising healthy children. They lived in bondage, struggling with poverty, and survival became their top priority. They seemed to age very rapidly. It occurred to me that the women in my family chose various mental institutions as resources for finding their husbands or mates, some of whom had been professionally certified as crazy. Although I observed this pattern as a teenager, I did not understand its dynamics, and subsequently repeated parts of it myself. Without examples or role models, I was not aware that healthy men existed, and had no idea that they could be available to me.

For many years I observed what I considered to be child abuse in my family. Although I did not name it at the time, I knew in the depths of my being that it wasn't right and felt the children would bear the burdens of the mistakes. And they have. The children were not only physically hit, but yelled at, pinched, jerked around, and disrespected. They were called names like "Stupid," Dummy" and sometimes worse.

I made many appeals to various family members, to think

about the long range effects of their behavior on the children, and I tried to suggest better ways to interact. Because I was the youngest in the family, without much life experience at this point, I was not in a position of authority, so they felt free to ignore my warnings. Child protective services were not well known then, and I wasn't sure that what I was observing was "abuse," although I knew it wasn't right. I did know that it was not the life I wanted for myself. I decided to avoid early sexual activity and premature motherhood which symbolized The Trap.

Years later, several of my nieces revealed also that they'd been sexually abused, but I was unaware of this tragedy while it was happening. I was aware there didn't seem to be enough emphasis on parenting, and the children's well being seemed an afterthought. I think my closeness to my mother and my unwillingness to keep secrets protected me from this.

As a child I was unable to understand the importance of education for a different future. I disliked school, (my first memory of it was sitting cross-legged on the floor) and I played hooky a lot. My mother valued education and saw it as the ticket to success and the only sure way out of the ghetto. I hated school with a passion--most of my teachers were angry, mean, middle-aged spinsters who didn't seem to bring much love to their work. School was not a safe place for me. I spent most of my time silently objecting to what I was being asked to learn, and the rest of my time wishing I was some place else.

Grammar school was the breeding ground for my separation of my feelings from my experiences. This coping pattern led to my later awareness of the coexistence of different realities. I knew that I had to find another way to think about what was happening to me-- lose my mind or kill someone, or both. I felt like a stranger in a foreign land. I am sure I had playmates, but I don't remember being close to any of my classmates. It seemed to me that many of the children had already developed tough personas in response to troubled family situations. They were quick to want to fight. I might have become a scapegoat since I was very skinny and black, but I had lots of brothers, sisters, and cousins at the school, many of whom also liked a good fight.

The teacher who had the strongest negative effect on me I clearly remember as Miss Urine, an overweight and frustrated old maid. I am not sure, however, if this was her name, but it was my experience of her. She talked with a lisp and if you stood too close to her, you would be sprayed with her spit. Every Friday she gave spelling tests; on Monday mornings she would call each child to the front of the room and give hard licks with the rattan stick for each word missed. I got more than my share of licks and have remained a poor speller to this day. I attempted to avoid the Monday morning humiliation and pain by pretending to be sick on Sunday evenings. This worked for only a short time before my mother refused to play the game, and then I had to resort to playing hooky.

One Monday I slipped away from the playground before school started. I had no idea where I was going but knew I didn't want to be there. I was standing on a corner crying, and a lady stopped and asked me what was wrong. I told her that I was hungry because I didn't know what else to say. She took me home and after she left, my mother beat the hell out of me, since I had eaten a large breakfast before leaving home. School didn't make much sense to me. I was unable to see the connection between learning to spell, write, and draw, to the importance of living. I just wanted to stay home with my mother. However, my mother would stop at nothing in her insistence that I go to school. She was determined that her children, especially me, would have a better life than she did. On a very limited income, she found some way to pay for my sister Bernice and me to take piano lessons, to join the Brownies, and to attend an after-school art program.

When I was in the fourth grade, I was transferred to Turner Open Air School, which was a special public school for children with physical handicaps or medical problems. Two of my older brothers also attended this school for a while. One was recovering from tuberculosis, and the other had rheumatic fever. I was sent there because I was severely underweight. I remember a nurse telling me when I was twelve that I weighed only fifty pounds. I must have been skin and bones, but I don't have an image of myself as skinny. However, I do remember my mother once saying, "I would give you a beating but your legs are so skinny I'm afraid I'll break them!" I recall feeling compassion for some of the disabled children there, like the girl whose legs were so bowed that she gave the appearance of a potbellied stove. After two or three years I must have gained weight because I was transferred back to the regular school. Most of my grammar school memories I have murdered and buried. I think I spent most of my time daydreaming about the beautiful house and life that awaited me away from school.

My mother usually paid her bills in person. I'm not sure if this was the result of a lack of trust in the system or if she waited until the bills were due and had to deliver them to avoid late fees. She often needed someone to do errands for her and considered this one of the few justifications for my missing school. I was highly motivated to avoid school, so at eight years old I learned how to take several streetcars and buses all over town to take care of my mother's business while she worked. My mother also got me up early when she needed something from the store for breakfast.

One morning while it was still dark I went to the corner store for her to get baking powder for biscuits. A man appeared out of a dark doorway and grabbed me from behind, putting what felt like a gun in my back. He covered my mouth so hard that he busted my lip. He dragged me into a back yard where he started to pull up my dress. I pleaded with him not to rape me, telling him that my mother had so many children that she couldn't handle any more, and that I was much too young to have a baby. I suppose I thought that pregnancy was the inevitable result of sex, and I knew I didn't want a baby. While I pleaded desperately with him, a light came on in an upstairs window, and he let go of me and ran off. I cried all the way home and told my mother what had happened. She called the police, who came and took a report, but I don't think they ever found the man.

      I have always known that I was special to my mother, and probably, as my siblings claimed, I was her favorite. She saw in me the last chance to realize her dream of having an educated child. After many years of resistance, I finally accepted that my mother was much stronger than me. This was my first realization that it did not serve me to go against what I experienced as overwhelming odds. I surrendered to a power greater than myself, which was the foundation of my growing trust in the Spirit. I went to school to have peace with my mother, which was the only way I could have peace with myself. After a period of time, I adjusted to the idea of school, but it wasn't until college that I began to really show up and excel. When I was considering registering in a Ph D program, my mother commented that first she had to force me to go to school, and now it seemed she had to force me to stop.

I am sure that another strong reason I decided to stay in school was to prepare myself to be the best caretaker I could be for my family. Ironically, it was also education which made me realize that I am different from my family, and I can choose not to repeat its dysfunctional patterns. We choose our behavior, whether we are conscious of it or not, so why not choose behavior that brings us the desired results?

My mother remarried when I was twelve years old. My stepfather, Thomas Ford, who we fondly referred to as "Papa Joe", was medium in height and weight, with large eyes and a balding head. He walked with a slight limp, the result of an accident at work, I think at a machine shop. Before they married I remember going with them on a streetcar ride. Something trivial had happened, and I began crying. He referred to me as a "crybaby," a name I had been called before. Looking back, I think I was actually crying because I recognized that accepting him as my father marked the end of my family as I had known it.

However, the addition of my stepfather improved our family's financial situation a little. Although not all my siblings agreed, I saw him as a very gentle, caring man. He bought my sister and me expensive orthopedic shoes because he was concerned about healthy feet. We hated the shoes and secretly took an extra pair to put on before arriving at school. Even so, I appreciated his sincere efforts on our behalf. He had a taste for "good Gordon Gin," which he used to drink at the kitchen table, a source of tension between him and my mother. I rather liked this picture of him sitting at the table enjoying himself. I became very close to him and remember him with love. We got along so well that my mother once commented he should have married me because I could get him to do anything. He was the first person who told me I should be happy. He also told me that I had beautiful teeth and feet. He strongly encouraged me to take good care of my teeth, which I still do to this day. When I came home on weekends from college, he always bought me cans of chili, tuna, fruit, and other goodies that I could take back and keep in the dorm. He also took me out for little special treats of ice cream or candy and sent me money at school. I knew he was proud of me. He was the most positive male influence during my early formative years.

CHAPTER TWO

ADOLESCENCE~~ THE SEARCH FOR IDENTITY

" Don't laugh at a youth for his affectations; he is only trying on one face after another to find a face of his own."

L.P. Smith, "Age and Death," <u>Afterthoughts, 1931.</u>

"Adolescence is a border between childhood and adulthood. Like all borders, it's teeming with energy and fraught with danger." Mary Pipher

Observing my sisters and friends become trapped by premature motherhood, I knew I did not want to travel that path. In my early teens I remember sitting in the bathtub having a dialogue with my vagina. I told it that I was not going to allow it to get me in trouble and control my life. I felt a pulsation in the warm water and knew it had heard the determination in my voice. My siblings seemed to me to be hypersexual, with little inclination towards self control. On two occasions I accidentally walked in to a bedroom (we had only three for ten people) while my sisters and their boyfriends were having sex, and I later learned that there was a lot more going on that I didn't see. But as my mother said, "What's done in the dark will come to the light…" and babies did appear. I am sure that my later choice of a lifestyle of celibacy was seeded in these early experiences.

I became a bona fide adolescent at the age of fourteen and stumbled into several of my waiting major landmines. One of my sisters, who was two years older than me, was already smoking when I turned fourteen. She told me if I smoked cigarettes for a week, I would get the habit. I told her she was crazy, but I tried it, wanting to be cool and tough like her, and I did get hooked. I started stealing cigarettes from one of my sisters and hiding in the bathroom to smoke, thinking no one knew. I was too scared to be openly rebellious, and I didn't want to rebel with things I thought would have dangerous or permanent consequences. I was sometimes in awe and disbelief about the acting-out, rebellious activities of my sisters and peers; I knew their kind of acting out would not work for me. However, I did choose to become a smoker (unaware of its ominous consequences), and it somehow gave me a feeling of being independent and being my own person. It also helped me deal with my mounting fears and anxieties by suppressing them.

School continued to be a pain in the ass and a cramp in my style. I was an average student, doing just enough to get by. One day in ninth grade, my algebra teacher came to my desk during class time and told me I could excel in algebra if I wanted to. I was amazed and flattered by his compliment, and gradually I began to believe him. This was a turning point in my resistance to school. I remember in English class giving an oral report on President

Harry Truman in front of the class and discovering I had talent in writing and public speaking. The next summer for the first time I decided to go to summer school, thinking I could get out of school sooner.

About this time I also got my first real job, working in a small neighborhood cleaners, owned by a man known to my family. I was very proud to have a job; earning money made me feel important. I spent a little on myself but gave most of it to my mother and siblings. After working only a short time, the owner, a married man and many years my senior, cornered me in the back room and inappropriately touched my breasts (which were "flat as a pancake"). I don't re-member telling anyone about what happened, but I knew I had to quit. I just didn't return to work the next day.

Also at fourteen, I stumbled over what turned out to be the most devastating landmine of my life. I met a twin, (also fourteen,) who was in the process of dropping out of high school. He had been observing me for months through the wire fence surrounding the school yard during my drum major practice. On my way home from school, I frequently saw him standing in the doorway of a brick two-family flat, talking to his buddies. He would call to me across the street where I was walking to avoid getting too close to him.

For several months I ignored him, because I didn't know

how to handle the attention, but then one day he walked across the street and asked me for my telephone number. I gave it to him, reluctantly, because I knew my mother thought I was too young to "receive company," and I didn't know what she would say if a boy called me. However, he did begin to call, and when my mother found out, we were already seeing each other with increasing frequency during and after school. Initially it was very hard for me to tell him apart from his twin, which I was only able to do by looking at the shoes they wore--one wore brown loafers, and the one I liked wore black lace-ups. I was thrown a curve when either of them changed shoes!

Melvin was a tall, dark, good-looking boy, who was extremely intelligent, which he generally used to be a crook. He was raised by a single, passive, low-energy mother who spent most of her time sitting in front of their house. When I visited his house after school or on the weekends, I was shocked to see that the house was often dirty and in disarray. Although he had an older sister, neither she nor the mother took kindly to housework. Melvin was impressed by my ambition and strong work ethic. He was also fascinated by my mother's support of me. He once commented, "If I'd had your mother, I could have been President of the United States."

From the beginning, he decided that I was the girl he would marry. I wasn't sure I wanted to marry anybody, especially him, because of my mother's strong negative reactions to him. She said that among other things he had shifty eyes. Actually I never felt safe with him. He was obsessively jealous whenever he thought some other boy was interested in me, and would give me the third degree regarding my whereabouts whenever I was not with him. Without a framework for healthy male/female relationships, I accepted his behavior as he claimed, that it was love. As a young girl, I was fascinated and flattered that someone could be so obsessed with me. I had no way of knowing that this was an early warning of the dangerous landmines that lay ahead. I also didn't recognize that this preoccupation with me enabled him to avoid looking at himself.

    After I'd known him for about a year, he was arrested for shooting and killing another boy. He claimed it was an accident, but he was taken off to juvenile hall for several months. I visited him there occasionally after school, standing outside and yelling up to him in his third story barred window. They tried him as an adult and he was later sentenced to about ten years in the state penitentiary; he served five or six. During this time we corresponded. He criticized me for not writing him often enough and not giving him enough details about my activities. I felt put-upon by his demands, and to my credit, I did not change my behavior. Of course locked up in prison he could do nothing about it.

In the meantime, I met a boy named Robert, whose best friend was going out with my best friend. We spent many happy times as a foursome, going to movies and even the opera. He would pick me up in his Chevy after school, and I thought I had hit the bigtime. We would go get a hamburger or ice cream before going home. I had my first sexual experience with him and lost my virginity in my kitchen when no one was at home. He said he loved my body and was very free with his compliments about our sexual activities. However, I wasn't particularly impressed with the experience.

Robert had an inflated opinion of himself, being the oldest son of a well-known Pentecostal minister. Robert tried to veil his arrogance in a cloak of being hip and cool. He later became a minister himself, with the philosophy of "Do not as I do, but as I say." He bought me a cheap watch for my birthday. When he gave it to me he acted as if he was presenting me with the Hope Diamond.

After graduating from high school I went to a local teacher's college called Stowe because I did not have the money to go away. Trying to study, work, and live at home was more than I could handle, and I had a lot of difficulty adjusting to college. One of the teachers talked so far above my head I thought he was speaking Japanese. I couldn't understand any of his words, much less his concepts, and I felt as if I was in a foreign land.

I had a job working at a soda fountain in Shoatz's Drug Store. I made sandwiches and ice cream sodas and sundaes. I worked in full view of the boss who was behind the pharmacy counter where he was supposedly filling prescriptions. On more than one occasion, he had to come over and remind me that I could not serve blacks at the counter--they could only order to go. He also observed me putting extra meat on sandwiches for black folks, which he ordered me to stop doing. Along with the stress of school, this pressure was almost overwhelming, but I hung in there for a year.

It was at this time that I became aware of my first symptoms of narcolepsy. One of my classmates came into the women's lounge where I had been napping, and told me that I was going to "sleep my life away." I was not aware that I was sleeping too much, but I knew I wasn't having a good time. I had no label for my excessive sleeping and didn't realize it was abnormal.

My freshman year, while still living at home in St. Louis, was a very difficult transition for me. Going to college was a clear departure from my family pattern, and a major change in my own identity. College was very unfamiliar territory for me and I felt unprepared and inadequate. I was afraid of failure and from that perspective had no idea how the future would turn out. I didn't drink at the time, so sleeping was my escape. After the first year I decided to drop out of school and get a full time job, so I could save enough money to go to Lincoln University where several of my friends were going.

I found a job as a dishwasher in the Georgia House Restaurant in one of the wealthy suburbs of St. Louis. I carried large tubs of heavy dishes from the front to the back of the restaurant, where I stood over a steaming hot dishwashing machine, filling it with dirty dishes. I was painfully aware of my second class citizenship as I watched blacks come to the back door to be served their food to go. However, the most pleasant moments of my workday were when I had friendly exchanges and jokes with my comrades in oppression. My hands aged from scrubbing huge pots and pans. The owner was a staunch racist and thought I should do all the dirty work. Once when a girl vomited in the dining area, he told the manager to have me clean it up. When she told me what he wanted, I went to him and told him that was not my job. His response was, "Well, I guess you don't have to work…"

I replied, "If you mean that my mother will feed me and give me a place to live, you're right." He wanted to fire me, but the manager liked my work and came to my rescue, sending me back to wash dishes while she cleaned up the mess. She also defied his orders that I should be the only one to clean the bathrooms and set up a system rotating this responsibility.

I saved every penny of my money, refusing to buy myself

even small treats like an ice cream cone. When I quit this job after a year to go to Lincoln, the racist owner gave me a parting shot by saying angrily, "Just come to the Georgia House and then quit after a year and go to school!" implying that I had used the job simply for self aggrandizement, without loyalty to the restaurant. He was one of my primary motivators to get an education. The manager continued to hire me during Christmas breaks and summer vacations, which was a huge financial help.

One of my older sister's boyfriends introduced me to one of his co-workers, Rubin, at MacDonald-Douglas factory where they made aircrafts. He was several years my senior but not much more mature. He was "high yellow", a good looking man, and laughed a lot. He had a good sense of humor and took few things seriously. We dated for several months, and I enjoyed his company and his late model Mustang. He had two children, but he told me he was divorced. I discovered that he was only separated but still married when his wife returned home and called me to warn me to stay away from her husband. I was devastated by the call. He upheld his agreement to drive me and my belongings to Lincoln University, bringing closure to our relationship, an important landmark of my transition into a new life.

Lincoln University, a predominantly black school, provided a very friendly environment. I lived in the dorm where I felt comfortable and supported. I made good grades and a lot of friends. During my years at the university, it was relatively small; it is now much larger and mostly white. It was located on top of the highest hill in a small town, Jefferson City. Going to the "Foot" to mingle with the town's locals was a major hike and the main entertainment. Most of the teachers were competent, and some were outstanding; all seemed to be interested in their work and the students.

I flourished in this environment and in time came into my own. Determined to succeed, I remember reading the dictionary on my first day in the dorm to improve my vocabulary. I took eighteen units every semester in order to graduate in three years. I made good grades and was on the Dean's List every year which made my mother very proud. Because of my good grades, in my second year I was invited to pledge to the Delta Sorority. I did, along with my roommate, but we both became inactive after a few months. I was annoyed by many of the requests of my Big Sisters (to perform tasks and run errands for them), and I did not have the money to spend on their frivolous requirements for extra clothing and other paraphernalia.

The young men on the campus had a daily routine of forming a line enroute to the cafeteria to check out the girls. They affectionately shared their opinions, commenting on what they liked (my "brick house") and what they thought could use improvement, (the color of my stockings). There was no way to avoid the "line" and eat, so I decided to use the comments constructively. This gutsy decision propelled my social development and enhanced my self esteem. I also belonged to one of the "ingroups" on the campus, the popular girls who were noticed and got dates. On my first day in the dorm I got into a wrestling match and to my surprise I took down two girls. This established me as someone to reckon with. My boyfriend was a Kappa and a good dancer. I too was somewhat light on my feet, and I enjoyed gliding across the gym floor with him at school dances. Although I was in the same city with Melvin, he was safely behind bars for the time being.

I kept the same roommate, Jerry Washington, for all three years. She was of medium height and attractive, with large eyes and a quick smile. She also lived a few houses from my house on St. Ferdinand St., only her house was much nicer. Her mother was a policewoman, and her stepfather also earned a good income. Although her mother completely financed her education, Jerry was very frugal and the perfect roommate for me. We pooled our money and bought canned goods to heat up on a hot plate for lunches. The cafeteria's food left much to be desired, so we usually ate dinner off campus at the Greasy Spoon or Mrs. Hazel's, where we could get her famous meatloaf, sweet potatoes, black-eyed peas, and rolls or corn bread for thirty-five cents.

Jerry and I had the same major and minor, sociology and

psychology. We shared most classes and studied together. We did each other's hair to save money and were sometimes called the "Bobsy Twins." She watched my back in protecting my cigarettes from freeloaders, and I shared my care packages from my stepfather and sister Ruby with her. I applied for and received a job working as the secretary to the Missouri Commission on Human Rights. The only problem was that I couldn't type. I talked my boss, Mr. Parsons, into allowing me to take the typing home to the dorm where I secretly hired the best typist in the dorm to do the work. I eventually got my boss to hire Jerry, who also used the "hunt and peck" typing method, and he finally got the idea to use us as filing clerks. We enjoyed this job a lot, and we had summit conferences lying in our bunk beds about how we would spend our Big Bucks.

Mr. Parsons was an MSW and encouraged me to continue on to graduate school to become an MSW after I received my Bachelor's Degree. He informed me that I could get a stipend which would pay me as much to continue my education as I would earn working with a BA. He even counseled me on how to go about getting the stipend. After graduation I went on to Washington University to the School of Social Work. I encouraged Jerry to join me at the university and later at Child Welfare. I worked at Children's Services until I left to accept another position.

The summer after my sophomore year, I got a job in a pizza

factory. This was my first exposure to pizza; I had never even heard of it. I quickly became skilled on the assembly line, and the owner hired three of my friends--Jerry, her sister, and another friend of ours. Going to work became somewhat like a party, because we made a game out of the repetitive activities. The next summer I got a job in a laundry where it was hotter than hell. Without being aware of it, I offered this experience to God, and I'm sure grace was the only thing that enabled me to endure it.

I visited Melvin once toward the end of his prison term, because I was still intrigued by his intensity and attention. Since he was about to be released, he was allowed ground privileges. He walked toward me, we had an awkward embrace, and we sat down on the grass. He seemed very different from my memory of him. His head and face were shining with too much grease, and his demeanor was subdued and remote. He had little to say, but he made it known that he expected me not to have any other men in my life. I felt intimidated by his efforts to control me (even from behind bars), but I thought I could handle the situation. I was too naïve to recognize the warning signs.

After a few months he was released, and as he attempted to readjust to society, he became increasingly aggressive, frustrated and jaded. I was an easy target for his anger. I was in college and came home on weekends, and Melvin would show up shortly after my arrival. Our relationship progressed and we became sexually involved. Melvin was an excellent lover, which was addictive for me. However, it only captured part of my attention. This was very disturbing to Melvin, who thought that sex was the alpha and omega of life, and probably was much of the fuel for his continuing obsession. He told me he had enough love for both of us, but his expression of his love was mostly limited to sex.

After I graduated, I did receive a stipend and went on to graduate school. It had the added benefit of giving me a good excuse to avoid getting married to Melvin. My field assignment was working in child welfare, and it seemed that the more progress I made, the more pressure he applied for marriage. He frequently stalked me, slept outside my house in his car, and beat up any male friend he saw me with. Much to my mortification, he even followed me on my field visits to clients.

One day he kidnapped me as I was leaving a foster home, and kept me captive for two days in a hotel. The foster mother had observed the kidnapping and reported it to the police. When Melvin finally took me home, my mother called the police. I was totally humiliated by this public window into my crazy personal life, but I felt unable to extricate myself. I was taken to the police station for a deposition, but naturally I was afraid to press charges.

Over time, his delusional jealousy then caused him to start physically attacking me. I was terrified, even called the police myself several times, but they did nothing. Melvin saw my involving the police as a racist act, my siding with the white enemy. I finally obtained a restraining order which Melvin totally ignored without consequences. I felt very vulnerable and unprotected. I thought I had no choice but to submit to his demands. I remember that during one of our physical battles I unwisely told him that he might be able to control my body but he would never control my mind. He became enraged, clenched his fists and his eyes glared at me, but behind them I saw a coward's feeling of defeat.

Melvin was the first person who told me that I had guardian angels. He said once when he had decided to push me in front of a streetcar, something held his hands and he couldn't do it. He also asked me if I could have children. It seems that he had been putting holes in the condoms during sex, hoping to get me pregnant, but it never happened.

Eventually, using profits from his drug dealings, he bought me a one-and-a-half carat diamond engagement ring which he asked me to wear, reassuring me that we did not have to set a date for the wedding. I reluctantly agreed. He soon asked me to go shopping with him, to furnish his apartment (which did not exist at the time.) He was careful to buy only furniture I said I liked. Shortly after the shopping spree, the pressure to marry him intensified. I participated in the fantasy of a potential wedding by purchasing a dress, getting bridesmaids, etc. Although I bought wedding invitations, I was petrified by the thought of mailing them. I could not maintain the deception any longer and confessed to him that I didn't want to get married. He became extremely angry, and he violently attacked me, blackening both my eyes. He threatened that if he couldn't have me, no one else would. He also informed me that the world was not big enough to hold the two of us if we were not together, and that he would find me wherever I went and mess me up so badly no one else would want me.

In spite of all this stress, I received a promotion to a very prestigious job--I was the first black professional to be hired by the Ellen Steinberg Department of Child Psychiatry in St. Louis. At the time they didn't have any black patients, not to mention black professionals. I applied for the job on a dare, and I was astounded (as was everyone else) that I got the job. I was interviewed by three psychiatrists and the senior psychiatric social worker. I was also invited to a party where I'm sure I was being watched to see how I handled myself socially. The chief psychiatrist asked me what salary I would like to make (another first!). I was so surprised that I asked for slightly more than I was already making, and got it.

On my first day at work one of the black childcare staff members said to me, "You must really know a lot!" After my first year the department paid for me to attend the Ortho-psychiatric Conference in New York. Coming home on the plane, I met the dean of Missouri University who offered me a teaching job. When

I informed my boss of the offer, he decided to raise my salary substantially, which showed up on my very next paycheck.

Melvin continued following me on my new job. Once I saw him sitting in his car in the parking lot as I got off the bus. My body shook like a tornado as I hurried inside, pretending not to see him. It was hard to make a good impression with my new colleagues while knowing I was being stalked and fearing for my life. I lived in constant fear and chronic anxiety. This toxic internal state developed into Cushings Syndrome, which is a rare disease of hyper-secretion of adrenaline. I was in a perpetual state of flight or fight, shivering with tremors. I gained forty pounds in one year, had a moon face, an elephant hump on the back of my neck, amenorrhea, a constant tremor, became three or four shades lighter, and was a general mess. I flinched every time I looked in the mirror, not recognizing the distorted pathetic face looking back at me.

I went to a specialist for each of my symptoms, with no one putting the symptoms together and properly diagnosing the disease as Cushings Syndrome. A dermatologist minimized my concern, telling me that most black people come to him trying to get lighter. I let him know that that was not my concern, and that the change in the color of my skin was part of a bigger problem. I suffered from the disease for five years before it was recognized and treated. Despite my many challenges, I maintained a good front in taking care of business. I learned to stand my ground among the well-known high-falootin mental health experts.

One day while returning from a walk with an autistic hyperactive seven-year-old, I was approached in the elevator by Dr. Melvin Eisenhower, the Head of the Department of Internal Medicine, who had been in Europe for several months. He noticed my moon face had become even more round, and he asked me if I was taking Cortisone. I said no, but I was totally mesmerized by his apparent knowledge of what was going on with my body. We rode up and down several times in the elevator while we talked, with the kid turning somersaults around us. By the end of the day, I had an appointment to go into the hospital the next day. I felt overwhelming relief that someone knew what was wrong with me and there might be a cure. I excitedly rushed home and told my family.

In the hospital they gave me multiple tests and found out I needed exploratory surgery to determine exactly what the problem was. The doctor said that after he had been operating for two and a half hours, he did not see the tumor. He said my right gland appeared shriveled and removed it. I still had all of my symptoms and a month later had to have a second surgery. This time he removed a tumor from my left adrenal gland. After the second surgery the symptoms gradually disappeared. Since I was hospitalized in the same place where I worked, I often got up, got dressed and went downstairs to work, in between tests. The surgeon, knowing I was a therapist, asked me to counsel a morbidly obese patient on the unit, which I did. Focusing on someone else helped me to forget my own worries.

Melvin maintained a cavalier attitude toward my belief that the stress of our relationship was responsible for my illness. He continued relentlessly to bully me into marrying him. He kept telling me that marriage would solve all our problems. I was between a rock and a hard place, not knowing where to turn. I was still living at home at age twenty-nine, because it was convenient for me to do so and financially helpful to my mother as well. I felt no need to express my independence by separating from my mother. I might have remained at home permanently, boxing myself into a very limited corner, but Melvin catapulted me right out of my cocoon, away from my family and into young adulthood.

Unable to cope with him any longer, I knew I had to get away from him. I met secretly with a job recruiter for the state of California and obtained a job in the Department of Mental Hygiene in Modesto. My oldest brother and his son drove me there in my car. When we entered the town, I was comforted by a huge sign saying, "WELCOME TO MODESTO, THE LAND OF PLENTY." In that moment I realized that I was free to become anyone I wanted to be, because there was no one there who knew me. I was determined to create a healthier life for myself, hoping my past would remain behind me.

CHAPTER THREE

YOUNG ADULTHOOD~ SELF DEFINITION

"For each age is a dream that is dying, Or one that is coming to birth."
                    Arthur William Edgar O'Shaughnessy (1844-1881),

Modesto was a very small farm community. I had never heard of Modesto. I accepted the job because the state was paying a larger salary due to its outlying location. My doctor in St. Louis who was also a friend had asked me about the social possibilities there for a single black woman. He suggested that I'd look pretty silly sitting alone in my room counting my money! I was so anxious to get away from Melvin that I hadn't thought much about a social life. I called my soon-to-be office supervisor and posed the question to her. She assured me that if I were a friendly person I would have absolutely no difficulty making friends. I also looked on the map and discovered that Modesto was only about fifty miles from San Francisco. What I didn't realize was the two cities were separated by huge mountains, and many winding, narrow roads which I was unaccustomed to and intimidated by.

    When we arrived, my brother commented on the smallness of the town, but then laughingly said that after I got settled I would probably enjoy it and even send for my mother. I was scheduled to start work the next day, and I was looking forward to it. I immediately discovered, much to my surprise, that my supervisor was a woman with obvious emotional problems and the staff acted out like small children whose parents were unavailable. The first staff meeting resembled a family brawl with no one capable or willing to take control. The tension seemed to move over everyone's head and slapped me in the face. In the first few hours on my new job in a strange city where I knew no one, I was forced to take charge and attempt to bring some order to chaos. This situation could only exist in Modesto. The staff actually reflected the same psychological problems the patients exhibited in the two state hospitals they served.

    I was naturally drawn to the one African American in the office, Morris, and he offered to help me find an apartment. He took me to see a three-bedroom apartment in a complex which I later discovered had mostly low income and welfare families, sometimes with three families or more living in one apartment. He told me that I would be very safe and comfortable there. However after moving in to the apartment, I observed groups of young white men gathered outside of the complex drinking beer at night, and I became afraid to go home after dark. I had experience with dealing with groups of black men, but this situation was new to me. I soon learned that Morris had a reputation as a sociopath and liar, whose choice of housing for me certainly reflected his insensitivity. I gradually distanced myself from him.

Another man in the office was Tom Lawson, a short, pale, redheaded white man from South Carolina. He spoke with a Southern accent, and was the one person in the office I initially was sure I would not like. Tom approached me with a list of apartments for me which he had prescreened for vacancies and suitability. He had recently moved to Modesto himself and told me that he wanted to help me avoid the difficulties he had encountered. I was impressed with his thoughtfulness and efforts on my behalf. We looked at apartments together and I moved after one week to a place more to my standards. I stayed in the second apartment for one month, and then moved into a house with a black social worker I had met in another office. She was into heavy duty control and very free with unsolicited advice about how I should live my life. I felt equally free not to follow it.

Tom became my best friend and we did many things together. He turned out to be a very cultured Southern gentleman. He introduced me to many new experiences and interesting places. He took me to my first auction which we both thoroughly enjoyed. We were quite the odd couple, he with his very white skin and red hair, me with my very dark skin and bushy afro. He often took me to San Francisco, Sausalito, to the mountains, and the snow. He was well organized and usually arrived with a list of activities for me to choose from. When I was ill, without my asking he would have medicines delivered. On one of our trips to Sausalito and my favorite restaurant, Ondine's, I looked up to the hills and saw houses nestled in the trees, and I commented that one day I was going to live there. Although said in passing, five years later it happened.

After I had been in Modesto for a month, my mother came out for a visit. She liked the smallness of a farm community, and the people. I met a handsome black pilot who took my mother and me up for a ride, and I dated him for several months before I learned that he was also dating several other women, including a white woman. He told me that he didn't believe in restricting himself to one race. This was my first exposure to the philosophy of a self proclaimed "world citizen" (which I eventually adopted for myself.) I continued to see him in spite of my misgivings--the pickings were slim-- and allowed myself to have a good time with him.

At work I received accolades for the reports I wrote, and I was also developing a reputation as a take-charge kind of person. I began to relax a little with the acceptance and respect of my colleagues. I think I was seen as a Big City Girl. The few friends that I had managed to make, especially my roommate, and even my mother when she met Tom, were all sure that he was in love with me. I was totally blind to the idea that this might be true, and assured them that he was just a nice man who treated all his friends with the same thoughtfulness.

To assist me in refining my new identity and expanding world view, I was sent an angel of my same sex, color, and persuasion. There were few blacks in the Central Valley and even fewer black professionals. I was delighted when I met Delo, a fellow social worker who lived and worked in Stockton, about ninety miles from Modesto. She was a tall, attractive, stately built black woman with large, erect breasts, which I admired. She was exceptionally bright and well-read. She grew up in South Carolina in a large family, all of whom were college educated. Delo and I became like the Bobsy twins, spending a lot of time together on the weekends and talking for many hours on the state's free interoffice phone system. I enjoyed talking to her, and learned a lot from her. She tended to be overweighted on the intellect-tual side, and somewhat naïve about men and street life. Since I had been around the corner a few times with my many older siblings, I was able to contribute to her social maturation.

I am amazed that she still remembers some pearls of wisdom I shared with her thirty-five years ago, that I had long since forgotten. Our favorite subject to talk about was men. Since the pickings were few and far between, and our criteria for healthy men were not well formed, needless to say, the men we attracted had "issues." She reminded me that I told her one of the men she was dating was "afraid of intimacy," and another had no "history of successful bonding."

After many years of unmerciful male bashing, during one of our lengthy conversations, I started feeling sad. I was stunned by the realization that we weren't saying many good things about the brothers. I told her that we reinforced each other's negative feelings about black men, and I was going to have to find someone else to discuss the subject with or stop talking about it. I knew it was unhealthy behavior on my part. It occurred to me, even then, that having children would be a healthier option for me, and I told Delo that I was considering motherhood as an alternative to dating. As a practice run, I took in some foster kids from juvenile hall on the weekends. While I was not ready to become a fulltime mom, I think I was able to make a small difference. The kids and I enjoyed each other. I felt my relationships with the children were a lot healthier than my relationships with men. This was one of many clues that maybe my purpose was to be a mother but not necessarily a wife.

Delo was a very good and supportive friend who I loved a lot and thought of as a sister. We could provide direction and guidance for each other. I particularly enjoyed our processing mutual experiences and events. It was always interesting to hear her per-spective on things and people. We also shared working for the state, although we lived in different towns She was the bridesmaid in my wedding, and a lifeline when I was trying to free myself from the prison Melvin was building for me. She called me during one of the times Melvin was holding me captive, and hers was like a voice from heaven.

After six months of small town suffocation, I transferred to the Fresno Office of the State Department of Mental Hygiene. Fresno was slightly larger than Modesto; it had a college, and offered a few more opportunities. It was also closer to Stockton where Delo lived. Fresno was more fertile ground for my professional development, and here I flourished. Again, no one knew me. I gave myself permission to be who I wanted to become--a competent, more cultured, refined, confident and assertive woman. (I think everyone could benefit from an opportunity to be new in a different environment. Change is much harder in the company of people who have known you for years and are invested in you remaining the same.) I found a very nice apartment with two bedrooms and a pool in an upscale neighborhood. Being the new kid on the block, I was introduced to the area's few black professionals, but Tom continued to be my closest friend.

On a professional visit to one of the nursing homes where my office placed patients, I met Susan. Susan was the social worker for the nursing home. She had returned to school later in life after raising her family. We had an instant mutual attraction, and she turned out to be another one of my angels in earthly clothes. She was a very attractive, well educated and cultured upper-class white woman who was fifteen years my senior.

Although she was married to a man who adored her and treated her like a queen, she longed for more passion in the bedroom. I was impressed by his caring qualities, of which I also became a recipient. The three of us often laughed about my being Bob's second wife, with all of the benefits and none of the responsibilities of marriage.

She later came to work at the State Department of Mental Hygiene where I was her supervisor. Our relationship grew over the years and we did many things together: we shopped, went to parties, took short vacations, etc. We also did many things that included Bob. Susan was very validating towards me and for her I could do no wrong. I learned many things, among which was to drink good wine out of pretty glasses, to surround myself with beauty, to buy designer clothes, and to carry myself with dignity. She loved my independence and free spirit. On one occasion she commented to me that I jumped in and out of more things in a week than some people did in a lifetime. My relationships with Susan and Bob continued until their deaths.

My relationship Tom was also one that went the distance. He visited me regularly in Fresno. Needless to say, I was astounded when he asked me to marry him. We were lying on a blanket on the floor. We had never kissed, and our most romantic interaction was a platonic hug. I asked him how he would handle the choice of a black wife with his family. He said he had given it great deal of thought and decided that if they didn't approve, he would just deal with it. I said that I would not want him to wake up one day and be angry at me as the cause of his separation from his family. What I realized but didn't say was that I loved him like a brother, and the two of us, while similar, were so different that the marriage wouldn't have a snowball's chance in hell. Although I declined his offer, we continued to be very good friends.

Tom later discovered that he was gay, and he eventually found the loving partnership he deserved. He and his partner have kept in close contact with me through letters and phone calls. They did not hesitate to make me a very large loan when I needed it. With all of our differences and physical separation, we have remained very close and our love for each other will always be unconditional. They always remember me with thoughtful cards and gifts on special occasions, and have never forgotten my birthday. Tom is truly one of my guardian angels.

Another good friend of mine was Joe, a tall, heavyset, well educated man, highly cultured. Although only in his early forties, he was completely bald in the center of his head with a few strands of hair on the sides. He was a handsome, closeted black gay man who was assistant director at the Fresno VA hospital, and I met him through work. Delo and I had a field day with our speculations on his sexual orientation. Joe and I bonded almost immediately, and became fast friends. We talked on the phone for hours, and he was very affirming and supportive. I had never met a black man like him, and I was enchanted by his knowledge, culture, and grace. He played a huge role in the development of my new identity and emerging middle class social status.

Appearances were very important to him--he bought extra-vagant gifts and cards to impress his public. He encouraged me to reflect the highest expression of myself, and felt free to make suggestions about both my dress and behavior. Once when we were going to an afternoon tea of the elite society, he was suited down and asked me to wear long black leather gloves which were not very comfortable. After about an hour of hors d'oeuvres, tea, and polite conversation, I looked Joe in the eye and told him to get me out of there because I was getting ready to take off those gloves and smoke a cigarette. He was very responsive to my request.

Another member of my new supportive family of friends was Martin. I met him, a hot-blooded Nigerian attending graduate school at Fresno University, when I was teaching a course in Pathology of Human Behavior there. Because there were so few Black professionals or students in Fresno, Martin and I frequently attended the same parties and social gatherings. He was a very ebullient Gemini who loved to dance the High Life. We danced a lot, talked, and had fun together. At one dance, Martin sat on the floor in front of my chair as if to prevent anyone else from asking me to dance. I let him know that while I liked him as a friend, I was not romantically attracted to him. However, he was very persistent, attentive, and accommodating, as if waiting for me to change my mind.

He started coming over to my house offering to fix things. He went out of his way to make friends with my mother, who was living with me at the time. On one occasion, Martin insisted on cleaning my swimming pool, which was filled with algae. He slipped, hit his head, and had a brain concussion which resulted in his having to have a craniotomy. Martin wanted to recuperate at my house after the surgery. My mother had also had an operation around the same time and I did not feel that I could manage to take care of both of them and work full time. He was living in the Catholic Registry so the priests and nuns provided the care he needed.

Nothing romantic ever happened between Martin and me. Although he made several overtures in the years that I knew him, I simply was not attracted to him in that way. Being the determined headstrong person that he was, he refused to give up, until I bought the house in Sausalito. For some reason I think this symbolized to him that he was no longer needed. We remained friends and he continued to visit, though less frequently. When my mother fell and became quadriplegic, Martin increased his visits and was very helpful with her care.

Some years later a friend told me that Martin had graduated

with a doctorate in botany and become wealthy, (which was one of his dreams), and moved into an all-white neighborhood in Sacramento. My friend thought that his children were having difficulties being the only non-whites in the school. She also told me that Martin had a picture of me that I had given him hanging in his bedroom. I told her that if she ever talked to him in the future, to ask him to please remove the picture.

One other friend who had a significant impact on my life was a man from South Africa named Dr. Mislani Jassani. I met him at school where he was teaching Medical Sociology. His father had been in the ruling class before the takeover of South Africa. He was short and stocky and definitely a touchy-feely kind of guy. At the end of our evenings together, he was always reluctant to leave, ignoring subtle hints. I finally resorted to putting a sign on my door that said: "All visitors must leave by 10PM. Signed, the Sleeper." During one Easter vacation, Jassani, who lived in San Francisco, brought the Prince of Swaziland and his First Wife to my house in Fresno. I didn't have an extra bedroom, so I offered to put them up in a hotel. Jasani said this would insult them, so they all slept on my floor. I still remember the conversation I had with the First Wife about polygamy. She explained to me that in this country men sneak around and the women are deprived of each other's friendship, whereas in her country, the women are all sisters.

In Fresno I came into my own professionally. I was promoted to supervisor, and was offered a teaching job at Fresno State. I opened the first group home in Fresno for disturbed adolescents. The house was jointly supported by the State Department of Mental Hygiene and the local Mental Health Association. I was surprised when I received the Volunteer of the Year Award from the Mental Health Association, mainly for my facilitation of this cooperative effort. The promotion as well as other professional successes raised new questions for me about my competency and certainly required another change in identity. My tendency to use sleep as an escape seemed to gradually disappear as I became more secure in the new position.

I developed my first private counseling practice, and referrals flowed easily. I also wrote my first professional articles based on some of my lectures at the college. My accomplishments in Modesto and Fresno were the groundwork for my transition to a healthier lifestyle. To all appearances, I seemed to have achieved the American Dream, but I felt my personal life lacked passion. I think the truth is that I had not worked through all of the past conditioning from my early years of conflict and chaos. I wasn't yet able to distinguish between contentment and boredom, or excitement and fear.

Melvin was apparently aware of my whereabouts from the time I left St. Louis, though I had gone to great lengths to try to keep him from knowing where I was. His devious manipulative personality seemed to enable him to get any information he wanted. On my birthdays and other special occasions, flowers would arrive with a card professing his undying love. I was not dating at the time. Homesick and sometimes lonely, I received the flowers with very mixed feelings.

After I'd been in Fresno about six months, I answered the telephone and Melvin informed me he was at the airport. With fear and anticipation, I went to pick him up. He was dressed to the hilt, and looked very handsome. Of course he assumed he would be staying at my house. We had a nice dinner, good wine (Melvin had excellent taste), and then we found ourselves in bed together again. The relationship was off and running. I kept it a secret from my family as long as I could. When my mother found out that I was seeing Melvin again, it broke her heart.

Melvin continued to pressure me to marry him. He claimed marrying me was his life's goal. For some strange reason still not clear to me, I agreed. I think on some level I believed that if I married him he would see that it did not solve all of our problems as he had promised, and he would be willing to let me go. My friend Joe got very excited about the wedding (not the marriage.) He loved to plan weddings and was very good at it. He proceeded in a whirlwind of planning without skipping a detail, and I got caught up in his excitement and enthusiasm, trying to forget what was really happening. A date was set and the fantasy was blooming. It was to be a storybook wedding with all the frills.

I tried to convince myself that Melvin was right and by some magic the marriage could work. However, I had seen several large packages of white powder in his suitcase which had been left open on the bed. When I asked Melvin if that was cocaine, he gave some vague explanation about keeping it for a friend, and assured me that he neither used it nor sold it. I found this hard to believe, especially since he seemed to have a lot of discretionary money which I was sure he didn't earn from his proclaimed occupation as a television repairman in St. Louis. He went back and forth between Fresno and St. Louis. On his visits to Fresno he was on his best behavior and wined and dined me in high style.

A few weeks before the wedding, I began to get cold feet. I attempted to discuss my anxiety with the minister who was going to marry us, to no avail. He assured me that all brides felt as I did, and not to worry. I told him that I didn't think brides felt the way I did, or there would not be so many weddings. I left his office feeling misunderstood, frightened, and hopeless. I consoled myself with the idea that the only way out of the relationship was through it, and that if it didn't work out, I could always get a divorce. I planned the divorce and the wedding at the same time.

When we picked up the marriage license, Melvin

announced to me that he now owned me. I said he was crazy if he thought he could buy me for three dollars! He made no comment.

The wedding was picture perfect and beautiful. However as soon as we started to live together as husband and wife, Melvin began his agenda of control. He would sometimes drive me to work and class so he could use the car. On one occasion he took me to the college where I was teaching, and acted surprised that so many students were waiting for me. I'm sure he was jealous, and he tried to find ways to prevent me from teaching, claiming that I wasn't available enough for him. He would refer to my friends as "middle class" as if that were a dirty word, and try to restrict my contact with them. He also interrogated me about my daily activities, although I usually went straight from work to home. Once my mother called and during our conversation she asked me if Melvin was working. Without my knowledge he was listening in on the extension. He became incensed by her question and beat me up. I ran out of the house scantily dressed and down the street, under the watchful eyes of my neighbors.

By two months into the marriage, I was no longer able to deny the truth: this marriage was a disaster. I was sitting at the dining room table crying one evening and Melvin asked what was wrong. I said I didn't know exactly, but what I did know was that I wasn't happy. He asked me where I got the idea that I was supposed to be so "happy happy", and I replied "Maybe I read it in a book somewhere!" The truth is that my stepfather always told me that I should be happy, that if I wasn't happy, something was wrong. And I believed him. Once he came to Fresno to visit, and he told me that my house was beautiful but there was no happiness there.

When I tried to talk to Melvin about my unhappiness, he looked at me with disdain and said he couldn't believe how middle class I had become. I said I didn't see that as a handicap, and he "went ballistic." He again punched me and threw me against the wall, saying if he couldn't have me, no one else would. During this time of misery, Susan and I happened to attend a workshop out of town where we were paired together in an encounter exercise. In a discussion of Melvin, Susan looked directly in my eyes and told me not to waste my life. I could feel the depth of her concerned counsel. I took her advice to heart, although it would be several months before I could act on it.

I finally got up the courage to leave my marriage. While Melvin was out, I took a few clothes and went to a friend's house in Sacramento for the weekend, where I knew he couldn't find me. When I returned at dusk on Sunday evening, as I approached the dark house I knew something was wrong. I peered in the window and was astonished to see a totally empty room. I went inside and discovered an empty house with all nine rooms of furniture, clothes, degrees, checkbooks, everything with my name on it, gone! At first glance I wanted to think I was crazy, or having hallucinations! But I knew that my empty house was a reality. I had a range of feelings from anger, and shock, to disbelief, but at the same time felt a strange sense of relief that he was at least not there. I went to Bob and Susan's with my weekend's supply of clothes, and they offered me refuge for as long as I needed it. Bob was my insurance man and helped me file a claim for the theft. Fortunately, the house was in my name only, as my separate property, because I had bought it while he was away.

Although Melvin had stolen and shipped my furniture back to St. Louis, he had not left town. He showed up one night at my friends' house and threatened to kill everybody there if I didn't come home with him. Susan and I ran and hid in a closet, but we could hear the shouting. Bob threatened to call the police (who were not Melvin's favorite people). For years I had heard about the brutality of the police and Melvin's hatred of them. I knew if I was a party to Melvin's getting arrested in a white neighborhood, I would be seen by him as committing the ultimate betRaythel al. Suddenly I felt torn between choosing to identify with my blackness or my safety. My fear shocked reason into me. Luckily, Melvin decided on his own to leave, so Susan and I could come out of the closet. We talked most of the night about what I should do about Melvin.

My family in St. Louis had heard through the grapevine

that Melvin had returned there with all nine rooms of my furniture. They made many phone calls to me urging me to get an attorney, to get my furniture back. Quite reluctantly I agreed, but I felt I was no match for Melvin's corrupt behavior. The attorney did nothing but take my money.

After about a week, Melvin telephoned me at work and asked when I was coming home. I asked where home was. He responded, "Where your furniture is." Emotionally exhausted from the drain of years of fear and stress, I summoned the courage somehow to tell him that he took the furniture, he must have wanted it, so he should keep it, and that he had left the most important person intact, and that was me. I had bought that furniture and I could buy some more. This brought an onslaught of more threats and curses, that he would hire a hit man to kill me, that I would never know peace because I would always be looking over my shoulder wondering when he would be there. I hung up on him. I truly believe that his taking the furniture was a sublimation for hurting me. With fear and trepidation I decided that I had to live my life. I had to go on, even with the threat of death at any moment. I had the marriage annulled. During the hearing the judge asked me why I married him. I had no answer.

On visits to St. Louis to see my family, Melvin would somehow find out I was in town, and one evening when I had returned to my mother's house, I realized Melvin had been following me. He threw a brick into the bedroom window, barely missing my head. Another time someone set my mother's back porch on fire, and everybody was sure it was him. Later, not realizing the porch was weakened, my mother fell from the porch to the basement and might have been killed if my brother hadn't broken the fall. Shortly after her fall she came to live with me in Fresno.

Melvin disliked my mother with a passion, though he claimed if he'd had her for his mother he could have been president of the United States. He was very jealous of my closeness to my mother and my attention to my family. He once told me that during what I'd thought was protected sex, he had been cutting holes in the condoms with the hope that I would become pregnant. He said that since I couldn't love him, he would be satisfied if I could give a child of his the kind of love I gave my family.

Five years later Melvin was shot sixteen times and killed while in his bed. I heard that he had been found with his penis and testicles cut off and stuffed in his mouth. I'm sure it was drug related, although no one was ever charged with the murder to my knowledge. A friend telephoned me from St. Louis to inform me of his death and ask if I were going to attend the funeral. I replied that I had had enough of Melvin in life and would pass on this one. In telling another friend about his death, I said I was glad he was dead, and she asked, "Did you kill him?" Although I'd wanted to many times, I never had the courage. I remember making the comment that God took the brother away because He had work for me to do which could not be done with Melvin here. THANK YOU, GOD. I was finally freed.

Since the time of his death to the present, I have had recurrent dreams about Melvin. He has continued to symbolize fear in my life, chasing me as I'm running and trying to get away from his domination and control. A psychic who was a new client volunteered that she was being contacted by someone who had passed over. I thought it was my mother, but she said it was a man dressed in a business suit and graying at the temples. I knew immediately who she was referring to. She said the man wanted me to know that he loved me very much and was proud of me. On another occasion, during a seance, he insisted on expressing through my friend, wanting her to give me a kiss from him. Even in his death I am not totally free from him. The gift of my relationship with Melvin has been the realization that fear will not kill me. Subsequently, I have been able to do things that frighten me instead of avoiding them. My stepfather told me once that whatever doesn't kill you will strengthen you, and I have witnessed the absolute truth of his statement.

In a telephone conversation with my college roommate about relationships, I commented that I was nobody's savior, and she reminded me that I used to think I was. She said I acted as if it was my responsibility to fix whatever was wrong in any situation that I found myself in. She described me as very picky and with extremely high standards for men, except when it came to Melvin Saunders. With him I had no standards at all, she said. Knowing I had been busted, I admitted that I had been on a naïve mission to "save" Melvin. In the end I was the one who needed to be saved.

Another gift from Melvin was the realization that I had projected all of my fears and negativity on him and that allowed me to disown them in myself. Melvin was so intense and aggressive that it overwhelmed any sense of my self and hid the part of me that colluded with the abuse. Melvin also had told me that I judged everybody according to myself, thinking they would or would not behave as I would. He had pointed out that this was a mistake. Although I did not grasp the meaning of this insight at the time it was given, over the years I have realized the truth in this statement. Wanting to see the best in people, and always willing to give the benefit of the doubt, I had a tendency to ignore or refuse to see character defects which would later come back to haunt me.

This denial was my abdication of personal responsibility-- the Bible says we should watch as well as pray. This was a hard lesson for me to learn because I just wanted to be laid back and mellow. I suppose I thought that if I didn't approach a relationship with an open heart, I might miss someone who was trustworthy. I now realize that in truth trust should not be placed in the other person but in myself and my ability to discern. Recently I heard a guru validate this by saying *not to trust anyone,* because we humans always fall short of perfection. Trust is misplaced if it's not in yourself.

CHAPTER FOUR

MIDLIFE~ SELF EXPRESSION

"My mother is a poem I'll never be able to write
Though everything I write is a poem to my mother."

Sharon Dubia

On some level, I have always known that I would one day be a mother. It just wasn't clear to me how I was going to get the children, although there were a lot of them around in the family in St Louis. I had no desire to repeat the family pattern of becoming a parent without the benefit of marriage, because I truly believed that marriage should come before the carriage! God had good reason for providing children with two parents even if one or both decides not to stay around. I had no desire to get married and play the traditional role. I had not met anyone with whom I could have an honest, supportive, exciting, and fulfilling relationship. So, settling for less seemed unappealing.

I was surprised that my first experience of motherhood was with my own mother. My maternal grandmother had died when my mother was around four years old. Because of her own deprivations she was determined to be a good mother, and she was. My mother was an unusually strong woman and she had only one fear (that I was aware of)--having to go to a nursing home. She occasionally commented throughout my childhood that one mother could take care of thirteen children but thirteen children couldn't take care of one mother. In my heart I knew as well as all of my siblings seemed to know that I would be the person to take care of her.

After Melvin set fire to my mother's back porch in St. Louis, she fell into the basement. She no longer felt safe being in her home. I invited her to come live with me in Fresno, and within a month I picked her up at the airport. Although she missed her home, friends, and the rest of the family, she adjusted well, and made some new friends. She enjoyed playing with her little white poodle and taking walks around the peaceful neighborhood. I introduced her to my friends and neighbors and took her sightseeing to Yosemite and other beautiful places around California. She seemed to be content living with me, and I loved having her company, as well as having delicious dinners waiting for me when I arrived home from work.

I was now well established and professionally successful, and had given up on finding Mr. Right. I felt I was now Ms. Right, and was ready to share my life with a child. I called my sister Ruby who was taking care of six children of her own and several grandchildren, and told her that I was ready to take care of a child. She could ask the children who wanted to come live with me in California. She gathered the children together and asked who would like to move to California to live with me. La Wanda, my great niece, raised her hand and volunteered. I knew she had been neglected, but at the time I was not aware of the extreme abuse she was experiencing and desperate to flee from.

On one of my mother's trips to St. Louis, she brought La Wanda back to Fresno with her on the train. Although La Wanda had said she wanted to come live with me, she arrived frightened, not knowing what she had gotten herself into, nor what to expect. We had seen each other only during my periodic visits to St. Louis, and she knew me as the "rich aunt" who always sent dolls home at Christmas.

La Wanda was a thin, light-skinned, high-spirited and adventurous ten-year-old with a very pretty face. A few hours after her arrival, she changed her clothes, ate, and immediately went outside looking for other children in the apartment complex where we lived. Although she was disappointed at not being able to find any black ones, she settled for whom she found. She soon had many friends. One day she came home and said that some of the teachers and children at school were prejudiced. I decided to go to the school to check it out. On our way to school, almost as if she were my equal, La Wanda said in a plotting voice that if I "took care of the teachers," she would "take care of the children." (I did, and she did!) In spite of the racism she experienced, she boldly chose to dress in African attire for a school play, and I was very proud of her courage. I also enjoyed dressing her up and exposing her to fine restaurants and cultural events. She thrived on the attention, and we started to become close.

After a few months La Wanda invited some friends over for a pool party. She came into the house and asked me what were the rules of the pool. I asked what she meant, and she said, "You know, at Mrs. Whitehead's house they have rules about what the children can and cannot do." This was my first realization that she was a child who needed and wanted rules. As I recall, there were no specific rules in my house where I grew up. There were, however, numerous ex-pectations, most of which were unexpressed, but if you crossed the invisible line, there was hell to pay. Experience has taught me that children need two things: love and clear expectations. I began to develop more structure for her life.

Six months later another niece named Kathy decided that she also wanted to come to California. Kathy was a short, dark-skinned, attractive girl who had lost her mother, my sister Bernice, at the age of about four. She was smart, but without direction, and did not really apply herself to anything. She was a pre-teen when she arrived, and she spent a lot of time on the phone talking to her siblings in St. Louis. Although I made great efforts to help her adjust, she didn't want to make the transition, and she only stayed about three months.

Unknown to me, La Wanda had experienced not only physical and emotional abuse but sexual abuse prior to coming to live with me. As a ten-year-old child under my rather close supervision, she seemed to behave normally most of the time. Some of her development was downright precocious, and she was identified as a leader by her teachers and peers. She knew things that most ten year olds were not aware of. Sometimes I noticed she overreacted to my occasional dates or outings with male friends, but I attributed it to jealousy over sharing me with a male. I imagined she probably feared that I might be swept off my feet by romance and leave her.

My mother, La Wanda and I lived in Fresno as a happy family of three for five years. One weekend my friend Pat from San Francisco visited me, and she told me that UC was looking for an assistant director of social work. She said she thought I would be good for the department and should apply. However, she said she knew that I was not interested in moving because I had just finished decorating my house. I responded that I couldn't imagine allowing a house to control my life. The thought of living in San Francisco was very appealing, so I decided to send in an resume.

Several years before, Tom and I had gone to San Francisco in search of employment and had applied at the UC Social Work Department. There were no positions available and the chief told us that the two of us should not apply for work together, because some people "might get the wrong idea." I guess she thought we were a couple, and in those days interracial relationships were not looked upon kindly, even in San Francisco.

The same woman was still chief of the department my second time around, but did not recognize me. Sitting in the office waiting to be interviewed, I decided to smoke a cigarette (which was acceptable in those days), and the Administrative Assistant was very attentive and brought me an ashtray right away, with a big smile on her face. This was a nice welcome, and I felt things were off to a good start. I was interviewed by the chief and a newly formed executive committee, whose purpose was to improve the staff morale, as well as make policies. It was a very old department with the same longtime chief of many years and little turnover of the large staff of about twenty-six people. This stagnation was fertile ground for discontent and conflict. The assistant chief who I replaced was fired, and had left the department in an uproar. She was angry, bitter, and dominating, and was disliked by most of the staff. I returned to my home in Fresno and thought about the many advantages of living in San Francisco, especially the vibrant social life of the big city. Two days later I telephoned the chief and said I wanted to be considered a serious applicant.

She responded, "Thank God that is the reason you called because the committee and I unanimously decided that you are the person we want!" In one month, I had moved to San Francisco.

My friend Judy had already relocated, and we shared an apartment. She had been the office manager in Fresno, where I was the supervisor. She was excellent at her job and appreciated the way I did mine. We held each other in high regard and over time we developed a very deep friendship, so I was looking forward to living with her. I planned to spend the weekends in Fresno with Mama and La Wanda.

La Wanda was very unhappy about not being able to go to San Francisco with me. I thought it was important for her to finish the school year in Fresno, and I needed time to find a house for all of us. The day before I was scheduled to leave, she came up behind me, playfully picked me up, realized I was too heavy and quickly dropped me, breaking my ankle. This did not make negotiating the steep San Francisco hills easy. Parnassus (where I worked) is one of the steepest. Even this didn't deter my enthusiasm for starting a new life.

My mother also was very upset about having to leave Fresno. I offered to let her keep the house there with a live-in caretaker. I would pay the bills and continue to visit her on the weekends. She declined, did not want to stay there without me, and decided to move when I found a house. Martin volunteered to look after my mother and La Wanda until I got settled and was ready for them to come. He took them shopping, for various appointments, (my mother did not drive), and he also helped around the house. He either brought them to San Francisco on the weekends, or I drove to Fresno, about a four hour trip.

Judy and I lived on Russian Hill, and just walking up it was a major challenge. We didn't have a garage, and being able to find a parking space often determined whether or not we went out after work.

My first week in the office at UC was primarily orientation, and everyone was on their best behavior. The Black Caucus in the department had organized a reception in my honor and invited other department heads and employees to meet me. This was impressive! Carrie and Harriet had graced the tables and decorated the room with African art, and I felt personally important and culturally validated.

The honeymoon was short but sweet, and then various serpents began to rear their ugly heads. Several of the senior staff had wanted the vacant position, but no one had applied. Some of the unresolved negativity surrounding my predecessor was passed on to me. Because I am black, a relatively new color to the department, and the only color at the level of my position, there seemed to be an assumption of incompetence until proven otherwise. Once when using the word "homosexual" with one of the gay staff members (who was not "out" at the time), I was told in a condescending manner that the word "dated" me. There were a number of history keepers who were eager to tell me why one thing or another could not possibly be done. I heard that one of the lifers who had been at the department since its inception some thirty-six years ago had said that the department had survived several assistant chiefs and would also survive me, only the third assistant chief in its history.

Shortly after I started my new job at UC, the director asked me how it felt moving from being a big fish in a small pond to being a little fish in a big pond. I told her I didn't know, but I would tell her when I found out. I think this might have been the beginning of my realization that I had greatly expanded the walls of my world and had to adjust to the new dimensions. In the process of learning my complex new job, I was often bewildered, hurt, and sometimes confused. I used some of my close friends as a reality check, and when I discussed my experiences in the department with them, they assured me that I was perfectly competent, and I was not the ogre I was being made out to be. I had arrived at UC an emotional, sometimes volatile, self propelled individual. I gradually realized that if I were to last in this position, I could not afford the luxury of indulging in my emotions or taking things personally. The philosophy of the Course in Miracles became my lifeline, and my daily practice was to see love and not fear. I could see that even though many of the staff had built angry walls around themselves, as true social workers they were also aware of their hearts.

The department was divided into four sections with section chiefs responsible for the hospitals and sixty-two clinics which the department covered. The section chiefs and the executive committee comprised the department's management group. Most of them were very competent, some of them wanted to do the right thing, and a few of them did. There were two strong, highly capable black women who were very supportive of me, like ideal sisters, and we have remained good friends to this day. Like my family, there was a great deal of confusion about boundaries and appropriate roles, with interactions characterized by projections. Unlike my family of origin, my work family theoretically shared common goals and policies which I could attempt to call people back to. This objective reality was my anchor. I gradually developed a professional detachment and internal self-monitoring system.

Shortly after I was hired, I met with the hospital administrator who asked me what was the advantage of hiring a black assistant chief. I said it was to help white staff learn to work more effectively with black patients and coworkers and other minorities as well. He then asked if blacks needed help to work more effectively with whites. I suggested to him that it is impossible to succeed in a white dominated world and graduate from white institutions without learning to understand white people, who do not have the same requirements-- for them, relating to and understanding blacks is an option.

After a few months I found and bought the house of my dreams in the Sausalito hills. It was a modern two-story, three bedroom, redwood and glass home. My friends thought I was crazy to take on such a huge mortgage. One who was particularly financially savvy pointed out to me that I couldn't even afford to pay the taxes, and that I should look for a house in Daly City. I told him I wanted to live in Sausalito. Even though I had no idea how I was going to pay for it, when I walked into the house, exhausted from house hunting, I leaned against the wall and said to God, "I'm tired of looking." God responded, "This one's yours." So I stepped out on faith. After closing escrow, I was sitting on the steps looking out at the panoramic view of Mount Tamalpais, the bay and sailboats, and the surrounding tree-covered hills, and saying aloud the words, "I can't believe I bought the whole thing!"

Judy decided to move to Sausalito and rent from me which helped with the mortgage. One of her friends who was consultant to a chain of nursing homes was leaving town and referred me for the job. My income was increased by $900 a month. My mother volunteered to contribute $300 a month from her social security check. In the second year the taxes were reduced by more than 50% by Prop 13, so God did provide.

Although the house was very beautiful, my mother did not

adjust well to Sausalito, where she felt isolated and lonely. She was not interested in senior centers and didn't have much in common with the neighbors. I loved the house--the expansive view, and the beauty of my surroundings. I wished it could have been different for my mother, but felt that I needed it for myself. She was home alone all day until I came home from work. I took her out on weekends and she made a few trips to St. Louis, but I knew she was not happy. Her health started failing and she was hospitalized twice. She had arthritis for years and insisted on walking up and down the outside steps to keep her legs from getting too stiff. I was very concerned about this and feared she might fall. In less than six months my deepest fear had manifested.

While I was at work my mother fell on a newly waxed hardwood floor and hit her head on a table in the hallway, instantly becoming a quadriplegic. Fortunately a friend was visiting me at the time building some new steps to my basement. He called me at work and told me that he had found my mother unconscious on the floor. I became hysterical and have no memory of my drive home. The ambulance arrived as I got home and I followed it to the hospital. I was afraid that my mother might die, and I was in no way ready to let her go. I felt as if the bottom had dropped out of my world. Although she was unconscious, I tearfully pleaded with her not to die and leave me. I'm sure she heard my cry.

The emergency room doctor was a vascular surgeon,

whose bedside manner left much to be desired. I took offense at his abruptness and we got into a big argument over my mother's care. My mother's personal physician was at a different hospital, and for some strange reason the emergency doctor asked to become the primary doctor.

Although he seemed to be taking very good care of my mother, antagonism between the two of us continued to grow. He was of the opinion that my mother wanted to die and should be allowed to do so. He did not feel that I could or should take care of her at home, and said that I was a young woman and should be out dating. (Later it became clear to me that he thought I should be dating him.) In the ICU he asked my mother if she wanted to die. I was infuriated by his insulting and insensitive attitude and started calling him every dirty name I could think of. I told him that I was going to have some of my friends catch him in a dark alley and cut him up. A nurse approached us and said, "We have sick patients here! You're going to have to go outside with this!"

In spite of his objections, I insisted on taking my mother home. Again he asked to follow her care with a promise to make house calls. With no training in nursing, I was overwhelmed with the responsibility of feeding tubes, hydraulic pumps to get my mother in and out of bed, blood pressure cups, etc. I was extremely anxious and made many calls imposing on the doctor's offer of goodwill. He was very responsive and came any time I asked him to. He took excellent care of her. Impressed with his unquestionable skills, and by now kind manner and gentleness, we developed a true friendship.

Though his interest in me was romantic, and there were a few kisses here and there, I was never interested in him in that way. Among other things, I think he became the symbol for powerful, arrogant white men toward whom I had much anger. We both enjoyed a good fight, and I would delight in taking out my verbal boxing gloves and boxing him around. One time I asked him why he'd wanted to be my mother's doctor when I had disregarded his advice. He said that he saw me as a strong informed woman who was not making a totally emotional decision to do something that she couldn't handle. He was intrigued with my determination and wanted to be part of my team. We remained friends after my mother's death, and even to this day we maintain occasional contact.

My dear friend Judy, who I'm sure was one of the angels sent to help me on my tumultuous journey, shared in my many responsi-bilities. She helped with my mother's care and the children as if they were her own. After my mother's fall, even though she was a quadriplegic and only able to move her head, she was afraid of falling out of bed. This meant twenty-four care because she wanted someone with her all the time. Judy was the one who suggested putting my mother's hospital bed in the living room so she could be a part of the family activity. Judy took regular shifts, getting up during the night to sit with my mother. She helped with all the chores, bought nice gifts for La Wanda and later the other children on special occasions, and taught them to wrap gifts and make beautiful bows. She shared in all family activities, including some gatherings with drunk out-of-control relatives. Since she herself didn't drink, I know this was way outside of her comfort zone.

She was an anchor for me: after putting my mother to bed, we often had philosophical discussions, and would laugh and talk about how we were content and at peace staying home on the weekends, while others our age were out partying. Some might have seen our lives as boring, but we didn't. Judy taught me a lot about love and friendship. I often ask myself if the roles were reversed whether I could be as unselfishly giving as she was.

One day I needed tires and went to the tire store in San Francisco. There I met Jim, a mechanic; he was a tall, thin, good-looking light brown skinned man who was very shy and unassuming. He offered to do some needed work on my car on his time off, and I was delighted.

Jim turned out to be one of my most loving angels. He was fifteen years my junior, and without a doubt the most gentle, supportive man that I'd ever dated. He was also very good in bed, and it was in my relationship with him that I experienced the essence of tantric sex. He was very appreciative of my body, and we both cherished our sexual union. During one of our times of love making, he became for me the Father, the Son , and the Holy Spirit. This was my first and only spiritual experience of my root or sexual chakra.

Jim came over often. On weekends when the attendant for my mother was off duty, he took the entire night shift sitting with my mother. He was the one person my mother preferred over me to sit with her because he would remain awake all night and I frequently fell asleep during my shift. Sometimes she would wake up, fearful, and find me asleep. After an all night shift, one morning as he was leaving, I thanked him profusely for taking care of my mother. He said, "Oh honey, you don't have to thank me. I enjoyed it." I was deeply moved by his selfless love.

My mother (for good reasons) had a lot of anger toward men during her life. Unintentionally this was passed on to me. I believe one of the reasons that my mother held onto life, even though a large part of her wanted to die, was to help me work through the anger. Unaware of how my unconscious anger expressed itself, one day after talking to a telemarketer on the phone and telling him that I wasn't married, my mother called me to her bed and told me not to boast about being single because it hurt Jim's feelings. I had been oblivious to the possibility that he might have a reaction. She pointed out to me that he was a better husband to me and a better father to the girls than most legally married men. This was the start of my sensitivity to the fact that the men in my romantic relationships also have feelings. I was developing a new compassion and empathy for them.

Once when I wanted to go to Chicago for a prestigious professional leadership training, I was in a quandary about who would take care of my mother after the attendant went home. Jim told me not to worry about it, that he would take a week's vacation and take care of her. I was reluctant to leave him with the responsibility of changing diapers and dressing the bedsores she had developed. He said, "If you want to go, go! I'll handle it." I was overwhelmed by his loving generosity.

While entertaining friends for dinner, I commented to one of the guests that I had the best relationship with Jim that I'd ever had with any man. He was embarrassed and in disbelief. Eventually there would be ten female beings living together in our home, including a cat and a dog, and we all looked forward eagerly to Jim's arrival at our door. On one occasion, when driving home after a party, I was inspired to tell Jim how much I appreciated him. He told me to stop talking like that or he might have an accident. I responded that I needed to tell him and he needed to hear it.

In many ways Jim was wiser and more mature than I was. His desire in life was to live on a ranch and become a father. At this time I had had a hysterectomy and was too old to bear his children and had no desire to be isolated from "city life." Jim started talking about wanting to be married and have children. For this reason I knew the relationship was time-limited. I suggested that we maintain our sexual relationship while he was looking for his wife, and discontinue it when he found her. His response to me was that he couldn't do that--he was a one-woman man. This reduced me to the size of an ant. I loved him too much to try to hold on to him when I couldn't give him what he wanted. I accepted that I had to let him go. I asked him if we could continue being platonic friends, but he said he couldn't handle that.

Since Jim was a mechanic I used the excuse to call him whenever my car was malfunctioning. He came over and repaired my car for awhile, then suggested that I find another mechanic. The loss of this relationship resulted in a lot of grief and three days in bed. Years later La Wanda saw Jim at Muni where they were both employed. He had an eighteen year old daughter who he had raised after her mother's death. La Wanda had gotten his telephone number and asked me if I wanted it. I said, "No, I want to continue to respect his wishes."

Matilda, a petite, cute, very competent twenty-six year old from Nicaragua was the best, longest-lasting full time caretaker for my mother we had. She was also a seamstress. She had a precocious six year old daughter named Maggie who also lived with us; she had an understanding and maturity that exceeded her years. Since Matilda was very soft spoken and easy going, often it was necessary for me to act as the disciplinarian for Maggie. Matilda was married to a man many years her senior who lived in San Francisco, and she and Maggie went home on weekends. Although Matilda had lived in this country for several years, she didn't have citizenship; fortunately I was able to sponsor her and help her obtain it.

Matilda took very good care of my Mother and me. She was also kind and caring with La Wanda and later with my other children, who were fond of her. Matilda and I became a "handyman team", repairing, or attempting to repair everything from washing machines to the kitchen sink, which we unstopped with a huge snake which was bigger than both of us put together. At least two times a week Matilda would make a dress or blouse or suit for me during the day while my mother was asleep. I looked forward to coming home from work to see what she had made.

When her eighty year old husband died, she remarried and had another girl named Maria. Maggie now speaks several languages and is a translator for the Army. She is married and has two children for whom I am godmother. Maggie and her family visit me whenever they come into town. Matilda was one of the true lights in my life during this difficult time, and we have maintained contact over the years on holidays and special occasions.

My oldest brother who drove me to California married late in life to a much younger woman. They proceeded to have ten children. She died at the young age of thirty-seven from cancer of the uterus. My brother attempted to keep the family together by working two jobs and trying to be both mother and father. My mother who was in her sixties helped him as much as she could and much more than she should have while she was in St. Louis. After a few years he began having strokes and had a total of eight before he became completely incapacitated. Both he and his wife had asked me to take the children if anything happened to either or both of them. They were in good health at the time and I doubted anything could happen to both of them; as the unspoken caretaker of the family, I agreed to it.

My brother was placed in a nursing home after his fourth stroke, but he had a strong constitution and we all thought he would recover again. In the meantime the children were left in the care of a rather unstable older sister. My mother had developed a good relationship with Henry's fourth child and second daughter, Yolanda, who was fast becoming a teenager. My mother was concerned about her being unsupervised and suggested that she might come live with us on a temporary basis. I talked to my brother and got his permission for me to come and get her.

Yolanda was a rich caramel colored brown skinned twelve-year-old. She handled the stress and trauma in her life by closing down and resisting new experiences. She was unhappy about having to leave her family and was determined not to adjust to a new one. She was aggressive and solved all her conflicts with physical force. She would eat only french fries and hot dogs, and fiercely resisted my attempts to introduce variety in her diet.

One day while I was in the basement preparing for a painting job, La Wanda came down and excitedly told me that Yolanda was upstairs planning her own funeral. I was tired and by now exasperated. I went upstairs and told Yolanda that I loved her, was willing to do whatever I could to make her happy, and hoped that would be enough for her, but in the event that it wasn't, if she decided to kill herself, there was really nothing I could do. I went back downstairs and continued my painting. The subject never resurfaced.

Two months after Yolanda arrived, I received a telephone call informing me that my brother was in intensive care with little chance of recovery. He could no longer care for his children, who now ranged in age from five to eighteen. I went to St. Louis, and arranged for relatives to take the two youngest boys on a temporary basis, until I could make permanent plans. I had decided to take the two youngest girls, Nita and Angie, back to California with me, my mother, La Wanda, and now Yolanda. The older children would remain in their family home and take care of themselves. At work I was the new director of a large department at UCSF, had a full social life, and was caring for my bedridden mother at home. Although my plate was completely full, I knew the job was mine to do. I didn't think about how, I just decided to.

Becoming an instant mother of four was clearly a life-changing event, and although I was taken by surprise, I was generally calm. La Wanda was not happy about having to share me not only with my mother but now several other children. I told La Wanda that if there was room in our hearts, there was room in our house. I trusted in the universe and just opened to the experience. My friends and mother cautioned me about taking on such huge responsibilities, but it didn't seem like such a big deal to me.

I flew back to California with Angie and Nita, both of whom were distraught and reeling over the breakup of their family. Angie was sullen and seemed to be fearing the worst, but had a wait-and-see attitude. Nita was more cheerful, open, and had a hopeful expectancy. My attitude was that I had accepted a new assignment and I knew God would help me rise to the occasion.

Angie, the seventh in her family of ten in St. Louis, was slightly overweight and had been the scapegoat for her older siblings. For some reason, they took delight in picking on her and finding all kinds of ways of frightening her. She rewarded them with the response of squealing hysterically and shaking uncontrollably. With the loss of both parents and most things familiar to her, she saw the world as scary and out to get her. She was extremely nervous and high strung, and she often trembled when she tried to express herself. She was very combative and argumentative with everyone, and masterful at creating conflict.

On the other hand, she was very warm and loving, sometimes volunteering to help me set the table, etc. She loved to talk, and talked rapidly in a high pitched voice. When she arrived home from school, at the top of the steps chaos would ensue in the house, in anticipation of her entrance. Chaos always accompanied her. I tried a wide range of techniques to reach Angie, from behavioral modification to bribes. Nothing worked. I suggested grief counseling to address her many losses. She told me she was not crazy and didn't need counseling. She refused to have any part of it. I attempted to solicit the help of the other children in bringing calm to Angie's life. They tried for a while not to be reactive to her provocations, but they soon reverted to old habits.

Benita was a very pretty, intelligent, creative ten-year-old who was the eighth in the family. She had been the recipient of the family's more positive attention. She had also received special attention from one of her teachers. She wanted a better life for herself and was hopeful that she could find it in California. Although she usually performed well in school, she had not been held accountable by her family in St. Louis and was not accustomed to doing household chores. On one occasion, I asked her to move a rug; she tripped over it and asked, "What rug do you mean?" When in doubt, she played both ends against the middle, and could always come down on the winning side.

When I took her to take her driver's test for the first time, she asked about the middle lane. Since the discussion took place in the abstract, I did not know what she was talking about, but assured her there is no middle lane. During the test she drove straight into the left-turn lane. After she flunked the test, I realized what she was talking about. I used the opportunity to explain to her that in life there is no middle lane, and one has to take a stand on one side or the other. Once when the kids played hooky from school, Nita claimed that she was talked into it, and I told her there were many temptations in life and she would have to choose her responses. Then I said I was punishing her for not thinking for herself, as well as playing hooky.

I bought two sets of twin beds, and I let the girls choose the wallpaper for their rooms. The two oldest, Yolanda and La Wanda, could not be talked out of a pink and silver metallic design of nude ladies. This was my first experience of having really to stretch to accommodate the differences in our opinions, lifestyles, values, and beliefs. There would be many more compromises, and the call for flexibility in what I thought was important and right. It was as if we came from two different worlds, although in many ways it was the very same. I knew I would have to choose my battles. The two youngest, Angie and Nita, were a bit easier to influence, and we decided to cover their walls with sheets. They had the design of a forest, which I thought was more appropriate and much easier for me to look at. The children seemed to enjoy helping with the preparation of their rooms. They all responded willingly to the sometimes overwhelming art projects I introduced, such as putting together a quilt with complicated patterns.

Shopping for groceries became a major event, requiring many hours and many dollars. I took them with me to teach them about comparison shopping. They listened with varying degrees of interest, but were more interested in getting an abundance of potato chips and sodas and cookies; I preferred for them to have more healthy and fresh foods. They did love meat, steaks and ribs especially, and I indulged them. I later learned that Nita had supplied her favorite Golden Gate Transit bus driver with filet mignon steak sandwiches for lunch which she had taken from the refrigerator and cooked for him.

Arriving home from work one day, I heard the children discussing the rules of the house. Hearing them for the first time, I realized that La Wanda had made them up, and since they sounded pretty good, I decided to go along with her. On one occasion, when I was upset and yelling at the children, La Wanda told me I should try to enjoy my children because I wouldn't have them with me for very long. I accepted the truth of this advice, and tried to follow it. La Wanda sometimes had wisdom and maturity beyond her years; in my presence, she was well-behaved; in many ways she seemed like a model child. I found it hard to believe when the children told me her behavior changed radically when I wasn't around.

My fantasy about how the girls should dress was short-lived. For the most part they were identified with the ghetto mentality of pimps and hoochie mamas. They humored me by leaving home in the morning dressed somewhat modestly and I was oblivious to their game.

Once while watching TV, Angie announced that she wanted to date a pimp. She said she thought they were cool. On a vacation to Tahoe, we posed for a family portrait in turn-of-the-century hats and dresses. Nita was very upset because I wouldn't allow her to wear a saloon dress. I told her that we were a respectable family and needed to look like one. Nita and I continued an ongoing battle about appro-priate dress. When she went to her junior prom, we must have shopped at twenty stores before finding a dress that we could agree on. I often commented to the children that the way they dressed was similar to wearing a sign on a t-shirt, and if sex was not what they were offering, they shouldn't advertise it. In other words, "If it's not for sale, you shouldn't put it on the shelf." My comments seemed to go right over their heads.

I was astounded to learn from one of La Wanda's middle school teachers that she arrived at school in revealing tank tops and miniskirts and metallic ice-blue eye shadow. The teacher said she wore enough red lipstick and makeup to put hookers to shame. She left home looking like a normal eleven year old, and evidently meta-morphosed on the way to and from school. La Wanda was identified as a leader at school, and her teachers suggested that I counsel her about using her leadership in a "more positive direction." It became the subject of many of our conversations at home. She loved poetry and acting, and was a powerful leader, according to her teacher, in her drama class. I was very proud when she was selected to give her graduation address.

However, after graduating from high school and meeting her first real boyfriend (to my knowledge), she developed a mind of her own and was hell bent on following it. It led her to the darkest corners of life, including drug addiction, maternal neglect, and prostitution. Watching these behaviors was totally devastating to me, and I wondered where I had gone wrong. In spite of my gallant efforts to hold on to her, her addictions eventually separated us, and we became quite estranged. She acted as if I was part of the problem.

After several years she finally "hit bottom," and with the

help of a street minister and her faith in God, she saw the light and entered recovery. She is continuing to wake up on many very deep levels. I had very lofty ambitions for her as a child, which she did not share. I remember asking her why she chose to live in Hunters Point when she left Sausalito, and she said she thought it was pretty there. This was such a stretch from any adjective I would have used, that I couldn't even dignify it with a response.

Recently La Wanda asked me if I knew she had more than one personality as a child. I told her that we all have more than one personality. For instance, one part of us might want to lose weight and be thin, while another part wants to eat sweets and carbs in bed at night. As we mature, the conflicting aspects become integrated into a cooperative whole, which works for our highest good. In retrospect however, La Wanda was referring to the different personalities that she had developed to respond to the traumas of her childhood.

Now her self image is becoming more like the person I saw in her as a child. She recently confided in me that she was at a filling station located in the ghetto where she lives, and realized that she felt out of place there. She is beginning to recognize her own potential greatness. She has returned to school to learn more about finances and buying a house. She has lost more than fifty pounds, and she is writing a book which is a way of healing herself of the past. She has also found an expression of her creativity in a gift baskets business. She is generous and socially conscious in her donations of her time and free gift baskets to those in need; for example, she was inspired to take a basket from Oakland to Half Moon Bay to a family who lost two children in a fire. Her spirituality and ways of experiencing the world are so similar to my own that listening to her is like hearing a recording of myself. She has started to remember with great clarity the things I taught her as a child. I am so glad that I lived long enough to see these changes in her. It affirms my belief in the Biblical advice: Teach children in the ways that you would have them to go, and if they stray, they will always return.

    Once I went unexpectedly to the Marin City Community Center where the girls were and observed Angie, who seemed the least interested in sex, wearing a very revealing halter top which she must have stashed in her backpack when she left home. Needless to say, I was shocked, and speechless for awhile. I managed to ask in a shrill voice, "What do you have on?" She acted as if she didn't understand the question. I loved her sense of humor and her joy and talent in making other people laugh. Aware of her loss of both parents and the abuses she had endured in St. Louis, I was impressed with her resilience. At first I only wanted to believe the best about all of my children, but gradually and with some difficulty, I learned to see and accept the whole person including their conniving and deceitful sides.

At times La Wanda's reasoning left much to be desired. At seventeen, when she was insisting on leaving home prematurely, it seemed very important to me to have a mother-daughter talk, to review the teachings of her childhood. I wanted to make sure I didn't leave out any words of wisdom that might guide her along the way. Her response to my anxiety was to assure me that she understood what I was saying, that she knew the truth. She just decided to structure it differently. I was horrified at the thought that she believed she could structure the truth and it would remain true. With this statement I realized the futility of words and knew I had to release her to the reality of her experience.

At another time during one of the many pajama parties, I decided to have a little chat with the girls about the birds and the bees. I told them that I was not trying to deprive them of pleasures with my advice to avoid early sex and premature motherhood; I wanted them to make informed and constructive choices. Nita made no response in the group, but came to me the next morning in the privacy of my bathroom and told me she had decided to do it my way. I doubt she ever shared this decision with the other girls. She kept her promise, delayed immediate gratification, studied hard, and was the most responsive to my advice. In high school she developed a successful babysitting business and became well known by the mothers of young children in Sausalito. She loved fashion and name brands, and went to John Powell

Modeling School. She alone graduated from college, although it was my dream for all of the girls.

After having the girls for about nine months, another niece, ten-year-old Carla, visited from St. Louis, and she enjoyed the family activities and outings with us and asked to stay. Her mother, my sister, was taking care of our sick brother, and Carla said the atmosphere at home was like a hospital. With some hesitation her mother agreed.

Carla was a slim, feisty, headstrong Taurus, who cultivated the image of being tough. Since she was smaller than the others, she often approached her battles with a butcher knife. She did not adjust well to school, and although she was excellent at track, she showed little interest in developing this talent. Behind her tough facade, she was a sweet, delightful, attractive little girl who later told me that she thought she was ugly. During summer vacations, Carla went to St. Louis to visit her family. Her father, an alcoholic, was extremely permissive, and her mother was unable to set limits, so Carla would come back to California with a pseudo-independent attitude of, "I'll do whatever I want!"

Sometimes when I would arrive home from work, I found the girls engaged in fist fights, even drawing knives and throwing chairs. After dodging flying objects, I was finally able to calm them down for one of our many family conferences, on how one acts as part of a family. I punished them by making them do household chores of waxing the hardwood floors, sweeping in front of the house, washing dishes, etc. I also limited TV and phone calls, and withheld allowances. To train them to conserve energy I deducted small amounts for leaving appliances on. I told them PG and E had more money than I did and I wasn't interested in giving them more unnecessarily.

During a summer vacation, Carla's father bought her a much-wanted bike. He wanted to ship it to California at the store's expense, but Carla persuaded him to allow her to ride the bike while she was in St. Louis, with the plan for her father to ship it after she left. Months passed, and the bike never arrived. Carla was very disappointed that her new bike was in St. Louis and she was in California. I took this opportunity to tell her that the situation was an example of why children should not make adult decisions.

In my efforts to expose the children to a range of experiences, I often invited friends from different cultures to dinner during which we would experiment with food from around the world. Once my yoga teacher came over and cooked an Indian meal which was totally incompatible with the girls' taste buds. They tried to be polite and pretended to eat, but in a short time asked to be excused. One followed the other and they went off into another part of the house, but we could still hear their muffled shrieks and moans.

I also took the girls to a variety of churches, which in retrospect might have been a mistake. They had come from very traditional Baptist churches in St. Louis, and found different styles of worship somewhat confusing. After leaving the Sausalito Presbyterian Church one Sunday, Nita looked at me in exasperation and said, "Marie, I just can't make these psychological shifts the way you do. At the Presbyterian Church they tell us we're going to heaven, and at the Marin City Church they tell us we're going to hell!" I must admit that the shift from the ethereal to the earthy could be a real stretch. So we all ended up going to church in Marin City together during the remaining years the girls lived with me.

In my desire to equip the girls with resources to negotiate life, I also dragged them around to various psychics. The girls indulged me for awhile and then La Wanda told me that she did not want to know the future. This came as a huge surprise to me since I wanted nothing more than to understand where I was going and how to get there.

On occasions when I came home to find chores undone, I would call a meeting and do a group reprimand. Following the meeting, some of the girls would come to me when I was alone and tell me that they had done their chores. I would acquiesce and usually say, "I know honey, it wasn't you, it was the others." In talking to each other they apparently shared what I had said to them and learned that I had told them all the same thing. Some years later La Wanda accused me of "raising a group."

Because of the many demands on my time, and only seven days in the week, I was spread pretty thinly. In my attempt to spend quality time with each girl, I arranged to share with each one on a Saturday any activity of her choice every five weeks; on Sundays we did things as a group. Nita found a way to get a little extra time alone with me by meeting me at the bus stop after work, and I would hear about her day on our short walk home. One thing I've always appreciated about Nita is that she makes sure she gets what she needs. Angie befriended a minister's family in Marin City and found a mother figure who was easier to relate to. In time she moved in with them.

Taking the children inspired me to want to be the best person I could be. This desire led me to the discovery that the best person I could be is who I am. I learned to tell the truth not just about what I thought, but what I felt. There was something very freeing and com-forting about telling the truth about my feelings, because it validated me, and opened me to hear the reality of my children. In the words of Gandhi, "There is no God higher than the truth." I learned to love the truth, even when difficult. It provided the basis for my interactions and negotiations with the children. I asked them to tell me the truth no matter what. I admitted that I might scream and yell, but assured them I would get over it. If the children could persuade me to change my thinking, I noticed that my feelings would change accordingly. Recently La Wanda told me that one of the things she appreciates most about me is my willingness to give the other person the benefit of the doubt. She admitted there were times when she abused it. My identification with being a mother drew me to my highest self.

Every morning the children and I formed a prayer circle and I asked God to watch over, protect and guide them throughout the day. On several occasions Nita resisted coming into the circle, asking, "Do we have to pray again?" However, on the rare occasion when I thought I was too busy to take the time, it was she who reminded me that I had forgotten to pray . By the time I got the children off to school, and got myself dressed and the house straightened up, going to work at my high-pressure, high-profile administrative position was a welcome escape.

Occasionally we meet lifetime friends at work. I had the good fortune of meeting Harriet who was one of the section chiefs at UCSF and I was her supervisor. We had a model working relationship. Harriet was a very attractive, vivacious, bright, articulate, warm hearted young woman. She loved clothes, dressed in the latest designer fashions, and probably spent half her salary on looking good. We worked together all day, our offices were only a few feet apart, and we often shared lunch. In the evenings we dropped our roles at work and talked for several hours on the phone about her life and mine.

Harriet has been very loving and supportive of me for many years, first at work, and then extending to an active role of aunt with my children. She was a definite positive influence for them, especially Nita, who admired Harriet's style of Gucci bags and short skirts. Harriet was always available during crises, projects, outings, or whenever I needed two extra hands. She took the girls every weekend for several years to give me respite. She alternated their outings between cultural events and fun entertainment. Harriet wasn't much in the kitchen and the girls still joke about the hot dogs which they called "Harriet's specials."

Harriet was in love with a man that she married after some twenty-two years. I remember commenting to her once that I admired her tenacity because I would have forgotten what my objective was after so much time had passed. She knew what she wanted, however, and was willing to wait as long as it took. I was given the privilege of marrying them, in an elegant ceremony uniting their two cultures, which ended with their "jumping the broom." In this ritual, I had the opportunity to ask them three times if they were ready, the third time asking if they were really, REALLY ready; certainly they had waited long enough to be sure.

I have often remembered and smiled about the comment I made to Harriet about the long wait. However, she is my shining example of someone who knew what she wanted, was willing to wait for it, and happy with it once she got it. As I struggle through the months and years of my health issues, I am reminded of Harriet's example and consoled by the quote from St. Augustine that the reward of patience is patience. Harriet has continued to be one of my closest friends who has hung in there with me through thick and thin, as I have with her. I am continuously inspired by her enthusiasm, her presence, focus, and joy. She still takes the time to celebrate my birthday with me every year. She's truly one of the lights of my life.

I was blessed with double good fortune to meet another lifetime friend at work. Carrie was a very competent, talented, highly principled, loyal black woman with a big heart. Carrie was well named, and could be synonymous with the C in caring. Carrie has always been an advocate for racial pride and justice. She had an excellent understanding of systems even before systems analysis was popular. I had a deep respect for her evaluations of her patients, from a systems perspective. She was very outspoken and had the courage of her convictions. Although rather mild mannered, she was labeled as a "Black Militant" by some timid white people at UC who could only take in very small quantities the truth which she freely dispensed. During a time when I had to deal with acts or perceived acts of racism at UC, I made a statement to God that if I had to deal with racism, to please send me Carrie.

The next week, Carrie (who had left UC to work on a dialysis unit at General) told me that she wanted to return. She wrote one of the first social science textbooks on dialysis, for which I wrote the forward. Her return to the department was indeed an answered prayer.

Carrie was married and had two children. She commuted from Palo Alto to the City daily. She was 100% committed to both her job and family. In addition, she managed to write and play music, and write poetry. She was very goal focused, with a great deal of tenacity. She stayed in a marriage that was less than satisfying until her youngest son finished high school. She thought it was important to keep the family intact. She developed a Family Wellness Center and constantly sought ways to serve those less fortunate than she. At the age of fifty-five she is now working on a PhD in education.

Over the years she has been more helpful and supportive than I could say. In the late seventies, the hospital administrator gave a party at his home and I wanted to wear African attire. Carrie took me shopping in East Palo Alto and we found one of the most beautiful green and gold African gowns and gele that I have ever seen. My dress was the talk of the town for days afterward. I am still showered with many compliments every time I wear it.

Carrie was famous for her soul food cooking. Barbequed ribs and chicken, beans and rice, turkey and dressing, and macaroni and cheese were just a few of her specialties. My family and I have spent many holidays at her table. On several occasions she brought a week's supply of food to me and the girls just to help out. Although her visits are less frequent now, she always comes bearing gifts.

Other friends and neighbors were also generous in offering support and helping lighten my load. When I first moved into the house in Sausalito I was very suspicious of the watchful eyes of my next door neighbor. He would stand on his side porch facing my house observing the movers as they carried furniture and boxes inside. I thought he was trying to determine what kind of impact this black family was going to have on his lily white Sausalito hills neighborhood. As is turned out, he was looking for opportunities to be helpful. Later he and his wife, who was an engineer, tutored the girls in math. During the heavy rains one year when public transportation shut down, another neighbor volunteered to drive Nita to school in Terra Linda, and for two weeks she helped out. I will always be grateful for the village God provided me to raise my children in.

After two turbulent years, the UCSF chief resigned (as she had said she would.) I had been groomed by her as her replacement, but according to hospital policy it was an "open hire" with a national search. I and another senior staff member applied for the position, along with others from outside. The interviewing and hiring was done by an inexperienced new female administrator who was anxious to make a name for herself. She interviewed most of the department staff regarding their experience and opinion of me. Needless to say, I got mixed reviews. Inside applicants always come with baggage. Once in an administrative meeting with her, she asked me what I thought of some of the other applicants, and I had to remind her that I was among them and didn't think the question was appropriate. This made me wonder if I were being considered as a serious applicant for the job.

After several tumultuous months, however, I was offered the job and promoted from assistant chief to the chief. The assistant chief, who had applied for the chief's position along with me and clearly wanted my job, was a very bright, competent, assertive young woman. She took on the role of my external monitor, and took every opportunity to point out my mistakes to me and I'm sure to others. Nonetheless, we had mutual respect for each other. I made great effort to learn from my mistakes and daily renewed my commitment not to take things personally. (Life is never personal.)

The executive committee, formed to improve the department morale, and I, decided to administrate the department based on a democratic model. This decision resulted in daily challenges of my authority; management meetings were often used as a forum to voice and promote personal opinions, and it became necessary to clarify on an ongoing basis that I was responsible for the final decision.

My position as director of the Social Services Department was the most challenging experience of my life to date. It has been said, and probably by my mother, that "the further you go up the lamp pole, the more your ass shows." I learned the truth of this statement as I became the dumping ground for negative projections by people below me. Racism was alive and active, the gay rights movement was off and running, and feminism was flexing her muscle. I felt caught in the pressure cooker of these struggles. With all the projections and accusations from those who needed scapegoats, sometimes it was hard to determine who was doing what to whom. In this complex arena I learned that we can consciously choose our attitude, so why not choose what we want? I chose to see the challenges as an opportunity and not a threat.

I met Celeste when she was hospitalized at UC. Celeste was a twenty-eight-year-old mother of a six-year old, married to an aspiring actor. She was admitted to the hospital with a rare skin problem which was never diagnosed. She was treated with very high doses of cortisone and prednisone, and in this case, the treatment was worse than the disease. She developed severe complications which resulted in kidney failure, diabetes, and a raging infection which resulting in her losing all the hard palate in her mouth. One of my staff members who covered the medical floor asked me

to see Celeste for consultation; I am sure she was hoping that the therapist in me would want to continue with her as a client, which I did. During her long hospital stay, she had both legs amputated, and her right arm was amputated at the elbow. All of her fingers were removed from her left hand, leaving her with only a thumb.

I visited Celeste often during her hospital stay, and was absolutely amazed at her loving spirit, positive attitude, and courage. After her discharge, I followed her through six months at the rehabilitation center, where I continued to be in awe by her strength and determination. She was discharged from the center and went home with an attendant. I continued to visit her at home. I observed her teach herself to type with her thumb, to learn to write again, cook, and perform the daily activities of motherhood. She also started writing songs and poetry. By this time I had met all her family and we had become good friends. We did many things together, such as having picnics (one on my living room floor), going to plays, musicals, and church. During one of her many hospitalizations, Celeste told me that she would be happy if I would marry her husband if she died. I told her that I loved her and her husband, but marriage was not in my plans.

Celeste later decided to return to school to get a masters degree in rehabilitation, so she could help other people with disabilities. I arranged for her first year internship at UC where I supervised her. As anticipated, she was an outstanding student. She later became politically active in the Movement for Access for Persons with Disabilities.

Celeste taught me many things, including not to help her do anything unless she asked. I considered myself a fairly sensitive person regarding people's needs, but she took my awareness and sensitivity to new levels. She taught me to see the person first, and the disability as it was handled by the person. I will never forget the time she invited me to the fiftieth birthday of another amputee that she met at dialysis, which she took three times a week. We were sitting at the table drinking punch when someone suggested people start dancing. The crowd was slow to move, and while I was waiting to see who would make the first move, Celeste whisked by me in her wheelchair up to the center of the dance floor, and invited the birthday boy to dance. She whirled around in her wheelchair as if on wings. One of the songs she wrote was called, "Magical Lady." She was certainly one of those.

Over the years Celeste became a major source of inspiration and one of my heroes. In one of our many conversations, Celeste told me that she was actually happier with all of her losses than she was before. She said each time she lost a part of her body, or experienced times of great pain, she would say to herself, "Well, I'm not that, so who am I?" And this inquiry drew her deeper inside herself, closer to becoming one with her spirit.

After a long courageous battle this spiritual warrior died from a heart attack during dialysis. The absence of her light was and is a tremendous loss to me. During her lifetime, when I experienced challenges and stress, I would call Celeste and just talking to her made me feel better, because it immediately put my small issues and self imposed limitations in proper perspective. Now I call upon her spirit in my heart when I need encouragement.

A year after I became director of the Social Work Department, I was elected president of the Black Caucus for the campus. During my tenure, there were numerous crises around racial issues. Tension was in the air and suspicions abounded: it was a racially charged atmosphere throughout the country and particularly on college campuses. I was wearing a large afro and many of the caucus members wore not only afros but African attire as well. Black Power was the rhetoric of the day, and hard lines were drawn in the sand around racial issues.

To resolve one crisis I requested a meeting with the hospital administrator. He asked me what I would suggest as a solution. I recommended a training program in race relations for the entire UCSF campus. In discussing the possibilities, he said he thought the program should start with the administrators and department heads. He asked if I would be willing to develop such a program and offered me a year's sabbatical from my position to do so. At this time I had planned to take my daughter to Hawaii for her graduation. He told me that while I was in Hawaii, to think of what I wanted to do and how much money I wanted to make (this was the era of abundant funds in health care). At one other time in the past, I had been asked how much money I wanted to make, but never what I wanted to do and how I wanted to do it. This inspired me to let my imagination soar; the higher it climbed, the more obvious my fears became. Lying on the beach, I decided to accept his invitation and confront my fears. I recalled a comment made by the former chief that I always rose to the occasion.

It is paradoxical that in the midst of the racially charged atmosphere of the early seventies, I found a "soul mate" who was white. Julie taught in the Sausalito Public Schools for thirty years, including teaching all five of my girls. We were introduced by another English teacher who suggested that she invite me to give a career talk to her eighth graders, and for many years I did annual visits to her class. She said she took an instant liking to me since I showed up in stylish business suits and Birkenstocks. We had a strong spiritual connection from the beginning; we became good friends and started doing many things together. Julie turned out to be one of my closest friends and richest treasures.

It is ironic that Julie, an upper middle class Midwestern white woman, taught me a deeper appreciation of my own cultural heritage. Julie and I spent long hours writing the CARE program, a series of Cultural Awareness workshops for administrators and staff of UCSF. When the Black Caucus decided to perform the Negro National Anthem for the UC campus for Black History Week, again Julie came to the rescue bringing inspiration and lightheartedness to helping me learn the words and choreography to the anthem. We shared many belly laughs as we went about our task. We both remember all the verses to this day. It's still hard for me to believe that I had the courage to actually do a dance performance in front of a large audience of my peers and superiors.

Julie was very knowledgeable and appreciative of Black History and culture. She was disowned by her father who was a prominent hand surgeon when she married a black man and had two biracial sons. I have always been impressed by Julie's ability and determination to raise her sons with pride for both their cultural heritages. She co-founded I-Pride, an organization for the recognition, support and education of interracial families and biracial people. She was very active in sensitizing the Berkeley School System to their sizable number of biracial students and families. She is an excellent model of authentic blending and bridging of different cultures. The most effective teaching is always by example.

It was Julie who invited me to the first intensive with Baba Muktananda at the Oakland Ashram. She wanted to share the experience of an intensive with me, so we could "process it" together. I had no idea what an intensive was, and little knowledge of a guru, but I was willing to go along for the ride. At the end of the intensive, Julie was relatively untouched and it was I who fell in love. I decided to be married to Baba, and only later realized that the marriage was to his teachings. Two weeks later, Julie and I went to lunch to continue our processing of the experience. At one moment, Julie angled her head in such a way that I saw Christ in her eyes. At this time I realized that Julie was one of my angels sent to bring more joy in my life.

Julie and I became very close and began spending weekends together. Our spirits were connected and we could talk about any and every subject. I felt totally accepted without judgment in our relationship, and she felt the same. Julie was a fun playmate, and we felt free and childlike together. Some observers of our relationship even assumed we might be gay, erroneously thinking intimacy and sex are synonymous.

Often during the years of her teaching at Martin Luther King, Julie came to my house to rest, soak in the hot tub, and hang out before Back to School nights and other evening meetings. At graduation time, Julie would come to my house and we would play in my closet dressing Julie in elegant fashions and jewelry for the occasion. This was a fun experience for both of us and was a very sweet part of our relationship.

Julie invited me to share a cabin at the Russian River which her friend had loaned her for a weekend. We both loved the Russian River area, and often went to Jenner to watch the sunset over the ocean, and enjoyed delicious dinners at the Rivers End Restaurant. We took many long morning and evening walks through the forest, and sometimes camped at Bullfrog Pond in Armstrong Woods. We meditated in the woods, being serenaded by the birds, frogs, and insects, and watched the mist rise through the tall trees. We liked to meditate in the morning sunrise.

We had such a good time that we decided to buy a cabin of our own in the area. One Saturday afternoon we took off in search of the perfect getaway spot. On the drive up, we visualized together exactly what we wanted, although we had no idea how we were going to find it. We ended up in a real estate office called Creative Properties. After a brief search, we found a cabin which seemed to perfectly fit our visualization. Before we got out of the car, I proclaimed, "This is it!"

The cabin had the appearance of a magical Hobbit house, with its front entrance through a huge wine barrel. It was located off of a very long, steep, windy road which would accommodate only one car at a time. Away from the road, the cabin was almost hidden, nestled in a stand of towering redwood trees. It had quite a history of ownership, ranging from an alcoholic couple who drank themselves into stupors and threw their bottles and cans into the canyon behind the property, to another couple, spiritual aspirants, who spent the day picking up the bottles and cans from the canyon when they weren't meditating. There was a Ganesh (an Indian elephant god) on the front door which was a magnet for me. I thought it came with the cabin, but during the negotiations, we were told that the Ganesh had been specifically named in the divorce from his first wife and he could not part with it.

Together the couple had made many unconventional expan-sions. There were numerous nooks and crannies, two lofts, one with a removable skylight, an enclosed glass room in the middle of the house, and several secret hiding places behind walls and under floorboards to accommodate their marijuana crop. Although he showed some of the secret places to us, we continued to discover others for some time. We decided to call the cabin the Russian River Hideaway, named for our intention to create a sanctuary for ourselves and our friends, though later we decided to extend the opportunity to others looking for a getaway. We then changed the name to The Rainbow's End.

I took great delight in decorating the cabin with treasures found mainly at the Marin City flea market. Shopping at the flea market was often an epiphany for me. Out of piles of junk, the perfect artifacts would appear. From these purchases it appeared that the cabin was calling for a multicultural decor, with universal religious and spiritual relics. After reflecting on the atmosphere emerging in the cabin, being the therapist that I was, it seemed appropriate to represent the various stages of human development to facilitate a healing and rejuvenating experience. Suddenly the cabin seemed a mirror image for the Cultural Awareness and Race Relations program I was to write. The serene atmosphere would be perfect for helping participants relax deeply. The décor and artifacts could stimulate exploration of cultures and attitudes.

Each room reflected a different culture, a specific stage of human development from birth to death, and one of the rainbow's colors. The bathroom inside the cabin had an oversized metal water trough with redwood siding, and a large picture window looking out into the redwood forest. Luxuriating in this tub was an experience in itself. Outside on an elevated wrap-around redwood deck was a spa with jets that massaged the back, relaxed the mind, and invited the spirit. It seemed extended into empty space and the redwoods.

Unfortunately after much negotiation, the hospital administrator decided it would be too expensive to pay for weekends retreats for workshop participants, and so the use of the cabin for this purpose was rejected. However family and friends were clamoring at the door, so we opened the cabin to weekend getaways for ourselves and rentals for the public when we were not using it.

In order to share the essence of the experience offered by

the cabin, we decided to write a guide for our guests suggesting how they could enhance their benefit and enjoyment. The journey started in the water trough as a pre-birth experience in preparation for birth in the spa. It was suggested that in the spa the guests curl up in the hammock suspended in the warm water for a rebirth experience. Pairs could alternate facilitating the experience for each other or it could be done alone.

The next stage of development was the Latino nursery, named for the loving and nurturing Spanish mothers. The decor of this room included a large adult-sized wooden cradle which extended between two heavy beams. It was built by a master carpenter and ex-client in exchange for therapy. (His therapy included the use of the cradle!) Above the cradle hung a variety of colorful mobiles, some of which played favorite lullabies. The walls were covered with Guatemalan rainbow-colored fabrics, and the shelves were lined with soft cuddly animals. There were baby bottles, blankies, pacifiers, and rattles available.

The Native American library represented early childhood, the next stage of development. Here one found a school desk, chairs, a range of books and art supplies, a record player, and a teddy bear which contained self-esteem tapes. The walls of the room were dressed in colorful Huichol Indian yarn paintings. The dolls in this room represented a wide range of cultures and myths, including the Eskimo doll called Sedna, who was given to me by the second client who experienced the process of the cabin.

The next room was called Fantasy Forest for your Coming of Age, for the stage of adolescence. The walls in this room were graced with beautiful murals of a green forest with graceful waterfalls, suggesting the gusto of life. There was a variety of sports equipment, stuffed animals, dolls, an easel and paints, books, board games, a boom box, and a telephone (which was blocked for long distance calls). There was also a futon, desk, dresser, and chair, and of course a mirror. Masks were provided for explorations of identity.

Young adulthood was found in the American Frontier room for exploration of your pioneer spirit. This room had the ambiance of a turn-of-the-century log cabin with a variety of natural woods. There was a full-sized built-in wooden bed with an old-fashioned quilt and lace curtains. Beside the bed on built-in shelves were beautiful antique vases with hunting dogs scenes. There was a stand with pitcher and basin, and on the wall was a small (toy) shotgun, and a real Native American bow and arrow. Over the bed was a cupola, which filtered rays of sunlight through the redwood trees. Although there were cracks in the roof and walls through which you could see daylight, the room never seemed to leak when it rained.

The African Loft, for discovering the True Identity of the Self, represented maturity. In this loft, always the warmest room in the cabin because it was above the wood burning stove, was a futon under a removable skylight. One could lie in bed with the feeling of being in a tree house, at one with the trees by day, looking up at the stars at night. On one wall of the room was an African mask which symbolized birth, and on the opposite side of the room another African mask symbolized death. Between the two masks was life symbolized by small African carvings of people and animals, dried African butterflies, and the living forest. The bed was covered with Zebra skin designs. In the wall was a hidden sliding panel which provided privileged guests with a secret view of activities in the bathroom below. Another panel slid open to provide one with easy conversation or convenient snacks handed up from the kitchen into the loft.

A fully equipped kitchen was one of the most popular rooms in the cabin. It included a breakfast nook which was called the American Breakfast Nook for your Cozy Family Gatherings. You could sit at the table and look out a large picture window into a terraced garden of plants and ferns amidst the forest. In the center was a large stone phallic sculpture. The view was especially beautiful and peaceful when it rained. This was a setting for many wonderful shared meals, as well as intimate conversations and creative thinking, planning and writing.

The French Loft was a private, cozy room for your Exploration of Relationships and Romance, accessed by a steep set of stairs. It was decorated with cream-colored lace and soft lavenders. The window looked out into the redwoods, inviting the trees into the room. An antique picture of a woman and child with love visibly radiating between them provided the atmosphere in the room. One could lie on the very seductive, comfortable futon and contemplate loving and being loved.

The Chinese Corner to Receive Wisdom of the Ages was a small, cave-like area under the steps, sparsely furnished, with pillows and a Chinese scroll. The scroll advised an open mind, written in Chinese characters. In this cave were the I Ching, the Runes, Tarot Cards, and a Ouija board.

The Japanese Tea Garden was an enclosed glass room where many early morning meditations took place in the light of dawn. The room appeared very zen, with its low black tables and meditation pillows, statues of Buddha, and a Bonzai tree. A very old hand painted Japanese plate, a treasure I found at the flea market for fifty dollars, had been given to someone by the general of the Japanese army. The picture was of a young lovely Japanese girl swinging in a garden whose face was a pure manifestation of serenity. Japanese tea cups and teapot were available for high tea, and a small fountain trickled peacefully.

The Indian Meditation Room for your Enlightenment held religious relics representing all major religions (and some not so major); it was a universal invitation to experience the Self in whatever image or form you felt drawn to. One side of the room was covered by a built-in altar. Under the altar was indirect lighting which created a golden glow. The aroma of Blue Pearl incense from the ashram filled the room. On the other side was a comfortable futon and a prayer rug. There were pictures of Baba Muktananda, Nityananda, and my mother, prominently displayed.

The Multicultural Living Room for Getting it All Together was the room where everyone came together before, sometimes in the middle of, and at the end of the day. Here we gathered around the Franklin wood burning stove in the winters, often leaving the door open to watch the fire burn. In the summer the sun streaming down from the skylights provided a warm circle of natural light. We shared our plans for the day, our experiences in the evenings, and all manner of subjects, beliefs, feelings, hopes, dreams, and fears. Gold African jewelry covered one wall, and another wall was draped with a Mexican serape. French windows looked out on a beautiful green garden on one side and the full view of the Japanese tea garden could be seen on the other.

The cabin for me became a microcosm of the School of Life. Its lessons were many, covering a range of experiences, some fun and some extremely challenging. Buying a cabin with Julie strengthened the bond between us, as we dealt with all the joys and problems that this presented. This shared responsibility was similar to that faced by most couples requiring communication, negotiation, and compromise. For twenty-five years or more we have been able to sit down together, calmly focus on the issues, and "process our differences." Because of our respect for each other, we met our challenges with love and grace.

During the eighties, the Russian River area was in transition from righteous marijuana growers, rednecks, bikers, and hard core drug addicts to a growing population of gays and yuppies from the Bay Area. This dichotomy of lifestyles was symbolized perfectly on Main Street in Monte Rio. The Pink Elephant, (the local redneck and biker bar), faced across the street to the Health Food Store (hangout of yuppies, gays, and hippies). The General Store was a catch-all rummage sale, not well stocked, as it depended on donations from local residents and was run by volunteers. The movie theater was in a perpetual state of being readied for use, but never open. The Bohemian Club for the rich and famous was an unsavory neighbor, along with the august Golf Club located in nearby Guerneville.

One of the major lessons the cabin taught me was a confrontation of my "Fear of the Dark." At first I was petrified by the narrow curves on unpaved, unlit roads in the forest at night. I was also scared in the day too! With the added challenge of the relentless winter rains, the roads became even more frightening, wet and slippery. Each time I decided to make the journey, it was a contemplated choice to overcome my fear, in order to get to the cabin.

I had no telephone for the first several months, and my next-door neighbor, the only neighbor for several blocks, happened to be in the enterprise of selling drugs. He was visited by characters of all descriptions, one of whom knocked on my door at two AM looking for a purchase. Spending the night alone in the cabin called forth all my fears about the bogey man, as I lay awake listening to all the strange noises and cries, both animal and human. In the beginning, I slept with the lights on, and had counsel with myself about my choice between looking for someone to drive, spend the night, or both, every time I wanted to go to the cabin, or telling the bogey man to go to hell. It became a practice of putting the bogey man out every night and telling him to stay gone!

On one of our frequent family night outings, Julie and I and several children were exploring the neighboring Camp Imelda, an abandoned homeopathic school tucked away in the woods a few doors down the road. We wandered into one of the classrooms and in the dim light of dusk and cobwebs we saw a bigger than life-sized statue of Jesus with his chest cut open and revealing a profusely bleeding heart. One of the children let out a blood curdling scream and we all bolted for home. The bogey man had reappeared at Camp Imelda.

As described by one of my friends who visited the cabin, the experience was long on substance and short on form. He was referring to the homemade plan-as-you-go-along foundation and structure of the cabin. The winters were extremely harsh, the rain came down in torrents and was unrelenting. There was a gushing waterfall coming down the hillside next to the cabin, musical and aesthetically gorgeous. However, the cabin's roof, walls, and windows leaked profusely. Mold and mildew abounded. The natural law of perpetual decay operates big-time in the Monte Rio forest, raising real questions regarding the suitability of combining city dwellings and redwood forest settings. Upkeep was constant and costly! We spent a small fortune wallpapering the Fantasy Forest room in photographic murals, which were totally destroyed in one winter. Local help was readily available, but repeatedly unreliable, inconsistent, and the quality of the work reflective of the substandard "river construction," as it was called.

With a lot of prayer and persistence, I was able to locate not only a responsible caretaker, but an electrician who was a jack of all trades and an angel in disguise. During the two-year tenure of this crew, all was well and the cabin radiated well being. Advertising for the cabin was predominately in the Berkeley Express, read by a select, well-educated group of people in the Bay Area. All business arrangements were made by phone and mail; we never met the guests in person. The key was left under a rock. Almost invariably the renters were honest, responsible, and appreciative of the cabin, with the exception of one group of obvious drug dealers who left much evidence of their illicit activities, including bleach stains on the wood. Although there were some expensive antiques there, nothing was ever stolen except one book by Rumi. The cabin was almost always left in good condition, and none of the checks bounced. This was amazing since I had received bounced checks by more than a few of my clients! My faith in humanity was renewed.

We enjoyed reading the love notes left by our guests and finding the small treasures, flowers, wine, and gifts left by them. One note said that the experience of the cabin was like traveling around the world in two days. Many couples experienced improved communi-cations and increased closeness. Another described the cabin as one of the wonders of the world. One mother commented that the cabin was the only place her son volunteered to do dishes. A few guests were inconvenienced by the occasional visits from mice, neighboring cats, skunks, squirrels, and scorpions, not to mention the weeping walls when it rained.

After purchasing the cabin, in hindsight, we learned that the Russian River overflows regularly, incapacitating several of the towns, including Monte Rio, and severely handicapping entrance and exit by the road. We were awed by the intensity of the elements--the rains, the wind, the fog, and the morning dew. The rain poured down in sheets turning the creeks on our hillside into gushing waterfalls. Fighting the leaks in the cabin roof was an ongoing losing battle. Living in the forest is not for the faint of heart.

Loss of the caretakers marked the beginning of the demise of the cabin. Although it was extremely difficult in more ways than one for me to try to manage the cabin from two hours away, I was conflicted about selling it, because it was such a haven for me and many others. I had bought Julie out several years earlier when our balloon payments became due and she didn't have the money. In my characteristic style, I held on by my fingernails until the bitter end. It was not only my lover but a most demanding teacher.

After a protracted period of four years, I finally sold the cabin to a person who was described to me by my realtor as "a good catch." I foolishly carried a second deed which was payable in five years. I suppose that this was my unconscious attempt to hold on to the cabin. A year later, the "good catch" decided to change his lifestyle and leave the area. He asked me to continue carrying the second for new buyers. I foolishly agreed (for some reason unknown to me), as this proved to be another monumental mistake. The new buyers did not pay the note --property upkeep seemed a foreign concept to them. They had very nasty attitudes; when I requested overdue payments, they often acted as if I was harassing them, and they were doing me a favor by answering the phone (which they only did sporadically). After great effort and expense, I was finally able to evict them. They left the cabin in a state of shambles.

Again I embarked upon a very stressful and expensive journey of repairing the cabin for resale. By this time it was a relationship with a lover gone bad. I knew it was time to terminate the relationship, and I was ready. The cabin finally sold after another year, and this time I felt complete. Out of nostalgia, my friend Julie and I visited the cabin a few years later. Our unwelcome was loudly expressed by ferocious barking dogs in the yard, and the new owners cracked the door but did not invite us in. The cabin had no resemblance to the past, and I knew the affair was really over.

In consultation with administrators, the Black Caucus, representatives of hospital and clinic departments, and others with vested interests, the Cultural Awareness and Race Relations Educational program was conceived. The concept and design of the workshops was created by my friend Julie and me sitting at the breakfast nook at the cabin. It was my desire to remove the participants from their familiar work environment in the city and enable them to experience the peace and harmony of the forest. The cabin offered a strong invitation to drop appearances, starting by leaving one's shoes at the door. Unfortunately, the administrator pointed out to me the per diem costs of off-campus retreats would make the program too costly.

The acronym was CARE. The objective was to demonstrate the effectiveness of caring about the people you work with. Initially the program was designed for all administrators and department managers who were theoretically supposed to share their benefit from the program with their employees. However, the program was voluntary, not mandatory, as I would have preferred. Many of the managers and administrators found one reason or another not to attend.

The success of the program was less than desired, but enough to warrant funding for a second year and was then opened to the entire campus of faculty, staff, and students. I still recall the hurt and pain of one employee who cried when sharing the experience of being forbidden to play with a little black boy who was his best friend. In this way, he was taught to distrust his own feelings, and he still had issues around knowing what was real for him. He was not comfortable around his black co-workers. People talked about their stereotypes and fears of minorities, especially black men. Minorities talked about inhuman treatment and distrust of whites. I think the program made a difference for those who attended, but in some ways it was preaching to the choir.

The assistant chief, then acting chief in my absence, had told me that she would only serve as acting for one year. I knew my decision to continue the program for another year was also a decision to leave the department at its end. Although I had no idea what I would do, this seemed OK to me because my mind had been expanded by this very challenging and rewarding experience, and return to the department felt like a contraction. At the end of the second year, I resigned and retired, much to the surprise of my colleagues who perceived my position as a plum. Most of my friends and family were flabbergasted at my early retirement, especially since I had no income. I withdrew the small retirement I had accumulated partially to repay a balloon note on the cabin. In my heart, I did not want to return to the department because my spirit was no longer there. This leap of faith was a major test of my early teachings and belief that the Lord will provide. In the absence of a regular income, I was forced to get to know my true Source. A friend referred a client to me for therapy, and this was the beginning of a private practice in my home, which the Spirit used as the form to support me.

My narcolepsy returned again when I was in my late forties. All of my children were grown and outside the home, and I had quit my job at UC. I had also sold the much loved cabin which had brought me a lot of joy. I was letting go of the most important roles in my identity. I realized that I was not who I had been and had not yet become who I would be. The narcolepsy returned with a vengeance. When I went to sleep while exercising at the gym, a man joked that I came to the gym to take my afternoon naps. I realized that this time something was really wrong. Shortly after this I went to see a psychic and told her about my sleeping. She told me not to worry, that I would just wake up one morning. I asked her how this was going to happen, and she said that *"They"* would be very upset with her if she told me how it was going to happen. I adopted a wait -and-see attitude and put this on a low burner in the back of my mind.

A few months later, I went to my personal physician fearing that I might have cancer. She told me I had no symptoms of cancer; my only symptom was excessive sleeping. She referred me to the Stanford sleeping disorders program. I was officially diagnosed and went through a clinical trial program for several years to test a new medication called Medafonil. During the study period we went without any medication. Two weeks later, some participants were given a placebo, some were given half the recommended amount, and others were given the full dose. We were instructed to call the doctor the following morning, to tell him which dose we thought we got, based on how we felt. I remember going into the bathroom about fifteen minutes after taking the medication and feeling as if I had woke up from a deep sleep. I called the doctor and assured him that I had gotten the "real deal." At this time I also remembered the prediction of the psychic that I would wake up, and that's exactly how I felt.

I continued to take the medication for several years during the extended trial program, when it was free. After the trial period,

I had insurance that paid most of the cost, but when I transferred to Medicare, which does not cover the cost, I stopped taking the medication. The narcolepsy seemed to have gone away. With the increasing intensity of the process, I have been revisited by the narcolepsy. This is probably the most challenging and demanding transition of my whole life. It seems to require no less than a total change in my identity. Although I have periodic glimpses of the person I am becoming, it is still hard to let go of the person I used to be, or used to think I was. I now realize that the narcolepsy returns whenever I am at a major crossroad in life and feel overwhelmed by it.

Reviewing my escape routes from life's major challenges, I realized that they were all established before I was five. I'm sure my mother had narcolepsy which was never diagnosed, but it was clear that she used sleep to get away from it all. Codependency was in the atmosphere of our home and inhaled with the air we breathed. Addictions ran rampant, with smoking and drinking symbolizing glamour and maturity. Triangles abounded, and everybody had at least one. I had developed my tool box full of escape techniques and knew which one to use for each situation.

CHAPTER FIVE

LANDMINES~~EXPLORATION OF FAMILY CODEPENDENCIES, ADDICTIONS, AND TRIANGLES

"Our families are experts at pushing our buttons--they should be-- after all, they are the ones who installed them."

Our families are the source of both landmarks and landmines in life. They are the breeding ground for the challenges we are to face in life. They magnify our strengths and weaknesses and shape how we face our trials and triumphs. Family patterns often continue uninterrupted for generations until one or more members question the dysfunctional patterns. They resist the conditioning and pressure to conform, refusing to continue the cycle. Thus the process of change and all its resistance are set in motion. Members are often emotionally attached to these patterns. Depending on one's willingness to do things differently, the friction created by the change in one could lead to more intimacy or cause separation.

Our families are only the first source of unavoidable landmines; many more await us out in the world. Most of us entered the world oblivious to the fact that it is a school. We are unprepared for the lessons we must learn in life, and unaware of the landmines which are strewn along the path, therefore we have no clue about how to avoid them. Some of our teachers may be gentle, while others carry a big stick. One of my mother's favorite sayings was: "Whatever I can't teach you, the world will." Life is not easy, but it doesn't have to be so hard. I have learned that pain is inevitable, but *suffering* is optional. "There are no victims, only volunteers." According to Dennis Kucinich, we are not victims of the world we see, we are victims of the way we see the world.

The major landmines provided for me by my family have been codependency and addictions, which are of course family diseases. I stepped on these landmines and was blown into oblivion. The road to recovery was long and treacherous.

Jack Kornfield says **addictions** are the compulsive, repetitive attachments we use to avoid feelings and deny the difficulties in our lives. They numb us to what is. Annie Wilson Schaef, the author of *When a Society Becomes an Addict,* says that the best adjusted person in our society is a person who is not dead and who is not alive, just numb, a zombie. When you are dead, you are not able to do the work of society. When you are fully alive, you are constantly saying no to many of the processes of society--racism, pollution of the environment, nuclear threat, the arms race, drinking unsafe water, and eating carcinogenic food. Thus, it is in the interest of our society to promote those things that take the edge off, keep us busy with our fixes, and keep us slightly numbed out. We are bombarded with advertising urging us to keep pace, to keep consuming, smoking, drinking, and craving food, money, and sex. The latest addiction of the masses is technology. All the people wired to the wireless cosmos are a sight to behold, oblivious to those around them. In this way our modern consumer society itself functions as an addict. In this way the stage is set for all susceptible individuals to anesthetize themselves against life.

Codependence is a set of maladaptive, compulsive behaviors learned by individuals in relationships, in order for the relationship to survive. It often causes great emotional pain and stress, for example, the consequences of a family member's alcoholism or other addictions, sexual or other abuse, chronic illnesses, adult children still at home, or forces external to the family, such as poverty, unemployment, or imprisonment. Whenever two or more people are together, there is fertile soil for codependency. We are social beings with an innate desire to please and be pleased. We yearn to feel connected, and strive for union. If the price of a union is suppression of either individual, the price is too high and it's unhealthy.

The codependent personality is either a victim or a rescuer, constantly trying to save others from the consequences they are about to face. They scout out opportunities to be helpful or to be helped. They will go to great lengths to perpetuate these patterns because it makes them feel secure. However, this is usually the shadow side of their personality, hidden from them and well defended by stories of reason. The stories they tell themselves about why they do what they do are so familiar and acceptable that they serve as the perfect anesthetic protecting them from their true feelings of resentment.

Of course, this type of rescuing only serves to keep the dysfunctional individuals enmeshed in the relationship, preventing growth and happiness. The lesson here is that we are all whole and complete. There is only one person in this world that any of us can control and that would be ourselves. When we change ourselves, we change our world?

My family is sharply divided into two camps-- the caretakers and the cared for. Although I was the youngest of thirteen children, I chose my role quite early, around five or six. I became a self-appointed caretaker. In my perception, the caretaker role seemed to be more powerful and benevolent, representing the high road. On the other hand, the cared for seemed to be weak and needy, the low road, much less desirable to me.

I had already started pointing out to my teenaged siblings the errors of their ways. Even then I could not understand why they made choices which had such negative consequences. I wanted them to be kinder and MORE GENTLE with each other and themselves. I also longed for them to prepare themselves for a brighter future. I did not know then this would have meant delaying their immediate gratify-cations. My mother often commented that it was a wise person who could profit from another's mistakes. My siblings seemed oblivious to the mistakes being made around them. They turned a deaf ear to my mother's good advice, and seemed determined to do things their own way. From my point of view, they were in a hurry to repeat their own mistakes, and those of others.

Some of my earliest memories are ones of feeling deep compassion for people in pain, especially children. I knew I wanted to be helpful before I knew what healing was. My favorite brother JC had rheumatic fever and became quite ill. Around age eight I volunteered to assist in his care, rubbing his back and feet, and bathing him (wearing shorts) in the bathtub. When my older sister was hospitalized, I used to go to the hospital to visit her and wash her feet before I went to school. It was so early the morning staff hadn't arrived, and the place was as lifeless as a cemetery. I greeted all the patients in the ward who were awake with a big smile, and they looked forward to my visits.

My original family home was a Classic College of Codependency, laying a solid foundation for its members in Relationship Enmeshments and Entanglements. My relationship with my boyfriend Melvin, starting at age fourteen and lasting three decades, earned me a Master's Degree in Unhealthy Attachment with a minor in Martyrdom. I was working hard for my ultimate Advanced Doctorate in Compulsive Rescuing. We had all of the ingredients for the perfect brew of strychnine. He professed a dying need for my love, and I was bewitched by my need to be needed. Although I was literally and completely imprisoned by the harsh demands of our dysfunctional relationship, I heard a distant voice of freedom calling me and I knew that one day I would escape. My first escape was school away from home in Jefferson City, ironically the very city where Melvin was incarcerated less than a year later.

With so much practice, my care taking skills flourished. When I got my first job around age sixteen (at a cleaners), at Christmas time on my very meager salary I bought gifts for my entire extended family, which was huge. Several members of my immediate family questioned this extensive outreach, but I failed to see it as excessive.

I refined my caretaking (codependent) skills simultaneously with my growing desire for independence. I wanted to go away to college after graduating from high school. My mother told me that she could not afford to help me with college expenses. She said she had done as much as she could for me, and that she needed me to help her now. I was shocked by this statement, and didn't feel ready to become independent. However, I remember thinking if my mother thought I could handle it, then maybe I could.

I decided to go to a junior college and live at home for the first year. I supported myself with a job at a drug store soda fountain. The second year I dropped out of school and worked full time washing dishes at a restaurant. I saved every penny I made so I could go away to Lincoln University. This was a major accomplishment and gave me the confidence and opportunity to develop the skills that would enable me to play the role of a good caretaker.

While growing up, I was closest to my sister Bernice, who was two years my senior. She was smart, and she was good looking. I was a scaredy cat and she was a ready warrior, always my protector at school. She was defiant in ways that I couldn't fathom myself being. Kids knew not to mess with her. She was very good at sports--baseball, volleyball, and jacks, and she spent hours doing crossword puzzles. She was a card shark, and she and groups of friends played bid whiz until the wee hours of the morning. I looked up to her and thought she was bigger than life. I was somewhat clumsy, but because of her, I was often chosen to play on the volleyball team. As a young child, I remember standing beside her when she gave speeches in church. I imagined that she would take the world by storm when she grew up.

Much to my dismay, she married a man that I didn't think would make a good husband and father. They had six children and lived upstairs in our two family flat. She stopped taking care of herself and became consumed by her role as wife and mother. She became an excellent cook, and I often ate dinner with them. My mother was cooking less as she had fewer people to cook for. Bernice took up the mantle of chief cook and caretaker.

Unknown to me, Bernice became pregnant with a seventh child. By this time she knew her marriage left much to be desired, taking care of six children was more than a full time job, so she wanted an abortion. She didn't drive, and I was the only one with a car. She knew that I was philosophically opposed to abortion, so she and one of my brother's girlfriends made up a story about the girl friend being pregnant. They asked me to take them to get her an abortion. Against my better judgment I agreed.

In a few days Bernice became very ill and was taken to the hospital. It became clear to everybody that it was she who had the abortion. The infection spread throughout her system. When she became critically ill, I walked around in shock and came close to fainting after leaving her room. She died at the young age of twenty-six. My entire family and I were devastated and my mother was extremely angry at the person who took her for the abortion. I overheard her say she really wanted to know who that was. I told her that I had been tricked into taking her, and that I had no idea she was pregnant. After her death her husband took the children to live with his mother, while he moved in with another woman. Although he was always around, he made no effort to make sure the children maintained contact with the family. I went over occasionally to see them, but they were not allowed to come outside of the fenced-in yard. I remember feeling very saddened thinking it was like they were in prison.

When Bernice passed away, Ruby, who was ten years my senior, became my closest sibling. People often said we looked alike. Liz was much older; she and I had similar personalities and had often butted heads when I was a child. Both my older sisters had very good hearts, but both were also angry and mean spirited. While Ruby was on the sneaky side, Liz was always up front with her meanness. The blessing for me is the realization that they were excellent teachers providing me with blatant examples of how I don't want to be, as well as admirable qualities I would like to emulate. I am determined to grow old gracefully.

Ruby was a short, medium brown skin, very attractive woman. She had long black flowing hair in her youth, and a seductive smile. She was a really sharp dresser in her day, with a taste for very expensive shoes and fine threads like silk and cashmere, courtesy of her boyfriends. I used to love to examine the numbers on the straps of her brand-new shoes. On special occasions she let me wear her clothes, and I felt glamorous and special.

Ruby was very proud of my going to college, and with her I had the experience of being on the receiving end of healthy codependency and was filled with gratitude. I became more aware of the power of the care taker. Even with meager resources, she was very generous and nurturing to me. She sent me care packages in college that contained candy, cakes, canned goods, sometimes clothes, and other goodies. When I came home on weekends, I would visit her in the mornings and she made my favorite breakfast of bacon, rice, and creamed biscuits. She even learned how to make special breads, yeast rolls and biscuits, which she knew were my favorite foods. I have always been very appreciative of her nurturing and have a very soft spot in my heart for her. All of my older sisters have supported me with food and love.

While I was away at college, back at the ranch in St. Louis the stage was being set for the performance of my lifelong caretaking role. My siblings were busy creating new characters for my ongoing family dramas, and I was busy preparing myself emotionally and financially to play my role in the family theater. Even when I moved away from Missouri to California, I continued to show my willingness to assume the role of care taker by sending money and gifts home regularly. As a child I often heard my mother comment that one mother could take of thirteen children, but thirteen children could not take care of one mother. I solemnly vowed to myself that I would be the exception. Although I never remember verbalizing this, it was assumed by all my relatives and siblings that I would be my mother's caretaker when the time came. I felt it was my destiny. When I moved to Fresno, I sent for her, and she came to live with me.

My oldest brother, who married late in life, had ten children. Both he and his wife had requested that I take responsibility for the children if anything happened to them. I agreed, with the unrealistic belief that nothing was going to happen. They died within a few years of each other, leaving several minor children. I became an instant mother, and my role as caretaker was cemented for generations to come.

A large number of my family moved from St. Louis to California and my house was the way station for them all. This involved many and varied acts of care taking. My brother and nephew, running away from their challenges in St. Louis, moved to California under the pretense of wanting to help me take care of my mother who had become quadriplegic. I was highly suspicious of this offer, since they were both alcoholics, but how do you turn down offers to help? The second day they both got drunk and got into a fist fight in front of my house. The next week my brother ran into the front fence and knocked it over. In the middle of my wealthy neighborhood my house was rapidly becoming the ghetto. Needless to say, help was not forthcoming except from me. Fortunately, after about two months my nephew and brother became homesick and left, with my blessings.

Family members felt free to ask me for any and everything--from moving into my house to bailing them (and their friends) out of jail, to co-signing for cars, which they seldom managed to pay for, and on and on. My family's attitude was that because I seemed to have it, I should be willing to share it with them, and for many years I was. However, all of the help and assistance I gave didn't seem to make them any more responsible. Our codependent relationships were in a process of perpetual decay. It seemed that my efforts to "help" were actually an interference with their learning whatever they needed to know to make better choices in life.

Although it would make me angry when they asked to borrow money they never paid back, my bleeding heart compelled me to comply. One of my nephews was addicted to cocaine, had kidney failure, and was raising four children alone; he was in the habit of telling me that the children were hungry whenever he needed money. I was a real patsy when it came to "hungry children." However, on one occasion, I got up enough courage to tell him no. The following day he called and thanked me for saying no because it forced him to manage from his own resources. Although I recognized this as a gift at the time it was several years before it had real impact on changing my codependent behavior.

Once the ploy of the hungry children stopped working, he brought a huge hungry German Shepherd to my house. He asked for emergency overnight shelter for the dog, and I agreed. However, overnight turned into a week, with the dog in the basement, growling, howling, urinating, and defecating. I was scared to death of the dog and fed him by pushing his food into the basement with a long handled broom. I called my nephew threatening numerous times to give the dog to the Humane Society. He finally came for him, and I adamantly told him never again. I learned from this experience that while I might rescue people, I was not a rescuer of dogs.

In spite of gross dysfunctions and numerous emotional handicaps, all members of my family (like everyone else's) have many talents. Over the years, I have had the misfortune of observing many members of my family fail to develop their god given talents and fall into habits of codependences because they haven't developed self-discipline. With awareness we have the choice to create healthier patterns of nurturing, growth, and independence. Encouraging each other to reach for our highest potential is more loving than reinforcing beliefs in personal inadequacy by taking on the role of rescuer or the rescued.

When I was separated from my family and living in another state, I could see the pathology in my family more clearly. After my mother died, I realized that I was not enjoying my visits to St. Louis. I was disturbed by the out-of-control addictions of various family members, even though my own addictions were secretly growing. I was particularly distressed by the aggressive behavior and verbal abuse of each other. After one visit, I was so frustrated that I told Ruby that it would be a long time before I returned. It was fifteen years.

During this time I continued my codependent relationships with various members of my family; since they showed meager interest in growth, it was mostly rescuing them financially. I felt that no one in my family really knew me anymore, and they related to their image of who they thought I was or who they wanted me to be. Although I might have been invisible to them on some level, of one thing I'm very sure--that they have always been proud of me and respected my accomplishments.

Recently I saw the movie "My Big Fat Greek Wedding," and I identified with the bride who felt alienated from her family and culture. As I was letting go of my codependent patterns, it seemed to me I had less in common with my family. Although there are many aspects of my culture that I love, I am well aware that some of its folkways and mores leave something to be desired--for example, being retained in church so long you forget what you went for, and a regular diet of soul food which while good to the lips is oh so hard on the hips and in reality, is a kiss of death.

My son-in-law's brother, who had been a minister and surrogate father to him, died recently. Typical of many Black Baptist congregations, his really loved their pastor. Following his death, there were many meetings to plan his funeral. Each person tried to outdo the others with more elaborate ideas. In the end, a three-hour funeral was planned (which was extended to five by the time he was buried.) My daughter asked why people went to such lengths after a person is gone, because it's only a dead body. I said that it was a cultural tradition which disregards time and is disrespectful to people's prior commitments. She said she didn't think it took all that to honor someone's life. We agreed that in this tradition it seems that the people who did the least for the person in life were the most dramatic in expressing their grief at his death. We wondered if this catharsis was an attempt to purge their guilt. It seems that the length of the wake is confused with the degree of love.

My youngest and only brother died around the same time and I decided to go to St. Louis for his funeral. I was very reluctant to take the trip because I had planned and paid for a women's retreat that I had looked forward to for some time. St. Louis is not my favorite place to visit and I had already made my peace with my brother and felt complete. We never had much in common, were not close, but maintained a mutually respectful relationship, even after I had ended the codependent aspects of our relationship (rescuing him financially from time to time.) My primary reason for going was to support my sister who was close to our brother and was recently diagnosed with bone cancer. I also thought about how it would look to other family members if I broke the tradition (as I had in the past) of being present at the funeral of a loved one, come hell or high water. I decided that I did not want to add this additional stress to the family. All of them (and there are many!) seemed appreciative of my presence.

The truth is that even though I have continued to love them, I feel alienated by some of their values and lifestyles. Although some in my family are very religious, engaging in activities ranging from speaking in tongues to testifying and holy dancing, they do not seem to me to be very spiritual. Others who wear their religion like a badge think it's okay not to repay debts. It appears they keep themselves small, unaware that they have settled for so much less than they could have. I wanted desperately to escape a similar preordained destiny awaiting me. I decided to take a stand for what I wanted and not to take the path of least resistance.

Self definition is something I had to learn rather early living in a white world as a black woman. It became very clear to me that I could not accept White America's definition of who I am. In the world, value and meaning are relative and vary with each individual. Depending on others to tell us who we are is a no-win situation. Many people do not know who they are, much less who you are. Self definition is the personal responsibility of everyone seeking self acceptance.

My sister Ruby exemplified the absence of self definition, and personified codependency; I'm sure she never heard of self assertion, and if she did, she didn't think it applied to her. Ruby was so passive and slow that the family nicknamed her "the Turtle." She held everything inside, and when she talked, she said nothing, at least nothing of significance for which she could be held accountable. She often sat with her arms wrapped around herself, a posture not of self love but one suggestive of her attempt to hold things in, repressing her self expression. She was so unassertive that she appeared to want to be almost invisible, giving away herself to others.

Ruby fostered dependency as if she thought it was a virtue. Anyone who was down and out could always find a good hot meal at Ruby's. Besides being the Chief Bottle Washer and Cook, she was the identified Family Babysitter, and Nursemaid for several disabled members. She became surrogate mother to Bernice's six children when Bernice died, even though she had six children of her own. She took excellent physical care of our brother who died from complications of diabetes, and our disabled nephew who had a brain tumor; all these tasks required the strength of Samson.

My family seems to divide on both sides of codependency; we are either givers, or takers. We have not learned the art of reciprocity. In life, human beings are needy when very young and very old; personal independence is a necessary journey between the two. Traditionally it is customary for the elders to take care of the young until they reach adulthood, and then when the elders become old, the young should take responsibility for them. In all families, coming of age without mastery of personal responsibility is not a sufficient foundation for maturity. Thus the family structure is weakened. The art of taking responsibility seems to have eluded many of the younger and some of the older generations in my family. In fact many of them overtly practice abdication and take the easy route of dependency. Also neither the givers nor the takers were taught the art of selfcare and the need to set clear boundaries.

Enmeshment prevails and is often confused with love, or "being nice." I fell victim to this confusion and for many years enmeshment and being nice were synonymous for me. Family members felt entitled to a share of whatever was available in the family whether or not they made any personal contributions. They had no qualms about borrowing money from my hard working, self-sacrificing mother, with no intention of repaying her. If for any reason she was unable to grant their request, they acted rejected and unloved. I think my mother bought into the pretense, thinking that a "good mother" would always give to her children. I often wondered why she continued to give money to them, knowing their track records. I vowed never to do it myself, but did it for seventy years before I broke the habit.

For years some relatives asked to borrow money from me. I loaned it to them, and then they never repaid it. When future requests were couched in terms of a "loan," I finally mustered the courage to remind them that they still owed me money from the last time. However, the requests did not stop until I flat out refused to play the game.

Once on a visit to St. Louis, I stayed with a niece whose daughter felt entitled to remove a new pair of shoes from my suitcase. When I got home and realized they were missing, I called and gave them to her mother. It seems none of the caretakers in the family have enough self esteem to be comfortable setting limits for themselves and others, confusing saying no with being withholding and unloving. Mindless giving from the ego depletes us; giving from the heart is love and nourishes us. As Dr. Phil says, "Self matters."

When the house Ruby was living in was condemned, I made the down payment on another house with the agreement that she would pay the note and other expenses. This arrangement worked well for several years. However, when her son Calvin became a teenager and started feeling his oats, he literally took over the house but made no contributions. Ruby never was much of a disciplinarian, and Calvin brought young girls in to spend the night in spite of her objections. Unable to get control, and with the encouragement and support of various family members, Ruby reluctantly decided to move to a retirement community. She was fearful that she might not like it, so I agreed to rent out the house for a year and to give her a hundred dollars a month out of the rent.

This would give her the opportunity to decide if she wanted to return. I took responsibility for managing the house, which was in my name, to support Ruby.

She moved into a very nice apartment and did well living alone for several years. To everyone's surprise she became very social, made new friends and seemed to really be enjoying life. She became famous for her wonderful homemade rolls which she made for family celebrations and for special occasions and people in her retirement home. Her apartment in many ways became the hub for her family gatherings.

Calvin, who was basically homeless, had been spending weekends from time to time at Ruby's. Over the years Ruby developed diabetes, kidney failure, hypertension, cancer, and the usual problems of aging. She had more going on with her body than Bush had troops in Iraq. Her health continued to deteriorate to the point that it was no longer safe for her to be alone, so Calvin moved in to the retirement center under the disguise of "taking care of her."

Calvin is a tall, good looking dark-skinned middle-aged man with large eyes. The intensity of his energy is exhausting, even when he's engaged in activities which are supposed to be pleasant and relaxing. He knows no boundaries and lives in his own self centered world which has little relationship to reality. He had two wives and innumerable baby mamas. He boasts about fathering at least twenty children, and seems to have consistently eluded the DA and avoided supporting any of his kids. Whenever I stayed with Ruby, I knew I had to buy extra beer and cigarettes if I wanted any, because her son Calvin did not hesitate to help himself to anything I had. He refused to respect my right to my own property, in spite of repeated requests that he stay out of my things.

He is in-your-face aggressive, intruding uninvited into others' personal space and property. Asking him to respect your property is like talking to the wind. He verbally agrees and then does just what you ask him not to. He gives a little, and expects a lot. I think deep down he has a good heart, but he is a master at irritating people and acts as if he is an ambassador for the devil. He has a limited vocabulary centered around the word "niggah," which drives me up the wall. I told him he would have to either stop, leave, or I would have to remove myself from his presence. He would stop for a short time only to resume his offensive cursing.

My sensitivity is also offended by the way he talks to his mother. Since I was a guest there taking care of his mother, who also knows no boundaries, I did not feel I could put him out as I would have done in my own home. I did not want to leave her unattended, so I felt trapped in a situation not of my own choosing. I felt great compassion for all of my family who are subjected to each other's disrespect and ongoing abuse, compounded by self-abuse. In spite of his helpfulness, I know having him around must have been very stressful for Ruby, although she never admitted it.

Calvin took it upon himself to break any and all rules of the retirement center that hampered his comings and goings. Ruby received several warnings which she did not heed about the back door being left unlocked, although Calvin was never identified as the culprit. Calvin actually wants to please, but he has a manner that makes a bull in a china cabinet look tame.

In his favor, whenever Calvin was around he tried hard to take care of Ruby, which was no easy task. Her conditions required a fairly strict diet. She had a very poor appetite; she never knew what she wanted to eat, and whatever was prepared for her was "nasty." The only thing she seemed to want to eat was exactly what she'd been told not to eat. She would deny and argue with her caretakers about her lack of compliance.

I believe Calvin loved and valued Ruby and me as much as he is capable. While I was there he even tried to take care of me, occasionally cooking and running errands, and generally did whatever favors I asked. After a while, I was able to see Calvin separate from his annoying behaviors and appreciate his good qualities.

Calvin is a self-taught highly skilled jack-of-most-trades, from remodeling houses to fixing cars. He is frequently called upon by family and friends for free repairs. I hired him, in spite of his known addictions, to remodel two rental properties. To the surprise of many, he was able to hold it together, and do a quality job, although it took him three times longer than would be considered reasonable. To his credit, he had requested that I buy him a house in exchange for his labor, and I had agreed. This turned out to be a good thing for both of us; otherwise he would probably still be living in my house.

He lived in the houses while he was working on them. In the last house he moved in several of his skid row cronies, giving it a ghetto stamp and making it unrentable to prospective tenants. Meanwhile several of my furnishings grew feet and walked away. In spite of my knowing he was an alcoholic/addict, I was lured to sleep by his temporary good performance, which I wanted so badly to think would endure. As his work for me neared completion, our relationship went downhill. I was deeply hurt by his stealing from me and his 180 degree turn in his attitude and how he talked to me. When he moved he refused to return my keys, and referred to me as a bitch to another relative. In general, he made completing our agreement very difficult for me. I had gone way out on a limb for him, and deserved much better. Nonetheless, I accept the fact that I was a volunteer and not a victim; however, my time as a volunteer with him is done. I have had no contact with him since.

During one of my visits, I was struck not only by Calvin's

but Ruby's disregard for rules. She took medicine not as it was prescribed but when she felt like it. For as long as I can remember, she hid behind a wide variety of prescription drugs, and in this way was an addict in the first degree. She acted as if she took some delight in ignoring her doctor's orders, as if she was a child getting away with something. I pointed out she was only hurting herself. I shared with her my observation, that she does not like to follow orders, and in this way she was hard to take care of. I suggested that if she was not going to take the medication as prescribed, she should tell her doctor so the two of them could be on the same page and not working against each other.

Despite her advanced age and many illnesses, Ruby continued to take care of one of our adult nephews who had a brain tumor. After about fifteen years Ruby became very frustrated with the nephew's lack of cooperation with his care and her interactions with him became laced with anger. I understood her frustration over his seeming refusal to do what he could for himself, but she seemed unaware of her angry tone with him. I took the risk of telling her that she appeared to be acting in opposition to her true feelings, because I know she loved him. She expressed surprise at my observations, and denied being angry. However, I feel she heard me, because in subsequent conversations, she sounded less angry when she talked to him. It is a family pattern to focus on how we think we should behave toward others and separate from our own feelings. In this way, we often behave in ways opposite to the way we really feel. I can recall this pattern in myself before I gave myself permission to honor and express my own feelings and set boundaries for myself in a loving way.

About four months after Calvin had moved into Ruby's one-bedroom senior apartment, Carla became angry with the person she was living with and moved herself and her two children in with Calvin and Ruby. Carla and Calvin do not get along, and they got into a knock down drag out brawl the first night. The following day Ruby became confused during her dialysis and was taken to the hospital. Lord knows I understand Ruby's conflicts and her choice to check out. Her health deteriorated quickly from this time.

The apartment manager wrote Ruby a letter of eviction based on the terms of the lease being violated. To avoid the eviction, Ruby reluctantly went to live with her oldest daughter in California, where she continued to worry about her "children" in St. Louis.

After Ruby moved to San Francisco to live with her daughter Carmen, I went to visit them. Ruby told me about the new dialysis center she was attending, which she liked very much; it was very close to where Carmen lives. Not very long after this conversation, Carmen came into the room and announced that she was going to transfer Ruby's dialysis site to Mt. Zion which is closer to where her grandson goes to school. This announcement was made without consulting Ruby. I'm sure Carmen saw the surprise on my face and she added a belated, insincere solicitation of Ruby's approval. Ruby is dependent on Carmen and extremely passive. She doesn't deal directly with much of anything, even under the best of conditions. It is highly unlikely that she would object to anything in her current dependent position.

Although I was very disturbed by this interaction, I said nothing--her care is Carmen's responsibility. However, it was the confirmation of my new direction to teach people in my life how I want to be treated. My responsibility is to provide for myself and to let people know how I feel and what I want, so there will be no misunderstanding about it . In this way I claim and reclaim my right to make my own choices as long as I can, and to plan for myself when I can't.

On another occasion Carmen called to say that she and Ruby would probably visit me on the weekend. I said OK and when we talked on the phone later, I said Sunday would be better than Saturday. When I attended church on Sunday, the speaker was a very dynamic woman who was offering a workshop in the afternoon.

I went home, called Ruby and left a message that I wanted to attend a workshop and asked if they could come after five. Carmen did not receive my message and called to let me know they were on their way. I told her that I realized I had said that Sunday would be better than Saturday but at the time I didn't know about the workshop. Carmen said that Ruby had wanted to spend the night. I told her that wouldn't work for me because I had planned a computer session on Monday morning. I explained that I needed advance notice when Ruby was going to spend the night with me, because I needed to plan, to shop for food, etc. I pointed out to Carmen that I didn't keep a variety of food in my refrigerator as she does. In addition, I was starting to become more active in the world and needed to clear my calendar. Carmen said she had told Ruby to let me know she planned to spend the night, but Ruby said it would be OK. I said at one time it might have been OK but it wasn't now. So we planned to have her visit the following weekend. Although I knew she was disappointed, I knew it was necessary for me to set boundaries to take care of myself. My years of codependency were coming to an end!

Once I decided to step up to the plate, I realized that all my old thoughts and feelings of being responsible for the world and wanting to heal all pain were gone! This was a hallelujah moment which I shared with Nita who has walked carefully in my footsteps of being a codependent caretaker. I told her that I was so happy that the feeling was gone and so proud of myself that I could hardly stand it.

In watching a program called "The View" on television,

one of the television hosts said she received so much personal gratification from being available during one of her daughter's crises that she wondered if she was happy that her daughter was in crisis so she could have the opportunity to help. She raised the question of whether people nurture to give to others or to give to themselves.

At a very deep level, we all desire to be needed. While the need to be needed is universal, the way it is fulfilled can be selfish and unhealthy. As a codependent-in-recovery, I no longer want to be needed to solve someone else's problem, which they are quite capable of doing for themselves. ("Been there, done that!") I don't think I even want to be wanted. I now realize that my need to be needed actually interfered with the expression of my truth and robbed others of their personal power. While I was acting as if I was the Bank of America, I was depleting my finances and delaying the lessons my family members needed to learn about their personal responsibility. I have put padlocks on all the doors of the bank. No one has asked me for money for a long time. Helping others is a virtue; helping others to help themselves is divine.

After a great deal of pain and suffering, Ruby passed away and took her love of codependency to her grave. The real pain for me came when I saw my own self destructive behavior in Ruby. I was forced to look at my continued smoking in spite of a chronic cough, and my drinking beer, which lost its effect long ago. I recognized my identification with the family's patterns of addiction, self abuse and flirtation with a death wish. I believed that I had healed many of the distorted thought patterns I once shared with my family, such as dependency, blaming others, and avoiding personal responsibility. However, I continued to identify with the addictive patterns. Seeing my behavior reflected to me by my family enabled me to realize how much I dislike it in them and in myself. I now know beyond a doubt that the things we find offensive about others are the things we dislike most and deny in ourselves. The power of this insight eventually forced me to take stronger action to heal my own addictions.

When Ruby moved out of the house I bought for her, I took on the responsibility of managing it. Still entrenched in codependency, I attempted to combine business with charity (déjà vu!). I decided to rent Ruby's house to a single mother with six children. She not only failed to pay the rent, but did very little to maintain the house and yard as agreed. I received frequent notices from the city threatening to fine me if the work wasn't completed. Caught between the city and an irresponsible tenant, I experienced one of my worst long distance nightmares. After a long expensive process of evicting her, I had a series of delinquent irresponsible renters (with one exception). Against my better judgment I decided not to sell the house for sentimental reasons. It was my hope that one day one of Ruby's children, probably Carla, would inherit it. This fantasy laid the foundation for an even more painful nightmare and financial loss. This house provided me with one of my hardest lessons around code-pendency.

Carla has two teenaged children who were good students and athletes. I invited both of them to visit me in California, and they had the time of their life. The youngest went home and told Carla she wanted to be like me, and it seemed to ignite Carla's insecurity and competitiveness. My close relationship with the girls seemed to become more distant. Nevertheless, aware of the soft spot in my heart for children and my high regard for education, Carla asked me to pay for her oldest daughter to attend private school. After several discussions, we agreed that Carla would move into Ruby's house which was close to a good public school. Carla was working at the time, and assured me she could and would pay the rent. She managed to do so for the first month or two, but then made partial payments which became delinquent, then no payments at all. Her attitude seemed to have been that I should allow her to live there rent free. After more than a year of mostly free rent, I asked her to leave several times. Ultimately I was forced to evict her. I don't think she believed I would follow through, but I did.

In her characteristic style, she waited until the deadline for leaving and had no plan for what to do next. On the last day she was frantically trying to find an apartment. As a last resort she moved to a shelter with her two young children where they stayed for several months. She had the nerve to ask me if I would sign for her to get an apartment. I told her that I was not inclined to do so, because she had a history of not paying her bills and I couldn't afford to allow her to ruin my credit. She said she would rent from month to month, and if she didn't pay, I could discontinue the contract. To my credit, I still said no.

Several months later she called and said she had used me as a reference for one of the apartments she had applied for. She said she told the woman that she had lived in my house for three years, paid six hundred fifty dollars a month, and moved because I wanted to sell the house. I was so stunned by this lie that I made no response. She then said that the manager probably wouldn't call me anyway since I lived out of town. When I arrived home, I had already received a call, and I was faced with a dilemma: I didn't want to lie, yet I didn't want to see Carla and the children homeless. I was annoyed that she put me in this position again, still acting as if I were responsible for her. I had decided not to respond to the call, because I wanted to end our co-dependent relationship, and I wanted to give her the message that I would no longer support her irresponsible behavior.

As the universe would have it, I got caught off guard, and answered an unexpected call from the manager. Her first question was whether I was related to Carla. I think this fact disqualified me instantly as a creditable reference. In a subsequent conversation with the manager, I half-heartedly danced around the truth, feeling I had betrayed myself again. I then called Carla to tell her what had happened and to say that that was the last lie I would ever tell for her. I told her she needs to take responsibility for cleaning up her credit and putting her life in order. She seemed to resent my advice and said that that was not helpful to her now. She added that she couldn't use me as a reference anyway because I had said she was related to me. She totally missed the point that she has to take the first step from where she is; however, she was looking for a quick fix, and I was no longer willing to accommodate her!

This decision was an important step for me toward earning my freedom from my family codependences. After moving out of the shelter, Carla moved in and out of different relatives' homes. She continued to sing her theme song that "no one has ever done anything for me." She lost her job of several years for not returning to work when she was supposed to. She decided to "handle this" by threatening to sue the doctor who should not have given out "confidential medical advice" to her boss, such as the date he said she could return to work. Throughout this drama, as difficult as it was, I maintained my resolve to allow Carla to be responsible for herself. No one ever told me that the pathway to wholeness would be easy, but I know that each conscious step is moving me in the direction of victory.

The sale of Ruby's house presented a whole new set of challenges. After several more thousand dollars spent in remodeling, it finally sold, and I was freed to let go of all the conflict, pain, and struggle that I had attached to the house. I finally released my unrealistic, grandiose desire to maintain a family home for Ruby's off springs. I felt a heavy weight had been lifted from my shoulders and I was filled with gratitude.

On one of my visits to St. Louis, I had planned to visit the woman who bought the house that Carla and her siblings grew up in. I wanted to meet the new owner, take her flowers, and give her my blessings for peace and happiness in her new home. I invited Carla, who was there on a rare visit to her mother, to go with me to bring closure. It didn't work out, because the woman wasn't home. When I issued the invitation, I didn't realize that Carla was not at the same point of closure that I was. She was still dealing with her feelings about not being able to live up to her responsibilities in the house and her subsequent eviction. She did admit that she had been in over her head with trying to work, raise her children, and manage the house. I told her that I saw in her the capacity and potential to do whatever she wanted. It seems that she did not see herself as I saw her.

She came over the next day and we continued our

conversation. It became an extensive and heated discussion about the time she spent growing up with me in Sausalito. She talked about feeling ugly, looking like a boy, not being able to handle the schoolwork, and being teased by the other children. She also told me that I was the one who introduced the children to drinking, how to mix drinks, and that they would drink my liquor sitting in the kitchen while my friends and I were drunk in the living room. She also accused me of constantly telling her that she was like her brother Calvin, strong willed, self centered and aggressive. This is not my memory of how I related to her. I thought she was cute, well-coordinated, an excellent dancer, and very talented in sports. Carla characteristically creates herself in the role of victim, which allows her to escape responsibility and blame others. On one occasion she said she had deliberately allowed herself to be victimized to protect Nita.

    She neglected to mention how stubborn and aggressive she had been, even pulling knives on the other children on several occasions. She minimized her combative, head strong attitudes, with the excuse that she was only a kid; she bragged about her rebelliousness while blaming me for the results. She admitted that she had returned to St. Louis because she wanted to do what she wanted to do. When she returned, she said her friends had teased her about "sounding white," so she made an effort to become more ghetto, (and she succeeded.)

She accused me of preferring Nita because she was pretty and got good grades, and proceeded to tell me stories about her and Nita's misbehaviors to prove that Nita was not the Miss Goody Two Shoes that she thought I thought she was. I told Carla that I did not prefer Nita because she was pretty and made good grades; whatever acting out she might have done, we agreed on the value of education as the way to prepare herself for a better life. I shared with Carla the fact that the morning after their pajama party when I had had a serious talk with them and their friends about the supreme value of education and the importance of avoiding premature sexual relations and early motherhood, Nita came into the bathroom and confided that she had decided to do it my way.

I reminded Carla that I had offered her a tutor which she refused. She suggested that I should have forced her to accept it, and I replied that given her strong will, I didn't think that would have worked. I told her that I grew up in the same general dysfunctional family environment that she did, and had my own baggage. I apologized for any character flaws or shortcomings that I had which hurt her. Even though she was "only a child," she knew my intention was to help them create a better life for themselves. She did know right from wrong and she has to take responsibility for her own choices.

Carla frequently has migraine headaches which usually take her to the emergency room, particularly after dealing with strong emotions which bring floods of tears. A few days after our conver-sation, Carla had an anxiety attack accompanied by seizures and ended up in the emergency room. When she came home I did a hands-on healing to remove her headaches. I was surprised at my objectivity, since in the past when my family hurt, I hurt. I took this opportunity to talk to her about her repressed pain and anger, and suggested she seek counseling. She said she had gone to counseling in the past and was ridiculed and called crazy by some family members. I told her that our entire family was crazy and needed several full-time psychiatrists. Some family members prefer to support dysfunction rather than seek help to heal themselves. Initially she took offense to my calling our family crazy, but proceeded to describe in detail all the ways in which they are.

Carla was hurt because she feels that the family has a negative opinion about her and she feels the tension rise when she comes around. I suggested that energetically she often appears as if she's angry or has an attitude; perhaps she could replace her frown with a smile. She admitted that her oldest daughter has a similar way of wearing her pain on her face. However, she made excuses for both of them saying her daughter was "only a child," and she was dealing with a lot of stress, and people should see beyond appearances. I agreed that people should look beyond appearances, but that they often just react to what they see. It's a lot easier to change yourself, I told her, than to try to change the world.

Following earlier out-of-control arguments about Carla's failure to pay rent and maintain the house, Carla's children, with whom I had felt close, withdrew from me. Whenever I saw them they seemed sullen and distant and unwilling to talk to me. Carla said that I was the adult and should have asked them what was wrong. She denied any possible effect of our conflict on the children, saying she never taught the children against me. I said children naturally take the side of their parent, right or wrong, without actively being taught. I said that I was always pleasant to the children in spite of their attitude, and let them know I was available should they want to talk. I felt that anything more would be intrusive and force them to choose between loyalties.

Carla's younger daughter called me just as I was leaving for the airport. I was happy to hear from her, but as it turned out, she had planned to go to the Jr. Olympics and didn't have any money. I was hurt that the real purpose of the call was to ask for money. I told her I couldn't talk at the time, but would call her from home. I'm sure her request was set up by Carla. While I want to encourage any child who is trying to develop herself, I plan to talk to Kenya about the unpleasant feeling of being asked for money whenever I'm contacted. I feel sure that she has not been taught that such behavior is manipulative, because I doubt that her mother has learned this lesson herself.

The final straw and evidence that Carla sees me as her benefactor and enabler was when she asked to "borrow" sixty-five dollars that she would repay as soon as she got home. Not only did she fail to repay me, she didn't bother to call. I considered this to be highway robbery without a gun. At this moment I understood that she felt entitled to my resources with or without my permission. It was my last time volunteering to be burglarized by Carla. Subsequently our contacts have been fewer and further between. I am at peace with that.

For the first twelve years of my life, my oldest sister Liz was my designated babysitter while my mother was at work. She lived in our upstairs two-family flat and had a daughter six months older than me. She was quite open about her dislike for me when I was a baby and as a young girl I was as headstrong as she was. Needless to say we had many clashes. I would often run and hide when she was on the warpath. She claimed that when my mother came home from work I told lies on her.

Liz is to my knowledge the only one of my many siblings who did not foster dependency in her children. She was a light-skinned very attractive strong-willed young woman with Indian features. They say she had long red hair in her younger days; however, it became shorter with the years. She always paid a lot of attention to her appearance, and always wore the latest "roaring-twenties" fashions. She was headstrong, feisty, and very firm in her beliefs, whatever they were. She had a mean streak which could cut you to the core. People knew not to mess with Liz. She had three children--Evelyn, Earline, and Arnette; she raised them alone after she divorced her husband. She forced them to be independent, perhaps too early, and each of them became serious full-time caretakers. Maybe codependency skipped a generation in Liz's family but it returned with a vengeance in her children.

Liz was a hard worker, and ahead of her time in terms of childrearing and health consciousness. Hygiene was so important to her that she washed her chittlins and greens with Tide washing powder. Her children thought she didn't serve much meat because she couldn't afford it, but she told them that too much meat was unhealthy. She regulated her body with cod liver oil long before colonics were fashionable. She exercised daily, and even at seventy she could put both feet over her head in a yoga posture, though I doubt she had ever heard of yoga. After arguments she would make her children kiss and make up; subsequently they developed a deep love and appreciation for each other. They were all independent and successful, and overly responsible. I believe that over-reactions against a pattern in one generation intensifies it in the next. The pattern needs to be understood, recognized, accepted, and healed in oneself before it can be eliminated for future generations.

I had planned a trip to St. Louis primarily to visit with Liz, my only remaining sibling at this time. I was also interested in continuing my exploration of our family dynamics and helping out in any way I could. An added bonus was the availability of inexpensive houses for investment. Liz was ninety years old and had Alzheimer's. She'd been declining for several years, and recently the family had requested hospice services. I decided to go to St. Louis to spend some time with her before she made her transition. Little did I realize that this trip would encompass a kaleidoscope of my entire family life and pull the final plug on our codependency. I was delighted to find Liz looking comfortable and well-cared for in her oldest daughter's home. I sat with her for two nights to provide much needed relief for my niece. I was limited in my ability to give her physical care, but kept her company; fortunately she has a caretaker she dearly loves.

Evelyn, Liz's oldest child, is very loving, gentle, and soft-spoken. She is an excellent cook and openhearted in her giving. Her list of the suffering needy extends for miles. She not only attends to family members in distress, but she sends scriptures and care packages to jails, nursing homes, and other welfare institutions. Her caretaking seems to have a benevolent spiritual quality. Unlike me, she is slow to anger and she appears unattached to the outcome of her giving. "Everyone Loves

Evelyn!" and her food!

Although Evelyn's children all live within a few blocks of her and each other, each of them contributes their own unique gifts. The nature of her relationships with her children seems to be more reciprocal. The care giving between them appears mutual.

Evelyn seems to have perfected the role of providing care and risen above codependency. I observed no trace of resentment in her, just pure sweetness. She is in my opinion the epitome of a nurturing mother. She is an excellent cook, inviting all who visit her home to share in meals. Her refrigerator is always full of delicious food, and she has homemade pies or cakes sitting out on hutch. Her breakfasts of grits, bacon, eggs, biscuits, and coffee were to die for. At dinner she didn't stop at ribs, spaghetti, fresh picked greens, cornbread, and okra--she also deep fried some of the most delectable chicken I have ever eaten.

Observing Evelyn in the kitchen was déjà vu of my mother's long hours cooking over a hot stove. Although I am an appreciative recipient of nurturing through food, I was reminded that it is not the path for me. I knew even as a young child that I would have to find a different way of nurturing. My way was to become a midwife to others' spiritual growth.

Evelyn confided in me that she enjoys taking care of her mother in spite of how hard it is. She didn't always feel this way a received gift through prayer. Although I didn't feel I had contributed very much to lighten her burden, she thanked me profusely and made several comments to others about how much she appreciated my assistance. Observing her reminded me of the importance of gratitude. I am truly inspired watching Evelyn do what she does with so much love and patience.

Liz received such good care from Earline and Evelyn that she was discharged from hospice and referred for physical therapy. Liz and Earline were featured in the local newspaper with a full two-page spread about her care and the assistance provided by the home care agency. However, Liz's Alzheimer's continued to be quite evident.

On my last visit she was in rare form and lucid for two days. She told me that God had given her a message for me and had reminded her several times not to forget it. She assured Him that she would not because I was coming to see her. As she described the message, she was quite clear, sitting erect in her wheelchair. She told me that God said I was dearly loved and I should not worry about anything. I will always be taken care of, and wherever I go He will go before me. I was told to enjoy my life and be happy because I had earned it. All my sins have been forgiven and I was now free to do whatever I wanted. She commented that in my travels around the world, wherever I go I will be well received and welcomed back.

Parts of her message seemed like a dream. She said there

was a group of children who were very happy when they heard my name, and responded, "Oh, Marie, she's a child of God." The children sang God's message to me with so much love in their hearts that it "took the form of a large greeting card." She said that she was very ill and thought she was going to die, but after she heard the song she was so inspired she got out of her bed and walked to her wheel chair.

    I thanked her and told her I was taking in as much of the message as I could. I said that of all the people in the world, she was the perfect one to deliver the message, that if I could believe it from anyone I could believe it from her. Because it came so clearly from her heart, it was received by mine. Liz said she was glad that I believed her. However, my head is still struggling to let it in. I am looking forward to the time I can simply accept that Love is who I am.

    Liz's middle daughter Earline is a shapely, brown skinned attractive middle-aged woman with a big smile and a soft voice. She loves fashions and shopping; she goes to sales whether or not she needs anything. In fact she needs nothing because she has three closets full of clothes and she's working on a fourth. Earline is completely identified with the role of caretaker; she seems to think that's who she is. She has perfected the role and is surpassed only by her Aunt Ruby. She took care of her elderly mother with Alzheimer's every other week. Also during this time her alcoholic husband Tom of more than thirty-five years was diagnosed with cancer of the esophagus and thyroid requiring extensive nursing care over a two year period.

Tom is a very opinionated, self-willed, hardworking man who provided well for his family. He worked for years for IBM and also ran a successful business from his home. His two loves in life were cigarettes and booze, which eventually cost him his life. Over time their communication deteriorated almost to silence. Cancer and addictions were prevalent in his family of origin; his father, two brothers and a sister all were smokers and died of cancer. Although Tom could eat nothing by mouth, he was still smoking. For me he was a graphic example of where I could have been. Filled with gratitude and compassion, I was moved to share with him my personal story of my struggle with addiction to cigarettes. When I had finished, he said he was a man who honored his commitments, his children were now adults, and he had done everything he had wanted to do. He told me that he had been writing his obituary for nine years and was almost finished. His message was clear, and he had no interest in my story of recovery.

I asked if there was anyone he thought needed him or wanted him to stay around. He said his only concern was his wife, and he worried about her emotional resilience. Asked how he could help, he said he didn't know, that he had asked her several times without getting a straight answer. Earline said she had asked

Tom several times not to leave her with the children. She added that every time she uses the word "children" it angers him. It seems that the word "children" implies dependency. He has resented Earline's fostering dependency after the children became adults.

I told Earline privately that her request for Tom to support her behavior was the same as his asking her to participate in his drinking, which she has resented and tried to get him to stop for many years. I encouraged her to open the door to meaningful communication with Tom. Once she got past the initial frustration of having tried so hard in the past, and why she had to be the one to initiate communication, she reluctantly accepted that he was in fact dying. I told her that after he is gone I didn't want her to regret not taking advantage of this opportunity. I suggested that she clarify her intention to communicate, pray on it, and be willing to accept God's guidance. I call her every day to check in on how she's doing. She said there had been some progress, but nothing profound. I reassured her that the journey of a thousand miles begins with the first step. I'm optimistic that she will take the second and then the third. One thing I know for sure, whatever we give God in truth he will keep.

Tom, arriving at death's door twice, decided to give life another chance. He had a lucid dream in which he and another fish were swimming downstream. He heard a voice telling him, "Don't come this way again." However he continued to drink and smoke. To his dismay life changed, but he didn't. His comeback amazed doctors and everyone else who observed it. Tom, getting chemo and radiation, and IV and tube feedings, felt compelled to maintain his contribution to the household. He cut the grass on the three-acre yard and cooked meals and washed dishes, even though he could no longer eat. He also got out of bed to strip wall paper from the bathroom walls.

Modern medical care seems to have abdicated responsibility for skilled nursing care, and Earline picked up the slack. She told me she had never wanted to be a nurse because she feared giving injections, but she stepped up to the plate. Although she's often exhausted and overburdened with too much to do, she can still find time and energy to even attempt to take care of me when I visit St. Louis.

Despite these already extremely heavy burdens, Earline continues to mother her three adult children. She even bought a daycare so her daughter, who has a master's degree in social work, (paid for by her parents), would have a job. Earline takes on most of the responsibilities for the daycare, turning a blind eye to her daughter's less than responsible behavior. She knowingly overpays her son-in-law to do small jobs, and I believe she supplements their income to enable them to take several vacations a year.

On my mission to cure codependency in my family, I got up the nerve to point out to Earline the unhealthy, codependent nature of her relationship with her oldest son, Eric. Eric is married to an immature, emotionally challenged white woman who has had several psychiatric hospitalizations. She openly admits that she is not sure who the father of the child is, and Eric has not been willing to get a paternity test because he apparently doesn't want to know. Eric's job transferred him to Milwaukee, but his wife and daughter remain in St. Louis. It is commonplace for Eric to call Earline from Wisconsin to tell her to pick up his daughter at school because his wife is unable to do so. He also makes other demands on Earline to subsidize the parental role.

I told Earline that she was protecting Eric from the consequences of his own actions. As long as she is willing to provide long-distance services and fill in the many gaps in his management of life, he will never learn his lessons and grow up. On the slim chance that he might divorce this wife (again), he would probably select a similar one because he has not been allowed to experience the difficulty and pain of an unavailable spouse. From where he stands, things aren't so bad because Earline is filling the holes, subsidizing the mother's role. After Earline's husband's death, Eric insisted on moving back in with her against her wishes. In spite of her many objections, he, like the boll weevil, found a way to stay. The battle over who runs the house continues. In Earline's own words, he is forcing her to be strong and teaching her to stand up for herself. She is finding strength she did not know she had.

Earline has attended therapy off and on and gone to Al-anon for several years and managed to get her family to try some family counseling; however, she has not yet been able to separate herself from the codependent role. In her late sixties she mortgaged her house to buy a daycare to provide her daughter and daughter-in-law, both of whom had college degrees, with employment. Her youngest son has been operating the family business for several years. Recently Craig decided he would like to open a dart club, which she also financed. Being needed continues to be a source of personal satisfaction for Earline. This payoff seems to overshadow any future promise offered by recovery from codependency.

Liz's only son and the apple of her eye was Arnette, a king of a man with an amazing ability to rise above the mundane and handle the challenges of life (and he had many) with dignity and grace. Arnette was married to a materialistic narcissistic hypochondriac. After working a ten- or twelve-hour day in his landscaping business, he frequently went home, washed dishes, did the laundry, and prepared dinner for his wife who was often still in bed. He also helped his sisters take care of their mother when she developed Alzheimer's, taking her to all her appointments and keeping her on the weekends.

In spite of his many personal responsibilities, Arnette also managed to help other family members and friends in need. He always picked me up from the airport when I went to St. Louis and was "Johnny-at-the-ready" with anything else I needed. Arnette raised four highly successful children almost singlehandedly-- a doctor, a hospital administrator, an entrepreneur and real estate investor, and CEO in a tech firm.

As with all expert caretakers, he did not take care of himself. He recently died of a heart attack. When I went to St. Louis for his funeral, I found myself looking for him at the airport. As part of his eulogy, orchestrated by his children, I said I had known him all of his life and had never seen him in a bad mood, impatient, or unkind. What a legacy! I hope all of the young men in our family will benefit from his example. Earline, Arnette, and Evelyn have always been very close and supportive to each other, although all of their marriages left much to be desired, in my opinion. Evelyn's seemed to be the most balanced. They all remained married for thirty-five, forty, and fifty years, and there is much to be said for longevity. Taking responsibility for your choice of a mate and hanging in there to the death working out your own problems is a real sign of health and maturity.

Another family member who was a codependent caretaker married to an alcoholic told me the following story: She was very frightened of snakes, and lived in a woodsy area. She found a snake in the basement of her home and became almost hysterical. Her husband had already started drinking for the day, but was not yet drunk, and he managed to kill the snake. He minimized and made fun of his wife's fears. He even seemed to take some delight in it. He told this story in great detail to anyone who called during the next several days. The day after encountering the snake, my client received a picture of two large snakes in the mail. She was bewildered to think about who would play such a mean-spirited trick on her. She threw the picture in the trash.

The following day she discovered her husband had taken the picture out of the trash and laid it on the table. She was hurt and angered by her husband's insensitivity and seeming pleasure in her pain. She tore the picture up in small pieces and returned it to the trash can with no exchange of words with him. This man might be suffering from chronic brain damage due to alcoholism, but in any case, he was so separated from his own feelings that he had no thermometer for tuning in to the feelings of others. The cared-for is often unaware that the care-taker has feelings.

In addition, he has a lot of repressed anger and jealousy regarding his wife's strength and superior competence. He has no clue about his jealousy and competition with her and would vehemently deny it if it were pointed out to him. In spite of his many hurtful and unsupportive acts, my client has chosen to remain in the marriage. Her excuse is that she doesn't want to leave the family home and dividing the finances would be a full-scale war. This story is a clear demon-stration of the damage done in codependent relationships to both the caretaker and the one being cared for.

My nephew Melvin, almost sixty, has fathered several children and has committed himself to raising his youngest four, whose mother is deceased. This has by no means been an easy task for him. He experienced a very traumatic childhood in foster homes, after the death of his parents. For many years he was an out-of-control alcoholic and drug addict. He has always had a good heart, a very generous man willing to help others, but usually only on his own terms. He can also be very verbally abusive, freely spreading his anger with the force of a fire hose. Somewhere along the way he found religion and developed his spirituality in a Black Baptist church. Melvin has extremely bad feet, but continues to work from time to time as a waiter, the only real skill he has. He also takes dialysis three times a week, which is physically and emotionally stressful. Added to this is the fulltime care of two teenagers and two young adults who are still living in the home. One of the older girls recently had a baby. It is easy to see why he lives in overwhelm. While I am sure he has a personal relationship with the Spirit, I can see the extreme limitations he places on the Spirit by his undeveloped personality.

There has always been lots of anger and conflict in the

family's interactions. A few days ago individual differences escalated to a major crisis which included Melvin beating the two older children by his own admission, and ended in his putting his fourteen year old out of the house. She soon called Nita for help. Melvin became extremely angry, accused us of putting our nose in his business, and interfering in his relationship with the children and God. Melvin is very stubborn and closed to any information that doesn't agree with what he thinks is right. He was unable to see beyond his own anger, and his flame was sparked by any mention of the children's needs. His only objective at this point seemed to be to punish them for their dis-obedience and lack of cooperation. Nita called me to ask for advice, and I suggested that she follow her own heart. She and her husband went to Palo Alto at eleven PM to get Joshua, so he could stay with them until things calmed down. Melvin seemed to have no concept that things can or will calm down, and at this point the wasn't willing to detach from his position long enough to let it happen.

This pattern of dramatic upset is frequently repeated in Melvin's family, after which everybody often ends up returning to business as usual without any new understanding or skills for dealing with the next crisis. Denial is the veil that prevents effective solutions and change. My many efforts to intervene have been to no avail. Perhaps the next generation will break the cycle.

If trying to help Melvin was like being in the Flood without the Ark, spending a week with Rosemarie was as equal or more challeng-ing. Rosemarie, Earline's first cousin and my niece, has moved again and is now living in a very upscale retirement home. Not only is it beautifully maintained, it is also caring and provides a variety of social activities. It was interesting to observe Rosemarie's difficulty in accepting this abundance. She talked at length about the other residents being older than herself, and that adjustment was difficult, giving up some of her privacy and freedom. When I questioned her about the freedoms, it turned out she has more freedoms there--more mobility, friends, activities, etc. I reminded her that in her home she had been fearful, lonely, and crying much of the time. She was confined and dependent on others to take her out, and her house was not very accessible for a wheelchair.

She admitted she felt safer, more peaceful, and happier in her new home. I suggested that she use her age to her advantage by reading to some of the other residents and learning from their wisdom. She could relate to this because she had been surprised to learn that a number of the residents also had difficulty with their children. I told her that her new home was indeed an answered prayer, and her appropriate response should be gratitude.

She told me that her daughter and son-in-law wanted to buy a house and wanted her to come live with them. She was aware that their underlying motivation was for her to help them with the house note. She said that the son-in-law had commented that her retirement home was for people who had no family to take care of them. I reminded Rose that when she was living alone and lonely, he had not come forth. After Rose had fallen she was totally dependent on her teenaged grandson for assistance. Her daughter Maria, who flirts with drug abuse and has anger issues, had argued with Rose and out of revenge went to Rose's house and took her son, leaving Rose destitute. I told Rose that in my opinion this was a graphic demonstration of Maria's inability to be responsive to Rose's needs. It is the ugly side of codependency. I suggested that she start practicing listening to her own feelings rather than external rhetoric. She got the message.

On one of my trips to St. Louis, I decided to take several family members to lunch, and I encouraged Rosemarie to bring her two grandchildren, who were visiting her along with her daughter. Melvin had asked to make the trip with me but said he didn't have plane fare. Due to his failing health, I thought this might be his last opportunity, so I agreed to buy his ticket. He was to be responsible for everything else.

When the waiter asked about separate bills, I announced that I would pick up the tab. Melvin, who had been outside smoking weed ("his medicine" for dealing with the side effects of dialysis), came in after everyone had ordered and asked who was paying the bill. Someone informed him that I was, so he proceeded to order lobster, the most expensive item on the dinner menu, plus a glass of wine. I was highly incensed and told him I was not paying for it.

After it arrived, I repeated that I was not going to pay for it. With an attitude, he reluctantly pulled about half the price of it out of his pocket and put it on the table, mumbling something about he thought he could order whatever he wanted. Then he lost his appetite and ate about one bite and decided to take the rest home.

First he put it in the refrigerator, then he decided to freeze it. When he thawed it, he said he didn't want it and was going to throw it away. He told her not to tell me. Earline intervened and said she would eat it. Instead of apologizing for his outlandish behavior, he made a comment that he didn't want to hurt me but he thought that we were going to split the lunch bill. This limp excuse was not followed by any cash. He repeated several times that the last thing he wanted was to hurt me, and I asked how is it possible that he can do so consistently what he didn't intend to do. After two days of my display of indifference, he finally mustered the courage and expressed remorse. This experience was the straw that finally broke my codependent back with him. This is the same nephew who called and thanked me for not lending him money because it forced him to find his own resources.

On the flip side, contrary to his behavior, Melvin seems to be more spiritually aware and sensitive than many members of my family. He frequently refers to my perseverance and my commitment to love in spite of it all. He often expresses appreciation for who I am in the world and who I am in his life.

As I have let go of my strong desire for my family to be different, several members have come to me for guidance and counsel. I know that I am healing myself from my family wounds because I'm now more able to be with my family in love and the truth about our dysfunctions. On one of my visits to St. Louis, my niece Cassandra asked me to counsel her and her two young adult daughters, both of whom have major attitude problems. She was very frustrated by her attempts to get them and other family members to be more affectionate and supportive of each other. One of the things I told her was that our family is dysfunctional; they refuse to talk about problems and difficulties in a constructive way, and they act as if you are crazy for wanting to change things, making it your problem and not theirs. Thus they excuse themselves from making any efforts towards solutions. She later told me that on first hearing the word "dysfunctional," she became angry. However, after she thought about it, she realized I was right.

Cassandra has had a bad heart condition since childhood. She developed hepatitis C from a blood transfusion and has a number of other complicated chronic conditions. She was recently hospitalized for heart surgery. I called to give her support, and she was appreciative. I told her that she can only make choices for herself. Now that she has decided to work to become healthier and seek peace, she will have to release anyone who isn't in alignment with her goal. She has to be firm and consistent and not become distracted by others' agendas.

One of her daughters is very angry and sometimes acts as if she's the parent in the relationship. I encouraged Cassandra to set boundaries for herself and refuse to allow anyone to be disrespectful to her. It's hard to feel out of harmony with those we love, but we have to choose peace for ourselves over harmony with others. It's necessary for her to forgive herself for any mistakes she might have made, let go of all guilt and the past, accept that she has been forgiven, and affirm her new intention for the future. When we are healed from our own fears and anger, right behavior is spontaneous. It is always intended for the good of all and the harm of none.

It took awhile for Cassandra to grasp the unhealthy nature of codependency, because her grown children and grandchildren are the center of her life and reason for being. I encouraged her to explore areas of personal interest and designate time for relaxation and personal care. It is from a healthy relationship with the self that all other healthy relationships flow.

The more I have learned about myself over the years, the more I have come to accept and love myself. Security in who and what I am has enabled me to become more conscious about my own thoughts, feelings and behavior. After many colorful, highly textured, tantalizing codependent experiences, I was finally able to discover its deep taproot. This is a thick root that goes straight down and is the lifeline of the living system.

This realization led me to the discovery of over-identification as the ultimate act of codependency. Coincidentally, Nita and I both had mammograms in July--our appointments were only a few days apart. Unfortunately, a lump was found in her left breast and my right one. Following a series of additional tests, she was diagnosed with in situ carcinoma, and a few days later I was told I had invasive carcinoma. The synchronicity of these occurrences was mind boggling. I knew the Spirit was trying to tell me something which demanded my undivided attention. I told the Spirit that I was willing to learn whatever lesson the experience came to teach me; however, my preference would be to learn it some other way. Nonetheless, I added that no matter what, I would accept His will. I prayed for courage and strength.

The process of my diagnosis was protracted, conflicting, and confusing. I decided to put my situation on the back burner to be available to support Nita through her surgery. In my heart I felt that the manifestation of my tumor was a sympathetic response to her situation. With every fiber of my being I did not want her to have to go through the loss and agony connected with the treatment, and I railed against it with all my heart and soul. At the end of the day, one thing I know for sure is God is always right. When I visited Nita after the surgery, I understood with new clarity why she had to go through the experience. I was very impressed with the strength, grace, and humor which she demonstrated in facing one of life's most difficult and scary challenges. I can die happy knowing that she is prepared to meet life on its own terms with grace and equanimity.

In witnessing this experience with her, I was able to disentangle some of my emotional enmeshment and see each of us as the unique individuals we are. Secure in our unconditional love for each other, and bonded by our common values, I could relive many of my own challenges as a young woman struggling to find meaning in life and to be true to myself and those who loved me. I could clearly see that we made different choices, based on the authenticity of who we are in the world, and in keeping with divine providence.

Neither one of us has had biological children. One primary difference is that Nita chose to be married and I did not. During the many conversations we had about what life was trying to teach us, we talked about the breast being symbolic of nurturing. We explored possible conflicts each of us might have in this area. I told her that being a mother was my primary role in life, and at this stage, the threat of cancer was an opportunity for me to evaluate how I feel about motherhood, the mistakes I've made and the successes I've had, and how I have used what I've learned to become a better parent. I now understand that over-identification is the most destructive aspect of codependency and helps no one. On balance, I feel that I have performed well in one of the most important role life offers. I know without doubt that the love I've given to my many children touched them each in a special way, and this gift will go on giving into eternity and beyond.

Over the past three years Nita has faced many health challenges requiring several major surgeries. I became exasperated with the protracted nature of her illnesses, which finally brought me to my knees and total surrender. On my visit to her in the hospital, I saw in the gift shop the perfect bear to represent my love for her. The bear had a very enchanting look on her face which seemed to say, "Hug me!" When I gave it to Nita, with delight and surprise she said, "Oh, Miss Marie is back!" After her discharge from the hospital, she came to spend a week with me, and we talked about everything from birth to death, spanning many generations. I pointed out the history of pathology in our family and acknowledged that it was impossible for any of our members to totally escape it. I shared many of my struggles and personal triumphs, most of which she knew and many of which she shared. The two of us are the highest achievers in the family, obsessed with trying to be strong and a source of support. We went out of our way to buy gifts for the family on special occasions and to act as the Bank of America for unsecured loans to unqualified applicants. With humor we acknowledged that this behavior was not effective in producing the desired results.

I expressed my concern for the umpteenth time that Nita's body was trying to tell her something, and she needed to be still and listen. This led to her discomfort in asking people to do things for her. Exploring the source of this attitude, she said that a tape of my voice beating the drum of independence always plays in her head. I apologized for overdoing it, and again shared with her the reason--I did not want her to be hurt because she felt dependent on someone else for her survival. I said that I had to learn to receive gracefully the hard way, but what I know for sure is that God is my source and of myself I can do nothing. I encouraged her to rely totally on the Lord, that He would make sure she had everything she needs. I also gave her permission to delete any tapes that I had recorded that were not working for her.

The next morning Piper killed a mouse and deposited it on the steps where it could not be missed. I saw it but passed right by it, but a few minutes later Nita let out a loud squeal that could be heard all over neighborhood. I told her that Piper was presenting us with a gift and wanted to be complimented. She went into a manic act of applause and cheering for Piper. I bravely swept the mouse into a dust pan and headed for the balcony to throw him overboard, but I somewhere between the kitchen and dining room I dropped it. I realized that the dust pan seemed light. I turned, and saw Nita jumping up and down, holding her head, screaming "You dropped it! I wanted to see it flip out the dustpan!" I started laughing, retrieved the mouse, and tossed it over the railing. Just then Piper came over and licked the back of her leg. Nita's eyes bugged out and she squealed, "He licked my leg after killing that rat! Ewwwwww! That's nasty, disgusting!"

I told her that Piper had given her the supreme gift of nurturing and caring. I said the message was that the stuff she was holding on to was dead and she could let it go. I said I was reframing it as a gift of my freedom from the past and suggested she might consider doing the same. She said she was glad that I thought it was so funny. Out of nervousness she started packing her bags talking about getting out of my house. She said whatever she came for she got it a day early, so it was time to go. She gradually calmed down but continued to look at me out of the corners of her eyes when she thought I wasn't looking.

Two days later Nita drove me to my writing appointment. She took this opportunity to express her concern about my "process" which continues after more than twenty years. She said that she had been observing me awake and asleep during the past week and concluded that it does not seem to be getting better, even though I have told her that it is. She thinks it might be even worse than before. She said she tried to believe me when I said it was temporary, but she doesn't anymore. She pointed out that it takes up a lot of my time and energy. She said she now thinks it's psychological and maybe I should consider hypnosis. I agreed with her, saying I too am concerned. I have done everything I know to do, from acupressure to chiropractic, faith healers, and a litany of CAT scans, MRI's and nerve ending tests, etc. I also carry-on continuous dialogue with the process itself, and with the Spirit. I am also willing to try anything any well meaning person recommends, and if she thinks I should try hypnosis, that will be the next thing on my list.

I said if she thought it was psychological, what did she think I was repressing? She said she thought that she and the rest of my children and family were disappointments to me. She said she had been thinking of ways to improve her status in the world in order to make me more proud. When I looked surprised, she said that anybody in my situation who had given so unselfishly of themselves would feel disappointed. I continued to look surprised and said that was not my feeling at all. What I wanted for all my children, including my foster children, was that they be happy and treat others with kindness and respect. I wanted them to get a good education and be successful in life because I had learned that resourcefulness is the foundation of a happy life. Knowledge is power, and money is added power, as well as comfort and convenience.

I told Nita that I feel my life has been a storybook success. I have been privileged to touch all of the children who have come to me in some way and I believe each has used what I have offered to the best of their ability. Sometimes it takes a while for the fruit to ripen. However, I feel very influential when I think of what might have been for me, or for the children, without each other, and I know I have made a difference. I feel blessed to have chosen the right profession for myself, and to have succeeded by most standards, doing it my own way. Bill Moyer said that to be authentic is the privilege of a lifetime.

I told Nita that I was very pleased with her ability to reach out and respect other people, and I was proud of the strength she had displayed during these serious medical challenges. Her faith was an inspiration to me and helped me handle the situation better. I am also pleased with the healthy relationship with her husband-- no small feat considering the lineage we both came from, of women making bad choices. I added if she felt personally incomplete and wanted to achieve more external goals in life, to feel free to do so, but not under the banner of doing it for Marie. We both shared a deep laughter as if we were letting go of all the shackles of the past. My heart overflows with gratitude for the opportunity to make this correction in my life's legacy for myself as well as my children. I have been blessed with children who are also my spiritual partners.

I didn't agree with Nita's diagnosis of my malaise, but I agreed to try the treatment she recommended. What could hypnosis hurt? And I was sure I would learn something. On the road to hypnosis I was suddenly attacked by a flaming sore throat. It had started on a low burn the morning Piper killed the mouse and licked Nita's leg. The entire scenario and her response to it had been such a colorful lighthearted demonstration of my answered prayer that I was overcome with laughter. I reassured her that Piper had given her the ultimate gift, the gift of freedom from which all others flow. She had been freed from the bondage of the past. Witnessing this healing I was healed as well.

Meanwhile, back at the ranch, I had a lumpectomy and received a final diagnosis of in situ carcinoma which is said to be an invasive cancer that is very slow growing and acts like in situ. The truth is that it is so rare that no research has been done and little is known about it. My surgeon recommended additional surgery and possible radiation. I sought a second opinion and that surgeon discouraged more surgery. She said that what is considered a clear margin will vary depending on who you talk to, the school they attended, the area they live in, and their individual philosophies. She said if I had any treatment she would recommend radiation. She also suggested that I could do nothing and have annual mammograms, since "nobody dies of in situ carcinoma."

The Chairman of the San Francisco Medical Society referred me to the top breast surgeon in the country for a third opinion. However, after I saw an oncologist who was very knowledgeable, patient, and thorough, I felt I had received adequate information on which to make an intelligent decision. She in essence concurred with the second surgeon, confirming that clear margins are indeed a judgment call. I felt that the Spirit had spoken. I told her that what I find most disturbing is when a doctor presents her opinion as the only right one. We both laughed when she told me that my first and second surgeons had both gone to the same school. I cancelled my appointment to do radiation and received a call from the radiologist. I explained to him that I was taking a number of medications that contributed to drowsiness, and it was my understanding that radiation would exasperate my fatigue. All things considered, I had decided to live life now and deal with the future when it comes. He also agreed that further treatment was a judgment call and told me to feel free to contact him with any questions. I have decided just to have regular mammograms and to put this issue to sleep, along with my codependency needs.

Breaking the chain of codependencies has been a lifelong pursuit for me because it's been the most destructive, crippling dynamic in my family. I have observed and participated in these patterns for three generations. Reflections of myself in the other angered me for years until I realized that I was seeing a self-reflection and that I was the one who needed to change. I was confused by the momentum of old habits that made my mindless behavior feel familiar and right. It takes energy to break old habits and to resist the lure of the path of least resistance. This is especially true when there is no overt resistance from the other.

At the death of my niece, Rose Marie, her oldest daughter Maria was anxious to take control of Rose's affairs. Rose had asked me to take power of attorney but I was in Costa Rica and Maria was elected by default. When I talked to Maria by phone she went to great lengths to convince me that she had been a caring and devoted daughter, which was not the way Rose had described her to me. Maria told me that several times she had asked Rose to come and live with her, but she refused. Maria also said that anyone who knew Rose knew that she was afraid to live alone. I pointed out that Maria seemed to be saying that Rose was too independent to live with her, and I asked if she could think of any reason why Rose would not want to live with her. Of course she could not. Before going to St. Louis, my prayer had been to be free from the bondage of codependency with my family and to relate to them on this visit in the witness consciousness.

When I arrived at the funeral, I was more than shocked to see that I and the entire Simmons part of the family had been eliminated from the obituary, even though it was we who had provided the most support to Rose during her life. Not only was I Rose's only living aunt, but she as well as Maria had been named after me.

As I was standing in line in the funeral home, Maria must have been overcome with guilt because she came and got me by the arm and I complied and walked with her in the family procession to the front row. I felt awkward and detached because nobody knew who I was. Nonetheless I comforted her like a loving aunt.

As if this wasn't enough, she invited me to ride in the limo to the cemetery and again she seated me front row and center. After the burial, unknown to me, we returned to Maria's house instead of the repast. Even though she knew I had an appointment she sashayed around, changing her clothes, holding me hostage until the time of my appointment had come and gone. When we arrived at the repast, we went our separate ways and our paths did not cross again. Maria was very clearly identified with Rose's father's side of the family, and at last I got an external signal that if I didn't buy into Maria's story I was expendable. At this moment I recognized that the price was too high. The chain was broken.

My nephew Melvin lost both his parents by age six. He and a younger sister lived in foster homes for several years. He told stories of extreme emotional and physical abuse, especially by one cruel foster mother who forced him to eat dog shit because she insisted it was his. After that she forced him to eat oatmeal which he despised. He has carried these scars all his life, along with some memories of himself as a four-year-old with his mother before she was sick. Melvin has a lot of repressed and overt anger which he sprays on anyone around, especially girls and women in particular. On the other hand he has a big heart and is generous, giving you anything he's got. Having been a waiter, he tips very generously, and he will give you the shirt off his back. He has a good sense of humor, and is usually honest. When he tells the truth it is sometimes refreshing, and other times hurtful and inappropriate.

Over the years Melvin has battled drug addiction, alcoholism, and mental illness. In spite of great odds, he managed to keep his three youngest children together with him; they had lost their mothers to drug addictions at a very young age. Although he had four other children, they were raised by their mothers. I believe he offered his children the best he had to give, and given what he had to work with, he did an outstanding job. Unfortunately, even though it was his best, it was a far cry from what the children needed. As one of his daughters commented, he used to blame them when things didn't go right. Melvin was unable to recognize his own projections because he couldn't' look at himself. Therefore he couldn't see that in spite of his strong desire to have his children close to him, it was he who pushed them away.

When I would try to point it out to him he would become annoyed and lose interest in the conversation.

With age he developed a number of chronic illnesses, including renal failure for the last twenty-five years. He has come to the end of his life. I have been impressed by the maturity and competence of his oldest daughter Francesca, who has stepped into a leadership role in the family. She is concerned about comforting her siblings and she visits her father daily in the hospital, in spite of having a two-year-old and a steady job. It occurred to me that Melvin might have been so focused on the things she did wrong that he somehow missed all the things she was doing right. I was inspired to try to facilitate the opportunity for Melvin to say goodbye to all of his children. I felt it would clear his path to make his transition in peace. I offered financial assistance where needed to make their visit possible. One of my daughters asked how was this my responsibility, and I replied it was not. It was simply a heartfelt offering of compassion. I felt grateful for chance to deliberately choose to align my thoughts, feelings, and actions to achieve an objective. It was free choice.

While Melvin's daughters from St. Louis were here, I had a dinner with them including Francesca, a friend, and several cousins. We had a lively discussion over pork tenderloin, twice baked potatoes, and uniquely creative salads. I asked them to share their observations of the most unhealthy emotional pattern in our family, and I would give a prize for the right answer. Addictions, laziness, and fear were offered, and I validated all those things to be true. Then LaWanda said codependency, and I said Bingo. This was followed by what it is, and how it feels in our relationships. Light bulbs were going on all over the place. Although the hour was late, everyone seemed to enjoying the conversation and learning new awareness about themselves. All said that they would take it with them and it would help them move forward in their lives.

I continued to try to weed out codependency relationships in my family. Pluck was the son of my late brother JW in St. Louis.

Dear Pluck, I am becoming more and more annoyed by my perception that you are taking advantage of me. I began having this feeling of hide and seek when it took several conversations in which you described to me that a bank account in your name which you claimed was yours was really mine.

To be sure I have sincerely appreciated all the help you have given in managing my property in my absence. Some of your decisions have been very helpful, some very costly. Although you were usually able to negotiate a higher rent it seems to have ended up being more costly to me in the long run. A series of bad decisions were made resulting in selection of several irresponsible tenants who failed to pay the rent and trashed the place. This happened on several occasions which was expensive to repair.

You were annoyed by my well-meaning observation that you seemed to attract angry black women. You asked me to keep my opinions to myself. I have tried to honor your request but I'm unwilling to pay for a practice that does not work.

You also would like to think of yourself as a good judge of character. Your denial in this area led you to pay two workmen before the jobs were completed, and consequently they never were. You paid another contractor (that you knew) $1200 in advance to deliver an air conditioner which never arrived. Regarding Section Eight and being clear about their policies, you arranged for Valerie to live in a three-bedroom house when she was only approved for two. The alarm system which you thought was month-to-month turned out to be a two-year contract. In both these situations, I had previous experience and could have avoided these expenses, but you seemed annoyed when I tried to point out things to you in advance, usually referring to your successful experiences of several McDonald's Restaurants. There seems to be little carryover of learning on your part. Your decision making pattern and style of communication is not working for me.

You decided not to pay your rent and informed me of your plans for repayment saying you had other obligations. I wondered if you didn't feel obligated to me and why you felt it was okay to make decisions about my money without my permission. I felt controlled, manipulated, and disregarded when you informed me by letter of your decision. Recently, although you haven't paid me back for the three months rent you missed, you now say you do not have this month's rent. Although you commented you were going to be contacting your landlord regarding your shop, you made absolutely no reference to paying your rent to me nor your rent that's past due. It seems that you don't want to be told what to do or take responsibility for what you do, that you just want to be doing what you do the way you do and you want me to like it. Well, I don't! Love, Marie.

RESOLUTION OF CODEPENDENCY

After many years of being blown to oblivion by the old landmines of codependences and addictions, I slowly emerged from my denial in active pursuit of resolution. The IEP's planted by my family gradually were losing their power. After each eruption, the ground under my feet became firmer. I acquired more skill and grace to navigate the uneven terrains. As I am approaching the end of my life, one thing I've learned for sure is that codependency is not sexy. In the end, it is painful, *and* you don't get what you thought you wanted. What most of us want is to love and be loved, and what codependency gives is anger, resentment, and disappointment.

The first real turning point in my healing came with the death of my beloved friend Susan in the late nineties. She lived her life based on what she thought was society's expectation of her, and always felt something was missing. I had known for a long time that I was repeating my family pattern of codependency which was anything but fulfilling. I decided that the best way to grieve her loss would be to try to correct the mistakes in my life that she made in hers. At her memorial I vowed to make some changes in my life--to extricate myself from codependency and live by choice.

The following Christmas I gave a Kwanza celebration and invited as much of my family as could come, and those who couldn't come we acknowledged in spirit. I announced to my family that I had come to the stark realization that contrary to my belief (and maybe some of theirs), *I am nobody's savior*, and I was freeing each of them to paint their own canvas. Years prior to this moment the spirit had informed me that even the birds dropped their young from the nest. I had been the identified caretaker in the family for as long as I can remember and even more so after my mother's death. I believe that one of the reasons I decided to get an education was so that I could earn enough money to be the best caretaker I could be. I went on to explain that they had every right to be who they are and were responsible for their own creations whether they wanted to believe it or not. I announced that I had decided to accept them just the way they were.

The responses ranged from tears and anger to shock and disbelief. The atmosphere was so tense that several people had to retreat to the decks for air. As we were preparing for dinner, Nita protested that I was "kicking her to the curb." Some of them thought that this decision meant that I no longer loved them. The truth is that it is a more loving act to recognize the power of other people to take responsibility for themselves.

Family members felt free to ask me for any and everything--from moving into my house to bailing them (and their friends) out of jail, to cosigning for cars, which they seldom managed to pay for, and on and on. My family's attitude was that because I seemed to have it, I should be willing to share it with them, and for many years I was. However, all of the help and assistance I gave didn't seem to make them any more responsible. Our codependent relationships were in a process of perpetual decay. It seemed that my efforts to "help" were actually an interference with their learning whatever they needed to know to make better choices in life. Although it would make me angry when they asked for money my bleeding heart compelled me to comply. One of my nephews who was addicted to cocaine and had a kidney failure was raising three children alone; he was in the habit of telling me that the children were hungry whenever he needed money. I was a real patsy when it came to "hungry children." However, on one occasion, I got up enough courage to tell him no. The following day he called and thanked me for saying no because he was able to manage from his own resources. Although I recognized this as a gift at the time it was several years before it had real impact on my codependent behavior.

I visited another nephew who was addicted to crack cocaine; he was living in a residential drug rehab program. He asked me to buy him a twenty dollar watch so he could be on time for meetings. I told him that he needed to save his money from his disability check and budget for a watch. In the meantime he should use the clocks I saw displayed on the walls.

He later made the comment that he knew my friend who was visiting with me and I had connections and he was wondering if we could hook him up with a job after his release. I suggested that he needed to learn to rely on his own resources, that he was very good about getting jobs on his own, but keeping them had been the problem. I told him that unfortunately he had not been at the Kwanza when I announced the end of my participation in codependency. He seemed quite surprised when he asked if the only thing I was willing to give him was advice. I assured him that I'm also available for moral support.

Over the years I've become more clear about recognizing and accepting that the Spirit is available to everyone, even my family, and we're all responsible for our own choices. "There are no victims, only volunteers."

Determined to remain conscious around all my "volunteer activities," I have learned to refrain from my knee-jerk responses to rescue anyone who asked for my help, and to think before I act. I had finally come to realize that saying yes was not always the way to help. Richie had told me once that everybody who throws you into a pile of shit is not your enemy, and everybody who pulls you out is not your friend. The Kwanza was to serve as my formal termination of my participation in fostering codependency and addiction, the two major dysfunctions in our family. After my declaration I felt very relieved and free. I reassured all concerned that this was really a loving act on my part, and that they would come to accept and appreciate it with time.

Continuing in my family's footsteps, I became aware that in the past I had attracted men who either wanted to take care of me and thereby control me or be taken care of themselves. As a young woman I was adamant about being independent, but I didn't have a clue about how to allow myself to be taken care of without abandoning myself. During the stressful period of my mother's illness and taking in the children, I was living in constant overwhelm. At this time I had the best relationship that I have ever had with a man: Jim took very good care of us all. The extremely demanding situation forced me to receive gratefully.

The relationship came to an end shortly after my mother's death. Jim announced that he would soon be leaving. His parting words to me were that he worried about who would take care of me when he was gone. I was somewhat surprised by the comment and responded that "I am going to take care of me." I was not yet mature enough to recognize Jim's need to be needed. Although I still wanted him, and was heartbroken to see him go, the truth is I didn't need him as much, and unconsciously the shift got communicated to him.

Some years later, I learned the art of allowing myself to be taken care of without abandoning myself. I realized and accepted that giving and receiving are one in truth. I now receive all love graciously and with gratitude. "What comes from the heart reaches the heart---there are no other requirements."

With the realization that I felt Nita took me for granted, which was not helpful to her and painful for me, I requested to join her on one of her visits to her therapist. This was an unusual situation in many ways, because the therapist was one of my former clients whom I had recommended when Nita asked me to suggest a therapist for her. During the session, each of us voiced our feelings about the other and our relationship. Nita talked about wanting the relationship to be more lighthearted and easygoing. She was unaware of the extent of my concern and feelings, that she did not appreciate me in the way I wanted. I announced that I was not going to listen to Nita's "rational" explanation of my feelings. At this time I felt determined to stop offering myself to be taken for granted. I was no longer available on demand, and discovered that she did well, even flourished, without my constant assistance. Gradually she became more attentive and appreciative of me and one of my strongest supporters.

Nita now goes out of her way to make sure I know she loves me. However, on a few occasions she has assumed she knew better than I what was best for me and has taken the prerogative to discard what she deemed not good for me. She was annoyed by the frequent calls of telemarketers, and thought I was overindulgent with them when I had a conversation with them. Once she even took it upon herself to hang up on one while I was still talking. I was both shocked and annoyed by this action, and told her so in no uncertain terms. I explained that I have my own reasons for doing things which she may or may not understand or agree with, but I reserve the right to choose my own actions.

A few weeks after this incident, I spent several nights in her home. She has a habit of making a final check after I'm in bed, and one night I had gone to sleep while watching TV. She turned it off. The next night she came into the room and turned the TV off while I was watching. I found this very disturbing and told her to check with me first. I also said that it made me wonder if I could trust her to carry out my wishes rather than her own if I were incapacitated.

Her feelings were deeply hurt by this comment. The following day she developed intense low back pain and had to go to the doctor. I felt compassion for her but did not feel responsible for her reactions. I told her that Louise Haye said that low back pain was an expression of not feeling supported. I asked if she thought the lack of support was related to our conversation. She agreed and pointed out to me that she had been very responsible about handling my affairs and had tried to be very sensitive to my wishes. I agreed and expressed appreciation for her efforts. I suggested that I was not talking about finances but about my person. I said that I didn't accuse her of anything, and that my comment was not intended to hurt her, but it was more about me and less about her. However, I wanted to be sure that she understood my feelings, and how she responded was entirely up to her. I added that I didn't know any better way to express myself and I would like to feel safe in expressing my honest feelings.

Nita, who decided that she would follow my outline for a successful life, has by all standards become successful. She said she was especially appreciative of my teachings about accepting things she could not change, changing the things she could, and the wisdom to know the difference, that this philosophy had freed her to really be able to let go. I am very proud of the woman Nita has become. Her achievements are validation of the effectiveness of my values. She has become a fine human being in her own right. She said she listened to me while she was growing up, and she thanked me for all that I had done for her and all of her sisters, and not just her biological sisters. Recently she was describing her delight with her work with the young people in her church. She said the reason she is able to give so freely of herself and her money is that I gave so freely to her. She said that it took her a long time to get it, but she wanted me to know before I left this world that at least one person heard me.

My nephew Keith, aka Deely, was thirteen when his father died and he felt he was thrown to the wolves. He described extreme abuse from some of his older siblings, whose mentoring revolved around teaching him to become a criminal in order to survive. He has lived with me off and on over the years, with our relationship improving each time as he matured. He has become increasingly thoughtful and reflective about life, and we enjoy hours of good conversation. He is another carrier of the family genes of a love for humor and raucous laughter. He even looks like Chris Rock. When Billy's time on Spencer Ave. had expired, Nita arranged for Deely to move in to facilitate a smooth exit. Deely is living with me temporarily as he is between wives, and I am also in transition. It is a mutually rewarding, respectful, and appreciative arrangement. The fact that our agreement was typewritten and signed by both of us assures that it will remain so; it is a testimony to the lesson I've learned about vague verbal agree-ments.

My daughter LaWanda took longer to integrate and practice what I preached. However, once she "got it," she had it.

Not only is it working in her own life now, but it is starting to be demonstrated in the lives of her children. I am exceedingly proud of La Wanda's courage, strength, and persistence in overcoming the many daunting challenges along her path. She has been triumphant in moving from darkness into light, maintaining her vibrant sense of humor. She faces life on life's terms and says she most appreciates my example and my willingness to give the benefit of the doubt. She also said that she admires the fact that I didn't feel I had to experience everything firsthand, and that I could learn from others' mistakes. She said I had been a good example for the family, and even though some of them didn't want to make the sacrifices I made, they still knew success was possible with hard work.

I have great hope for the future of my family. Most of us are moving toward personal development, self-reliance, and an end to codependency. LaWanda's son Jesus had two drug-addicted parents. His father left when he was quite young, and it took his mother years to get into recovery. Nevertheless, Jesus is a very athletic, bright, ambitious entrepreneur. He is persistent and self-willed, and most importantly, hard-working. He wanted to be a mascot for the Warriors basketball team. Initially he was rejected, but he persisted, willing to sweep floors and do whatever it took to achieve his objective. He was finally trained and hired, and has traveled all over the US and several times to China. He was on the front page of two newspapers in Mexico, appearing as if he was flying without wings. He is so talented that he was twice on "Ripley's Believe It or Not."

He is able to walk the streets of San Francisco and Oakland peacefully, without getting in trouble with the police or the gang bangers. He has taken on the awesome responsibility of being a positive male role model for the family. He developed a dance team to give boys a venue for creative expression and resolution of conflicts. He also has a dunking team and he teaches street kids his "Acro-dunking" skills. At the tender age of nineteen he has become a minister, and people say he's wise beyond his years. He seems destined for greatness.

I had the great honor of attending a celebration dinner for Jesus' sister Dy' Easha who triumphed over nearly insurmountable odds to graduate from UC Berkeley. Her childhood was also tumultuous, living between her mother, father, relatives, and surrogates. She lived with her father during her formative years, and he taught her the love for and importance of education. He instilled in her a thirst for learning. She always did well in school, and helped her siblings with their homework, even though she was the youngest. She did a summer internship at Stanford and received a four-year scholarship to Berkeley.

She left home at seventeen and moved in with her boyfriend. He became "violent and abusive," separating her from her family and isolating her, but he always encouraged her to continue her education. She worked full time at a variety of jobs. She became pregnant and thought about dropping out of school, but decided to continue when she contemplated the consequences. She knew she couldn't cook, and wasn't much of a housekeeper. She thought she could be cute but knew this wasn't enough by itself nor would it last. Being "an academic" was what she did best.

She was also motivated by all the people who told her she couldn't make it. She decided to go through with the pregnancy and had to withstand the rude stares and raised eyebrows from others who would have made a different decision. Resolutely she hauled her extra thirty pounds up and down the hills of UC's campus and remained focused on her goal. She grew weary under the heavy responsibilities of fulltime employment and burning midnight oil required to stay on top of demanding class work at a top university. She credited God with the strength she found to leave the unhealthy relationship and remain steadfast with her education. Eventually she gave birth to a son, reunited with her family, and received some much-needed support.

At her graduation celebration, she said one of her primary motivations in graduating was her desire to show her siblings that it could be done. I was touched by the closeness between them, and the pride they all took in her achievement. One commented that it wasn't just her, they had all graduated! I was amazed at the similarity between me and her. One of the things that inspired me most was the desire to show my siblings that life could be different for them. I told her that all of our ancestors and all of the generations to come would be proud of her and encouraged by her magnificent achievement. She used her steel determination to overcome great odds, any one of which might have crushed someone else. She is a true instrument of God's hands. I am more proud of Dy' Easha than words can say, and it is a joy for me to again pass on the baton of hard work in attaining excellence in higher education. Thank God that there has been at least one member of each generation who has been willing to be an example for the rest. The importance of living examples of what's possible to encourage future generations cannot be overestimated.

When LaWanda became a young mother and dropped out of school, she limited her ability to provide for herself and her family financially. Several children and years later, she wanted to move into a better neighborhood (long overdue) and needed a 3600$ deposit to move in. Although her desire to move was very strong, her resources to do so were weak. She called to ask if I could help her. I was not happy to hear the request, because I knew on some level it was a temptation to revisit my codependency, identify with it, and be lulled to sleep; *or* I could resist it, wake up, and grow large. Lord knows I have helped and over-helped family members financially in the past, and it did not help them become more responsible. I'm sure her expectation was that I would continue. I told her that I presently had no income, and I have to be very conscious about how I spend money. I said I would think about it, and get back to her. She was planning to come over on Sunday and go to church with me.

Attempting to control my reflex actions, I contemplated her request. I considered the tremendous progress that she had made in recent years, including the loss of eighty pounds. In the past, I would have been tempted by the desire to reward her for a job well done. Also, this is the child who told me she thought Hunters Point was "pretty", and so I am overjoyed by her desire to provide nicer surroundings for herself. Initially I thought perhaps I could loan her the money, but I was faced with the realization that to date she has never repaid a loan to me. I also remembered the promise I made to myself never to loan any money I wasn't willing to give.

When I saw LaWanda I said, "The Spirit is not telling me to give you money. The reason I was so adamant about you getting a good education is that I knew you (and all young people) need to prepare for financial independence in your youth because everyone needs adequate resources to live comfortably in the world."

It has always been my desire for my children to grow up to be independent, responsible, and loving people. I told her that my use of money to achieve this objective in the past had not been very effective. Now having little discretionary income is forcing me to make more conscious decisions about money. I said I was a bit sad to realize I had to be without discretionary money in order to develop a more conscious relationship with it. I told her that giving people money is a way of fostering codependency which I am choosing not to continue. I told her that health she is a very strong, talented, creative, and resourceful woman and I have every confidence that she will be able, with the Spirit within herself, to provide for herself whatever she needs. Initially LaWanda was disappointed and maybe a little angry, but in her heart she knew I was doing the right thing. She eventually was able to move to improved housing using her own resources. It was a victory for both of us.

Carla seemed to mature and come into her own after the death of her mother Ruby. On a recent trip to St. Louis, I was very pleased to see that Carla had a stylish haircut, was well-dressed, and appeared to feel very positive about herself. This is indeed an answered prayer. She has now been drug-free and working for several years and has her own apartment. Her children have grown into healthy well-functioning young ladies, and both are following the path of higher education. One has excelled in track as well as playing the violin. The other has become a skilled ice skater and had one of her poems in a book when she was only ten years old.

Carla now attends family gatherings and spends quality time with her aunt Liz. She even remembers to send her cards on special occasions.

Carla has started reaching out to other children in the family by exposing them to athletic and cultural activities, and she has invited one of her nieces to come live with her. Carla told me that it was from my example that she learned to reach out to help others. Although all of my children in one way or another have identified with my caretaking of others, I hope that they will not carry the burden of codependency, and will learn to take care of themselves first.

Angie married and moved to Southern California. Understandably, she needed to put physical distance between herself and her family of origin. In her childhood she had been cast in the role of scapegoat, and the patterns lingered throughout her development. She has kept very good jobs, and owns her own home. She worked very hard to overcome her early emotional deprivation and abuse to become a good mother to her two children. She is warm and caring, with her own unique brand of humor. She has also reached out to her husband's daughter by his first marriage, treating her as her own daughter. Her children are also doing well, and her grandson is the apple of her eye.

Yolanda has taken over the role of Family Nurturer through her good cooking. The family often gathers in her home for

Thanksgiving and other holidays, and everyone raves about her desserts, especially her banana pudding and peach cobbler. She works as an in-home care provider and takes pride in her job and the progress of her patients. She is married and has two children, and four grandchildren. Like all of my children, she knows the Spirit, but unlike most of them, she is not bound by the Baptist tradition. She is more similar to me in her spiritual explorations and was proud to tell me that she is reading The Secret and pursuing Eckert Tolle's workshop.

ADDICTIONS

The light of awareness shines indiscriminately. More and more of my shadow was becoming illuminated, pointing me in the direction of my addictions. In spite of the fact that my parents were both teetotalers later in life, it seems that several of my siblings and many of their offspring's are addicted to some substance ranging from alcohol, cigarettes, marijuana, and cocaine, to everything in between. Others have hidden their addictions behind prescription drugs. One or two even became addicted to heroin. My mother never drank or smoked, but she dipped snuff and chewed tobacco for a number of years while I was growing up. My father did not smoke but had a history of drinking. In his youth he drank liquor sometimes until he was out of control and became physically abusive to my mother. He was later struck by lightning which frightened him into salvation and onto the wagon. He became a preacher.

Quite early I experienced my attraction to addictions. As a child I remember watching my mother's habit of trimming her corns and longing for the time I would get to do that. In retrospect I realized this yearning was very deep and significant, as I associated it with a ritual of being with the self. There was so much chaos in the household that I longed for some structured or routine experiences as a means of escape. Habits seemed to fit the bill. I started smoking cigarettes at age fourteen when my sister (who was already smoking) bet me that if I tried smoking every day for a week I would have a habit. Although I strongly disagreed, I accepted the challenge. In one week I lost the bet--I got a habit that took me forty years to get free of.

As predisposed to addictions as I was, I knew I had to be selective about my substances. Being a self appointed care taker, I had to remain available to life, work, and all my dependents. Breaking the law was not an option. I could not afford the luxury of becoming addicted to drugs. This was also not my inclination, since I had observed some skid row addicts in my neighborhood who seemed enslaved by their drugs. Before I started using alcohol, I hid behind a legal and socially acceptable smoke screen provided by my cigarettes, and also developed narcolepsy as a way to "get away from it all." This was a legitimate medical problem, as well as a convenient way of "checking out." (I believe my mother and one of my sisters also had narcolepsy but it was undiagnosed.) Later I used alcohol to anesthetize my fears and get the courage to face my challenges. At a family celebration I remember one of my nieces commenting on how happy I seemed. It was the first time I realized that I was using alcohol to enable me to let go of my inhibitions. I felt there was an unspoken family taboo to expressing love and happiness, which probably would have been seen as a weakness.

As a teenager I was too fearful to openly rebel, and I had the good sense not to rebel with things I observed to have dangerous consequences. I was in awe and disbelief at the rebellious activities of some of my sisters and peers. Cigarettes seemed harmless enough at the time and shielded me from the world. They gave me a feeling of being cool, independent and belonging to the in-crowd.

Addictions run rampant in my family, and I was naïve enough to think I would magically rise above addictions and avoid going through them. On a recent visit to St. Louis, due to the sudden death of my diabetic nephew, I was bombarded by the addictive patterns of my relatives. On the way to the funeral, a nephew and his girlfriend ("old lady"), both of whom are alcoholics, were riding in the limo with me and other family members. My nephew pulled out a cigarette and being from

California, I told him that he could not smoke in the limo. Overhearing his girlfriend say that you could do anything you wanted in the limo, the driver confirmed that smoking was not permitted. Although both of them brought alcohol in fast food soda cups, my nephew pulled out his bottle of liquor and attempted to refill his supply. I announced that there was a time and place for all things, and some things are not appropriate for all occasions. With this proclamation, he put away his bottle. Observing the total absorption of their addiction turned out to be an unwelcome gift. For the first time I was actually able to see an addiction separate from the personality that possessed it. It is a living entity in its own right. It is a disease.

A niece who is diabetic and asthmatic and severely overweight continues to use alcohol and weed regularly. She thinks, like most addicts, that nobody knows. She is quietly killing herself, and there is an unspoken family agreement to act as if she's not. A nephew who has perhaps twenty children (none of whom he supports) is addicted to both alcohol and cocaine.

For years, smoking cigarettes was my screen from the world. I used them to alter my feelings about any and everything. Throughout my life, they protected me from seeing things I didn't want to see, and they repressed feelings I didn't want to feel. It even clouded my mind when I didn't want to think. With a lot of grace and overflowing gratitude I managed to be smoke free for many years in my thirties. However, throughout this time I picked cigarettes up again whenever I went through a very significant and stressful transition period. No matter what was going on, telling myself that I could have a cigarette was comforting and reassuring. I was in truth totally out of control around smoking.

For a long time I was caught between holding on and at the same time wanting to let go. The more I wanted to let go, the stronger my urge was to smoke. I developed a chronic cough and wheeze, strong warning signs of the deterioration of my health. As I listened to myself cough, I was aware of my struggle between life and death, and death seemed to be winning. I knew I would have to make a conscious decision to get busy living if I didn't want to die. I thought of all the reasons I wanted to live, and all the reasons I didn't want to die. And yet I smoked. I smoked when I was happy and I smoked when I was sad and for every feeling in between. I lived behind a cloud of smoke. I was the Queen of Distractions and Addictive Behaviors.

I have always hated the smell of stale smoke which I tried to camouflage with Listerine, gum, toothpaste, incense, etc. I was repulsed by the smell on other people's breath and clothes, and was sure that my "shit didn't stink." My sense of smell had long been effectively anesthetized by the cigarettes, so I could minimize the fact that its sour aroma penetrated my clothes, hair, skin, breath, car, bedroom and entire aura. I was also personally insulted by the astronomical cost of a pack of cigarettes. Every time I paid five dollars for a pack of cigarettes I had a huge battle with my own principles. Being a thrifty person, I hated to see that much money go up in smoke. I looked with soft focus eyes at the cigarette burns in my clothing, bedding, carpets, etc., telling myself I could always replace them.

  Meanwhile I nurtured my addiction. In my desperate efforts to stop smoking, I switched from buying cartons at Costco (they were cheaper) to buying single packs. I was horrified every time I forgot to stock up and found myself going out into the night to 7-11, paying almost twice the price, and subjecting myself to the dangers that lurk in the night.

  My friend Julie, a former smoker and twelve-stepper, was relentless in her determination to penetrate my denial. Once she asked me what it would take for me to stop smoking. She asked if, like some people, I would continue to smoke while walking around with an oxygen tank or put a cigarette into my tracheotomy. I was horrified by these images. On another occasion after we had conducted a very successful workshop together, during which I used my spiritual name Arundhati, she said that I looked pretty ridiculous and certainly incongruent to facilitate people's opening to their connection with the Spirit while I was sneaking outside to hide and smoke. The hypocrisy of this behavior cut deep and was very sobering. As I reflected on this image, I was rather surprised to find that I could not hold the two images of myself simultaneously. I had to pick one or the other! I needed help.

Floundering helplessly behind my smokescreen, I talked incessantly about quitting smoking, yet I didn't. I had enough sense to realize that on some level I wanted to smoke more than I wanted to stop. I started praying for the willingness to stop.

Coincidentally, Julie invited me to accompany her on a visit to one of her former eighth grade students who had been struggling with substance abuse and addiction since childhood. It was Cathy's forty-third birthday and Julie wanted someone to go with her to take Cathy a cake and a gift. She was living in a fleabag hotel in downtown San Francisco. We drove around the sleazy streets of the Tenderloin looking for the hotel and a parking space.

Inside we were greeted by two East Indian clerks who had adapted well to this skid row environment. One of the men asked Julie if she were Cathy's social worker, and she told him she was her teacher. He seemed impressed by this, and directed us up the elevator, around two corners, through the fire doors to Room 417. He said we would probably hear her before we saw her, because she is "very loud." He quickly added,"....but I like that." We knocked at the door and heard the sounds of rustling, suggesting the removal of things not suitable for guests.

After several moments the door was opened and we were

greeted with a thunderous welcome. Cathy was living in a tiny, dingy room with a thirty-five-year-old rather handsome man who appeared to be somewhat new to the drug scene. He described himself as Cathy's platonic protector, self appointed to watch her back. In reality he probably needed a place to stay and access to her monthly check, however meager.

Julie and I had not seen Cathy in several years, and we were shocked by her condition. She was now a full blown intravenous drug addict and alcoholic, yellowed with cirrhosis of the liver, obvious mental deterioration, and probable HIV infection. She was very thin, her eyes were cloudy, her skin had an ashy overtone, and she appeared to be fading away. Cathy was overjoyed to see us--she talked in a baby-like whiney voice, jumping from one unfinished thought to another, squeezing Julie's hands very tightly. She vacillated between entertaining us with the lingo of the streets, displaying her inexpensive rings and bracelets, bragging "Look, I've got the bling-bling!" She continuously wept with tears of joy and sorrow.

We lit the candles, sang Happy Birthday, and her boyfriend reminded her to make a wish. After she blew out the candles, she surprised and shocked us by turning and asking me an amazing question: would I speak to her about wisdom, strength, humility, and survival. Julie and I were stunned. Cathy had seemed so far gone. I told her I would be happy to answer her question. I said that wisdom was recognizing and following the spirit within, finding one's own truth. Strength naturally flows from this choice. Humility comes from the understanding that you are not the doer, and survival is then transformed into thriving. Cathy seemed comforted by my response.

We stayed about an hour, sharing life stories, expressing love for each other, and talking about addiction. Julie urged Cathy to get back into a recovery program and make sure that she has follow up support. Cathy said, "I knew you'd go there." Julie and I were deeply touched by the whole experience of the visit. In the car Julie burst into tears and asked if we could pray for Cathy, which we did. We talked about her depth, her love for poetry, and search for life's meaning. Initially I was unable to identify my feelings but knew I had been profoundly affected. I later recognized them as depression and despair. Witnessing the addictions in my family did not have the same visceral impact on me. Being with Cathy I felt a crack in the thick shell of my denial, and I realized I was, like Cathy, killing myself, only just a little slower. Sadly, Cathy shortly passed away at the young age of 43. There was no memorial except the one Julie and I shared.

On the way home from Cathy's apartment, Julie gave me an article from Kaiser she had saved for me about quitting smoking. We talked about what I might do and I remembered that Smokers Anonymous had helped me quit in the past. I made a few unsuccessful attempts to locate a meeting, but I couldn't find one, but I did stop buying packs of cigarettes, and started to bum single cigarettes. Driving around in my car and stalking people on the street for signs of the possibility of bumming a cigarette made me feel like a sexual predator.

I went to St. Louis for my fiftieth high school reunion. Several old friends were sitting outside the hotel smoking, and the familiar feelings of cravings and wanting to belong lured me into asking for a cigarette, even though I would have preferred to present myself to them as a nonsmoker. As I observed myself smoke, I realized that I was not really enjoying it. Subsequently, I smoked two more cigarettes when I got back to my niece's house where I was staying, (one of them guiltily stolen from her husband's pack.) Again I was aware of not really enjoying it. The cigarettes were losing their hold on me. However it took several more months for this reality to make its way into my consciousness through layers and layers of very deep rooted fears. During the process of quitting, I struggled to identify my fears and became aware of my resistance. I became aware of some deeply repressed anger and refusal to allow right action to flow through me. I realized that I was holding on to outdated feelings I thought I had let go. I came to see an aspect of my personality that felt unworthy and sought abuse.

Although on some level I knew I was being self destructive,

like all addicts I was powerless over my addictions. My ego had myriad rationalizations and excuses for my behavior. The cough resulting from my chronic pollution of my lungs with nicotine and other poisons had become an almost constant reminder of my self punishment.

At a Christmas party I ran into a former acquaintance from Smokers Anonymous who told me where a Marin group was meeting. She described this particular group as very powerful. As I left the party it was raining. My bracelet fell off and rolled down the hill. As I ran after it I slipped and fell, breaking my finger. This resulted in surgery and a long period of incapacity and dependency. Cigarettes seemed to retighten their grip on me and my cravings intensified. I spent an inordinate amount of time looking for my cigarettes and lighter that I frequently hid from myself.

During this crisis, I also had time and opportunity for self reflection. I remembered the power of group commitment which had helped me to stop smoking ten years ago. Despite my broken hand and no clear directions, I finally arrived half an hour late to an SA meeting, and everyone gave me a silent but warm welcome.

Listening to my own story being described by others in such detail with great clarity and objectivity by fellow addicts pulverized my ego. My insanity was laid bare. All the crazy things I told myself about why it was okay to continue smoking, --- I would beat the odds, and not be one of the sixty million people who die prematurely every year from cigarette related diseases. I thought that I could somehow avoid the many chronic illnesses which usually result from filling one's lungs with tars and nicotine (note that this denial was in the face of a chronic cough which was so severe that it affected my vocal cords.)

The witness is always present. I felt weak and ashamed every time I asked for deliverance while reaching for a cigarette, realizing that I was hardly willing to go to any length to stop smoking. I had refused to take a single step in that direction. I often dealt with my sense of helplessness by telling myself that I could quit if I wanted to. This was only partially true because my addiction had convinced me that I really didn't want to. Once I accepted I was crazy, I gradually became willing to receive help. For me, this was listening to the voice of reason, which had been whispering in my ear the entire time, and now I heard it in the voices of the group.

After my fourth meeting I was overwhelmed by the strong presence of truth in the group sharing. At the meeting I had eaten some peanuts rather rapidly on an empty stomach. Due to several bowel obstructions in the past, I have learned that I need to chew most foods well and to avoid things that are difficult to digest. When I went home, several hours after the meeting, I recognized a familiar pain which my mind tried to confuse with an upset stomach. The peanuts set the stage for an obstruction. The truth of the sharing had illuminated my conflict between holding on and letting go. I had truly arrived at the crossroads. The gate closed and I knew that there was no turning back.

The pain was excruciating-- holding on was killing me. Because the regular elimination channels were blocked, I began vomiting violently. After several hours of suffering, I apparently went to sleep during which time my subconscious decided to let go of the cigarettes. When I woke up I was no longer in pain although my stomach, which was the battleground for the duel, was tender. I knew smoking was no longer an option for me. I had to be willing to go to any length to give it up, and once again, my body was my master teacher.

I finally accepted that I had willingly enslaved my free spirit to my nicotine addiction. My voluntary enslavement had the same chains, abuse and humiliation as the slavery of my ancestors. I now called forth the courage and strength of my forefathers to escape from slavery to freedom. I became willing to live in the mystery of life instead of the predictability of ritualized addictive behavior. I opened to the release of all my addictions.

I wanted to love rather than punish my body. I was humbled by the wisdom that inspired the Twelve Steps Programs. Not only did the creators provide the map of the twelve steps, they identified the source of power in the collective strength of the group--("Where two or more agree in my name, I Am there also.") They even anticipated possible distractions and advised against outside influences by placing principles before personalities. It is a brilliant strategy which works! If you work it. I began "trying" to work it. Cigarettes were now hanging on by a thread.

Several weeks after Julie and I visited Cathy, I heard that a guru, Leslie, was offering a three-day intensive in Marin. I had met her years before and continued to see her from time to time when she came to California. Although I was unable to attend the first two days, and had a dental appointment on the third, I was inspired to register even if I could only attend a few hours. The topic of the intensive was Global Renaissance. I resonated to the title, for both global and personal reasons. The first thing I noticed after taking a seat was a statement written on butcher paper on the wall that said that the ego is afraid of its own destiny. I knew I was in the right place at the right time, successfully engaged in the right activity.

Leslie's guides had instructed her to ask three questions of the audience: What do we see as an ideal world? What do we think our destiny is? And how are we dealing with our fears? I said that my vision is a world living in peace, my destiny is to live in love and truth, (according to Gandhi "There is no God higher than truth,") and my fear of allowing right action to flow through me is symbolized by my addiction to cigarettes.

During the question and answer period, I briefly shared that the stronger my desire to become one with the Spirit, the more intense my fear became, symbolized by an increased urge to smoke, although I was resisting it. I asked for guidance and was told to communicate with the part of me that smokes. She suggested that I honor it and sit quietly with it, then talk to it lovingly, and ask it to align with me to experience the light. She also said that I could give it permission to go home if it so desired because it was probably tired after working for me for more than fifty years! She said its original intention was to be helpful. It probably came into my life to protect me in some way. I resonated with the truth of this statement. She said she has never known this technique not to work.

At the break a woman came into the bathroom and offered me some Nicorette gum to try. She said she was hesitant to make the offer out of concern that I would become addicted to the gum. She had stopped smoking three years ago but continued to chew the gum. It crossed my mind that the gum might be effective if it was potentially addictive, and I felt a glimmer of hope.

On my way to the dentist I couldn't find my one cigarette I had brought with me so I tried the gum instead. To my surprise it was effective in satisfying the craving. When I returned to the workshop, during the second break, another woman approached me and suggested I try Lobelia Tincture, an herbal remedy. She said it had been created by Native Americans to cure tobacco addiction, not part of the peace pipe rituals. Several other people shared their experiences offering techniques and encouragement. All of this seemed very synchronistic to me. When the workshop ended, a woman turned to me and said she hoped that I would fall in love with the Nicotine gum.

On the way home I went to Walgreens as directed and got some Nicorette gum, which happened to be on sale with a fifteen dollar savings. At Whole Foods where I went for the Lobelia Tincture, there was a parking space waiting for me right in front of the store, a very rare event!

In the ensuing days, I realized at a deeper level that the part of me that smoked was initially an ally, a way that I could rebel without the serious consequences of acting out sexually or using drugs and alcohol. It also linked me to my favorite sister who introduced me to it. I gradually became aware that my fear of cigarettes was starting to fade.

The first time I quit in the 80's, I did it cold turkey and became very irritable when I was hit with a strong craving. Dr. Phil says that we don't break habits, we simply substitute new behaviors. This time my craving for nicotine was satisfied by the gum and it was easier to let the thought of smoking a cigarette pass. During the transition stage I encouraged myself to prefer the gum to cigarettes. As the lady suggested, I began to love the gum. Out of my gratitude for not being obsessed by the craving I opened my heart to the gum. I smelled better, spent less money, and developed higher self esteem and personal integrity, not to mention my chronic cough had almost disappeared. I was coming to see my desire to smoke as an outdated program which I was no longer willing to run.

In my conversations with the part of me that smoked, I explained that I don't want to be protected from my feelings any longer. My deeper choice is to walk in truth and grace with the spirit. Smoking was no longer my best friend but had become my worst enemy. Instead of serving me, it was in fact killing me. To my surprise the part of me that smoked admitted that it was tired-- smoking was hard work! I had to remember to buy cigarettes, look for lighters or matches, try to avoid burning things down, and do things awkwardly with a cigarette in my hand.

Three days after the Leslie workshop I was on the freeway on my way home from the dentist, and I missed my exit for buying cigarettes. I took this as a sign that it was time. *I stopped smoking.* I now recognized that all addiction is both a request for God or a desire to hide. God had appeared. I felt I had been delivered.

In a recent conversation with my college roommate, she expressed concern about her sister's continuing addiction to cigarettes in spite of her doctor's advice to stop. We laughed about my addiction in college to cigarettes and her participation in lying to other smokers in the dorm about whether I had any. Smoking was a big deal in those days. I told her that I smoked for every conceivable reason. She expressed surprise that cigarettes could do all that. I told her that cigarettes for me was like yoga--it can cure anything that ails you. I told her it was not simply a question of not smoking, one had to change one's relationship with cigarettes and realize they are not your best friend. In fact Healthwise they are your worst enemy, as well as the enemy of your closest friends who are exposed to your secondhand smoke. The only way I was able to change my relationship to cigarettes was to substitute God (the breath) for the cigarettes.

After giving up my drug of choice (cigarettes), I noticed that I started drinking more beer. With this observation I realized that I had not yet developed an effective strategy for dealing with my feelings that I repressed with cigarettes. When I perceived it was not safe to express my feelings or ideas because other people were not ready or willing to accept them, instead of blowing my feelings up in smoke, I was drowning them in beer. This also was self destructive. I knew the road to recovery, and now it was a matter of surrender and timing. Inspired by Barack Obama's courageous, calculated example of self control and expression, I asked for the willingness to be committed to my health and well being. The tools for overcoming addictions are mine. When I think about it, I have already started to substitute conscious breathing, walks on the beach, listening to music, and using Mandaza's technique for reconnecting with the strength of my ancestors. I am also practicing the art of gentle self discipline and expressing my truth in love. And I am calmly waiting on deliverance from all my codependences, addictions, and triangles.

CHAPTER SIX
LANDMARKS CONFRONTATION OF SHADOWS

After years of listening to stories of codependency and addiction in my therapy practice, and dancing to the same tune with a colorful array of roommates and foster children, I started to feel as if I were awakening from a deep sleep. I owe many thanks to my clients, roommates, and foster children. Their objectivity and unconditional love and acceptance have provided me with clear mirrors and the safety I needed to practice avoiding the landmines my family had strewn along my path. Such relationships as these can be less confusing and not as threatening as entangled complicated family dynamics. In many of my family relationships, I was often blinded by my enmeshment, compassion, sense of responsibility, and desire to be helpful.

Over the years I slowly put 2 and 2 together and realized that compassion is both my strength and my weakness. Too much of a good thing is bad for all concerned. Gradually, in relationships where I felt safe, I learned to sustain a more objective perspective and become more aware of some of my unconscious motives and repetitive behaviors. I often recall the words of a crazy friend who told me that "Everyone who throws you into a pile of shit is not your enemy, and everyone who pulls you out is not your friend."

Psychotherapy was not only a source of income, it was a venue for personal healing and growth for me as well. I brought to the counseling relationships my training in social work and psycho-therapy, a well-developed spiritual practice, and knowledge and experience of a variety of cultures and lifestyles. Maturity gave me the courage to add additional "tools" to my bag of tricks.

About a year after meeting Baba Muktananda and receiving shaktipat (transmission of spiritual energy), I was attending the Baptist Church with my oldest child, Faye. It was a revival with a guest evangelist. He called the two of us into the pulpit and told me that he had been directed to pass the gift of healing to me. He held my hands and touched my head. When he was finished he told me that I should go to hospitals and heal the sick wherever I found them. I was surprised by this experience and did not connect it with an earlier prediction by a psychic. I went home after church and didn't think much about the experience. However the following morning both my hands became extremely cold which lasted for about ten minutes. I acknowledged this as an unusual occurrence but did not understand its meaning. However, I started experimenting with "laying on of hands" when my family and friends had headaches or other ailments. My confidence grew as my effectiveness increased. Gradually I was able to integrate healing touch in my therapy practice.

As a student of the universe, nothing human was foreign to

me. Whenever I accepted a new client, I knew that I would also be different at the end of our relationship of mutual influence. I have always felt that the clients referred to me were specially selected by the universe because their issues were ones that I was either dealing with or had dealt with in my own life.

For years I was not aware of my unconscious and unhealthy behaviors. I crawled around in darkness, unable to see my contribution to the unsatisfactory results in many of my relationships. I was bewildered by the universe's response to my good intentions. I now recognize my participation in codependent relationships and know that all personal problems are the result of not loving ourselves enough. Instead of encouraging my family to love themselves more, my focus was to convince them how much I loved them. At the end of the day they were more aware of my strength than their own, didn't love themselves any more, and loved me less. Codependency breeds resentments on both sides. Without self love one cannot take in the love from another.

Over time, I started recognizing old patterns of codependency, and gave myself permission to choose new behaviors. Of course there continued to be times when I was seduced by old patterns; but in the light of day I stopped losing myself in the role, and was able to see that I was not the role. I observed my dysfunctional behaviors more objectively and affirmed that I had the ability to change. As I healed, I was able to recognize the patterns more quickly in my clients.

My approach to therapy is to love every client unconditionally. In the light of love and acceptance, with emphasis on personal responsibility, my clients gradually learn to love and accept them-selves and are able to solve their own problems. My first client was a man, but my practice soon developed more around women and their special issues. For years my practice was almost entirely women, then gradually it changed to predominately men. In time as I worked out aspects of my own masculine and feminine characteristics, my practice became almost equally balanced. I came to recognize the common well-springs of human emotions that we all share irrespective of gender. I also realized that men and women express the same emotions differently. For example, women tend to express their low self esteem by abdicating their personal power, whereas men express theirs by unfairly taking control of the personal power of others.

Unfortunately, many women offer their bodies hoping the exchange will bring them love. On the other hand, many men offer loving attention, hoping the exchange will bring them sex. Love is not to be confused with sex. One of my clients was an intelligent, drop-dead-gorgeous woman, who told me that she felt she had to sleep with any man who bought her dinner. Another vivid image of low self esteem was a woman's description of herself as "the hole of an inner tube." Her husband's sexual preference was for "quickies." Once she was crying during sex and her husband failed to notice. She allowed him to finish, she continued to cry, and she remained in the relationship for several more years.

The immature belief of many women in the "need to please at the expense of self" inspired me to specialize in relationship therapy with the primary focus on relationship with one's Self. At the time I didn't recognize that this "need to please"--looking for love outside oneself-- was a classic codependent pattern, one I also shared for many years. It is only from a correct relationship with the Self that all other healthy relationships develop. When one loves oneself, one becomes aware of the connectedness of all things and is able to heal one's relationship with any and everything. We are the center of our own universe and we receive exactly what we ask for, even though we might not be aware of it. When we feel unworthy of love we invite abuse. In every religion and spiritual philosophy, a connection is made between asking and receiving. The universe does not reason; its only response to our requests is yes.

I regularly remind my clients that we have to take responsibility for our own behavior and happiness. When we change our thinking, we change our self and our world. Faith without works is dead. We are all attending Earth's School to learn who we are.

We are Love, and love flows from the inside out. The secret is that you must be able to feel love within in order to experience it outside. I encourage my clients to be patient and gentle with themselves as they learn to love. Mistakes are part of learning, and forgiveness of self and others is the key to progress as well as happiness. The following story demonstrates a typical masculine struggle in the universal search for love.

A thirty-five-year-old, extremely bright, very talented carpenter came to me because his wife had requested a divorce and he wanted to save the marriage. He had been focused on his work, neglectful and insensitive to what his wife wanted and her feelings about their marriage. She had been his care provider and the container for the family emotions. He brought home the bacon, worked hard, and was a good provider. He truly didn't understand why she wanted to leave him. His grief and disbelief were so strong that he was jarred from his usual independent, well-defended, and self reliant security which blocked him from giving and receiving love. He was now being forced to seek help outside of himself. I was his first experience with therapy.

His facade was one of "having it all together" (excluding emotions), a real "take charge" kind of guy. He lived comfortably in his head, unaware of any other way to be in the world. In the emotional tornado created by his wife's wake up call, he lost control. He stopped working and sought out intensive therapy.

We met daily for several months. After a period of time we decided to move from a money exchange to the exchange of services. He worked long hours at my cabin where we also did therapy. He had an excellent sense of design and built a beautiful elevated deck for the hot tub which overlooked the forest. He also built some classic Japanese benches for the tea garden, and an adult sized wooden cradle which he hung on two pillars in the nursery. His enthusiasm and competence in his work inspired me to a higher consciousness in mine.

As the creator of the cradle, he was the first person to use it. It was the vehicle for moving him from his head to his heart. Our mutual high regard created a synergetic connection which enabled each of us to be more than either of us were as individuals. In our work together he experienced several epiphanies and came to know and love himself in a new way. Following one of his experiences of the Self and his awakening of his emotions, he claimed his personal power. He found a huge stone at the beach which resembled a gigantic penis. This symbolized his understanding and acceptance of his masculinity in a new and more powerful way. He brought the stone to the cabin, where we proudly displayed it in the front garden. Eventually his wife did leave him, and after several years he remarried. His new wife inspired him with her open heart as well as her ability to dance with his mind. I was invited to the wedding where I ate my first chocolate wedding cake.

Things are not always what they seem. The next story is an example of a couple where one appears to be the identified patient, or the perpetrator, and the other the victim. Upon closer examination their joint participation in codependency is revealed. A waltz requires two partners:

A forty-five-year-old female client and her husband were on the verge of a divorce and came for marriage counseling. They had been married for thirteen years. She had two children by a previous marriage who were now living outside of the home, and two younger children by the present union. The husband presented as an easy-going, nice guy and she appeared to be the angry aggressor.

After a few sessions, it became clear that she was a screamer and he was a passive aggressive; his weapon was silent withdrawal and refusal to respond to her increasingly hysterical demand that he participate in solving their numerous marital problems and issues. The most obvious and devastating for the wife was his refusal to communicate. Although the emotional divorce had taken place years ago, in his passive aggressive way the husband wanted a physical divorce but was setting his wife up to be the one to ask for it, so again he could be the "nice guy." He also grew up in an emotionally sterile, unsupportive family, who stamped out any budding self expression on his part. During a trial separation, the husband dropped out of counseling and acquired a girlfriend (who might have been in the wings all the time).

Ultimately, with great conflict and grief, the wife finally filed for divorce. Although the marriage had been extremely stressful, and the wife's health compromised with many physical symptoms, she was devastated that the husband was not willing to work at saving their marriage. She was convinced that he would do the right thing financially and provide support for her and the children. Down the line she was devastated by the rude awakening of his request that she move out and they sell the family home so he could get his share of the money. Her family had originally bought the house and he had not made an equal financial investment in it. It seemed that their marriage had been based on mutual dependencies rather than the love and respect they both sought.

The wife had experienced a very traumatic childhood whose parents were present but emotionally unavailable. Her father vacillated between being playful and funny, to being physically punitive and verbally abusive. In discussing her difficulty in letting go of the marriage, she told me that her self definition was dependent on her husband's response to her. I described this condition as secondary identification, meaning she had no identity of her own. Few women have articulated this lack of sense of self so clearly, but many women in abusive relationships seem to share this tendency to rely on their partners to define their worth. As this client gradually built her self esteem, she wondered why she had stayed in the marriage so long.

Lacking a strong sense of self is also a setup for addictions. Addicts are magnets for codependent relationships. An addict's primary relationship is with his alcohol or drugs of choice. The caretaker must be willing to accept being second fiddle. True intimacy is never possible with an addict.

Another client, who was a codependent caretaker married to an alcoholic, told me the following story: She was very frightened of snakes, and lived in a woodsy area. She found one in the basement of her home and became almost hysterical. Her husband had already started drinking for the day, but was not yet drunk, and he managed to kill the snake. He minimized and made fun of his wife's fears. He even seemed to take some delight in it. He told this story in great detail to anyone who called during the next several days. The day after encountering the snake, my client received a picture in the mail of two large snakes. She was bewildered to think about who would play such a mean-spirited trick on her. She threw the picture in the trash.

The following day she discovered her husband had taken the picture out of the trash and laid it on the table. She was hurt and angered by her husband's insensitivity and seeming pleasure in her pain. She tore the picture up in small pieces and returned it to the trash can with no exchange of words with him. This man might be suffering from chronic brain damage due to alcoholism, but in any case he was so separated from his own feelings that he had no thermometer for tuning in to the feelings of others. In addition, he had a lot of repressed anger and jealousy regarding his wife's strength and superior competence. He had no clue about his jealousy and competition with her and would vehemently deny it if it were pointed out to him. In spite of his many hurtful and unsupportive acts, my client had chosen to remain in the marriage. Her excuse was that she didn't want to leave the family home and dividing the finances would be a full scale war.

This story is a clear demonstration of the damage done in codependent relationships to both the caretaker and the one being cared for. The longer one stays in a codependent relationship, the harder it is to get out, as one loses perspective, personal identity, and rationalizes remaining in the situation. Many people settle for much less than they want because of fear, low self esteem, and lack of self confidence. Codependency is also a lack of confidence in others' abilities to be self reliant. When one feels little worth, the empty coffers are filled by focusing on those who seem to be more worthless.

Guilt is fertile ground for breeding codependency. One of my clients has a young-adult son who has developmental and emotional disabilities and possible brain damage. Over the years several professionals offered differing diagnoses, which were confusing to the mother, and she vacillated in her expectations and responses to her child. She also felt guilty because she had divorced the child's father; the stepfather seemed jealous and was verbally abusive to her son. She had never been able to allow him to grow up. She fostered his dependency on her, and was overly permissive and indulgent.

He was caught acting as a "mule" to import heroin, and was in danger of going to prison for years. To help him, my client had maxed out her credit cards and mortgaged her house to come up with thirty thousand dollars to hire an attorney. She made several trips to Florida, and wrote many letters on her son's behalf. While he was out on bail, she worked hard to get him a job, and bought him a car so he would have transportation to get there. In the meantime, she discovered that the son was on heroin. He and his girlfriend seldom left their apartment, and according to my client, they did not bother to clean up or wash dishes. His mother went over and cleaned his house, and paid for his rent, food, therapy, and methadone. The son decided to sell the car to get money to repay his younger brother whose credit he had destroyed. When he went outside, he discovered the car was missing and reported it stolen. Before an insurance claim could be paid, the car appeared in the Oakland Police Garage, having been towed away because of unpaid tickets. The mother was charged six hundred dollars for storage, which she somehow managed to pay.

Clearly the writing was on the wall. I asked her how far she was willing to go to rescue her son, and she said this was the last straw. She was finally able to see how her codependent behavior was contributing to her son's irresponsibility and self destruction. I helped her see that she could not change the past and repeating it was self destructive; her guilt was making a bad situation worse. She learned to forgive herself and gradually started to develop the self discipline she needed to stop rescuing him. With fear and trepidation she became willing to let him experience some of the consequences of his choices.

When we do not feel worthy of love we become very creative in disguising the abuse we invite into our life. We are often blinded to the repetitive patterns that result in the very things we are trying to avoid--loneliness, disappointment, and frustration. Triangular relationships are often decoys for lack of availability. I received a phone call from a client I had seen in therapy for several years who was in great distress following the abrupt termination of a relationship he had imagined would end in marriage. As in his previous relationships, the woman in question was unavailable. She was very recently divorced from a highly controlling partner of several years. As it turned out, she was also involved with another man as well as my client. She was clear, in the beginning of the relationship with my client, that she did not want to be in a committed relationship and needed to be free. My client also pointed out to me that this woman was a "7" in the enneagram. This means that she has a natural resistance to commitment.

Although he told me several times that he felt, after all the work he had done on himself, that he both accepted himself and felt he was worthy of the desires of his heart. However, he also told me that when he lost a very profitable business and was working for several years as a carpenter's helper for ten dollars an hour, he was not motivated to reach out for a relationship. He said that during this time in some ways he felt freer and more at peace with himself. Even so, he did not feel ready to be in relationship until he had built another successful business and bought a house in a prestigious neighborhood, (in other words, had "his front" together.) He was surprised when the woman that he fell in love with was more interested in the form he presented than the substance he wanted her to relate to. It took him a while to understand that he was getting exactly what he was asking for-- he offered the care, and had attracted a taker.

He was extremely distraught over the break up of the relationship, and said that he had never grieved so hard for anything or anybody in his whole life, including the death of his parents. He recognized that the extent of his grieving seemed excessive since he only knew her for one year. He was somewhat comforted by my suggestion that the loss of this relationship was symbolic and the catalyst to revisit the grief over his emotionally unavailable father. I pointed out to him that as a child he was totally dependent, had only one father, to whom expressing his needs could be dangerous. As an adult, he is independent, has many choices of a mate, and is completely capable of protecting himself.

He was gradually able to accept the recent loss as an opportunity to examine the undeveloped beliefs of his inner child. As a child he always felt as if something was wrong with him, that he was not as good as other people. This belief is shared by many small children who do not experience love. These children often believe that if they were really lovable their parents would love them. Frequently these beliefs remain unexamined and subconsciously rule the life of the adult. I explained to him that his father was emotionally impaired before he was born, so there was no way he could have been responsible. He admitted that his mother experienced the same deprivation in her relationship with the father.

Being a businessman, he could readily grasp the metaphor of a business contract in which the client had clearly stated that she did not want the product, in this case a committed relationship. Ignoring the client's wishes, and attempting to sell her something that he wanted her to have, does not work. He was also able to make the connection between an employee who shows up for work late if she bothers to come at all, and is seldom around when needed. While he quickly recognized the prudence of dismissing an unmotivated employee, he was baffled by his inability to terminate an unmotivated romantic partner. With encouragement, he was able to recognize the little boy in him who felt unloved and undeserving because he was unable to change his father into a loving parent who was available to him. The small child insisted on having what he thought he wanted, even though he was looking for it where it did not exist. He was willing to lose or deny himself and do anything necessary to please the other person in the hope of getting his needs met. This practice is self defeating and assures that he will not get what he wants because he is not present for himself or the other person. It is impossible to be seen and validated when we hide and are invisible in relationships.

It takes a very mature person to respect and validate someone who does not respect or validate himself. As we talked about ways to develop a relationship with the small child he had deserted but who ruled his life, his self-disrespect became clear. He was able to see how this part of him had prevented him from asking for and getting his needs met. I suggested he focus on parenting his child with patience and love, and not to overindulge him or allow him to have irrational tantrums. It is ineffective to give control to that which we want to change. It is crucial to identify with the mature parent who sets limits and provides direction. Sitting at home moping about losing his favorite toy isn't helpful. He could reason with the child, distract him, or nurture him, by not abdicating his validation, and personally acknowledging his worth and strengths.

We clarified his objectives and outlined steps to achieving them. He wants a loving, committed relationship. This means that he has to select a woman who also wants the same thing. The fact that she might be pretty, well educated and talented is icing and not the cake. In the past, he has selected "trophy" partners. He admitted that he depended on having a pretty woman to enhance his self esteem. He thought that people observing him would think that he must have something going for himself if he were able to have a beautiful woman on his arm. He has lived his life based on the illusion that he was esteemed by others because of who he was with, when in reality his relationship was only a fantasy because in truth the woman was not really *with him*. Even after his most recent relationship was terminated, he continued to linger between the hope that she might come back and the despair that she might not, with no reasonable expectation that she WILL.

It is important that he practice expressing his wants and needs in all relationships, and listening to those of the other person. He must remember to ask questions for clarification when there is a possibility of confusing what is real with what he wants, to avoid misunder-standings and disappointments. In developing a more loving relationship with himself, it was necessary to become his own best friend, and to refrain from critical self-talk. I suggested he talk to himself lovingly, supporting himself in all situations and not abandoning himself to please others. He told me that he practices this program of self acceptance during his walks in the park, and he always feels much better. He understands that he is re-programming old tapes from unworthy to worthy. This requires commitment, focus, discipline and determination not to continue to tell himself lies.

    Another of my clients was a forty-five-year-old bachelor and also a highly successful businessman. He was married briefly years ago and expressed the desire to be in a mutually loving, caring, committed relationship. He also wanted to have children. He felt time was starting to run out on him. Initially, he ignored all of the red flags, fell in love, and decided within a month that she was the woman he wanted to marry. My client also tends to be very generous with a care-taking complex. He offered a very comfortable package to an unemployed woman with two kids. He rationalized the unbalanced giving in this relationship and minimized the fact that his needs were not being met. For example, when his computer company went bankrupt, she made herself scarce by supposedly taking several low-paying jobs which provided her with excuses to be away from home. She took the opportunity to see her other boyfriend. When my client found out about it, she said she wanted to continue both relationships. After five months of double dipping, she decided to move into her own apartment. My client was very sick for about a week, and she was too busy to visit or provide any care for him. Their romance continued another few months until she was over the financial crisis of her divorce.

My client (who was a very intelligent man) seemed shocked and bewildered when she terminated the relationship. He could not understand how or why it ended. We concluded that he once again had created a triangular situation in which he ended up being the caregiver to an unavailable taker. In addition, he repeated the pattern of minimizing his needs and settling for less than he wanted and deserved. This pattern resulted from his relationship with an emotionally absent father who rewarded him for keeping his mouth shut and doing what he was told. The father preferred his older brother. The fact that he was a thin, unattractive teenager who wore glasses and felt he had to go the extra mile just to get a girl's attention did not help his faltering self esteem.

Initially he thought or wanted to believe that he had resolved his feelings of not being good enough, and unworthy of the love he wanted for himself. However with support he was able to recognize old patterns and eventually to identify and heed warning signs early in his relationships that indicated unavailability, or unwillingness to commit. He started exploring with his partners mutual goals for the relationship. His new tools were loving and accepting himself unconditionally. He learned to listen to what potential mates were saying and not to what he wanted to hear. He came to believe that he deserved and could have what he wanted. He started practicing behaviors aligned with his new beliefs--asking for what he wants and recognizing when his wants and needs are not being met, without rationalizing why they're not being met. In this way he would not abandon himself, or settle for less than what he wanted. He finally got that all effective relationships flow from a correct relationship with the self.

    Many months later he called to say that he was feeling much stronger and wiser. For the first time he has started saying out loud while looking into his own eyes in the mirror that he loved and accepted himself unconditionally. He forgave himself and his father, and felt relieved as if a heavy weight had been lifted from his shoulders. He also said that once he faced the truth about the termination of his last triangular relationship, he felt freed. He realized that it was his resistance that created his pain. He seemed rather surprised to realize that what he had heard all his life was really true, that is, the truth will set you free. He had always had the ability to see other people's blind spots and defenses, and was amazed that they couldn't see them. We laughed at the fact that the eye (I) cannot see itself! He was slowly burying the past.

It is absolutely amazing how some people can be so mentally intelligent and emotionally undeveloped. Genius is not necessarily accompanied by high self regard. Sometimes the strong desire to have what we think we want blinds us to our own self defeating behavior which prevents us from having what we **really** want,-- what is actually present. I have observed that the people who talk most about wanting to be in a loving relationship repeatedly attract people who are not available or at least not available to them. This dynamic can lead to the belief that "all women or all men are unavailable." In truth, the person looking for the relationship is the one who is unavailable. These individuals resist the idea that they are the unchanging variable in their series of similar relationships. They are attracting similar individuals as a catalyst to resolve some conflict or dynamic within themselves. Often people go from one marriage or relationship to another without taking time for self reflection and inner change, and seem surprised by the similar outcomes. It is as if these individuals project blame and place all responsibility for the failure of their relationships onto the other. The cost of blame is staying stuck in the problem.

When people feel unworthy of their desires, they disguise their intentions and try to manipulate others into meeting their agendas. Another client who felt unworthy and was frightened of intimacy had difficulty maintaining relationships for more than a few weeks. He tried too hard to please his partners, insisted on believing what they said instead of what they did, because he was unable to trust his own feelings and reality. He usually ended up disappointed and in pain, feeling like a victim. We had many conversations about the pitfalls of trusting another person. Authentic trust is always for, with, and of the self. One must trust oneself to discern differences between what is said and what is done, and act accordingly. People have difficulty trusting their own truth when they lie to themselves because they want to be someplace or someone they are not. This client loved to work because it provided him with a container, concrete evidence of results, and personal satisfaction. At work, he understood that what he got out of it was what he put into it. In relationships he was confused about what he put in and disappointed by what he got out. This brought him to despair because he was not allowing himself to see how he blocked himself from getting what he wanted and therefore was unable to take responsibility for changing it. You can't heal what you won't feel.

This client, like many others, entered relationships with desires which were sometimes spoken but usually not. He also had a tendency to assume that the other person was in agreement with his spoken agendas, when this was not always the case, not to mention his unspoken agendas. His need for control interfered with his ability to see and hear. Subsequently he was usually bewildered when the relationship hit the rocks. To quote a verse from the Bible: "In all our getting, we should get first an understanding." It is hard if not impossible to negotiate differences to the satisfaction of all involved without the foundation of agreements, about wants and intentions and commitments. It is dangerous to enter relationships with hidden agendas that one expects the other to meet. Like trust, commitment can only be to the self in truth.

To date, on a personal level, I have never been able to commit to a romantic relationship with a man. I now realize that this inability is because I am committed to truth. When I go against what I know to be right inside of me for whatever reason, regardless of what I think I want, I don't feel good about myself. In many romantic relationships it was expected that I would meet my partner's needs, even when I explained it was not what I wanted to do. Sometimes these men felt rejected and hurt because we wanted different things. I often felt conflicted about complying with their expectations, but at the end of the day, I was not willing to abandon myself to rescue them. Men with a need for dominance seem to think it is their God-given right to have women do what they want, especially when there is a romantic connection (in particular, good sex). I only met one man without this agenda, and our lives took different paths. God only dances between equal partners.

"We can see in other people what we sometimes cannot see in ourselves." A female client who was a licensed nurse suffered from chronic pain in her neck and shoulder. She attended a pain support group. She informed me that she observed that all the people in the group had certain characteristics in common: painful childhoods, abusive relationships, the inability to say no, feelings of helplessness, perfectionism, and anger. I complimented her on the astuteness of her observation. She then elaborated that she is aware that many of these people, mostly women, have options that they do not see. One of the members of the group was a therapist who suffered from unrelenting muscle pain. This woman was in an abusive relationship and felt trapped. We laughed at my comment that she probably chose to be a therapist searching for solutions to her own difficulties but was not yet successful.

I asked my client what her observation said to her about the commonalities in the group, and what she could do differently. We talked about thoughts being the origin of pain: negative feelings are created by the thoughts, and when they persist over time, they are expressed in the body. If left untreated, deterioration occurs resulting in chronic illness. We reviewed her history of pain, abuse, and hopelessness. In addition to a very abusive childhood, when she became pregnant out of wedlock at seventeen, she was beaten up by her father who was joined by her two brothers, one of whom kicked her in the stomach. Following this trauma, she became nervous when talking to people and her head shook uncontrollably. She told me that she started holding her neck rigidly to stop the shaking. She worked in ICU for a number of years under stressful conditions while she was in an emotionally abusive marriage. Her neck and shoulder became worse from lifting patients and holding the emotional pain of her failing marriage. She took time off work periodically.

Whenever she tried to return to work the pain became worse. She was finally placed on permanent disability. She became very disillusioned when her husband showed no sensitivity about her painful situation. She became increasingly frustrated and angry at her husband, and of course the physical symptoms intensified. Ultimately their marriage deteriorated into oblivion. She held tenaciously to her anger and blame of her husband for her misery. Stuck in this position, her body's cries for help grew louder, in a stiff neck, severe headaches, and pain radiating down her arms, limiting her movements.

When she complained about how pain was controlling her life, I asked what she would do without the pain. Predictably she had a list of things she would love to do. I told her that she is in control of her body and could develop a loving relationship with it. In this way she could work out an agreement to do the things she wants. I told her that her body is crying out for her attention and offering an opportunity for her to develop an intimate relationship with herself. Until she does this, she will not be able to have true intimacy with another person. I pointed out to her that she is so focused on her anger and external blame that she cannot move forward with her own life. I asked her if this was really how she wanted to live her life.

She could see then that her lack of forgiveness had not solved her problems or produced the desired results. In light of her intense, debilitating pain, and growing inability to move her neck, she ultimately decided to work at trying to move rather than to freeze in her position. She was forced to let go and take the high road, for the health of her children as well as herself. Our body is constantly seeking balance. Our job is to take the blinders off and to meet it halfway. It is true that what we are looking for is looking for us.

I reminded her that during childhood she was dependent for her survival and any attempt to protect or express herself was dangerous. She has continued to act out this fear. The early dependence was a real tiger. Her continued fear is of a paper tiger that is unable to hurt her. I told her that her past had created enough pain for her and it was unloving to herself to choose to continue the pain in the present, preventing any change in the future. Living in the past is giving power to an illusion. As stated in the Course in Miracles, the only true thing about the past is that it does not exist now. I suggested that she create a ritual to forgive her family for not being the people she needed and wanted them to be, and to forgive herself for anything she thought she needed forgiveness for. Forgiveness of self should include believing that she was unworthy of love and support because it was not provided. She also identified with the image of herself reflected to her by limited, unemotional parents, and now treated herself the way they treated her.

    This is the same woman who told me that she depended on her husband's approval to define her self worth. This was particularly dangerous because her husband was also separated from himself and very difficult to please. Again I suggested that she practice in front of a mirror telling herself that she loved and accepted herself just as she was. In the beginning this affirmation sounded false but as they say in the Twelve Step Program, "Fake it 'til you make it!" I encouraged her to do this. Said another way by Dr. Phil on the Oprah Show, "We have to behave our way to good health." As she has observed about members of her pain group, she does have choices that she's not choosing to see or follow. We did exercises around her feeling of being hopeless and stuck, using the image of fighting her way through quicksand with the tools of a spiritual warrior. She felt relieved and more hopeful, and by her own comment, she was gradually getting stronger.

    The ultimate example of mutual insensitivity that I heard came from a woman who was having a miscarriage in the bathroom. Her husband woke up, she told him what was happening, and he turned over and went back to sleep. She took this blatant disregard in stride. She became pregnant again, and he was not present at the birth. Sometimes people can become so accustomed and immune to abuse that they accept it as normal life, thinking it's what they deserve. If only we all remembered that we are heirs to all the riches of the universe, love is who we are, and it is our birthright to be happy and respected.

The resounding lesson I learned from my clients is that codependences and addictions are both searches for love and the fear of finding it. Fear is the antithesis of love, and when we look outside ourselves for it we are then asking for love with fear and it distorts the authenticity of what we give and receive. Most of my clients improved and moved on, and it was also the time for me to move on too.

ROOMMATES

Having a lot of unused space in my large house seemed wasteful, and I needed more income, so I decided to rent my two extra bedrooms. Apparently I still had more to learn about relationships, especially triangles. Reflecting on threesomes, I was reminded of being a little girl and the painful triangle between my older sister, my mother, and me. When I was left in my sister's care, it was my perception that she punished me for being my mother's favorite. I remember in the neighborhood I grew up in and at school feeling hurt when two friends joined together to exclude or scapegoat me or someone else. Triangles are a universal dynamic in families and in all groupings of more than two.

My lessons were then transferred from my clients to a colorful succession of roommates, with many opportunities for me to heal the illusion of separation while establishing clear, firm, loving personal boundaries. Everyone has their own idea about what it means to be a roommate. Many were in search of a room and a "mate" to take care of them, with an unconscious desire to resolve conflicts rooted in families of origin, theirs and mine.

Triangular dynamics have their beginnings in the oedipal stage between mother, father, and child. These dynamics exist in all cultures and are later reflected in sibling rivalry. Depending on its successful resolution or not, it is continued in schools, workplaces, churches, and intimate relationships. In any relationship of three or more, at some time one or more will feel "ganged up on" or "double teamed by" the majority. In psychological terms, this is experienced as separation and rejection of one or more, and (real or imagined), it hurts.

Paradoxically, a **triangle** is more stable than a dyad, but a triangle creates an "odd man out," which is a very difficult position for individuals to tolerate. Anxiety generated by anticipating or being the odd one out is a potent force in triangles. The patterns in a triangle change with increasing tension. In calm periods, two people are comfortably close "insiders" and the third person is an uncomfortable "outsider." The insiders actively exclude the outsider and the outsider works to get closer to one of them. Then a new outsider is created, and on it goes.

Someone is always uncomfortable in a triangle and pushing for change. The insiders solidify their bond by choosing each other in preference to the less desirable outsider. The one not chosen experiences intense feelings of rejection. If mild to moderate tension develops between the insiders, the most uncomfortable one will move closer to the outsider. One of the original insiders now becomes the new outsider and the original outsider is now an insider. The new outsider will make predictable moves to restore closeness with one of the insiders.

On a recent trip to St. Louis I was reminded by my college roommate of a mutual friend's preference for dating other people's boyfriends. Once to cover her tracks she claimed she had been raped. I believed her and tried to comfort her. However when her parents were called to the campus her mother indicated that this was not the first time such a scenario had occurred. One could speculate that this young woman had been exposed to many dysfunctional triangles in her family. I'm aware that this dynamic occurs frequently in relationships at a very high price to the scapegoat. Interviewing roommates was both interesting and exhausting. The universe sent me a wide variety of inappropriate candidates, from hippie to yuppie to buppie. (Perhaps it was the universe's humorous way of showing me what I didn't want.) There was one depressed looking woman with long flowing unkempt red hair, whose attire was an eclectic arrangement of styles and muted colors. She told me that she was planning to return to Europe to spend time with her family and was really looking for a place to which she could return without paying interim rent. She said she had observed that there was lots of turnover in the rental market, so she was checking out a few places before she left with the magical idea that it might be vacant again upon her return.

In my characteristic open style, I invited her to sit down for a brief chat which we extended far beyond the norm for a business transaction. At the end of a rather lengthy monologue, she commented that she had done all the talking and I had said very little. The next day she phoned and asked if she could meditate with me sometime. I agreed and the following morning we sat together for an hour of mediation. She said the meditation had been helpful and she had received some insight regarding her situation. As anticipated, my initial impression of instability was correct; however, I was happy to extend a helping hand to her, and I never turn down an invitation to meditate in community.

And then there was the well-dressed, thirtyish, BMW

(Basic Marin Wheels)-driving yuppie who entered the door and said, "I have a BMW convertible and I need a garage." She also informed me that she had lots of clothes and would need a very large closet. It was clear to me from the beginning that with her slew of demands she would require more attention than I was willing to provide. A visiting friend commented that it wouldn't be long before she wanted her own living room.

There was also a new-age Marin hippie, with a long brown unbraided pony tail whose constant companion was an aged white fuzzy dog which he carried around like a small child. He had learned the spiritual lingo well, but had not quite managed to integrate the beliefs. Although the dog was well-mannered and unobtrusive, I was not yet ready to invite animals into my home.

Out of all the applicants in this initial round, I was truly impressed with only one. Although he did not talk about spirituality, from our brief discussion about his values and experiences, it seems to me that he lived his spirituality. He presented himself in a neat and attractive way; his manner was quietly open yet modest. He spoke several languages, and another plus for me was his love for cooking and working in the garden. He seemed very interested and we agreed that he would call me when he decided.

When I didn't hear from him after a week, I decided to call him and say that he was my first choice for a housemate and would like to extend an invitation to him to join me if he chose. He said he was still looking around and would call me toward the end of the month. I said that was fine. The reason for my call was that I wanted him to know that I had been impressed with him and appreciated who he is in the world. I considered meeting him to be a gift that I will always have no matter what he decided. The gift of appreciation is joy which knows no time. I said I was confident that he will find the perfect place for him and I would find the perfect house-mate for me. Love is always perfect and knows only itself. It also comes in its own time and form. We must be willing to wait on it, recognize it, and accept it on its own terms.

  I felt very good after this exchange. However, I still did not have a roommate, and wondered what the universe was up to. One of the lessons was possibly not to judge the book by the cover. Things and people are not always what they seem. It also occurred to me that maybe I was advertising the wrong thing in the wrong place. I was using the traditional advertising resources such as the IJ and Marin Rentals. I was emphasizing the house rather than the importance of living together in harmony. I was convinced that when I became clear about what I wanted the universe would comply with what I needed. Often our lessons are unconscious so our teachers come in disguises.

  I adjusted the ad to emphasize compatibility. A woman

named Deidra answered. I was a few minutes late for our appointment and she was standing in front of the house when I arrived. She had a beautiful smile and I liked her right away. She also seemed to like me. We had tea on the deck and she asked to move in that evening because her son with whom she was living was having a party that evening and she wanted to give him and his wife their space. She said she would start to work the following week and would pay rent from her first paycheck. I agreed.

She went to get her things, and she brought some pasta and sauce and bread for dinner. We became quickly acquainted over the meal and she started referring to me as her sister. Although not highly educated in a formal sense, Deidra is very knowledgeable, creative, and skillful with her hands. She can fix almost anything. Very soon Deidra was preparing all of the meals, and I washed the dishes. She has a lot of nervous energy and a need to be active. She volunteered to clean the house and assisted me with whatever I started. We shared long talks after dinner, with a beer or a glass of wine, in front of the fireplace. We talked about many things but mostly the Spirit (my favorite subject).

We became very close over several months and Deidra decided that she wanted to create a garden. She started in the front yard which was a steep hill filled with weeds. Many mornings the two of us would share coffee and witness the awakening of new life from seeds or cuttings she had planted. We prayed for the garden, asking God to bless it. After a few months the blessing became manifest and the garden bloomed with beauty and life.

My initial plan had been to have two roommates. After Deidra had been there for several weeks, I advertised for a second roommate. Angela answered. She was a very petite, pretty, vivacious, sophisti-cated, seductive young woman. When Angela and Deidra met, they both took care to be superficially nice to each other, at least in my company. As time went on each continued to relate to me warmly but kept their distance from each other. Angela may have held some private disdain for Deidra rather masculine, working-class demeanor, both in dress and behavior. Although extremely skilled in many ways, especially being able to fix almost anything that broke in the house, Deidra seemed threatened by Angela's more feminine and competent presentation. I loved both of them for the different strengths each brought to life. I tried to help each of them to see the other from my more positive perception, and my interventions were sometimes helpful but short lived. I offered them both the opportunity of a 20% commission to participate in my promotion of Shona sculpture. Angela planned and marketed the first showing which was highly successful. She had a number of attractive boyfriends who were anxious to impress her, and who were subsequently very helpful to me.

After several months Angela left for South America to be

near her aging parents, and the triangle dissolved. She kept in touch for a while, and still calls occasionally. Although both women were fine people, they had very different ways of expressing themselves in the world. Unfortunately each was threatened by the other's personal style of expression. I appreciated both, and with practice I became more skilled at reflecting their strengths to each other, and we parted on a friendly note. So we were back to the drawing board looking for a third roommate.

Deidra reluctantly participated in interviewing for the next roommate. A short, stocky man named Jed answered the ad. He was a middle-aged eccentric man with many strange ideas. He was a recently divorced father of two children, ages ten and sixteen. He was a school psychologist who retired early as a result of his eccentric and inappropriate behaviors at work. Among other things, he started painting his fingernails as flags representing his favorite countries, and wearing scarves tied around his neck accompanied by a large brimmed hat that tied under his chin. He became
increasingly unwilling to repress his ideas and speech, even if they were not complimentary or appropriate to the institution he worked for. There were a few red flags here that I chose to ignore.

The new triad consisted of two women and a man. Deidra and I both had considerable doubts about him, but he was very enthusiastic about living with us and was anxious to move in. Neither one of us wanted to be judgmental so we agreed to give him a chance. His strangeness seemed humorous and harmless.

Initially, Jed had many dates which he obtained through the Internet. For one reason or another, none of them worked out. He gradually withdrew to his room which he only left to go to the bathroom and take hikes. Days would pass without seeing him, and he could have been dead in there for all I knew. He decided to give his car to his son and subsequently ordered food from the Internet and delivered from Safeway. He did not use the kitchen, and ate from cans or bags of dried food. He told me he had started eating dry dog food (Alpo) because it was cheap and had good nutritional value. He accumulated very little trash and was an extremely all-around low maintenance housemate.

He spent numerous hours on the Internet and writing poetry. He obsessively wrote about sex and spirituality--Jesus having sex and at one point having sex with his mother. It was so disconcerting that I could not continue reading it. He had asked me for my comments, but when I told him I was ready to discuss it, he showed little interest. I was glad!

Jed loved to sing and hum. Strange sounds could be heard coming from his room--mysterious groans and loud nose blowings. In the beginning Deidra and I wondered if he was having sex on the Internet. Once he wrote "Fuck me" on the steamed bathroom mirror. This was very upsetting to both of us, especially to Deidra because it was in their shared bathroom. When we confronted him, he said it was like an adolescent impulse, and made light of it. Deidra, who has her own issues with men in general, disliked him intensely and found it necessary to report this behavior to the Sausalito police, who simply made note of it. We both had witnessed an earlier demonstration of his inappropriateness when he attended my daughter's wedding. At the reception he unexpectedly put her whole hand, which had cake on it, in his mouth.

Jed and Deidra grew increasingly antagonistic toward each other, and after the mirror incident, the war was on. Deidra was the most intense and obvious about her disaffection. After a few months, the relationship between them deteriorated to the point that Deidra could hardly manage to speak to him or look at him. Each of them was very considerate and nice to me, but the atmosphere became strained when the three of us were together. In her own way, Deidra tried to apply subtle pressure on me to ask Jed to move.

Although Jed was not the easiest person that I know to be around, he did have his good points such as paying his rent on time, using very few facilities in the house, and for the most part was not seen, nor heard, except for the strange sounds seeping from under his doorsill.

It also goes without saying that while Deidra had many virtues, she also had her "growth areas." Since they both had strengths and weaknesses, I tried not to identify with one and against the other. However, Jed was so eccentric it became increasingly hard for me to accept his behavior, and even harder to help someone else be comfortable enough with him to live in peace.

Probably in part to maintain her own sanity, Deidra decided to channel her frustration into constructive behavior and tackle the back yard. It was not only much larger than the front but filled with berry bushes and weeds. Inspired by her enthusiasm, I arranged to have the bushes removed and she started work. She worked long hours in the yard, climbing up and down the steep hill like a mountain lion. I must say that I did not have a vision for the final product, and had serious questions along the way about what it would look like when completed. Deidra assured me that it was going to be beautiful.

Soon I was making trips to Home Depot's garden department with such regularity that I became well known by the staff. Deidra and I realized that the garden could provide a needed home for several tons of Shona sculpture that I was storing in my house. I enjoyed shopping at flea markets and garage sales for other unique artifacts for the garden. Deidra did not like to shop and greatly appreciated and enjoyed all the supplies I brought home. Her eyes lit up when she looked at beautiful plants and she always found just the right place for whatever I brought for the garden. Deidra's prediction of beauty started to reveal itself as the garden developed. It was truly a reflection of our combined talents and energies. Our relationship came to center around the garden. It was the one thing that the two of us were in total agreement about.

Deidra continued to cook and it seemed fair that I buy the food in addition to washing the dishes. Deidra has four children, the youngest two were living in Santa Fe with their father. She com-mented several times that she was concerned about her daughter and wished she could come to California. At least once Deidra suggested that her daughter could move in with us and pay a small amount of rent until she was able to get settled and find her own place. I don't think I made any response to this suggestion, but remembered thinking that the process was so consuming I really didn't have the energy to relate to an additional housemate. Of course Deidra was aware of my preoccupation with the process, and my feelings that I was already stretched to the max.

One Sunday afternoon, Deidra casually asked if she had told me that her nineteen-year-old daughter would be arriving the following week to share her room. She said she would pay an additional $150 dollars for rent. I was stunned with the feeling of betrayal, but decided to give it a chance. The nineteen-year-old had a major attitude problem--when she was upset with her boyfriend she would refuse to speak to anyone. She also did not lift a finger to do any work around the house, ate meals in her room, watched movies all day, and entertained several boyfriends at different times.

Another triangle had been introduced and in this one, I was the odd man out. I found this position very uncomfortable. I became part of the problem and therefore ineffective in creating a solution. The daughter and I did not get along, which was quite evident to anybody who had eyes to see and ears to hear. Deidra made various excuses, claiming the two of us were very much alike, and in her opinion this caused the conflict between us. I failed to see the similarities. At another time she told me that I was the adult in this situation. I agreed, and told her that was the problem, that as an adult I could not tolerate such an arrogant attitude of a teenager who seemed to think she could do whatever she wanted in my house. On the other hand, I did not have the energy nor the inclination to struggle or compromise with an adolescent at this point in my life. Deidra was obviously disappointed that in spite of her best efforts to negotiate a friendly relationship between me and her daughter, it was not happening. I felt responsible for what went on in my house, and I was unwilling to invest the enormous energy required to resolve the negativity. Because I tend to rationalize and hold on to relationships longer than I should, my clear acceptance of this limitation was an indication of real growth on my part.

This marked the beginning of the deterioration of our relationship. I know it was very hard for Deidra who felt trapped in the middle of our mutual dislike. I suggested several times that Deidra and her daughter might consider moving together. Deidra's response did not indicate that this was a probability, but in fact, it is exactly what happened a few months later.

The first time Deidra decided to move she gave me one week's notice. She told me about a very special place that was available immediately, and I was very happy for her. It turned out this apartment was not available. A month later she told me her daughter had found an apartment and the two of them were going to move together. Again she gave me a week's notice. I was hurt that she didn't choose to let me know of her plans to move and the short notice felt like an expression of anger she could not talk about. I shared my hurt feelings with her and told her that it is customary to give a month's notice. After thinking about the situation for a few days, I told her that I would like for her to pay rent for the full month, and she did. When she moved she did not leave a forwarding address or a telephone number although I had her work number.

Several weeks after she moved she called to say she'd like to come work in the garden. I was of course delighted because the garden had started to cry out for attention. The garden was an expression of our highest relationship, and Deidra said she felt very happy and at home there. She gave her car to her daughter, so I would pick her up on Saturdays and take her to my house. We resumed our friendship, without discussing any of the issues about which we disagreed. I did not have much discretionary income at this point, but made modest donations towards her efforts with a promise of more when my finances increased. I realized that this was another area of lack of clarity between us. On one hand she said that she considered her work a privilege and does not expect to be paid, and on another hand she has commented several times that she might have to take a second job to make ends meet.

I was not satisfied with this arrangement, and I sincerely planned to pay her more adequately in the future. I know that despite whatever lack of clarity that existed between us, we did love and appreciate each other. Her work in the garden gradually came to an end. We maintained contact for several months, with our continued verbal expressions of care. Without her, the garden began to fade away. The connection between us was also fading. I acknowledged the loss of the garden as our joint creation and said I would like to develop a new basis for our friendship if she also wanted that. Although she said she did, I heard from her less frequently, and then not at all. She was no longer exuberant when I reached out to her, and I accepted that what had been for me a meaningful relationship had apparently ended. I was clear almost from the start that she wanted something from me that I was not giving. First of all, I didn't really know what it was, because she was unable to articulate it. Even knowing this, I remained open hearted in the relationship.

Sometimes I forget the wisdom in the Biblical quote: "In all our getting, get first an understanding." We never agreed on the true basis of our relationship which ended in disappointment for both of us. Often the existence of triangles serves the purpose of distracting the two people in primary relationship with each other from dealing with the issues between them. In the future I will work harder to identify clear mutual goals and expose any hidden agendas. I remain both respectful and grateful for my friendship with Deidra and will always love her.

When Deidra moved out, I was left alone to experience the intensity of Jed's insanity, which was becoming scary. I was dismayed during a conversation with Jed when he made several references to "landmines," which let me know that he had read my writings without my permission. I started wondering what other personal boundaries he had crossed and what else he was doing in my absence. Earlier he had casually mentioned that he was out of his psychotropic medication and had decided to stop taking it. I hadn't even known he used it. Once he even commented that if something happened to me, he feared my relatives would put him out of the house. All this concerned me and I worried that his behavior might deteriorate into a psychotic break.

I was watering the garden one evening at dusk when I heard a strange sound. I turned around to find Jed butt naked urinating from the deck off his bedroom. In shock I told him to go use the bathroom, and he responded, "I didn't know you were there!" This was the last straw and I decided that it was time to part company. I prayed and asked God to help Jed find the perfect new home. I suggested to him that a remote cabin in the forest would be perfect for him, and he loved the idea and became excited about a new adventure. He got busy on the Internet researching possibilities. He settled on the Fort Bragg area and made several calls but was unable to find anything. He decided to move up there into a hotel until he could find permanent housing. Since he did not have a car, I volunteered to drive him. He treated me to lunch and we said goodbye.

Jed was so strange that I knew our relationship was not an accident. Without the confusion of romance I was able to see clearly my own attraction to crazy men that I had observed in my sisters for many years. He was without pretense--what you saw was what you got. He was very honest and sweet in a childlike way. I liked those qualities and found them refreshing. However, they came at a high cost.

Looking back, I observed certain patterns in my

relationships. One of them was my attraction to the underdog, things and people nobody else seemed to want. "Dog" is a metaphor for the undesirable. When I had more energy, I loved nothing more than going to flea markets and thrift stores to find what had been discarded as junk and to transform it into treasures. I also reached out to express love to the "unlovable." I was surprised to learn that some of my family are repeating this same pattern. One of them has become a top manager in a large financial firm by accepting supervisees that other managers rejected.

Jed taught me two lessons: First, his behavior wasn't personal to me so I wasn't drawn in emotionally. And secondly, that people without boundaries or pretense can be emotionally available for connection, but unfortunately they are often also "crazy." A connec-tion with such people is usually primal, unsocialized, and un-developed. Most people wouldn't even bother with them. I realized that I do want to be able to relate to people at this level, but not in an intimate situation. My preference is for an open heart and clear boundaries.

Years later I heard Jed had remarried. He was "hiking" in the neighborhood one day and knocked on the door. We exchanged pleasantries, and he told me that his mail order wife had come to an untimely death by suicide. I expressed my condolence, but was not surprised.

After Jed's departure I lived alone for several months to

recuperate. I asked the Spirit to send me a sane companion of like mind with whom I could share activities and have fun. I had almost decided that I would not rent to men, but 90% of my calls were from men, so I thought the universe was trying to tell me something. When Artem appeared at my door, I did not immediately recognize him as an answered prayer, and I certainly didn't recognize him as the next master teacher for my still unresolved issues. My interactions with him would span the range of all my relationships--family, client, roommate, employee, friend, caretaker, etc. The fact that he owned a remodeling business and had a van appealed to me. In addition to having access to a handyman, I thought it would be very nice not to have to haul things in my car. I was also looking forward to sharing creative projects with another person.

Artem was a thirty-eight year old, energetic, good-looking Ukrainian. He entered the house quickly, as if he were in a hurry. He took a cursory look around. He commented on the African art, and said he loved Africa and everything African. He asked me if I was from Africa. I told him I was at some point, but not recently. We laughed, and he left. I doubted his real interest in renting the room. He called me five minutes later on his cell phone to ask if utilities were included. He called again fifteen minutes later and asked if he could put his tools in the garage. He waited another ten minutes, called again, and said he wanted to come fill out the paperwork. I told him I didn't have any paperwork, but I would get a rental agreement. He said he wanted to come over and talk a bit more and bring me his references. I agreed. A week later he moved in.

Soon I learned that he was deeply grieving the recent loss of his girlfriend who he had planned to marry. In my opinion, the loss was compounded because he had been in this country illegally for several years, and he was desperate to get his green card. He described himself as severely depressed, but his energy was very light and sweet. This was an obvious ruse, but I chose to overlook it. Instead I focused on the intensity of his pain and confusion, thinking that he might be too innocent and gentle for this world. He claimed to care nothing about money or status.

Meals offered an opportunity for us to pray together. He was somewhat surprised by my ritual of saying grace, which he described as a rare practice in Europe. I introduced him to meditation and we meditated together. For his first experience he seemed to go rather deep. We were both devoted yoga students, and we attended one of his classes together. Unfortunately the class met on Sunday morning which conflicted with my church time. He also attended church with me once, but he preferred to use his Sunday mornings for yoga.

He was an excellent cook, with a taste for expensive wines. It seemed to give him great joy to serve me, as if this was his mission. He even commented that he wanted to take care of me. He loved our long talks over meals, and he was very open and receptive to my counsel. He seemed to appreciate the time I spent with him, and took great care to let me know. At one point I told him to trust in God. He said that he didn't trust God, but he trusted me. I told him that was OK, because I was God's representative. He told me that he thought that in his despair he might have committed suicide if he had not found me. He knew how to make me feel special and needed.

He observed things in need of repair around the house, and fixed them without being asked. One of his first projects was to clean the garage, which was no small undertaking. He also suggested we clean the basement which was filled with thirty years of debris and excess. He commented that the basement was quite large, and could be made into a very nice two-bedroom apartment, which he indicated that he would like to do. He also volunteered to go to St. Louis with me to repair a house that I was planning to sell. While I appreciated the offers, I thought the logistics would be overwhelming, so I gratefully declined. I began to wonder if he was too good to be true, but my defenses were down and I threw caution to the wind.

At breakfast one morning, I said I was excited about things being built and repaired, that I loved the process of creating. He said that humans are in the world to create. I was impressed by this statement. We discussed the possibility of going into partnership to remodel and sell houses. This had a lot of appeal for both of us. We discovered that we both had dreams of living on the ocean, and talked about the possibility of buying oceanfront property.

Artem appeared to be a very loving, caring, attentive man, to whom I was very responsive. He called me during the day and reminded me to eat, which I often neglected to do. He brought me roses and other flowers at least once a week, to be sure I had fresh flowers in the house. He seemed totally accepting of me. He is the only person who has ever actually encouraged me to "do the process," withdrawing from the world into my bathroom attempting to balance my body. (Most people try to get me to stop!) He even volunteered to do chores so I would have more time to devote to it. It was his opinion that the process was one of taking power into my body so that I could heal other people. Once I attempted to explain to him that I am not my normal self. He said that to him I was normal, since the present was his only experience of me. We both recognized that our connection with each other was very special. We talked about our relationship spanning many lifetimes. I came to think of him as my answered prayer.

In my relationship with Artem I began to feel safe and comfortable enough to express my true feelings and assert my needs. This new freedom was a huge awakening. I was more able to be the witness of my own behavior. I can only imagine how others must have experienced my unconscious behavior in the past while I was busy rationalizing, or justifying my actions. The truth is that when we don't feel our feelings, other people have to.

I have a tendency, which has gotten worse during the process, to be late for everything. I used to make excuses for myself, all of which seemed very legitimate to me at the time. I now accept my lateness for what it is, disrespect for the other. I became shamefully aware that Artem always ended up waiting for me whenever we were going out, even though he told me in advance what time we were leaving. He said he didn't mind, but putting myself in his position I would be very annoyed if not angry.

I remember waiting for him once. I did not have a watch, and arrived at the destination early. It was very windy and cold, and it seemed that I had waited a long time. When he arrived I jumped all over him letting him know in no uncertain terms that it didn't work for me when he did not show up on time. Being the well organized person he is, he took his computer from his pocket which had recorded the time of his phone call to me, and he pointed out to me that there were only four minutes difference between the time agreed upon and his arrival. I could hardly believe it, and I apologized profusely.

Artem and I had planned to go to dinner after a yoga class, but he ate dinner earlier without my knowledge. After the class, he said he was not very hungry so I decided not to go to the restaurant, and wanted to go to the sauna instead. Artem later commented that I had changed my mind twice in one day. I reminded him that he was really the one to change our original plan, and my decision was a response to his change. After thinking about this interaction, it occurred to me that he had some objections to me changing my mind. In my continued effort of teaching him how to relate to me, I told him that I reserved the right to change my mind, as he did. I added that I am a unique individual and he should respond to me on the basis of who I am and not his past experiences with other women.

I pointed out to him that relating to a woman in some ways is similar to playing a violin--the more familiar he is, the better he understands, and the sweeter the music. He has a habit of knocking hard and slamming doors. Sudden loud noises are very disruptive to me, and I told him that when he is preceded by loud noises, I have a temporary disconnect from him. I told him that in general he would get my best response when he entered quietly and talked to me in a soft gentle voice. I have come to realize that this is true probably not only for me but for other people as well. I am very aware of how my consciousness elevates when I am treated with respect.

I persisted in my objective of having two roommates and decided to have two people of the same sex because of the shared bathroom. The next triad was between two men, Artem and Ken, and myself. Artem moved in about three weeks before Ken, and the two of us had already formed a very close relationship. A similar situation occurred in that the chemistry between the two of them was not great, but again, Ken was extremely anxious to move in and Artem decided to give it a try.

Artem was very neat and meticulous. He worked out regularly at the gym and was very conscious about his body image. Ken, on the other hand, was a very overweight, sloppy young man who acted as if he was waiting on his mother or someone to clean up after him. He also appeared to have his days and nights confused. He slept most of the day, until 2 or 3 in the afternoon, and was up most of the night. He frequently came home at 2 or 3 in the morning, walked around upstairs as if it was midday, cooking and watching TV, and taking twenty-minute showers. Artem and I were both early risers.

The first week Ken was in the house he did laundry every day. I found his habits most annoying, and talked to him about them on numerous occasions. Invariably, he had some excuse or lengthy explanation to justify his behavior. He made several less than effective efforts to change and become more compatible.

The sibling rivalry and antagonism between him and Artem escalated. In essence this was a mirror image of the triangle I experienced with my two previous female roommates, only this one was more explosive. If we don't get the message from a gentle tap on the shoulder, the universe will accommodate with a kick in the pants.

Artem was openly disdainful of Ken, and I am sure the feeling was mutual. The only difference was that Ken made every attempt not to let his feelings show. Each of them tried to get me to take his side against the other. I explained to them both that I was not willing to mediate their conflicts. It started to feel as if I was a kindergarten teacher trying to teach two squabbling and tattling five-year-olds how to get along. Artem commented several times that he was not happy in the home, attempting to apply subtle pressure on me to ask Ken to move. Again, I refused to take sides, although Ken was sure that I favored Artem and scapegoated him. I attempted to reassure him with examples that my reaction to him was based on my interactions with him and had nothing to do with Artem. Ken's habits and body rhythms simply annoyed me all by myself, and I did not need Artem to tell me I was annoyed.

I asked Ken to move three times; the first time he asked to stay five months until he could save enough money to move out of state. He said it would be extremely difficult for him to move twice because it would cost several thousand dollars which he doesn't have and would prevent him from moving out of state. He implored me to grant him time, promising to pay more toward the utilities and to limit his wash to twice a week and take shorter showers. The second time I had become impatient with his late hours and destruction of two plants on separate occasions while he attempted to negotiate the steps in the dark while inebriated. Again he promised to improve.

The third time I became outraged at the petty power plays between the two of them. Once I had no hot water for a morning shower, which infuriated me, and I was sure it was the result of Ken's long showers and laundry. As usual, he protested, saying it was Artem who took the long shower, and again he offered an elaborate story about how unfair I was being to him. I told him that I was sick and tired of discussing infantile conflicts when I am dealing with life and death issues with my own process. He said he understood but thought I had a responsibility to be fair. I told him that my responsibility is to myself, and maintaining harmony in my house is my priority, even if they both have to move.

Internally though, I realized that I didn't want to hear anything Ken had to say, and I was not open to change or reason; this was disrespectful, and he didn't deserve such treatment. I forced myself to listen to him. Ken assured me that he would eliminate the conflict between the two of them by essentially avoiding Artem. Then he asked for three more months, promising to move at the end of May. Although it would be my preference to have him move immediately, my insidious codependency let him stay.

Taking responsibility for whatever contributions I made to this dysfunctional relationship, I thought it was only fair to have the patience to allow the relationship to end on friendly terms. Subsequently Ken made extra efforts to be nice to me, even though many of his basic habits had not changed. Ken finally moved out, which was a protracted ordeal. He used every opportunity to demand an audience from me or my daughter. During the process of our final transactions I misplaced one hundred dollars that he had given me. Unfortunately I intimated that he might have taken it. I found the money a few months later in my dresser, but I had no forwarding address for him, and no opportunity to apologize. He saw a mutual friend and sent warm greetings to me, which I took as forgiveness. I resolved to
recognize these dynamics in myself and be more vigilant in my refusal to participate in dysfunctional triangles.

Several months after Ken moved out, Artem referred a newly divorced European friend who needed a temporary place to stay. I seldom saw this roommate, who owned a new restaurant in Sausalito and worked long hours. He brought me pastries which he left on the dining room table. I liked finding his croissants, breakfast rolls, and pecan tarts. Our interactions were always affectionate and real. I felt better after a contact with him. He reminded me that it is not as important what you say or do for people as how you make them feel. The presence of his spirit in his smile and touch connected with the spirit in me. The tonality of his recognition, greetings, and compli-ments had the power to elevate me for hours afterward. We often forget how healing another's greeting can be.

He invited me to eat in his restaurant (on the house) and at his request I placed pieces of Shona sculpture there. One of his customers fell in love with "Magnificent Flower," an abstract stone carving. He called me from Lake Tahoe to arrange an appointment to buy it. Our meeting was magical, more than the buying and selling of art, and felt predestined. He bought the art, and I knew it had gone to the perfect person. After a few months this roommate found another room in Sausalito at half the price, so to save money he moved there. He invited me to come by his restaurant for lunch on the house, and we parted as friends.

Then Artem's best friend from Europe, a website specialist, visited for a month in my home. He showed me several beautiful websites he had created for hotels and restaurants in Switzerland. Since my trip to Zimbabwe and my epiphany with the artists and the sculpture, I had wanted to promote African artists and their work. I was unable to proceed in this endeavor because I shuddered when I thought about opening and sitting in a gallery all day; also taking responsibility for selecting and hiring someone else to do so did not appeal to me.

It had not occurred to me to create a website for my

collection of Shona sculptures, which I had attempted to sell in a variety of ways. It was on the last day of the friend's visit that I made the connection. I asked him if he could create a website for me and he told me that it would "delight his heart" to do so! The two of us had a lot of fun taking pictures of the sculptures, and he created a very beautiful calling card to be used as the first page of a virtual tour of what he referred to as my "store." I was very excited and inspired as I watched the opening of the door to my virtual art gallery. I decided to call it "World Sacred Art." I liked the idea of living with artistic expressions of the Spirit. The gallery was to include art from around the world, but would be centered around Shona sculpture. This seemed appropriate since my interest in promoting art began in Zimbabwe. Adding the word "world" opened the opportunity for me to travel extensively in search of sacred art. This seemed like a majestic endeavor, and I welcomed the new path. I was amazed by modern technology and mass communication on a global scale. The thought of sitting in my living room being in contact with people all over the world was mind blowing!

Shortly after Artem moved in, on his first trip to the basement he had suggested that I could remodel the area for expanded living space. Since I had no immediate need for the additional space, I wasn't too enthusiastic about the idea. However, he continued to talk about remodeling the basement as a possible living space for himself or a showroom for the art gallery. He introduced me to one of his friends, Alfredo, who is an architect. Alfredo was very interested in designing the project, but my energy around it remained lukewarm. I gradually became enthusiastic after I saw the possibilities of creating a virtual tour on the internet and a showplace for the art. I grew ecstatic as I participated in the co-creation of a project that could express all of me. Artem and Alfredo also seemed very motivated (for their own reasons) to create something beautiful and unique. Everything seemed to be moving along with effortless effort.

My enthusiasm for life and new beginnings was observed by other people, especially my children. Artem was very complimentary and told me on a regular basis that I was looking younger. He said that he was becoming wiser with me, and I was becoming younger with him. At a family party La Wanda announced several times that in spite of her initial skepticism and the continuing doubts of others, she "believes in the process," that I had made a believer out of her. She said I was looking forty years younger. Several other relatives and friends at the party also went out of their way to tell me how well I looked. These comments clearly demonstrated to me that the light indeed shines from the inside out. I was swept off my feet and thoroughly enjoying the magic carpet ride, being in love with love itself.

Artem, who seemed to have some unresolved ambivalence

and fears about women and intimacy talked a lot about not being able to find a good woman who understood and appreciated him. After a few months he met a young woman who seemed to adore him. Initially he was excited about the new relationship, but after a week he told me that when a woman is too available he loses interest. The relationship ended after a short time. In spite of his ongoing rhetoric about not being able to find a good woman, I think he was afraid to find one, and this may be one of the reasons he felt so safe and comfortable with me.

For a while I went two health clubs, one of which Artem and his ex-girlfriend also went to. I often saw the ex-girlfriend, who he still claimed to love and toward whom he nurtured significant anger and resentment. When we first met, I don't think she knew Artem lived with me. Gradually we started talking together about the weather and other light topics. She is a very proud hair stylist, and invited me to her salon for a haircut. Artem was very encouraging and even offered to pay for the haircut. I declined, not wishing to be a pawn between them. Among other things, he was recently hurt when she went to his favorite restaurant with another man. In poor taste, the owner of the restaurant informed Artem that he had just missed them. The owner said she was probably enjoying great sex with her new lover, and asked Artem if he couldn't hear her moans of delight. Artem was devastated, worked up his anger to the boiling point, and once again I was subjected to the broken record of how she had done him wrong.

The following evening, I went for a steam and sauna and ran into his ex-girlfriend. We chatted idly, as usual. Artem was always curious about our conversations. This evening he asked me twice if I had "told her." I responded both times, "Told her what?" "That we live together." He said that I knew she had disrespected and hurt him by going to his favorite restaurant with another man. I told him that I didn't think that was any of my business, and he said that the two of us were family, not her, that I should be on his side, and that I should not talk to her. He gave as an example someone being rude to me and he continues being friendly with them. He was so upset by my perceived betrayal that he didn't eat the food I had bought for him, and went straight to bed. As he was leaving the room, I laughed and said to him that he had to be kidding. He neither got my real message, nor saw anything funny, and left without comment. I was stunned.

The following morning I asked if he had a few minutes to talk. I affirmed that I do love him, and all my actions involving him come from a loving place. However, as to taking his side, I stand on the side of truth, without obligation to agree with someone because I love them. The fact that I may not agree with them does not mean I don't love them. I suggested that agreement is not a requirement of love, and such an expectation is immature and narcissistic. He became rather quiet and thoughtful. He then minimized his reactions and told me I should forget it. I said it was important to me for him to understand that within the framework of love, differences are accepted. Also, I wasn't about to be controlled by him.

This situation reminded me of one of my clients who interpreted all negative experiences and disappointments as an indication of personal rejection. She believed these experiences meant that something was wrong with her. For example, when her hair stylist failed to return three telephone calls, she thought this meant she was no longer wanted as a client. Even though the hair stylist was in the process of moving to a different location, with the possibility of endless personal reasons for not returning the calls. My client reviewed her history with the stylist, wondering if she had tipped too little, or not at all, or whether her shyness had been a turn-off, or if her chronic neck pain while getting her hair done had been silently communicated without her complaining about it. Upon our exploration, the client became aware that her agitation, triggered by the hair stylist, was really about early feelings of rejection, and the real pain was caused by a recent feeling of betrayal by her ex-husband.

We are never upset for the reasons we think. When we respond to life experiences as if they are caused by us personally, we rob ourselves and the other person of the real experience. We deny the other's reality and distort our own, missing the essence of what's happening and the opportunity to learn what the universe is trying to teach us in the moment.

Artem continued to act very caring and attentive. Frequently I was engaged in the process from morning to night. Sometimes I couldn't wait for him to leave for work so I could go into the bathroom and get started. I was usually still in the bathroom when he called to say he was on his way home. I would then run upstairs to wash the breakfast dishes and turn on the lights to welcome him. He either cooked when he arrived home, or picked up carry-out from restaurants. He took on the role of an anxious mother regarding my eating properly, and seemed to take great pride in this role!

Artem's mother sent him a bottle of special liqueur made only in the Ukraine. He was very anxious to share it with me. I knew from past experience that I cannot drink hard liquor and certainly should not drink any alcohol on an empty stomach. I ignored the lessons of my past experience and became very intoxicated. The next morning he told me that he couldn't sleep he was so worried about me. According to Artem, my IQ fell to about 20, and I acted as if I were an "African Bushman" with no education. I didn't fail to notice this racist comment, but chose not to react because I didn't want to be defensive while he was trying to hold a mirror up for me.

With tears in his eyes he told me my behavior was very ugly and said he wondered who that person was, that he didn't see the person he loved and thought of as his teacher. He said that he was convinced that my smoking and drinking and not eating were indications that I didn't care about myself. He said the people around me seem to care more about me than I do myself. He wondered if I were trying to kill myself. He said he knew what he was saying probably hurt me very much but he needed to say it because he loved me and was worried about my health.

I did feel very bad--he had confronted me with my deep ambivalence. I wanted to see myself as a healer but had to admit that I sometimes behaved as if I was the one in need of healing. I thought a lot about whether my behavior was in fact a death wish. I came to the conclusion that it was. My choice was literally between death and life. I concluded that I wanted to live, and I renewed my commitment to giving up my addictions, although it would be a long time coming.

There were many perks in the relationship for both of us. I enjoyed the companionship, his generous gifts, exotic flowers, emotional support and seeming devotion. His frequent calls to check on my well being whenever we were separated were very touching; however, I sensed another disguised attempt to control me. Against my daughter's advice, he even bought and paid for a cell phone for me so he could always reach me when I was not at home. The problem with this was that I never remembered to take the cell phone with me. We had a lot of fun playing board games and different roles with each other, and enjoying elaborate meals in good restaurants. We savored hot sake, good wines, and high minded, animated conversations.

I think in the beginning of all love relationships, the natural tendency is to want to please and be cooperative. I felt he was becoming attached to me, or thought he was. Growing increasingly uncomfortable with our vaguely defined relationship, I decided to invite to dinner a young, vivacious, cute French woman whom I met at church so she and Artem could meet. Artem went out and bought fancy Italian pastry, expensive French wine, and several other bottles totaling around $160 dollars. I was surprised at the extent of his extravagant preparations, and gently told him so. He said that the French wine was for the guest, and the rest was for us. I was beginning to be concerned about his emphasis on maintaining a constant supply of alcohol, but I'm not one to refuse fine wines.

When the guest arrived he introduced the two of us as a couple, which surprised the guest and shocked me! Although he joked a lot, when I explained to the guest that he was joking he assured her he was not. When she asked if we were married, he said convincingly that he hoped to be someday. I explained to Artem that he should not give the guest the wrong impression of our relationship, to which he made no response. The three of us finally settled down to eat, laughed a lot, and had a really good time together. I went to bed and left the two of them to talk. She stayed another half an hour and went home.

The following morning I asked Artem what he thought about the young woman, and he said that he didn't want to get involved with anyone at this time. I suggested that at least he might want to follow up with an offer of friendship; he agreed but never followed up. His introduction of us as a couple startled me and awakened the possibility of inviting romance into my life again. I fantasized for a moment about what it would be like to be married to Artem or someone like him, but the role simply did not fit. I was acutely aware that the exchange of marriage for a green card was less than honorable and with the passing of time would end in decay.

I felt the need to put our relationship in a well-defined context, (mother and son seemed to fit the bill), so I told him that I would unofficially "adopt" him on his birthday. I had often told him that I was married to the Spirit. When we told one of his friends that I had adopted Artem, the friend asked who was the father. I told him the Spirit is his father. When Artem first arrived he was not accustomed to saying grace, praying, or meditating. He was soon reminding me whenever I forgot to say grace before eating, and often suggested we meditate together. We talked increasingly about the Spirit and he said the Spirit talked to him. I wanted so much to believe that he was waking up spiritually because it made me feel more comfortable. I minimized my observation of discrepancies in his conversations and actions, and took him at his word. I continued to enjoy what he offered.

After almost a year, Artem found a new girl friend, Jennifer, or rather she found him. She was divorced with a four year old son. She went to the Nautilus Gym where she knew he exercised, and left a note with her telephone number, asking him to call her, which he did, with my encouragement. Both Artem and Jennifer proclaimed their read-iness for a relationship, and both wanted a family. They quickly became a threesome-- Artem was delighted with his readymade family and enjoyed playing daddy. He was also highly motivated to stay in this country and obtain a green card. Since 911, the immigration laws had become more restrictive and the only way to get a green card was to get married.

After knowing each other for about three weeks, they were practically living together, and already discussing marriage. A wedding date was set for less than four months after their initial meeting. When Artem talked about Jennifer, it was all about how much she cared for him. However, knowing Artem and how he clothed himself in the caretaker's role, I was sure she also appreciated how much he took care of her. It crossed my mind that their marriage might be based on need and mutual care, yet lack passion. I wondered if out of fear Artem would be settling for less than he wanted and Jennifer settling for what she thought she could have. A lot of people do this, without being clear about what they are asking for, and subsequently are disappointed with what they get.

Artem and Jennifer were married in a very small private ceremony at Sausalito Presbyterian. Jennifer knew the wedding coordinator and arranged to have her wedding in the afternoon following a morning wedding. The church was already beautifully decorated and looked like the gateway to heaven covered with flowers. One of the two musical selections was "Someone to Watch Over Me." The minister was eloquent both in his selection of tailor made vows and his delivery of them. The bride and groom radiated joy as they became husband and wife. The reception and dinner were held at a very romantic restaurant, formerly Sally Stanfords, in Sausalito overlooking the water. The food was good and love was in the air. I was very happy for them.

Sometimes love (and even passion) grows with time but it is unlikely to happen if it is not nurtured. People are usually unconsciously attracted to each other for mutual healing, which requires hard work on both sides. When this is not understood, there are expectations that one person needs to change to make the other person happy. It has been my experience that one can never feel safe or heal with a partner who wants or needs them to be different than they are. Also it is impossible to truly accept someone that we expect to be a certain way for our comfort. Each partner expects the other to complete him or her in some way or do their internal work for them. Many people resentfully settle for less than they want and live in chronic anger, preoccupied with what's missing in their lives, and continually seeking what they don't have. The answer to this riddle is to be content with what we have, because the only person we can change is ourselves. When we change ourselves, we change our world.

A friend asked me if I missed the attention provided by Artem (pre-new girl friend) and if I was looking for a new roommate to replace him. Although I enjoyed and appreciated all of the time and attention he devoted to me, I knew the relationship was time-limited. I was very pleased to realize that I was neither attached to Artem nor what he did for me. Artem was feeling guilty about not being as available to me as he once was. In his rather childlike attempt to see how I felt about the change, he said that I always credited the Spirit for the care that he provided, and wondered if it was because of the Spirit that he was no longer providing it. I agreed, and he breathed a sigh of relief, wiped his brow, and with a big grin said, "Oh, then it's not my fault!" And then he said, "You're weird! You're the only person in the world who would say that!" I told him that not only was it not his fault, it is his responsibility to follow the Spirit inside his own heart.

When we become attached to another person or what they bring to our lives, we resist change and try to hold on to what was. This prevents us from experiencing what is. We linger in illusion. The inability to let go often results in resentment and suffering. For this reason the Buddhists teach non-attachment. We need to remember and trust that the Spirit is our infinite source and will send whomever and whatever is needed to continue our journey towards completion.

I don't recall ever feeling competitive with another woman. Maybe this is because I had never met one who had something I wanted and thought I could not have. I had never become personally attached to a man, even my father. The closest I have come to feelings of envy over a man was after I met Baba. He had no personal relationship with me or any of his devotees; of course he chose Gurumai as his successor. The lineage is preordained. In no way was I appropriate, or ready for, nor did I want such heavy responsibility. However, she *did have* something I wanted and thought I didn't have--closeness with Baba. I decided to devote my life to obtaining intimacy, not with Baba with his spirit. In the process, I realized that I had it all along. It was simply a question of opening to what was already there.

Even before he was married, Artem made several suggestions that Jennifer and her son could move in with us and he could fix up the basement for their apartment. I didn't fall for this okeydoke, so he kept a foot (and some belongings) in both camps. We continued our discussions and plans for the art gallery. Things seemed to flow naturally with a number of synchronistic events. I attended a workshop on Living Your Dreams, and met a woman who works for a printing company, and she offered to print 8x10 pictures for a portfolio to display my art. This seemed to be a green light to proceed in the direction of promoting the artists in Zimbabwe.

I was merrily rowing my boat gently down this stream when Artem casually suggested that we look for houses to remodel for sale, to earn the money to build the gallery. I was not open to this major detour, and I made excuses for my mounting anxiety. After all, the architect had completed the plan, the structural engineer had completed his calculations, and the Title 24 Engineer had finished his job. The plans had gone to the City for a building permit, and we had even purchased a lot of the lumber to be used. I was revisited by fear. In retrospect, I believe that this was Artem's circuitous pattern of flitting from one grandiose scheme to another to avoid confronting his own limitations as a "self made" contractor.

I thought that I had mastered fear in my practice of the Course in Miracles, and my desire to see God everywhere and in everybody did not leave room for fear. However, I was also watching my portfolio of stocks decrease more than one hundred thousand dollars, and I found myself for the first time without income. I was not able to see God acting in my financial situation. I had thoughts of being too old to get a job, not having enough money to live on, losing my house, becoming dependent on my family, or worse, becoming a bag lady in the streets. I even had fears that my belief in the Spirit might be delusional and I was really all alone in the world. Deep feelings of sadness and helplessness lurked beneath my fears. I began to feel trapped by the situation.

Against my better judgment, Artem and I started looking at houses. It felt more than a little strange that at the same time I was trying to remodel my own house I was actively working to start a new business--buying and remodeling homes to sell. This adventure was either an act of serious magical thinking, or a true demonstration of blind faith, or perhaps a bit of both. Actually it was a blatant disregard for obvious facts and conventional wisdom. I had not yet sold my house in St. Louis, and I had no idea where the money was going to come from to develop and sustain this business, but I was proceeding enthusiastically.

However, when Artem and I found a house right in Sausalito with excellent potential and a breathtaking view, I thought that this move could allow me the opportunity to live one of my best dreams every day, which is remodeling houses. Exploring resources to put this plan in motion, Artem suggested that the most efficient way with the least risk would be to sell the home I live in. I was outraged. He had a hard time understanding the emotional attachment I, my children, and many other people have to this house. For him it was rather cut and dried--to use all available assets to multiply future earnings. Probably this was the reason he didn't have any assets of his own. In his opinion, I was making a decision between making my family happy by keeping the house, or selling it and living my own dream. He didn't seem to grasp the fact that I can never really live my own dream if it didn't include my family and the values and history we share. While I was not willing to sell the family home, the symbol of our multigenerational life together, I was willing to consider leasing my house. The money from the lease would be used to pay the note on the new house, which I (we) would live in during remodeling.

Putting the remodeling project for my house on the back burner, Artem fell in love with the new Sausalito property and stayed up for two nights working on a plan to maximize its potential with the least expenditure. After several drafts, he came up with an idea that we both liked and thought practical. I was somewhat concerned about his amateur design, level of insecurity and strong need for my approval, but I minimized what I was feeling. I reassured myself of his competence. We had many discussions regarding the pros and cons of this investment, and we mutually decided that it would be a good one. The initial asking price based on an earlier assessment was one million dollars. However after several months on the market, the price was lowered to eight hundred ninety-nine thousand. Bank of America is the trustee for several houses owned by a deceased benefactor who left her entire estate to the Humane Society. I decided to offer seven hundred fifty thousand, which was far more than I could afford. It was my way of testing the Spirit and the market. I told myself if it was the Spirit's will they would accept it, and if they didn't, I didn't want it.

In the meantime I thought about the quantum leap in responsibility I would have to make if they did accept it, and what other path would open if they didn't. My offer was rejected. I accepted this as the Spirit's statement that it was either not the right thing to do, or not the right time, or both. I now know that my adventure of flying in the face of reason was mostly magical thinking, and fortunately nothing happened. The spirit continued to protect me in my slumber.

Artem was, for the most part, a self-taught carpenter. He presented himself as being more skilled than he actually was. Before I realized this truth, we had many fanciful conversations about grandiose ideas, including building a monument to the Spirit. The architect Alfredo, an acquaintance of Artem's, had recently moved from Italy to California. He also was without a license or a green card and needed work. Alfredo was excited about the project and offered to draw up plans, charging only twenty-five dollars per hour. (I thought I was getting a deal, but the jury was still out at this time.) His design was very elaborate and quite elegant. I have a flair for fine aesthetics, and was impressed with his drawings and was very complimentary. However, I had no idea what was required in the actual building of the design nor its appropriateness for the steep hillside I lived on.

Artem had hired Alfredo to help him with some carpentry on another job. He complained about Alfredo's inability to follow directions and insistence on doing his own thing. The two became very competitive, although their skills were very different. On this occasion, I was not unaware of what appeared to be jealousy on Artem's part. Things became increasingly more complicated when they began to work together. During our three-way meetings, it became necessary for me to mediate their differences, and I felt caught in the middle of two bickering children. Artem later told me that he only went along with Alfredo's design because I liked it. He began to question Alfredo's competence, and I quietly began to question my judgment in getting into the most costly and toxic triangle to date.

What had appeared to be an organic flow was taking on the characteristics of a crusty corroding old sewer system. Things progressed very slowly, down to a trickle. We had to make many trips to City Hall, in part because Alfredo was not familiar with the many regulations and requirements by the City. I think he was further handicapped by being a new architect with a limited command of the English language. The building inspector for Sausalito informed us that an engineer would be required. I accepted Alfredo's recommendation of an engineer because I felt the two of them needed to work together. The engineer was from Iran, talked very fast, and was often difficult for me to understand. He agreed to do the job for $4500 dollars, assuring me that this was less than his usual fee, and he was doing me a favor because he thought that I was a nice lady. Although I didn't realize it at the time, the idea of him doing me a favor prevailed in all of our subsequent conversations. I came to realize that the favor was not mine.

Sausalito is notorious for its detailed and elaborate require-ments for building permits. None of us were prepared for the extent of the difficulties. On one of my visits to City Hall, the Building Manager pointed out major flaws in both the architect's and engineer's plans. He said it might not look like it but the City "had my back" on this. It was necessary for the engineer to have many more phone conversations and write several letters, which seemed to exasperate and overwhelm him. In the process of going back and forth with the building inspector, I started to lose confidence in the architect and question the competency of the engineer. Artem became increasingly critical of them also, and seemed to take delight in complaining and blaming, which was very annoying to me. As time went on, I began to see blatant evidence of Artem's incompetence. He seemed unable to follow building plans. Although I had seen some of the work he had done, it was all done extemporaneously from his own ideas.

After several tumultuous months we finally received a building permit. By this time, Artem was working for another customer, and the next thing I knew, he had brought several Mexicans in to work for me, claiming it was to save me money. Things seemed to quickly get out of hand. When Artem did show up he was more interested in going to the store to buy supplies and playing straw boss than doing any of the actual work. He was making decisions without my input, and spending my money without my permission. When I objected, he assured me he was saving me money, that I should trust him, be patient, and in the end I would like the job. I started to see him as unfocused, defensive, manipulative, controlling, and avoiding the work. As my doubts grew stronger, I wanted to stop the project, but by this time things had gone too far.

I became so upset and angry with Artem that I yelled at him on several occasions, and at one point had a strong desire to hit him. I have a real appreciation for the rage women develop in relationships where they feel controlled and discounted. After awhile, I could hardly look at him, and made little response to his efforts to be nice, which I could only feel as attempts to manipulate me further. I struggled with my feelings until I felt that I was literally choking.

I realized that these very strong feelings must be deeper than my relationship with him, whom I'd only known for about a year. Subsequently I became aware that they were primal feelings related to my father. Finally I knew I had to express my feelings to Artem. I invited him over and he came, bringing dinner. I told him I felt betrayed, deserted, controlled, and disregarded. It's my impression that under the disguise of wanting to please me the truth is that he wants me to accept whatever he decides to do.

I took responsibility for my feelings, and told him that the conversation with him was more about me and less about him. I told him that if I had known what our joint efforts were going to end up being, I would not have taken the journey. He could relate to this because he had shared with me that if he had known his wife better, he wouldn't have married her. Not once did he admit that he was in way over his head.

The disappointment I felt in this experience is shared by many people who enter a relationship with an intention thought to be mutual, only to find out it wasn't. Artem had said that the purpose of human life is to create. It was my understanding that the two of us would work together to build a monument to the

Spirit. I told him that the Spirit could not be controlled, and that if the two of us had been in the Spirit, it would have been a whole different experience. In the beginning of our relationship, we talked a lot about the Spirit, and it seemed we had a heart connection. Artem told me that religion and spirituality had not been a part of his upbringing. However, he seemed intrigued and quickly learned the lingo. He often referred to me as his spiritual teacher, and on some level I accepted this responsibility. I was gratified by his responsiveness, and probably I was willing to see more growth than truly existed. I am now more acutely aware of my eagerness to believe what I want to hear. I have developed a healthy caution for paying less attention to what one says and more to what one does.

Whatever involvement we shared and enjoyed in the past ended for me when I became aware that Truth was not our mutual goal. The Spirit is present in any relationship where love exists; however, there is no love without Truth. When personal agendas are not openly expressed, the relationship usually ends in conflict. In my opinion some of Artem's personal agendas were hidden from his own awareness. I think his hidden agenda to obtain a green card was one of the reasons the woman he accused of breaking his heart terminated their relationship. I also believe it was this covert motive of his that undermined our relationship, not to mention his unspoken interest in my financial resources.

From his perspective, he was loving, kind, generous, and helpful. He admitted he had enjoyed the home, social life, and other advantages the relationship with his ex offered. He failed to realize that in all his giving, he did not give her what she wanted. A recent Oprah show featured an expert in the area of men who are in extreme need for control. According to her, all controlling and abusing men are scared little boys at heart. They have a primal fear of being left and abandoned by the person who is the source of their nurturing. Unlike women, many men do not form nurturing relationships with other men. They often have single primary relationships with one or more women and are very frightened of rejection.

In my continued reflection on the disappointing (bordering devastating) state of my relationship with Artem, I became aware that my lessons with him were a repeat performance of my tendency to lose myself in relationships with controlling men just to keep the peace. Although I was fully aware of Artem's strong need for control, at first I was amused by it because I wasn't yet caught up in it.

However, in our "joint" venture to remodel my home, I was not only at affect of his control but trapped by my financial investment. It turned out that our venture went from exciting to stagnant to downright painful and destructive. The dream had become a nightmare. Artem tried to feign competence and gave very little consideration to my input. He insisted he was saving me money and I should trust him. He seemed to have little respect for the fact that I was the customer, and he was spending my money without restraint. The loss of potential, the disappearance of an illusion, is always painful. My grief ran deep.

Serendipitously I attended a workshop called "Tell it Like it Is." I had a light bulb moment when the facilitator said, "We can only communicate at the level of the least common denominator," that is, at the level that each participant is willing and able to communicate. Being oblivious to this has been very costly to me in a number of my relationships, especially with Artem. While it is true that everybody knows the truth on some level, people are not equal in their ability to recognize and act on the truth. In the past I have engaged with people with the dangerous assumption that they shared my truth, and I was hurt when they did not respond in kind. In the past I have contributed my inability to connect with others in truth to some personal deficit; perhaps I didn't express myself in the right way, or became frustrated and angry when people were unable to hear my truth through my strong emotions. I am now willing to let go of my expectations for people to communicate with me in a way that I find personally satisfying. I will try to hear and accept their truth in the way they express it. I will look for personal satisfaction where it can be found, and remember the teaching of the Sufis: "Leave when the work is done, and leave empty handed."

There are stark similarities between the lessons Artem taught me and those taught by Melvin, Richie, and Faye, all master teachers for me. In these relationships I was willing to be blinded by what I wanted. Certainly the truth about their need to control did not escape me; however, I rationalize the impact, denied my vulnerability, and minimized my difficulty in handling the situations. Richie, Faye, and Artem all perceived me to be wealthy and felt entitled to my resources. Melvin was highly skilled at projecting blame and making me responsible for his shortcomings. Richie was convinced that his metaphysical knowledge and physical strength entitled him to command and control his environment and everybody in it. Not only did he speak with great authority, he was a physical bully. Faye and Artem shared the art of seduction with their showering of attention and anticipating my needs. Faye thought it was my responsibility to take care of her because I had more, an attitude of tribalism which did not include contributions from her. I was often confused about who was doing what to whom.

Artem had a sense of proprietorship, resulting from his delusion that his behavior was actually helping me, masking his extreme need to be in charge. He is very comfortable with a "care taking" role, bringing meals, flowers, sweets, etc. These are the tools of his trade and his mask of defense. I have come to see this behavior as deposits for his entitlement to control. His effort toward helping me obtain my dream was really a dream identified by him and became a nightmare for me. The physical evidence is that I am not better but much worse off as a result of his so-called "help."

He decided to sell his truck for a cheaper one; among other reasons he he said he needed the money to finish my garden. This was a boldfaced lie. I did not think selling his truck, which he needed for his work, was a good idea, and I told him so. In his typical fashion, he assured me he was getting a good deal. He was buying a "new" used truck for half its value, and he had checked the engine which was good.

The next day he informed me that the truck stopped when he got it home, and it needed a new starter. I told him that I did not want to be a part of that decision because I disagreed with it. I also did not want him to complete the garden. I said that this situation was another example of his doing what he wanted to do disguised as helping me. If he should realize that his choice was not a good one, I did not want him to be able to misconstrue his motivation as being altruistic. He said that I always made him feel guilty, but he also admitted that the real reason for selling the truck was that he needed money for his family and his immigration fees. The degree of his self deception about his behavior and intentions was absolutely flabbergasting. We agreed that he is not the man to complete the unfinished work. I assured him that when the two of us got disentangled from the web of confusion, the Spirit would send the perfect carpenter to complete the garden and the deck.

I told him that my real pain came from my inability now to find the Spirit in our relationship. Because he did not listen, I felt unsafe and unable to trust our friendship. I asked him to refrain from bringing me gifts or doing me favors. Perhaps this would help us both find the Spirit (Truth) again. He admitted that he did not know how to fix the relationship. I don't think he realized that such a "fix" required a level of integrity which he didn't have. I am aware that when the "honeymoon is over," and the power struggles get resolved, there might be little or no basis for continuing a relationship. When Artem was unable to refrain from the caretaking role, I suggested that we discontinue our relationship. I hope I have learned to recognize that when the Spirit leaves a relationship, it is also time for my departure.

In retrospect, in many of my relationships, I see I had given up my ability to honor myself. When I focus on what I want rather than what is, I separate myself from the truth. I hope I have learned that in the face of strong external desires, I will be careful to seek internal directions. When I fail to do this, the results are painful, but after a while the pain fades and the lesson is forgotten, until it reappears in a different form. This time I fully experienced the pain and accepted my responsibility for my feelings of betrayal.

For several months, there were four huge holes for a nonexistent platform in the front of my yard which I saw every time I went in or out. The holes were both actual and metaphoric. Now they have been filled in and provide a fine home for beautiful Japanese maple trees and luscious ferns. Even so, it's unlikely that I will ever forget what's underneath them.

Although I have not seen Artem for a long time, I heard through the grapevine that he and Jennifer were doing a lot of drinking, fighting, and blaming each other. I don't know if he ever got his green card.

Artem could be considered a weapon of mass destruction to the sleeping soul. As the Buddhists say: "All pain is a result of desire." Desire and attachment distort perception, and one is unable to see the truth; however, the truth exists whether we choose to see it or not. To quote my mother, "A lie can travel around the world as it often does but the truth is always there waiting on it to reveal itself." When we hide from the truth, we hold on to the past and rob ourselves of a true presence, the only time in which self recognition and self change can be realized. We can learn from the past, and avoid repeating our mistakes. The seed of the beginning is always present in the shell of the ending.

Shirley McLain expresses my new sentiments: "I believe that each of us human beings serves ourselves and others as we try to understand our soul's journey through time. I believe that the people in our lives who hurt us the most are true servants to our learning. I believe it is time to get off the wheel of victimization and pay tribute to those who open our eyes regardless of how hard their methods might be. They are masters in their own way. They stimulate us to know ourselves. I became free of blinding dependency."

Keith, one of Artem's friends, was looking for a place to rent around the time Artem moved out. Artem and I were still on good terms at the time, and he arranged for Keith and me to meet. I had actually already met him when he was substituting for one of my yoga teachers. He was an architect, between thirty-five and forty, mild mannered and soft spoken. His light brown pony tail suggested the era of a hippie. I also saw him periodically at social gatherings with Artem in Sausalito.

Initially Keith wanted to move in right away, but when I interviewed him, he seemed hesitant and said he wanted to think about it. I think the truth was that he was going on vacation for a couple of weeks and wanted to reserve the room without paying for that time. As it turned out, he was detained in Mexico when his girlfriend lost her passport, and although he had left some of his clothes in the vacant room, he asked if he could start paying from the date he actually moved in, because he had spent a lot of his money in Mexico. Although I failed to see what this had to do with me, I agreed, to maintain peace and start the relationship on a good footing. I thought I was being considerate and understanding. I didn't recognize at the time that this was my codependent tendency rearing its ugly head again.

After he had been living in the house for about three months, I was preparing to leave for my trip to St. Louis. He told me that he had some issues with the house. He was sensitive to the mold in his bathroom, and claimed there was an odor in his bedroom. We agreed that he could take the responsibility for getting the room painted and cleaning the mold in exchange for a reduction in rent. He also said that he wanted to live in more of a community atmosphere, sharing things like cooking, cleaning, and companionship. He was ready to be married and settle down with a family, but he and his girlfriend had numerous issues that needed to be negotiated first.

After my experiences with Artem, I was hardly eager to become emotionally involved with another roommate. Keith and I did not share activities, but maintained a friendship of mutual respect and positive regard. He paid his rent on time and occasionally offered supportive gestures, like folding my laundry, washing dishes he hadn't used, and trying to help me find a carpenter and other skilled workers to repair the disastrous damage in my yard that Artem had spearheaded. It was our agreement to share the cost of utilities. We also agreed that he would not pay one month's rent in exchange for his drawing an architectural design for fixing my front porch. Several months passed and I told myself that I was giving him time to do the plans, and he understood our agreement about the utilities, so there would be no problem whenever I presented him with the bill.

I recognized in this rationalization my pattern of abdicating my responsibilities for written contracts. It's easier for me to assume that both parties bring equal integrity to the table and will act accordingly. I know this defies good business practices, and that written contracts are the time honored method and container for both people's integrity. If either person seeks to gain advantage over the other, verbal agreements will be altered according to the person's agenda. Memory is always under the influence of the ego.

In my characteristic style of procrastinating and Keith's style of avoidance, we did not get around to settling the utility bills until he was ready to move out, a year later. His share by this time amounted to around $1200 dollars. Also I never received the architectural plans, and even though he had brought over several potential contractors, none followed through with the job. I started feeling vulnerable and recognized the situation as all too familiar. At this point I opened to seeing my participation in creating another codependency and setting myself up as a victim. Because it was less emotionally entangled, I was able to see it sooner. When I finally presented him with the bill, without resistance he stepped up to the plate and accepted his responsibility. I appreciated the fact that he did not "go south;" he paid the bill. We agreed on a compromise for reimbursement for his time spent on the porch project (but without results).

After about eighteen months he found his own apartment, but moved out slowly. He asked if he could pay me to store his antique jeep and some other things in my garage. We agreed on a hundred per month, and he paid for the first five months. After this time, he became irregular, and when I brought it to his attention, he expressed good intentions but lacked consistent follow through. I also asked him several times to move his jeep, but to no avail. Apparently the jeep was symbolic of his desire to have a home of his own and a place to store it. I helped him explore the possibility of getting a less demanding, less expensive symbol for his desire for a home.

Clutter was a major issue for both of us. After he left, we agreed to support each other in getting rid of our stuff. He helped me clean out the garage. We had a successful garage sale, and with my prodding, he has come over about five times since to continue our joint efforts to handle our excess. I was impressed that Keith continued to show up and take responsibility. He seemed to be one who wanted to "go the distance," and I acknowledged his desire to do so. He was very appreciative of my compliments and thanked me for helping him to grow up. We completed cleaning out the garage with the exception of his jeep. He paid most of the back rent and eventually moved the jeep; however, he left still owing me money. When I attempted to collect it, he too went south. Unfortunately this turned out not to be the corrective emotional experience we had both hoped for. The promise that he would be different in his acceptance of personal responsibility faded as it became clear that he did not have enough stored integrity to push the rock all the way up the hill.

Meanwhile, the roommate relay continued. Keith's girl friend Heidi, who had been the topic of many of our discussions, lost her home of seven years when the houseboat Vallejo was sold. She needed a temporary place to stay, and I had already met her. One Sunday after church she asked if she could move in to Keith's old room, and I agreed. She stayed about two months, and moved out when I brought home a seventeen year old potential foster son for a pre-placement visit. I didn't know he had serious boundary issues, and he went into Heidi's room without permission and recorded his message on her answering machine. Understandably, she felt invaded. She told me that she was an only child and had never lived with children, much less disturbed teenagers. I told her it could be an opportunity for her growth; however, I could certainly understand if she didn't choose to accept the challenge. She declined the mission, so this triangle had a short lifespan.

I was enjoying living alone for several months, when Donna, one of my angels, asked me to allow her oldest brother to live in my spare room for one month until he found permanent housing. It seems that Billy had taken care of their mother while she was ill, and has been between jobs since her death. He had lived in Donna's apartment for several months, but she was now getting a new roommate and needed the space. She said Billy had been very helpful to her and she thought in exchange for a room he would be a blessing to me. She claimed he could fix anything. He would soon find his way in the world and make it big, she thought.

I had seen Billy several times years ago when Donna worked at my house. He is an average looking sixty-three-year-old man with thinning gray hair. We had an initial meeting where he talked profusely about reverse mortgages, attempting to convince me that he knew everything about everything. Overwhelmed with the barrage of information, I told him I was not feeling well but before I retired, we agreed he would move in for a month in exchange for helping me with various projects and work around the house. We planned to evaluate the situation at the end of the month, and although the basic agreement was vague, we decided to extend his stay indefinitely. I didn't realize it at the time, but this vagueness was the prototype for my codependent relationships, and I was backsliding into another one.

Billy proved to be quite green, changing all the light bulbs to halogen, and suggesting switching to low flow toilets and shower-heads. He made himself useful around the house, carrying my groceries, etc. He was quite willing to drive me wherever I needed to go. His primary relationship was with his computer, and they were together 24/7. Until very recently he had three email accounts, and was very computer savvy. His desktop publishing skills were very useful to me in creating personalized greeting cards, especially at Christmas, and he was a big help in handling my emails.

He had a combative nature and a real affinity for the uses of the law. He delighted in verbal and written sparring which on occasion worked to my advantage. For example, I bought some Christmas cards which had a minor defect and he took it upon himself to write to the company. As a compensation they sent a large box of variety cards. On another occasion I discovered that the dental care I had received for twenty years was substandard, and he researched the dentist's history and found the perfect attorney to represent me in the case. He was very thorough in reviewing a real estate investment I was making in St. Louis, and when I traveled he crossed all the T's and dotted all the I's to ensure my ease and safety.

On the other hand, there were several incidents of his poor judgment and the absence of clear boundaries. By now I had a teenaged foster son living in the home. He told me that he had paid Billy to drive him to his girl friend's house after I went to sleep, and to pick him up before morning. It seemed that Justin had become Billy's resource for his gas money. There were other occasions when Billy aligned himself with the teenagers rather than me as the responsible adult. Using my phone, Billy removed the call waiting feature so his personal calls would not be disturbed. On one occasion he charged his answering service to my credit card without my permission, claiming he planned to tell me before I got the bill.

He was unwilling to be accountable for the time he spent on my behalf. He had a beautiful rent free room in my house in the Sausalito hills. I paid his monthly internet bill, and he freely helped himself to my household supplies and food. He also drove my car for his errands and did not replace the gas. He claimed that I *knew* what he was doing for me, and was insulted that I wanted a written account. He insisted that he was giving more than he was getting. From my perspective he had become increasingly comfortable with the arrangement and I didn't feel that I was getting what I was paying for. We had heated discussions about this situation without resolution. I told him that we needed some kind of objective measurement. Failing to get one I became increasingly frustrated, and everything he did irritated me. I had promised myself that I would never remain in a situation where I was unable to resolve conflict or negotiate differences. (I now know why trapped housewives are called "bitches.")

I made repeated requests for him to get fingerprinted and pass a background check, routine requirements for anyone living in a home with foster children. In his passive aggressive manner, Billy had managed to avoid doing so for the past year and a half. In spite of this, the social worker and I had been exceedingly patient, but I became increasingly uncomfortable with my participation in circumventing rules which are designed to protect children. I also became resentful of his refusal to resolve our differences or even be accountable. I gradually awakened to yet another codependent relationship and the nuances of my pattern of rationalizing things I don't like and making myself comfortable with things I do like, all in the disguise of keeping the peace. I again had failed to get a clear understanding and a written agreement of our arrangement.

Things were coming to a head because in addition to all of the perks I supplied him with, for three months I "loaned" him money for his special email account, which he did not repay. Even so, he was also asking me to give him about $150 dollars a month more to pay his other bills. When I refused he became angry and accusatory, telling me I belittled him and didn't appreciate him and was insensitive and inconsiderate of his financial dilemma. He was unwilling to discuss our differences or provide a written account of his activities. He refused to speak to me for an entire day.

Intensely uncomfortable in my own house, I was forced to review my participation in this unhealthy relationship. When I told my daughter he had become angry and yelled at me, she decided to intervene and have a talk with him. She too was unsatisfied with his refusal to be accountable for his part of the bargain. In the heat of the moment Billy said he was leaving and Nita gave him a deadline. In addition, she arranged for her brother Deely to move in to facilitate a smooth transition. He was ready to escape his current living situation with his ex-wife.

Within a few days Deely showed up carting all his worldly possessions and made himself at home. When I told him his stay would be temporary because I planned to lease the house, he became very emotional and threatened by the idea of being homeless, and he acted out a humorous version of his fears. Billy was thoroughly entertained by Deely's lively display of emotions, which was a graphic demonstra-tion of his own repressed fears. Billy told me he really liked Deely.

Initially, Deely and Billy got along fine. However, when I left them alone for a week, the dynamics of an insecure elderly white man and a hotheaded insecure young black man collided. Apparently it got ugly, with Deely slinging words of truth that hit below the belt. This again proved that when we do not express our feelings, those around us will express them for us. Deely said everything that I had been thinking about Billy but considered too rude to say.

In case I had any ambivalence about his leaving, the universe miraculously provided a place for Billy to go. My nephew Melvin, who has been on dialysis for fifteen years, lives alone and needs an in-home support person. He suggested that Billy could move in with him, and he would provide free room and board and a small salary. I presented this offer to Billy and he said he would consider it, although he would prefer to remain in the North Bay near his brother and sister. The fact that Melvin had no car was of concern to Billy. I told him he could consider his options as long as he liked, but he needed to be out by our agreed date. Billy dragged his feet until the very last moment, and he ended up choosing to go to a shelter.

Since our "clean and sober" (non-codependent) relationship, he became much more pleasant. We attempted to explore opportunities to work together for which I would reimburse him financially. After a few exchanges it became quite clear to me that his inflated sense of his value and my view of his effectiveness were worlds apart. At our last meeting his charge was so exorbitant for the service rendered that I knew we had finished our dance.

It is my lifetime work to refrain from codependency, whenever and wherever I see it coming, in me or anyone else. I must be finally learning the lesson, because this one was much gentler, shorter, even light-hearted by comparison to others. Instead of the stick becoming a two-by-four, the two-by-four has become the stick! It gives me hope to recognize that I have made progress in confronting my shadow, but it continues to lurk around dimly lit corners. I continue to bite certain delectable, irresistible bait, such as a combination of need, humility, and hard work. Throw a few children in the elixir, and I am completely anesthetized.

I decided to write a program which would teach children, especially foster children, how to navigate life more effectively. I called the program "The Art of Gentle Self Discipline." It occurred to me that I could benefit from applying the principles of the program to my own life by taking a disciplined approach to creating more financial abundance. My house is my largest resource, and I had been using it very inefficiently. I confronted my emotional attachment to living in my beautiful house head on. It was another opportunity for an examination of the spectrum of my patterns of codependency. It was clear to me that I either needed to lease it or use it more fully. Dealing with my own and my family's feelings about the possibility of leaving the house brought all sorts of repressed and not so repressed feelings up for discussion. Ultimately I decided to remodel the house and share it with foster children.

For some reasons unknown to me at the time, I irrationally

insisted on hiring a painter named Jose. He was brought to the job site by a friend who was the primary bidder, who bid himself so high he went straight out of the ball park. A few days later Jose returned, presenting himself as the underdog, and offered to do the job for two thousand dollars less. He said he needed the work to take care of his family. He commented that he had known his friend for ten years, and that his friend had lots of jobs and he had nothing. He assured me he would do a good job, but asked that I not tell his friend about his offer. I told him I did not want to be part of a conspiracy, and suggested he tell his friend and offer him a finder's fee. My suggestion was not received with enthusiasm. Although I was put off by his willingness to throw his friend under the bus, I was tempted by his lower bid, even though it was not the lowest of all. The real hook seemed, now in retrospect, to be his humility and neediness, and the feeling that I could be helpful.

A dear friend Harriet whose judgment I trust was visiting at the time. I ran this scenario by her and asked her opinion. I was thinking that hiring Jose would be going against my own values of honesty and openness. Although I knew I had already made up my mind to hire him, because the decision seemed irrational even to me, I sought outside counsel. Harriet told me that business was business and while I was not obligated to inform the original bidder of my decision, I needed to inform Jose that I would not agree to secrecy or be part of deceptive practices. I told myself that the reason for my uncertainty was a concern about rationalizing choices made out of self-deception.

Two lengthy hospitalizations and several sudden disappear-ances from the job site, not to mention failure to show up for work when expected, and forwarding all the phone calls to an answering machine, I realized that my real concern was my pattern of combining business and welfare. My bleeding social worker's heart had emerged again and overpowered my better judgment. Another classic act of codependency on my part! Typical of a codependent personality, once the seesaw is in motion it is very hard to get off. During his prolonged absences I called him daily, sometimes twice a day, and talked to his answering machine. I tried to express understanding and a willingness to help. Although he failed to return my calls, during a two-week absence, he had the hospital social worker call me to say that he had not run off with my money for paint, and really wanted to continue the job. When I didn't respond immediately, he had the social worker call again the next day.

A few days later he arrived at my door wearing his hospital bracelet as proof of his story. He promised to show up for work bright and early the next day. He worked for two days and then disappeared for three more. When he was here however, I took every graceful opportunity to talk to him about his drinking problem. Among many others, one of his issues was describing himself as a victim. I learned that his "family" is really in Mexico and he has no relatives in this area. He told me his daughter and wife no longer love him, and that his wife has had two babies by another man.

My gentle probing revealed that every evening he was passed out drunk when his wife came home from work. I asked if he thought it was fun to be married to someone who was often comatose--that it was the same as being married to a dead man, and asked him what was the point? He looked surprised, as if he'd never heard this perspective before. He said he drank at least a quart of tequila a day, and therefore had no money to send to his twelve-year-old daughter. I suggested that this was a clear statement that tequila was more important to him than his daughter's needs, and that perhaps she was angry about this and this was the reason she refused to talk to him on the phone. Again he appeared surprised.

While I was in my waltz with Jose, I observed my reaction to his addictive patterns of anxiety and fast getaways. He starts moving quickly and talking fast, a very effective way to get what he wants. My inclination (and I'm sure that of other codependents) is to escape from my own anxiety which is created by his agitated behavior and urgency in his voice.

Although I know he liked to be paid in cash at the end of the day, I didn't get money from the bank in advance, so the two of us had to make a trip to the bank. After completing our transaction Jose went on his way. I went to get some vacuum bags at a local market, and was told by the clerk that they were very expensive and I should try Long's. Following his advice, I left the store and proceeded to have an accident that cost me several thousand dollars. I was probably distracted by the replay of my scenario with Jose, and I did not see the coming car. My Prelude was totaled, but fortunately no one was seriously hurt. Needless to say I was very shaken. I did not feel grounded and was unable to be consoled by the excuses offered to me by well-meaning friends and family. I knew the accident was my fault, and I accepted responsibility.

Now I was faced with a question: should I stop driving? I don't want to be one of those little old ladies who put other people's lives in danger. I am still contemplating this dilemma, as I cautiously resume limited daytime driving. In a quandary, I decided to pray . My prayer was answered and I was led directly to buy the right car for me at this time. I realized that my willingness to live in the mystery is a requirement for hearing the voice of God. My practice now is to become more comfortable in a state of not knowing. Although the accident was very costly in many ways, I was also willing to accept the blessing the experience brought. I decided to use it as an opportunity to learn again that God is my true source.

After a couple more weeks of two steps forward and three steps back, he told me he was going to AA and had stopped drinking. He looked much healthier, and had even bought himself some new brushes. His old ones were in such bad shape that I had offered to invest in some decent brushes for him. I told him my mother said that it was a poor carpenter that complained about his tools, and that if you take care of your tools, they will take care of you. Like a proud mother I was very pleased because the new brushes seemed like a promising sign.

I am both excited and challenged by the universe's insistence on waking me up. For about a week he worked every day and seemed more focused, and more than anxious to please me. But then he disappeared again and hasn't been seen since. I know that recovery is a slippery slope and that relapse is part of the process. Fortunately most of his work here is finished. I am now in a position that I'm not too inconvenienced by his erratic work ethic. I am reflecting on the seductive disguises of my inclination towards codependency, with the intention of pulling back the veil of half awareness to full consciousness. I might continue to rescue strays, but I hope it will be done with free choice and without emotional charge or expectation. Given who I am, I have decided that is as much as I can hope for. In fact, I doubt that we ever truly change. What we really do is manage.

On my last several trips to St. Louis I was working on

remodeling houses for low income families. This project required frequent contact with several family members who were paid to assist me. They all shared similar issues resulting from our family codependency malaise. I was overwhelmed by the number and the intensity of the problems in our interactions. I found myself becoming increasingly impatient and irritable. The manifestation of the collected stress showed up in an unprecedented breaking out of sores and blisters on my face, including a sore throat, sore teeth, and earache. Initially the doctor thought I had shingles, but changed his diagnosis to a bacterial infection. I knew I had been attacked. The symptoms seemed to be directing me to examine everything I saw, heard, felt or chewed on. At this point I was highly motivated to do so.

On the trip to the doctor, Keith and I were discussing my emotional attachment to my family. I told him that the time had come for me to truly let go. He assured me that I had worked very hard to "help" my family, and now it was time for me to simply say my truth and leave the acceptance to the others. He shared his passion for Black History, saying he had felt disappointed when others hadn't shared his enthusiasm. In time he came to realize people have their own things to be enthusiastic about. It occurred to me that most people are probably not interested in understanding their own behavior much less human behavior in general. Since this is my favorite pastime, it should come as no surprise that these same people would find me hard to take.

I told him that when I'm able to state my truth without attachment to the reactions of others, I will have achieved my goal--freedom from codependency. Taking it a step further, I realized that one of the ways I had learned to express love and caring was through service, being helpful. I acted as if the more I did was an indication of how much I cared. I have known for some time that when someone I love is hurting, I hurt. I was unable to untangle the enmeshment of our shared pain because I felt I was responsible for making it better. I don't know when or how my pain became confused with caring. Compassion does not require taking on the burden of another.

Since my recent wake up calls, I experienced several light bulb moments, recognizing that I can feel compassion without pain. In fact, sometimes my strong emotions might be in conflict with what is truly helpful for the other person. I could see how my strongly expressed emotions might even be overwhelming or even frightening to the other person. My solutions to their problems could deny their right to self determination and personal responsibility.

The primary lessons that my painter, my family, my clients, roommates and foster children and *life* have taught me is that all problems are the result of not loving ourselves enough. I decided to focus on loving me and to rescue and heal myself.

Codependency is an attempt to get from others the love we fail to give to ourselves. It is an ineffective way of trying to get love vicariously, and it contami-nates the authenticity of unconditional love. Why not go for the real thing? All we have to do is remove the barriers we have erected against it. I have almost suspended the habit of self-judgment, affirming who I am unconditionally.

From a small child, I recognized that some relationships between men and women could be deadly landmines. Subsequently I promised myself that I would avoid financial dependency on a man at any cost. I was less vigilant about emotional and social dependencies, because I didn't know how. I had to learn the hard way to separate dependency from desire. The process has a meaning.

The pastor of my church in Sausalito invited his sister who is also a minister to give the sermon. She is the complete antithesis of what I expected. She is the white pastor of a predominantly black church in Harlem. She was an actor before going to seminary. She has very short blond hair, and she projects an encompassing aura; she is dramatically engaging in her presentation. Her sermon seemed almost a blue print of my path, my belief system, and my way of relating to the world. I was blown out by the similarities of our experiences: we're both minister's daughters, we both grew up in St. Louis, and are strongly drawn to art as a gateway to the Divine. At a luncheon after church, we both felt a magnetic draw between us and recognized each other as kindred souls.

I had a strong feeling that this encounter had been staged for some time. I was pleased with her reframed perspective on Lent—she described it as a time for self exploration and discovery, not depri-vation. But the price of admission for me was the awareness that the caterpillar withdraws into its cocoon prior to transformation. During this stage, it liquefies and changes its DNA. The butterfly is indeed a NEW creature. This is similar to my own experience with the process. In the initial stages the substance was liquid. Over the years it took on more form until it was solid. In this way I could feel my DNA being transformed. Outwardly I might appear to be the same but inside I am totally new.

CHAPTER SEVEN
MATURITY ~ SELF ACCEPTANCE
"As we grow older, we stand for more and fall for less."

Growing older is a necessity, but maturity is an option. Maturity is earned, and some of its fruits are patience, wisdom, acceptance, and generosity. Blessed are those who know the Self. Youthful folly and the search for identity require great effort and energy. On the other hand, the wisdom of maturity and the awareness of who we are is a state of being. It requires little effort and generates its own energy. When we learn to stop focusing on our imperfections, we are able to see our divine reflection.

I have always liked to be around older people. I have received great benefits from the wisdom and counsel of people who have been where I'm going. Being in their company also helps me understand some of the challenges of aging, and different responses to it. Having a blueprint has helped me choose my responses more consciously and I hope gracefully.

My mother always said, "It is a wise person who benefits from another's mistakes." I have always wanted to be wise so I took this to heart. Lots of people want to run off to do things their own way. These people are often ignorant about what they don't know, and would be better off remaining with the pack, especially until they learn what the pack knows. Al Gore said in "Inconvenient Truth," that it is not what we don't know that hurts us, but what we think we know for sure (that is not true) which will destroy us.

Becoming mature requires daily and constant practice of the desired behaviors. As birthdays grow in number, so do losses. The loss of 20/20 vision, perfect hearing, hair, a full set of teeth, even friends and family; all these losses bring new challenges. It is not easy to accept them, and impossible to do so without maturity and grace. In the words of Joan Crawford, "Growing old ain't for sissies."

In the practice of becoming mature, one has to cultivate a relationship with one's own spirit. Said differently, one has to come to oneself, so that one's giving is from a full cup. We have to be willing to listen to and express our own truth, or we become disconnected from it. Many people take better care of maintaining their cars than their own spirits. We give up ourselves in the attempt to please others or try to live by other people's truth. This habit is a state of illusion, and of course separates us from the Self. We have to be willing to spend enough time with the spirit so it can grow stronger than our ego and direct our lives.

New habits require commitment and daily practice. Anything you are devoted to can become a gateway to the divine. Step by step, the more we repeat an action, the easier it gets. Once we know the path, when we stray we can always find our way back. Eventually it becomes our natural state of being. In the words of Aristotle, "We are what we consistently do. Excellence is not an act but a habit." The spirit is all-knowing, all-loving, and affirms the good in all and harms none. Why would we not want it to direct our lives?

On my way to maturity, I have found several Gateways to the Divine:

1. Pain and Struggle

If one struggles sincerely, hard enough and long enough, against or for anything, one will come to discover the "Truth" and its connection of all things. With this awareness one recognizes one's personal power to change anything.

2. The Other

Union with a lover, an oracle, spiritual teacher, scripture, meditation, (union with the Self), yoga, and other experiences lead us to the awareness of love as the spirit which connects all things. The higher self emerges when personal selves are joined.

3. Nature

Mother Earth is our sacred gift. Many people lose themselves in the beauty of a sunset, the vastness of the ocean, the warmth of a fire, or the peace of the forest. This loss of the personal self gives birth to the higher self which connects all there is.

4. Illness, Death and Loss

A serious illness, severe grief, loss of a loved one or

cherished pet or possession, or deep helplessness of any kind, thrusts us into surrendering the personal self.

5. Art

Inspired artists are able to communicate the Spirit through their works--music, dance, painting, sculpture, and other art forms.

6. The Breath

The breath is the swinging door to our innermost being and infinity.

A major landmark of my soul's yearning for a shift in consciousness manifested around 1970 when a friend named Bob, a physicist, started talking to me about physics, which I had always thought of as too cerebral for my liking. However, I had already read *Seth*, so ethereal concepts were not foreign to me. One day Bob showed up with a comic book which presented some of the laws of metaphysics. He also told me about the Course in Miracles before it was published in hardback, and he urged me to get a set of the books. I was very intrigued by his description and somehow knew the books were going to change my life in some significant way. I ordered them immediately and spent five years learning the first lesson, which was: "You and your brother are one."

Then I began learning the second lesson, which is: "There are only two emotions: love and fear. If you're not experiencing one, you are experiencing the other, and they do not co-exist." I accepted this statement as true, without realizing how it was possible. As a therapist, there seemed to be a range of emotions between these two extremes. It also seemed to me that I had no trouble experiencing both emotions simultaneously.

I loved every aspect of the course--the language, clarity, logic, and suggested practices. The Course consists of three books--the text, workbook, and teacher's manual. It is said to have been channeled from Jesus Christ by a psychologist at New York State University and her colleague who acted as a scribe. It was unsigned. The Course made a profound impression on me. Every day I practiced trying to see everyone as my brother (and sister). I had a field day with this on my job at UC. The Course became my connection with my higher self and my lifeline for living in the world and maintaining my sanity in the UC pressure cooker.

I remember coming home from shopping and going to my mother's bed to check on her. I thought she was asleep. I did not know she was looking at me and she did not know I was looking at her. Our souls touched in that moment. It is this level of interaction that I long for in all my interactions. I realized that I am living my dream. My dream is to be present in truth and to be helpful to the people I encounter, without conditions or expectations.

With the death of my mother, the purpose of my life changed. It seemed as if the world had fallen away beneath me and I was suspended in thin air without a safe place to fall. This loss was compounded by the termination of my close relationships with Jim and Judy. Both had moved on. Jim pursued his desire to get married and have a family, which I was unable to offer. Judy moved several times to different parts of the state and developed new relationships. I reached out to her many times, but my efforts to hold on were eventually to no avail. Apparently our work together was done. This was hard for me to accept because we were such a good team. No one ever told me that quality was not synonymous with longevity. I just thought it should be. These losses forced me to revisit the question of Who am I? I plunged into a spiritual and metaphysical search for deeper understanding.

To assist me in the practical application of my metaphysical theory, the universe presented me with a master teacher. During this time, I was raising five teenagers alone and feeling overwhelmed with all my responsibilities. I walked out of my front door one warm evening as the full moon was rising. I looked directly into the moon's face and was sure I saw the picture of a man. I asked God to please send me a man who would love me, himself, and help me with the children. I had no idea what I really needed for the shift in consciousness I longed for. I was clueless about the form this request would take.

A week later, I went out with a girlfriend to a nightclub where we drank wine and listened to jazz. We were there an hour or so when two men and a woman came in. Among them was a well-built black man wearing jeans and a shirt with the sleeves cut out, revealing his alluring muscles. On his shoulder he was carrying a handmade flute which I later learned he had carved himself. They sat near us, later joining our table. The flute-carrying man invited me to go outside and said he would play me a tune by the water. I was very seduced by his smooth and mellow music. The three strangers accompanied my friend and me to her house where we all sat up and talked metaphysics and philosophies of life all night.

About a month later, I met this man, Richie, again at a conference on East meets West in Spirituality. I was surprised to see him; however, it didn't seem to be a shared feeling. We talked during the break, and I gave him my phone number. He phoned me a week later, said he was passing through town, and wondered if I could put him up for the night. I agreed, and again we spent the night talking about experiences and the meaning of life. I was very stimulated and interested in his knowledge, his complexity, understanding, and his depth. His physical type was unlike any that I'd been attracted to in the past, and our lifestyles were opposites, yet there was a magnetic force about him, drawing me into his sphere. He called himself a "Zen Sufi Blitz", and this he certainly was!

The lessons were intense, and anything but gentle.

Periodically he would show up in town unannounced and telephone me from some short distance away. He invited me to come and pick him up, but only if I really wanted to. I disregarded my usual response to what I would have considered an imposition, and welcomed him with expectancy. His primal presence demanded that I show up, and I did! I couldn't discern if he was psychotic or brilliant. In retrospect, I think he was both.

After several months of sporadic visits, he revealed he had been living in an old school bus with the two white friends that I had met him with, but the bus somehow got wrecked, the three had parted ways, and he was now homeless. Being a tried-and-true codependent caretaker, I offered him a place to stay temporarily, until he could find a home. He spent every day sitting in my home watching TV, drinking wine, smoking grass, and "studying my vibrations" while I was at work.

When I arrived home, he'd say, "Come on, little girl. I'm going to introduce you to yourself." He proceeded to enumerate my virtues and my weaknesses. While pointing to the hills of Tiburon and Belvedere, he acknowledged me as a "mountain climber", and he also told me he had not encountered anybody that I did not try to understand. He also accused me of keeping the bedroom disorderly, and pointed out that although I gave him sex and money, I was not gentle with him nor emotionally available. Needless to say, I had to stay focused on my objective to experience love and not fear during these sessions. My sense of self began to fade.

Meanwhile I was trying to carry on business as usual, mothering five teenagers and working a demanding administrative job. None of my children or friends liked Richie. They found him too intense, intrusive, aggressive, insensitive, and lazy. They couldn't understand what I saw in him. We seemed mismatched in most ways. Also he was a catalyst for bringing up and unleashing repressed issues that people didn't want to or couldn't deal with. There were frequent unpleasant confrontations between him, my friends, and the children. I attempted to put these blowouts in a positive context, suggesting to the kids that their experiences were opportunities to learn more about themselves. However, it didn't change their opinion of him, and they continued to resent him as an intruder and freeloader.

Our lives continued in this tumultuous atmosphere for several months. One day Yolanda aggressively defied his assumed authority, and the two of them got into a physical fight which I was unable to break up. He had her pinned to the wall while she swung at him wildly, kicking and screaming. I was hysterical and in tears while the fight ran its course. That evening I escaped and went to visit friends in Watsonville, and while I was gone, two of my teenaged daughters--Yolanda and LaWanda-- decided to move out without telling me. This was very disturbing to me; their moving out seemed premature and self-destructive, and the whole situation made me feel like a helpless bad mother. We were all being bamboozled and intimidated by Richie, but I didn't know how to handle it.

A few months later, when a friend of mine was visiting in my home, the three of us were discussing life, and as usual, I was very free with my opinions in the conversation. After the friend left, Richie became extremely disturbed, accused me of undermining and disrespecting him in front of my friend. This was neither my feeling nor my intention, and the accusation seemed to have little relationship to what actually occurred. He viciously berated me for hours, and I again felt what were becoming familiar feelings: disbelief, betrayal, and fear. In my helpless state, I asked God to give me more love to help me deal with the situation.

The following night after I had cooked dinner, Richie became ill and accused me of poisoning him. He proceeded to beat me up, punching me in the face and shoving me around as if I were some lightweight feather. He was a fourth-degree black belt in karate, who had previously informed me that he had not only hospitalized but killed women in the past. I knew I was no match for his strength, so I totally surrendered and once more I cried out to love. Months earlier, we had taken tai chi lessons, and during the battle I suggested to him that we do tai chi together. I was very gentle in soliciting that calm knowing part of him with which I could reason. I gave myself to love with complete abandon, and his blows turned back on himself. He eventually became exhausted and became willing to join me in tai chi. When he went to sleep, I got out of there lickety-split, taking with me a change in clothes and the visceral experience of the truth: Love is the strongest force. The following day I forced myself to go to work with two black eyes, so that I wouldn't miss the humiliation of the experience. I wanted never to forget the lesson.

During this time, my craziest period, I saw two psychiatrists at the same time. One was Price Cobb, who wrote *Black Rage* and helped me with my own. Price asked me a key question: Who is Richie really? And I responded that he is whomever I decide he is for me. My decision to see Richie as a powerful teacher was what had enabled me to tolerate, rationalize, and excuse all his insanity. I also saw Jerry Jampolsky, who was a pioneer in the Course in Miracles. He helped me to explore and understand the experience in a spiritual context. In both instances, this help was very generously offered as collegial support and without charge. After awhile I realized that Jerry and to some extent Price had their own unique ways of paraphrasing what my mother had taught me and I had known all my life: To be true to myself and know that the Truth would set me free. At this point, I accepted the truth, I knew the right thing to do, and the only thing to it was to do it! I got up the courage to call the police and had

Richie evicted. He left without resistance.

Years passed with no contact and then out of the blue I received a phone call from Richie inviting me to meet him at a friend's house. After a great deal of consideration, my desire for closure won out and I went to meet him. During dinner with his friends at their home, I observed Richie being rude, narcissistic, and belligerent, (with which I was well familiar). At this time I simply experienced him as a crazy man without mystery. I had forgiven myself and him long ago when I accepted the wisdom in the lessons he taught me. I felt only gratitude for my growth and my willingness to remove my rose-colored glasses. He is now only a dull memory, and I find myself wondering if he was only a figment of my imagination.

Around this time another opportunity to move from fear to love was offered to me by the universe. Heather was one of my highly evolved teachers, only this one was four-legged. She was a pretty brown, black, and white calico cat. Although she did not have language, she spoke very clearly. As a young child, I grew up listening to frightening stories about cats sucking the breath from babies in search of milk. All my life I had lived with this lingering fear in the back of my mind. My family never had cats; dogs were the preferred pets; however, my beloved friend and roommate Judy loved animals of all descriptions. I reluctantly agreed when she asked me if she could have a cat in the house.

Her first cat was a totally black green-eyed six-month-old who had been given to her. This cat developed malignant tumors within a few months and died, after numerous visits and enormous expense at the vets. Judy was very distressed. She later decided to get another cat to lessen her grief. This time I readily agreed, and Heather arrived. Initially I simply respected Heather, but kept my distance. Some months later, Judy's job required her to transfer to LA where she took an apartment which didn't allow pets. She asked me to keep Heather until she could find an apartment where she could have her. I accepted this "temporary" adoption and was very dutiful about making sure Heather's physical needs were met for the next two years.

After a year Heather was hit by a car. She chose to go to my next-door neighbor's house who loves cats but whose husband was allergic to them. She had taken loving care of Heather whenever I was out of town. Lillian called and told me that Heather was at her house with a broken leg. I took Heather to a vet who hospitalized her. After several days the vet called and informed me that Heather was grieving and I should come and pet her. This was the time of our true bonding. During the process of holding and stroking her, my heart opened. When she was discharged she came home to a friend (me) who truly loved her.

During Judy's visits, it became clear to both of us that

Heather was now "my cat." She became the lady of the house with her favorite chair, her own side of my bed, and fancy cuisine. She greeted all visitors at the door, extending welcome and inviting them to pet her. She also took her place in the neighborhood by perching on the front porch where she loved to sunbathe. Many neighbors who commuted to work petted her as they walked by. It was through Heather that I met many of my neighbors who recognized me as "Heather's mother." While I was still working and also commuting, Heather would often, like a devoted dog, meet me at the bus stop. At home, Heather would jump up in my lap and the negativity and stress of the day would drain from my body.

When Richie moved in, Heather was distressed. She stopped sleeping on the bed and on one occasion defecated on the floor by his side of the bed. This did not go unnoticed by either of us. Another time a longtime friend with whom I had a flirtatious relationship was visiting. We were sitting on the sofa chatting cozily when Heather decided to insert herself between us; she was very adamant about her position and refused to move. The friend and I laughed about Heather's objection to our being close. Although this relationship continued for a number of years with mutual half-hearted efforts to explore the possibility of becoming more than platonic, it never got off the ground. Heather's wisdom prevailed.

When I transformed my house into a Healing Center, with numerous people coming in and out of the house, Heather seemed to emotionally withdraw from me and started having accidents all over the house. I consulted with Penelope who is well-known for her abilities to communicate with animals. She informed me that Heather was angry at me about something which she refused to tell her, but said I would know. I explored numerous possibilities but was never quite sure I understood the reason.

Heather lived to become twenty-two years old, which is ancient for a cat. As she aged she stopped going outdoors, spent most of her time in my room, and became extremely finicky about foods. I spent hours in the store trying to guess what might suit her tastes. I thought somehow that the more expensive, the better, but to no avail. I spent more on cat food than people food. I even resorted to cooking for her, which she sometimes ate and sometimes not. One of my daughters commented that Heather was treated better than a lot of people.

I had planned a trip to St. Louis and rented out my house for a month. Heather had become quite frail at this time and it was clear that she probably wouldn't live much longer. I was in a true dilemma about how to arrange for her care. She disliked kennels with a passion, and I didn't want to ask the people renting the house to take care of her. During our early morning talks, I explained to Heather that I was going to St. Louis, and arranging for her care was going to be difficult. I acknowledged that our relationship had been a very good one, but if she was ready to leave I was ready to let her go. Weeks passed, the date I was due to leave was near, and she was still here. In discussing my dilemma with friends, one asked if I had told Heather I was ready for her to leave. I had not, but decided to do so.

One morning before leaving for work, I told Heather that I was ready for her to go. When I returned home, I sensed something was different and went directly to my bedroom. Heather's body was hanging by her claws on the side of the bed. I was so dumbfounded that I couldn't touch her. I ran next door in great distress and told my neighbor that Heather had died. In his confusion, my neighbor called 911 which summoned the police and the fire department. A police car, a fire truck and a medical van arrived with sirens blaring, prepared to deal with a mortal emergency. We sheepishly admitted that it was a dead cat. This was a dramatic and fitting experience for Heather's departure. I received a letter from the vet who cremated her, expressing condolences and informing me that he knew Heather had received a lot of love and care. Cats do not live twenty-two years without it. To this day I still have Heather's ashes. The right time to disperse them has not yet appeared, or perhaps I'm still not ready to let her go, despite what I told her. Her final teaching to me was to hang in there with unconditional love, and leave empty-handed when your work is done.

Death and loss can be gateways to an epiphany, although it is probably not most people's first choice. One of my most beloved human companions, Bob, Susan's husband, died after a short illness with cancer, during which I assisted Susan with his care. It was indeed a privilege to share this meaningful time with them. I was the only non-family member to be asked to speak at his funeral along with his children. I spoke of my long-term meaningful relationship with the family, my perception of who Bob had been in the world, and the importance of his presence in my life. Next to my mother and Baba, this was perhaps one of the most significant losses in my life. After his death, Susan remained in the large family home, with a full-time caretaker. Soon, her own health started to deteriorate, and she decided to sell her house and move to a retirement community in San Luis Obispo. She was careful to get a two bedroom apartment so I could have a room when I visited.

Susan was one of the few people that I knew who loved me unconditionally. I could talk to her about anything. On one occasion, when I described to her my contribution to a problem situation with my current boyfriend Jim, she looked me in the eyes and with a serious face said, "Oh no honey, you didn't do anything wrong!" Susan disliked Richie, my Zen Sufi Blitz teacher, with a passion --she had no idea what I saw in him. She was certain that he was not the right man for me, and I should get out of the relationship. Of course she was right, but his enchanting spell over me still lingered. Even though she had strong opinions about everything in life, I never felt judged by her.

As her health continued to fail, she moved to Arizona to live with one of her sons and his family. Near the end, she telephoned me from her hospital bed and asked if I could come over to see her. Her son called me later to inform me that Susan was not totally coherent and probably thought I was a few blocks away. He told me that it probably was not necessary for me to be on the next plane. I said that it did not matter, that I was on my way. When I received the phone call, I was in the middle of refinishing a dining room table, up to my elbows in stain. I abandoned the project and went out to make a few purchases for the trip.

When I returned, I discovered that I was locked out of my house. My next-door neighbor was not home, so I went to the fire station at the top of the hill to get help, but there was no one there. I knew I did not have time to call a locksmith, so left to my own resources, I found an extension ladder in the basement. I leaned it against the house and with great determination I climbed up two stories to let myself in. Within a few hours I was in the air and on my way to Arizona.

At her bedside, Susan reminded me that she would always

love me and was very proud of me. This was the last time I saw her. At a very small memorial in her daughter's home in Fresno, her children and I remembered and celebrated her life. I shared what an important influence Susan had been in my life. Susan's relationship with her daughter had been very tumultuous, and the contrast was uncom-fortably apparent. I have remained in touch with Susan's three children through Christmas cards, occasional notes, and periodic visits from her youngest son. Susan's death left a void in my life and I vowed to make some necessary changes to improve the quality of my life and relationships by putting an end to my codependency.

Tom, Susan's youngest son, recently invited me to the graduation of his daughter from law school. It was an opportunity to spend quality time with all of them, celebrating not only Jessie's achievement, but Susan's life. In the absence of their elders, I was bestowed with the honor of representing the grandparents. Susan would have been very proud of who her children and grandchildren have become, as well as their achievements. The grand- children were interested in learning how Susan and I met, and Susan's daughter Kathy said she had always wondered about the basis of our attraction to each other and our friendship. I told her that our attraction was instant and other-worldly. We had a mutual positive regard for each other and a respect for differences. It was a well-known fact in the family that for Susan I could do no wrong. Susan took great delight in my risk-taking personality, seeming to receive some vicarious enjoyment. She commented several times that I was in and out of more situations in a month than most people are in a lifetime.

I, on the other hand, was fascinated by Susan's traditional and steadfast goal-directed behavior. Kathy responded that Susan was highly disturbed by her unwillingness to follow tradition. The more Susan tried to control her, the more she rebelled. Kathy said that she was afraid she was a terrible daughter, and often wishes she could tell her mother she was sorry and that she now had compassion for the struggles of her mother's generation. I commented that Kathy probably lived out Susan's repressed wishes which were very threatening. I commented that it's never too late to apologize.

In our relationship, Susan did not feel responsible for my behavior, nor did she perceive that my behavior was a statement about her. I shared with Kathy that her father had made the comment that if Kathy did some of the things that Susan easily accepted from me, it would be a declaration of war. I said I thought Susan recognized this dynamic between her and Kathy but was unable to change it.

Apparently Susan's three children observing their parents' marriage had numerous opinions about it. Kathy asked if her mother had ever had an affair. She assured me that I could tell them since they were all grown. I told her that in my opinion Susan did more fantasizing than acting out, and they were inclined to agree. We had several discussions about the dynamics of their parents' marriage, and possible solutions. All acknowledged that they had inherited or acquired traits from both parents.

Kathy asked me if I thought her mother was happy. I said I thought her mother was content and had accepted the life she created. I added that one of the differences in Susan's and my upbringing was the primary message from my family was to be happy, and hers was to be responsible. It is my opinion that you can't be happy without being responsible, but you can be responsible and not be happy. Although she had gone back to graduate school to become a social worker, I don't think that was the cloth from which she was cut. Tom commented that Susan was under-challenged in life and should have been a top executive in a large firm. This was the general consensus of all present.

Tom was spot-on in his description of his mother's life in his recently published poem:

The Accordion

My mother
Brought it home one day
And said
She was going to learn

To play
She didn't say
She wanted to become
Someone else, someone
More in tune with her talents
More in tune
With her estimation of herself
She didn't say
She wanted to go somewhere else,
On a boat to Tahiti
Somewhere with money glamour love
She didn't talk
About the Miltowns stashed in her purse
The Seconal at her bedside
The drinks, the fights,
The dishes slammed to the floor
While we kids tried to sleep,
She didn't say
She was a beautiful, intelligent, sophisticated
Woman
Who had wasted her abilities and joie de vivre
Stuck at home with three sour children
A dull husband and a dull life
She just brought home

An accordion--
Sometimes I would
lift it to my knees
And pull the bellows
In and out, let it fall to the sides
Press the black buttons
Finger them, pretend to play on the keys
And sing a tune
Waltzing Matilda,
Lady of Spain,
Oh, Dear, What Can the Matter Be?
A sad melody,
One of the tunes
Mother was learning.

LIGHTHOUSES:
PSYCHICS, DREAMS, ASHRAMS, AND CHURCHES

Thank God that during this time of my searching there were many lighthouses shining through the fog. Once when I expressed my frustrations and confusion about my job at UC to a trusted friend, she introduced me to my first psychic, who was located in downtown San Francisco. Her address was misleading and in no way prepared me for the experience. First of all she was very late and made no apology. Her name was Reverend Rousseau and she was very airy-fairy and other worldly. About ten people were crammed in her tiny room, and she walked around, rubbing the sealed envelopes containing the questions, closing her eyes, cocking her head, and repeating what she said "the Spirit says…." in response to the questions in the envelopes. Later I was astounded by her accuracy. Consulting psychics was new for me, but I learned to trust and be comforted by their predictions.

After my mother's fall, I was desperate to find a full-time attendant for her, so I returned to Reverend Rousseau to ask how I could find a good one. When she got to my question, she started reading a letter that she had received. I interrupted her and said that was not my question. She told me to wait a minute and continued to read. As it turned out, the letter was from a Korean couple who were looking for work and a place to live. The woman had experience in nursing in Korea. I was absolutely overcome with amazement.

I went to the address she gave me, rang the doorbell several times, with no answer. However, I was persistent as if I knew someone was home, laying on the bell continuously until there was an answer. After what seemed like hours, a Korean woman appeared, and I told her what I wanted. She replied in broken English that she and her husband were available for the job, and could move in the following week. I was so thrilled to have found them that I moved out of my bedroom and into the den. They arrived with two suitcases and a few personal items, which included special cooking utensils for their Korean dishes. They introduced us to many new foods, some of which, (like chittlins,) had almost unbearable odors. They put horrible smelling stuff out on the deck until it was ready to be cooked. We all whispered about it, but knew we had to adjust. We actually learned to enjoy the kim chee and some other foods which La Wanda still prepares to this day.

They lived with us for about a year. My mother didn't like the woman very much. She said the woman was mean to her when I wasn't there, and had hit her once. When I confronted the woman, she denied hitting my mother. The problem resolved itself when the husband found work in the City. I advertised for a new attendant, received several responses, and after several months of mismatches, I recognized one, Matilda, as the answer to my prayers.

On another visit to a psychic who read Tarot cards, she told me that God was at the beginning of my cards and God was at the end, that I would inherit both heaven and earth. At the time this seemed like gobbledygook to me, as I was in a state of confusion and pain, which was the reason I sought her counsel. Nevertheless, I tucked it away and recalled it from time to time for reassurance. I'm sure it was God's hand which eventually pulled me from my mother's womb, when I changed my mind about coming to earth. I'm also convinced that it will be His hand which pulls me out of here when its time for me to leave. However, along the way, like everyone else, I have had times of feeling separated from Him.

Another psychic told me that I had a very high calling and she experienced the depth of my love and compassion as being similar to that of Mother Theresa. This scared me to death! My psyche heard this statement but to date I have not fully integrated its meaning into my consciousness. I truly believe that God exists in all of us. However, my failure to integrate this vision speaks to my continued fear and struggle between beholding the beloved and becoming the beloved. I suppose this is just the human condition in which I am still struggling.

A friend was learning to channel with a ninety-year old woman who happened to live in Sausalito. My friend described the woman as very knowledgeable and powerful and thought I also would enjoy working with her. I had several appointments with the spiritual teacher, who told me many wild stories about her work with the lay lines. These are power lines that run through the universe. Apparently she was called by the spirits to help people who had passed on but were stuck between the two worlds. On my third visit she told me that the masters were very pleased with me and my writing and that I should go to the head of my class. This intimidated me so much that I never returned, but today I can laugh at myself for being so afraid of the yearnings of my soul.

While I was attending a workshop on the Course in Miracles, a woman had planned to do a psychic reading for my roommate who was also attending the course. However, when she arrived, she seemed more interested in reading for me. She told me that I was being tuned to a master spiritual teacher who would take me through an initiation which would increase my healing vibrations 100%! She advised me to be ready for the experience although she didn't tell me how to prepare.

Ten years passed since this prediction and the teacher's appearance. I had totally forgotten that he was expected, and when he arrived I was in no way prepared for the radical change he would affect in my consciousness. While sitting at my dining room table one evening, I noticed the Blue Angels jet planes making figure eights in the sky. Out of nowhere I received a clear mental imprint of a date, Jan. 8, 1972. I had no idea what it meant but knew it was significant, and later I found out.

In addition to predictions by psychics outside of myself, I also remember some lucid and recurrent dreams which seem to have been my unconscious preparing me for this journey. The first dream was a recurring dream of driving up a very steep blacktop road and losing control of my car, which traveled backwards down the road at a high rate of speed. During the dream I had no idea where I might end up, what destruction might occur in the process, and whether I would live or die.

The second series of recurring dreams took place in a leading university whose name I did not know. The expectation of academic preparation was clear, yet I had no class schedule and no idea what I was to learn. As I wandered from classroom to classroom, searching for answers, no one could tell me where I belonged or what classes I should attend. There were more dreams questioning whether or not I had taken all the required classes.

The third series of dreams were related to graduation. In the first, I had forgotten to order my cap and gown. The second dream had to do with my ordering the gown but not the cap. In the third dream, I had ordered the cap and gown but didn't have the receipt. Faye was with me and told me she had the receipt. I later understood why she had the receipt. It symbolized one of my biggest lessons.

After the graduation series, there was a shift in the theme. The symbolism was depicting movement toward freedom. In the beginning I was able to fly but flew into one brick wall after another. Sometimes I was running away from something or someone and found myself flying into rooms of buildings where I was trapped and unable to get out. There were several dreams of this nature.

In the final sequence of these dreams I became aware that I was flying freely. I could soar above the clouds, gliding without effort. I later told someone that I could fly and then became apprehensive that I might not be able to fly at will. However, as my informed friends looked on, I was able to mount to the sky with ease.

I was encouraged by the new direction of my recurrent dreams. In one, a small naked black boy was dancing euphorically in a cave. I wondered why he was so happy, because he was naked, and people in society wear clothes. I wondered if I should put some clothes on him. Upon awakening, I realized that his nakedness probably symbolized the loss of ego and defensiveness. I looked forward to achieving such a state.

The second dream of exposure was of a small black boy emerging from a cave wearing no clothes. Although he seemed very joyful, the adults outside hurried around talking about how they needed to put some clothes on him.

In another dream I was appearing in public places either nude or scantily clothed. I was unaware of my nakedness until someone pointed it out to me. I became embarrassed, and attempted to cover myself. In later dreams when I became more secure with my "socially unacceptable appearance," the other person gradually seemed to become more comfortable with my nudity. These dreams suggest my eventual acceptance of my being defenseless and different in the world. I now realized I really have nothing to hide, and none of us can hide anyway. Everything is already known and none of it is personal.

As my journey continued, I had another dream about graduation. In the process of preparing for my celebration I realized that I was not sure I had completed all of my course work. I went to the Registrar's Office and there was no one there. I made other feeble attempts to find someone who could inform me if I had completed my requirements. Again, I was unable to locate anyone who could give me information about my situation.

A physical manifestation of this dream came with my gradua-tion from the foundation course given by Reverend Carol of the Church of Spiritual Living (Religious Science). Due to the "process" I had been unable to write legibly for several years. Subsequently I was unable to complete the written assignments, and I missed the final written exam. On the last day of class the students were requested to present a project which reflected what we had learned. I had created a card with an image of a ninety-five-year-old woman doing the hula hoop. I inserted a lotto ticket in each card with the statement that "You have to play to win." It became very clear to me during this class that I have to be an active co-creator with the spirit, preparing my mind for clear passage of the answers to my prayers. I thought the card reflected my most important lesson of the course on multiple levels in a fun way. I did not realize that I had left the cards at home until it was my time for my presentation.

Needless to say I was very perturbed and disappointed in myself. It was a dark and rainy night and I had no time to go back and get them. I couldn't believe that I had been so absent minded, and I ran back and forth to my car several times thinking they might somehow magically appear. Exhausted, I was overtaken by the reality of the situation. In my helplessness I asked the spirit for direction. I remembered two of the other principles taught in the course--that everything is in divine order and there are no mistakes. I became willing to see the blessing in the situation. My project then changed from a presentation to a demonstration of what I had learned. Without my props I got up and explained to the class what had happened-- my surrender, acceptance, and willingness to be present with what was, rather than longing for what wasn't. With this shift in consciousness a large part of my ego died.

Several students thanked me for my presentation. One said that she was truly inspired because her pattern is to become defeated when her plans fail. The teacher wrote me a very touching note acknow-ledging my spirituality and thanking me for sharing with the class. One of the practitioners volunteered to come to my house and take dictation for all of my missed assignments and the final exam. I graduated with honors!

Following my graduation I had a series of negative dreams. I was angrily acting out and confronting other people. These dreams seemed to be remnants of lingering unresolved anger and resentments. Fortunately they were followed by a series of vivid romantic dreams. I was surprised to learn that my sexuality is still alive and well. I was in a relationship with a range of different men, some familiar, some not. In one dream Richard Simmons, the weight-loss guru, didn't want to go to work. It seemed that he had deluded himself into thinking he really loved his job. There were also a few famous movie stars-- (Michael J. Fox and Gregory Peck, for example). In one dream, I remarried Melvin Saunders, and we were very lovey-dovey and cozy. These seem to indicate that I am identifying with widely diverse aspects of my masculine self.

For years I had maintained footing in three camps (spiritual communities)--the ashram, Sausalito Presbyterian Church, and the Church of Religious Science. I also placed a foot in various Baptist churches from time to time. All have offered unique nourishment for my soul. A comparison can be made to foods: soul food--delicious but will put you to sleep, and Chinese takeout--tasty but doesn't stick to the ribs. Choosing one at the exclusion of the others felt to me like deprivation. Depending on where I was on my spiritual path, I was drawn to the one that best met my needs at that time. However I came to believe that there would be advantages to being identified with a particular group and not being a spectator on the periphery of several. I decided to "join" the Sausalito Presbyterian Church, but another invitation, too good to refuse, came along.

In December of 1978, my friend Julie invited me to attend a weekend "intensive" with her at the Siddha Yoga Ashram in Oakland. She wanted us to share the experience and analyze it together afterward. We have continued our efforts to understand what happened to this day. It is no accident that the two of us are sharing the task of writing this book.

I was looking for a new direction so I accepted her invitation, even though I had no idea what an ashram was, and knew even less about gurus. Although the dates of the intensive were Jan. 7 and 8, I made no connection to the psychic's prediction and the earlier vision I'd had. The first day of the intensive I felt nothing. I was extremely critical of the Indian-style vegetarian food, the decor of pictures of near-naked old men in loincloths, the seating arrangement on the floor which was too close for comfort, no room to stretch your feet, sitting in an unfamiliar cross-legged position for extended periods--it was a bit much to endure.

However I did enjoy the sweet smell of the incense, and the Jean Nate perfume which was wafted about. In my most arrogant voice, I asked Julie if the guru was so powerful, why didn't he speak English? He looked like any other little unattractive, pot-bellied man to me. As Julie and I were leaving at the end of the first day, feeling a bit ripped off, we overheard the hall monitor reassure another participant that there was no need for worry, he would certainly have an experience because the guru knew just the right place to touch and open each participant's heart. I remember thinking, "Fat chance."

I spent the night with Julie who lives in Berkeley. After dinner we spent many hours ripping the program up one side and down the other. We analyzed it to death. After laying it to rest, I felt a strange sense of peace as I drifted off to sleep that night.

I woke up the next morning feeling surprisingly refreshed and light-hearted. As I took my two-by-two seat on the floor in the meditation hall, I felt as if I were at the head of my class, even though I had no idea what the class was about or what I knew. As the guru walked toward me between the narrow space of the cushions, I could feel and see his form even with my eyes closed. The closer he came, the more I expanded. I felt myself becoming one with him and we extended into the universe. As customary in those days, he bopped the top of my head with some peacock feathers, and placed his thumb on my third eye. To my astonishment, I received shaktipat (the sacred transmission) and my heart opened.

When my consciousness came back into the room after an unknown period of time, I had the strongest impulse to go to the highest mountain and yell at the top of my lungs, " Hey World! This is Me! And Love is who I am!" I euphorically told my friend Julie who was with me in the intensive, that I had FOUND IT. Her response was, "Yes, until the next thing comes along." I assured her in no uncertain terms that this was the real thing and there would be no other!

My first question to Julie was whether the guru was married. I only knew that I wanted to be close to him for the rest of my life, and in my ignorance, marriage was my only frame of reference for the closeness of a committed union. Since marriage has never been one of my life's goals, this strange desire was out of character for me. I now understood people who were willing to give up their personal self to follow whatever they believed in, be this a woman with a husband, a lover, or a spiritual leader. At the time, I had a prestigious position at a well-known university, had adopted many children, and had a large house with many obligations and responsibilities. Suddenly I wanted to give up everything and follow this Baba.

However, the Spirit kept insisting that the work was "right here." This advice had little meaning to me at the time, because I was blinded by my intense desire to be close to the guru. I only believed that the message was saying I was not to follow him then. In my mind, this message was clearly temporary and I decided to fulfill my responsibilities to the children, find a suitable professional replacement, etc. I consoled myself with the thought that when the children finished school, I could sell my house and take the money and move to India to be with Baba and live in the lap of luxury. While continuing my worldly responsibilities, I attended programs at the ashram during the week, and used it as a personal refuge on weekends. Keeping my commitment to myself, when I took my last daughter to college, upon my return I had arranged to move into the ashram.

The very evening I arrived home, Julie called me and told me Baba had taken samadhi (selected his time to die). Although he had no apparent illness, he had told his devotees that he would be leaving his body at the next full moon. He met with his swamis and chosen successors, completed all his affairs, and at the appointed evening lay down, closed his eyes, folded his hands across his chest, and slipped away. Somehow I was oblivious to this information and was deeply wounded that he hadn't bothered to ask me. I had planned the second half of my life around him, and now felt lost and bewildered, with no idea of the direction of my life. Fortunately, the universe had arranged for me to take a sabbatical from my regular job to become a consultant for a cultural awareness and race relations program (CARE). This gave me the freedom to create my own schedule and to move into the ashram as I had planned.

Broken-hearted, I threw myself into the fifteen day continuous chant to celebrate Baba's departure. Although my singing voice leaves much to be desired, I was so effective in losing myself that an unknown man wrote me a beautiful card stating that my chanting was divine (much to my surprise!), and that I had inspired him to improve his. Absorbed by the chant, I was aware of my unbroken spiritual connection with Baba. I stayed for six months at the ashram, arising at 4am for meditation, chanting, and breakfast, then driving across the Bay Bridge to UC to develop and teach the CARE program.

While washing dishes, which was my usual "seva" (selfless service), one of the residents attempted to ease my grieving by telling me that my real desire was not to follow the guru physically, even if he still was alive. He said the long lines to greet the guru were exhausting and prevented close contact. He suggested that what I really wanted was to live in the ashram surrounded by pictures of the guru which would inspire the awakening of the guru within myself. This is the same advice the guru had given everyone.

This now made good sense to me, because there had never been any personal exchange between me and Baba, and I wasn't even sure that he had been aware of my existence. The one exception was when I requested a spiritual name. He handed the written name to me, then took it back, rubbed it, and offered it again. When I read the meaning of the name, Arundhati, who was married to the Lord Rishi and "a model of family excellence," I felt very intimidated. She was powerful in her own right and raised the morning star (consciousness). Although other women became distracted from time to time, she was one-pointed in her love and devotion to God. I was reluctant to tell anybody my new name and what it meant. Even so, somewhere in my soul it resonated as truth, and I knew it was me.

After many hours of chanting, I asked myself the question: why did I love this man so much, and what was my inheritance? What did he leave me? The answer swelled up inside me--the message was clear: "GOD DWELLS IN YOU AS YOU FOR YOU. SEE GOD EVERYWHERE AND IN EVERYBODY." This has comforted and guided me, as well as whoever hears my outgoing phone message.

During my stay, the ashram was totally renovated, destroying any attachment I might have had to the outer forms, and insisting that I rely on my own internalized experience of God. In other words, I had to grow up, and find the guru within. From the point of my awakening, my primary focus in life has been to return to total consciousness of the Self.

The six months that I lived in the ashram were blissful for me. This spiritual community is a combination of ancient tradition and forward thinking. I loved smelling the aroma of incense and listening to the soothing chants as if I was being rocked to sleep every night in very loving arms. The sour cereal which I detested at first became nectar to my body and soul. I want this experience to be included in my epitaph; it's one of the best things I've ever done for myself.

Baba left two successors who had lived in the ashram with him since childhood. Shortly before his death, Baba announced that Nityananda and Chidvalasananda, a brother and sister, were next in the lineage. However, Nityananda was apparently unprepared for the personal sacrifices required by the monastic life. He was still lured by the temptations of the world. Maulti, as Chidvalasananda was called, rose above the cultural taboo against female power, and embraced the heritage and became Gurumai.

She was an exquisitely beautiful woman, and she was privileged to serve as Baba's translator and trusted assistant for many years. She was always by his side, and very close to him. She is a real life manifestation of the guru's ability to transmit power. Although she is very sweet and I love her dearly, my experience with her is not the same as with Baba. There is still a void left by him in my heart. Perhaps we only have one True Love.

The new guru was scheduled to give her first program in Oakland. Because the Oakland ashram was too small to hold all the devotees, the Berkeley theater, larger in size, was chosen for the overflow. The decision regarding who would sit with the guru in the ashram or watch a video in the theater was made on the basis of a lottery. Attendees who won were to be notified by phone. Although I did not receive a telephone call, the one-page confirmation of registration seemed to indicate that I would be seated in the ashram. (I was sure I had won the lottery! and shared the news with my friends and family.)

A friend of mine had offered to drive me to the event. He reminded me that people to be seated in the Oakland ashram had received telephone calls. I was not totally convinced, and he phoned the ashram, who verified his statement. I had looked forward to being in the company of the guru, and wanted the opportunity to share my "process" with her and have the benefit of her insights. This experience was yet another reminder by the universe that I should focus on substance, not form. This was not exactly the lesson I wanted to relearn at this time, but nevertheless it was the one at hand and I decided to enjoy the satellite program at the Berkeley theater. I was gradually getting the idea that the experience with Baba that I longed for was not to be duplicated. I have come to accept that "you can't go home again."

I have come to accept the impermanence of all things in a new way. Baba continues to teach me from the other side the importance of non-attachment and that the dwelling place of true power lies within. He advised his devotees not to worship the guru but to become the guru. My soul resonated with this advice, even before my ego was ready to accept it. At one time I was very attached to Baba's form. Following Baba's teaching, I have come to accept that my experience of him is eternally protected. Baba and the ashram are deeply embedded in my heart and with me wherever I am.

My recent visits to the ashram have been few and far between, and I thought the primary reason for this was distance. Most of the programs are in the evenings, and it is difficult for me to drive at night. All of my attempts to live in the ashram were futile and went against the flow of the cosmos. My mind thought that if I were to become the guru, I needed to live in the ashram as he did. In retrospect, I could never really see myself in a sari or living the cloistered life. I now accept that my unique expression of love will be living in the world, following the example of Jesus in the tradition of my own cultural heritage. As in the fairy tales, often one must search the world looking for the treasure that exists right at home.

One of the things I loved most at the ashram was the Cave, a small dark meditation room where the chant "Om Nama Shivaya" ("Honor the god within.") played nonstop. I spent many happy hours in there--sometimes as many as 10 to 15 a day. I was disheartened when they had to close the cave due to earthquake regulations. However, the universe in its benevolence provided me with a private cave in the comfort of my own home. Following the instructions of my healer from Zimbabwe, I sit over a steaming pot of seaweed covered with a blanket while listening to the chant "Om Nama Shivaya." This for me is a combination of a sauna, a sweat lodge, and the cave. The seaweed aroma connects me with the primal elements of life. I open and experience the oneness of God right in my own living room.

The book emphasizes the importance of taking personal responsibility. Blaming others keeps undesirable situations in place, while taking responsibility for our choices and shadow is empowering and affirming to ourselves and to those around us. The author discovers with absolute certainty that love is who she really is, love is who we all are, and love is what we all want. Love also wants all of us. Life is a journey of awakening to the realization that we already are what we are looking for. Although this story has already been told many times and in many ways, the author believes there is an audience waiting to hear her unique wakeup call.

We are born free to know love as our own self. However we are also born dependent on others for our survival. Through the process of socialization we are often taught to believe that we are someone or something that we are not. Unfortunately we identify with the mask created for us by our caretakers and would-be caretakers. The more we identify with these masks, the more fearful we become of losing them. In time and with practice, the distance dims the light which distinguishes truth from illusion, luring us into permanent amnesia. Human beings come to Earth's school to remember what we already know in a world which is uniquely designed to distract and confuse us. It is the truth which sets us free, not fame nor fortune, just the simple truth. The universe loves a happy learner.

Meanwhile, back at the ranch on Spencer Ave., my affairs were going to hell in a hand basket. In my excitement about moving into the ashram, I impulsively allowed my oldest adopted daughter Faye, her husband, and three children to move into my house for a measly four hundred dollars a month plus utilities. Faye was the oldest daughter of my oldest brother. She was a tall, light skinned, stately young woman with a deep voice and pretty face. When it served her she could be very outgoing and charming. She was also extremely manipulative and self-serving. After her mother died, she was forced to grow up very fast and assist with the responsibility of her nine younger siblings. She missed several developmental stages, which impaired her moral development. When her father died, I brought the youngest girls to California and Faye remained in the family home in St. Louis with her teenage siblings and young son.

She later married Deak, who was a nice guy but a drug abuser. Trying to escape from old problems and find a new life, she decided to move her family to California. By this time she had two additional children. Of course at first they all stayed with me--my house was the first way station for all family members and some of their friends who decided to move to California. Having four additional people in the house was a major challenge but Faye made a real effort to be helpful with the cooking and cleaning. After two months they found an apartment and moved to Marin City.

Faye visited often and very methodically cultivated a close relationship with me. She cooked dinners on holidays and the family gathered at her house or mine. We all went to church together in Marin City and Faye and I spent many hours listening to good gospel music and talking about the spirit. She seemed very receptive and even appreciative of the attention I gave her and the wisdom we shared. At one point she commented that she "almost had me where she wanted me," and even this blatant confession went over my head. Faye was a very strong charismatic woman, a mother figure who had a lot of influence on her siblings. I was so obsessed with trying to create a healthy family and thinking she could be a real contributor to this goal that I failed to heed the many warning signs.

I had received several other taps on the shoulder by the spirit of truth. I even ignored a two-by-four when Faye and Deak set me up for a sting involving several thousand dollars. She claimed she had found a diamond ring, and then asked me to buy it because she said she needed money. After I swallowed the bait, she later changed the story, claiming the ring belonged to someone who was demanding it be returned under threat of violence. I returned the ring, but I never saw my money again.

I had received a premonition of a devastating betrayal in a dream, but I had no clue how to avoid the landmine. When I failed to get the lesson with the two-by-four, the walls eventually came tumbling down. I had allowed her to live in my house when I went into the ashram. I was aware that her income was limited, but I was unprepared for her repressed rage and sociopathic dishonesty. After four months I intuitively sensed that something was awry but had no idea how bad it was. She had neglected to tell me many "small details"-- that for the six months she'd lived there she'd failed to pay the house note, the insurance, or the utilities! When I told her I was returning home, she said she had no place to go and acted as if I was imposing on her by asking her to leave. It took her two months to move.

Reluctant to leave the sanctuary of the ashram, it was evening when I moved back home. In the dusk, I attempted to turn on the lights and realized there was no power. I lit a candle and went to the fuse box, and was surprised to learn that there was nothing wrong with the fuses. I was forced to consider the possibility that for the first time in my life my utilities had been turned off. I picked up the phone to call PG&E, and the phone was dead. In a state of shock I sat down on the bed with my lighted candle and discovered a foreclosure notice on my house. I told myself that I was delusional and my eyes and ears were playing tricks on me. This was a deja-vu of looking into the dark empty house in Fresno after Melvin had stolen all my furniture and clothes. Stunned, exhausted, and still in denial, I eventually fell asleep.

The next morning I was devastated by the magnitude of the situation and the betrayal of my trust and generosity. I comforted myself with the memory of having the strength to get through the Melvin betrayal, and told myself that I could get through this one. A week later I started receiving large bills from several department stores. In addition to everything else, Faye had also charged several thousand dollars on my credit cards without my permission. When confronted, she was obtuse and unresponsive, acting as if she had done nothing wrong, and making no effort to assume responsibility for her actions. I was enraged by her attitude and my naivete.

Needless to say, I wanted nothing more to do with her; however, she continued to call me trying to engage me in conversation. At one point she had the audacity to tell me that I could not go to heaven if I did not forgive her. It took me years to undo the mess she made of my excellent credit history and even more years to forgive her. We occasionally both showed up at family gatherings, but I held my tongue and kept my emotional distance from her. Her drug and alcohol problems intensified, and eventually she met an early death at the age of thirty-five.

I continued going to evening programs and spent

weekends at the ashram. From time to time I attempted to move my residence back to the ashram, but without success. In one way or the other, I was cosmically kicked out of the ashram. In spite of my experiences, I still thought the universe's message was related to timing, because my desire to live in the ashram continued to be strong. Gradually I have come to accept that my journey is a walk in the world, and the ashram is to become my inner state, rather than my dwelling place.

    Five years after Baba's death, I saw another psychic who informed me that she saw what appeared to be rope or twine wrapped around me, that I was totally tied up by Baba. She asked me if I wanted her to remove the bonds, but I would have to stop listening to the chants and detach from the energetic flow from Baba. I thanked her and respectfully declined her offer. It was my strong belief that I had given up my dependency on Baba at his death, as well as my depen-dency on the ashram. After the major renovations on the meditation hall and the closing of the changing cave, it no longer seemed like the same place to me. However, I saw no need to let go loving memories of my experience and the ongoing nurturing I received from the recorded chants.

    Subsequently, I have associated my "process" with the binding she referred to. In this way it is strangely similar to my relationship with Baba-- no words, no interaction, nothing personal--it's only feelings, and blind trust. I accept that the process is my new teacher. Baba advised all his devotees not to worship the but to become the guru.

Shortly before I met Baba, I was looking for a Course in Miracles study group, which I found at the Sausalito Presbyterian Church. It is a very old, beautiful church nestled in the serenity of the Sausalito hills. It is deeply established in Christian tradition. The minister at the time was in my opinion a very knowledgeable freethinker. He was a spiritually-centered social activist. I felt connected to and inspired by him. He led the Course in Miracles group which I regularly attended. I also began going to Sunday worship services. After several months, I was asked by one of the church leaders to become a member, which I did. I felt honored, but also had some minor hesitations, as I was the only African American in the church, and I had been raised a staunch Baptist. However, on my way to church one Sunday, I received the message from the Spirit that my role was to "integrate" the church. This message did not come with any instructions as to how it should be done. As time passed, I came to realize that it was not about race.

I became a member of this church for twenty-five years, actively participating in all of its activities, ranging from giving a sermon to being chairman of the worship committee, chairman of the usher committee, of the Christian Nurturing committee, etc. It was a small church, quite wealthy, and most of its members were my neighbors, accomplished professionals or businesspeople who were reasonably secure with themselves. I felt comfortable with our mutual attainment of relative personal freedom--they wanted nothing from me, nor I from them. Unlike some other churches, I did not feel conscious or unconscious pulls of unspoken personal agendas on my energy.

At a workshop given by one of the members of the church, the meaning of names was discussed, and we were asked our feelings about favorite names, spiritual names, where they came from, etc. It was here that I revealed publicly for the first time and explained my spiritual name, Arundhati. I had had this name for ten years but used it infrequently and only in the ashram community where I received it. I was asked if I wanted to be called by my spiritual name and very timidly I said that I did. After a short time, the entire congregation started calling me Arundhati, which became an invitation to me to rise to a higher consciousness. It was in this atmosphere that I received the courage to practice seeing God in everybody and everywhere, a directive from Baba. SPC was fertile ground for learning that differences are not threatening in the presence of love. Everybody was so different from me, yet I felt loved unconditionally for who I am. I knew most of the congregation, and felt supported in the development of my spiritual maturity, as well as my professional and social life.

I became good friends with the minister and his wife. He

had grown up in the black Baptist church and loved gospel singing. A small group from SPC attended several concerts, and during the year I was responsible for the music program, I arranged for a number of gospel singers and choirs to sing for the congregation. Everyone loved the music, especially the minister. He also was interested in the ashram and its music. At his request I bought twenty-five tapes of "Om namah shivaya" and sold them at the church. The congregation was very happy to receive them and the chant became "integrated" into the church.

After thirty years of service, the beloved minister retired from SPC. This was another major loss for me of a significant spiritual teacher, and my attendance at this church became less frequent. The minister had been one of the primary lighthouses guiding my spiritual journey, and I shared a deep and meaningful relationship with him and his wife. An interim minister was hired, more traditional in his thinking, but nonetheless a good man who appeared spirit-directed. Meanwhile, I was invited by a friend to visit the Church of Religious Science in Corte Madera, and gradually my loyalties became divided between the two churches.

After many months, the Sausalito Presbyterian Church Search Committee selected a new minister. Initially he appeared to be the perfect fit for the rather progressive yet still conventional conger-gation. He seemed the answer to the church's prayers. Many celebrations were planned to welcome him and his wife to the church family. It was an opportunity for me to reconnect with my SPC community, and I was overwhelmed by the outpouring of authentic love and expressions of delight in seeing me. I was reminded of the love and connection that I felt when I was actively involved and inspired to make the transition from "Marie" to "Arundhati."

One of my original objectives in joining SPC was to assist in integrating the church. I was effective in arranging for the church to experience some "good gospel music," especially during the summer that I was responsible for developing the music program when the choir was on vacation. Although the congregation enjoyed the music, the church was never integrated in the manner I had anticipated.

As a black woman, I think I assumed that the focus of my personal expression of the Spirit would be with people who look like me. Yet I had been the only black member of the church for twenty-five years. Could my picture have been more wrong? Awakening to this reality I remembered a Black Caucus meeting at UCSF where the group was discussing helping blacks understand the white world. Out of seemingly nowhere I heard my voice say that I wanted to help the white world understand blacks. This should have been my first clue, but I really didn't identify with the voice. Subsequently I was surprised that I ended up in an all-white church; it certainly was not the way to help blacks get along with whites. SPC continues to be almost lily-white to this day.

With the arrival of a new minister, there were a few missteps in working out the dance between him and the existing church leadership. Two of the elders from the SPC came to see me about different perceptions between them and the new minister concerning the direction of the church. I was honored by this request for consultation and saw it as an opportunity to witness the power of prayer and explore the possibility for meaningful participation before terminating my longtime affiliation with the church.

The two women were well educated, articulate, competent, energetic, and clear. In their own words, they were "committed to quality." I could not imagine that the minister would not be open to a win-win negotiation in this situation. Our opening prayer was the acknowledgement of our oneness with the Spirit, each other, and the minister. We accepted this reality and gave thanks for this truth. I asked for direction and guidance to the best resolution of differences. We asked to be gifted with the understanding and acceptance that differences are not threatening in the presence of love. We asked that the Spirit of love express itself in rich abundance for the good of all and the harm of none.

Later one of the longtime very active pillars of the church called me to request advice on issues she was experiencing with the new minister. She said that another member was also having similar problems and asked if they could come together. I recognized the second member as an equally powerful presence in the church community. Contemplating the request, I asked God for guidance. I was told to start with prayer, and ask each of them how they wanted the situation to be resolved, and what we could all do together to achieve the expressed intention. It occurred to me that whatever differences they were experiencing with the minister, it would be in his best interest, and that of the church, if the conflict was resolved with a win-win result. The situation was ripe for inviting the spirit, aligning our attention with our intention, and letting God do His work. The possibilities were exciting!

The women said they were inspired by my counsel and saw the issues in a new way. They felt hopeful and clear about the path they needed to take. The next worship service was a demonstration of our answered prayers: it was well coordinated and the minister stayed on purpose. Both women made a point of telling me how encouraged they were.

I was also invited to attend a meeting of the Shepherding Committee of the church. This group of elders and leaders was responsible for mentoring the new minister. Again I considered this invitation another opportunity for me to make a meaningful contribution to the future direction of the church. I have always loved "Sausalito Pres"-- it has played a very significant role in my spiritual development. At one time it was pivotal in my life, and it was here that I felt safe enough to practice unconditional love. In my opinion Sausalito Pres has the potential to become a national model of unconditional Christian love. Perhaps being free of the material woes of the world, having the privilege of higher education, and the luxury of relatively healthy families contributes to their openness to love.

About a month later I was invited to become a member of the session (the governing body of the church), which I reluctantly accepted, because I'm not fond of administration, but was willing to give back to the church what I had received. I was also asked to join the large planning committee for the annual retreat. I agreed to join another person on the program subcommittee. It seemed to be a given that the other person would be the chair, which was fine with me. Initially I saw my role as supporting her. I was simply interested in finding where I fit best. The larger committee experienced many somersaults including the resignation of their chair, who left because he wanted a more intellectual program. Other members were lost in the process of attrition, confusion, and divisiveness. The program chair became rather seriously ill before she had completed the planning. I ended up writing the entire program out of default.

When I initially presented the program, it was well received by the remaining members of the committee. The new chair, however, was very skeptical. He cancelled three subsequent meetings with the statement that there was no need to meet for people to "just agree with me." I found this statement odd and unsettling, but said nothing. After I wrote the program, the previous chair took responsibility for the scheduling. When the minister, the chair, and I finally met to combine the program and the schedule, the chair was quite anxious and irritated. The atmosphere was uncomfortable and I asked the minister if we could have prayer before starting the meeting.

The chair was not deterred by the prayer. He literally attacked me verbally, saying that he needed to finalize things and every time he asked me a question all he got was "snow." He said he was a businessman, and needed to know what was going to happen, and was uncomfortable with an attitude of "it will just work out," which I never said. I later discovered that he had not even read the program. He seemed also not willing to consider that I was not responsible for the scheduling nor aware of what had or hadn't been done. He seemed "loaded for bear", and was dismissive and rude to me. The minister said nothing to address the attack. A major issue for me in the world had been being dismissed by white men in positions of power. My ego used to take delight in verbally annihilating them. It was all I could do to maintain my composure and not return the attack. I was surprised at the force with which my ego returned. I wanted to leave several times, but the Spirit wanted me to stay. I managed to get through the meeting with a little dignity and a lot of grace.

I later asked the minister to mediate a meeting between me and the chair. I said that I can't remember the last time I was attacked in that way, and it was important for me to let the chair know that he can't talk to me in that manner. Despite several attempts, the minister said he was unable to arrange a meeting, and said he had left a message for the chair to call me and apologize. This was not what I had asked for, and it did not happen anyway. After several weeks, I decided to call the chair on my own, and left a message that I would like to talk to him.

Another week passed, and when he did call, he said that he did not have any issues with me, he only wished me well, and really called to tell me about the next meeting. He glossed over my concerns and said that I was the one that everyone was talking about, how I had "stormed out" of a discussion with him when he denied failing to inform me when a meeting was cancelled. I decided not to dignify this projection with a response. What I had done was simply to look at him, say nothing, and leave. However, I am sure that the energy I projected felt very stormy to him. After we hung up, I thought about it and realized that I would have to make peace with who the chair was at this time in his life. It was not my responsibility to blame or change him.

He later cancelled his participation in the retreat, and was "too ill" to attend the next meeting. It seems that the entire committee had dwindled to three people at the last meeting--the minister, the person responsible for scheduling the rooms, and me. We finalized the program and wrote a letter to welcome the participants. The committee member who had been assigned to announce the retreat on Sunday called to say that he was detained by the flood. Again by default I volunteered to make the announcement in church. The minister seemed relieved.

During prayer request time, I asked the congregation to join me in prayer for God's blessings on the retreat, to make it fun, stimulating, and meaningful for everyone who attended and indirectly for all the members who were not able to attend. I asked God to make me a clear channel for facilitating His love, peace, and clarity at the retreat.

Gradually I came to recognize my experience with the chair as a gift. I realized I no longer have a button that can be pushed by men like him. It seemed that the retreat was to be the first group expression of my embodiment of the Spirit since emerging from "the cave" of self-reflection. It was an opportunity to give back what I had learned, with no responsibility for how people received it. I accepted the call.

The retreat was attended by about twenty-five people at the beautiful Westerback Ranch. Julie and I were co-facilitators and role models for trust, openness, and unconditional acceptance of racial and cultural differences. Attendees were willing to be vulnerable and enthusiastically participated in all planned activities. They shared memories, both happy and sad, of their common stages of human development. They learned that love is who we are, differences are not threatening in the presence of love, and that we are all one. The retreat was highly successful; everyone who attended reported some degree of increased self-awareness and acceptance of self and others.

Following the retreat I met with the minister to let him know I was still disturbed by the many discrepancies with which the two of us perceived the same situations. I told him that his inability to handle the conflict between me and another member made me question his leadership and integrity. I concluded I didn't want to be a member of a church where it was acceptable by the minister for members to attack one another without reprisals. I told him the time had come for me to leave, but that I would always love the church. After more than twenty-five years in this church, leaving it was a great loss to me. The minister offered a lame regret and said I would be missed. In the meantime, general dissatisfaction with his performance was mounting in the church, and some months later he was dismissed with pay. Occasionally I still visit.

After leaving SPC, I became active in the Church of Religious Science, a rather young new-age church which seemed almost severed from established Christian tradition. The singing, the sermon, the "satsun" (spiritual community) all reflected a rather trendy style. It had the high energy, excitement, and expectancy of the growing youthful heart. The young, however, often lack integrity. The following story reveals the youthful folly of one of its members, and my continued impulsive attraction to empty promises.

One Sunday I commented to Clara, one of the women who attends the Church of Religious Science, that I was looking for an illustrator for my book. Her eyes lit up and she said quite enthusiastically that she was an artist in abstention and would love to have the opportunity to get back into her art. In that moment our spirits connected. She asked for a copy of my text so she could get a feel for what she would be illustrating. I told her that it had been recently put on a disc and I would give her a copy. She asked if I had it with me, and by some synchronicity I had left it in my car the night before. She asked if we could go get it, which we did.

Almost immediately after receiving it, she suggested that perhaps Catherine, a member of the same church and a well-known artist, should be the illustrator. I ignored this red flag. She insisted that we go talk to Catherine, who told us that she is in ministerial school and does not have time. Clara then told me that she was going to an event in the afternoon where there would be a famous artist and she would love to show him a copy to see if he would be interested in illustrating the book. I reluctantly agreed, and we parted with her promise to return the disc the same evening or the following morning at the latest. I had told her she had my only copy and I needed it for Wednesday to give to my minister. He had offered to read it and share it with his sister who was a publisher of a small company.

I became concerned when I had not received the disc at the end of the week. It gradually dawned on me that she had an unedited rough text and I was not sure I was ready to share it with the world in its present form. I also realized that Clara is a young woman who loves to talk but often has little to say, and might love to bring attention to herself using my raw text as her vehicle. I did not have her telephone number so I waited until the following Sunday to see her at church. She was very apologetic that she hadn't called me and told me that she had mailed it to my Post Office box. However, it never arrived. I telephoned her, quite annoyed, and told her the disc was not there. Again she apologized, saying she didn't know what had happened, but she had loaded the information on her hard drive and would make a disc and mail it to me. At this point I was ready to pick it up myself, but she offered to bring it to me, which she did, giving me a hug and telling me she loved me. Needless to say, I was very uncomfortable with my unedited text being on her hard drive, and I decided to ask her to remove it.

The following Sunday after church I told her I wanted to talk to her. I told her that I had experienced her energy as scattered and it made me uncomfortable. I told her that I did not like the way she handled my private property, and that I was surprised, considering that she is a lawyer. I questioned both her intention and her level of maturity. It was my perception, I said, that she had changed our initial agreement to co-create art for the book. I do not consider it her responsibility to find someone else to meet my need because she is unable to do so. At this point I saw no reason for my book to stay on her hard drive, and I requested that she remove it. I told her I almost wanted to come to her house and watch her remove it, but then decided I would just leave it to her integrity.

She said she had taken the disc with a note to the post office and feels that she followed through on her agreement to look at the disc and give me her thoughts about illustration. She said it was not her fault that it was not delivered. She suggested that I use a family photograph to illustrate the book, and added she was an excellent photographer. I told her I was not interested in finding fault; however my experience of our interaction is the same regardless of her intentions.

I said that I did not want to struggle with anything around this book. She said that sometimes struggle is necessary. I agreed, commenting that I choose my struggles and I am not willing to engage in the mire of ambivalence. I said it was my opinion that her scattered energy contributed to the outcome. She asked if she was totally responsible for what happened. She admitted that she tends to overextend herself and then realizes that she is unable to follow through. I said no, that I was taking responsibility for my contribution. I shared with her the similarities between my experience with her and other relationships where I had connected with the spirit in another person and had continued in the relationship after the spirit had left. She asked for permission to keep the text on her hard drive because she would still like the opportunity to think about the photography. She reminded me that she is an attorney and would keep everything confidential. I was still distrusting of her motives, but felt caught in her web, and turned it over to God. I pointed out to her that the universe is not wasting our time with things we already know. My recognition that the spirit had left and my choice not to continue our relationship is an indication of my growth. This lesson was shorter in duration and much less painful than the previous ones.

It seemed some CRS members took themselves less seriously than the Presbyterians, and their relationship with God seemed to be more celebratory than reverent. On the other hand, the leadership was committed to building a community for lifelong spiritual development and support. I considered this goal admirable and was very attracted to the church for this reason. I also had some rather pleasant friendships in the congregation, and participated in many of its activities.

Both these churches teach and attempt to practice the Truth. The difference is in conceptualization and presentation. Many Sunday mornings I found myself deliberating about where I would attend church. Frequently the decision was made on a time basis because one church starts at 9:30, and the other at 10:00. My attendance was often dictated by my process and its activity of the morning.

In my ongoing analysis of the two churches, I discovered that I am more philosophically aligned with the Golden Gate Church of Conscious Living, which emphasizes God within rather than without. I have recently become a tithing member. However, this church is also lily white, and I do not feel truly at home there. I am still searching for my unique expression of the Spirit in church service. I was asked to teach Sunday School which I agreed to do, but the number of children attending had been so small that there was not much opportunity to teach. I was considering doing outreach to teach children to become ambassadors for peace, which is near and dear to my heart, but it might not take place in this church.

The Church of Religious Science sponsored a four-day retreat at Gualala Camp for about one hundred women. The retreat centered around powerful ancient rituals of several goddesses. The presenters dressed as the goddesses whose power each embodied. It was a wonderful invitation and opportunity to share the experience of the powers of the feminine.

A group of teenaged girls were invited to the retreat to be initiated as Maidens. Participants who identified themselves as Crones were asked to share their wisdom in one sentence with the Maidens. My sage advice was that the maidens should always wear hats to inspire their queenly consciousness. The laughter of the group sounded like a cosmic release, suggesting on some level they appreciated the universal spiritual tradition of head coverings for women. I also advised the maidens to see love everywhere and in everybody. This practice has served me well in life and is the key to real joy.

One of the offerings available was a sweat lodge. Here again, the rituals were outstanding. I was the oldest woman in a group of ten nude women-- I was asked to be the grandmother and holder of the water during this sacred experience. This role and the powerful energy created by the group of like-minded naked women elevated my consciousness. I became one with the role of grandmother.

On the last day of the retreat, each woman announced to the group the qualities she was aspiring to. The ceremony began with a statement that I am a powerful woman of passion and included what the woman was taking from the retreat back into the world to contribute to world peace. I announced that I am a powerful woman of loving passion, and that I was taking from the retreat a renewed commitment to experience my oneness with all things and to see love everywhere and in everybody. I could feel Baba's presence permeating the atmosphere. I left the retreat knowing who I really am, claiming the wisdom of my full maturity, and ready to take on my remaining challenges in life.

Selling the cabin in Monte Rio was yet another major loss in my journey to maturity. It had been a beloved source of personal nourishment, not only for me and my family and friends but also for many other people who stayed there. I struggled with this dilemma for years--I knew selling it was the right thing to do, because it had become a financial albatross; on the other hand, I feared that giving it up would leave a big hole in my life. I missed it terribly. When Nita, my last child, moved away from home, I attempted to recreate the cabin by turning my home into a Healing Center. I was looking forward to energetically connecting with likeminded healers. I was so excited about the adventure that I neglected to take into consideration the fact that I lived in a totally residential neighborhood with very observant, law abiding neighbors. I failed to anticipate the many problems associated with opening my home for public use. I was unaware of the many ordinances restricting such an endeavor. Little did I know that a caravan of angels were assembling to come to my aid.

Two friends joined me in the transformation of my home. Mary, a traveling angel who lived with friends and house-sat for a variety of people, was probably the least attached, unmaterialistic, genuinely happy person that I have ever known. She had worked on the art of conscious breathing for years. She was very talented and skilled with her hands. She was also very responsible, conscientious and a hard worker. She always seemed to take the high road in any situation, little if anything really bothered her, and I don't think I ever really saw her angry. She quit her job working in corporate America several years before I met her. She became a personal organizer, helping people clear clutter out of their lives. She earned just enough money to get by, which was fine with her.

Maria was an attractive, somewhat euphoric middle-aged woman who wore false eyelashes. She spent many hours putting on her mask for the public. She worked as a color consultant and was also employed at Big Four Rentals. She did not like working there and was very happy to quit her job and join in the adventure of a Healing Center.

Mary, Maria and I, the three M's, went about the business of moving everything out of my house, including a baby grand piano, antique china cabinet, dining room table and chairs, and thirty years of collected stuff. We had several garage sales and gave away truckloads of things to friends, family, and Goodwill.

My house has very high cathedral ceilings so Maria

arranged to have a ten-foot scaffold from Big Four delivered and set up. We painted the entire house inside in a pale rose quartz, which she had selected. The three of us painting on a ten-foot scaffold was indeed a sight to behold. We refurnished the house in a very zen fashion: following the tradition of the cabin, we named and decorated each room with a multicultural theme. For example, we put five pink and white French ice cream parlor tables and chairs in the dining room for seating large groups. The room came alive with luscious green ferns hanging from the ceiling and beautiful rose and white designer mirrors which brought into the house the spectacular views of water and trees and sky. Mary's motto was: "Give everything we do in the Center at least 200%," and we all tried to live up to it. We carefully selected each item of furniture which required group approval. We feng suied every room with many mirrors intended to reflect to people their higher selves.

As the work continued, many friends helped out with various jobs and some made financial contributions. We prayed before every meeting and blessed the house whenever there were seminars or workshops. Mary was good at networking and marketing. In a relatively short time, the Center became well known in Marin, and was rented for a wide range of spiritual workshops and growth groups, ranging from Rajneesh's Dynamic Meditation to Rolfing to Rebirthing to Art Therapy to Bodywork, etc.

Some of the healers were on the cutting edge of the Human Growth Movement. I had the opportunity to selectively participate in a wide range of offerings. This was a time of accelerated growth for me, and I met many wonderful angels who offered different gifts. A few were prima donnas with a lot of special needs, but for the most part they lived up to the description of helpful angels.

Dot was a high-flying angel who rented office space from me on a regular basis. She did channeling, hypnosis, and spiritual readings. She hung out with other angels in the spiritual world a lot of the time. The two of us shared a powerful spiritual connection and became very close. I am sure we shared many lifetimes together, which enabled us to be unconditionally accepting of each other in this lifetime.

Once I rented the Center to a group of male East Indian healers who had culturally arrogant chauvinistic attitudes of control. The group was there for two weeks which totally changed the energy from feminine to masculine. While I was away in St. Louis, Dot handled this challenging situation with dignity and grace. She was very friendly, accommodating, and lovingly set limits for them around their noise and messiness. Maids were not included in the rental contract. Another time I rented the Center for a month for Rolfing trainings. I left town because the group moved in and used the entire house with the exception of

Dot's office. Prior to signing the contract, I had inquired about the noise level, concerned about both the neighbors and Dot's hypnosis practice. The teacher assured me that it would not be a major problem. Although I had some doubts, based on my limited knowledge of Rolfing, the deal was very attractive because it paid me ten thousand dollars for the month. With fifteen students practicing at one time, the noise level proved to be more of a problem than the teacher had described. Rolfing by nature is an emotional release, often accompanied by moans, groans, and sometimes screams. After class there were social gatherings in the hot tub on my deck in full ear-and-eyeshot of the neighbors. My next-door neighbor was highly annoyed and resentful. Dot's hypnosis clients were also distracted by the noise, but again she persevered with grace, and never blamed me for her inconvenience.

    I also made an appointment to have a new roof put on the house two months in advance and forgot to tell Dot. She was able to reschedule some of her clients and took long lunch hours to avoid the noise. Once again she was very pleasant and understanding without criticism. Dot was truly a light in my life, and I couldn't have operated the Center without her support. In her light, I was able to see my shadow clearly. I resolved to be more considerate and mindful of others' needs. My heart is filled with only love for her, and I will always remember her as a living example of unconditional love and acceptance.

From time to time my next-door neighbor came over and complained about noise, and cars turning around in his driveway. Once he asked me if I knew that what I was doing was illegal. My comments were designed to placate him. I believe this was the neighbor who reported me to the city. I received an official letter informing me that I could not rent my house for public use in a residential zone; it was against city ordinance, with the exception of a school or church. At this time, the Center was in full swing. I didn't know which way to turn. I talked to my pastor at the Sausalito Presbyterian Church, who suggested that I present my situation to the session which is the administrative arm of the church, and ask for support. I did, and the session voted unanimously to support me. This enabled me to continue operation for several more years. Then I received another complaint from the city informing me of a pending investigation. The City Manager scheduled an appointment to visit my house to see if it was set up for public use. They kept the appointment and decided that they did not observe anything out of the ordinary and they backed off.

Shortly afterwards Dot decided to move to another office. I was out of town during a scheduled Bioenergetics workshop and my dear friend Harriet was housesitting and taking care of my cat. Before the workshop started she received a phone call warning her of a bomb threat. I had no clue where the threat originated or why. Harriet was near hysteria. She cleared the Center of people but she was unable to get the cat in the car and feared leaving her in the house. When she telephoned me I attempted to calm her down, although I was somewhat shaken myself. This seemed a clear warning that a landmine was afoot. I later learned that the workshop leader himself had called the police with the bomb threat because he was feeling unprepared to lead the workshop. I was receiving a variety of messages from the universe that it was time to close the center.

    Many angels, both students and teachers, had come in and out of the Center, giving me the opportunity to practice seeing God in everybody. I told a friend that we are all angels with special qualities and I consider it a real blessing to be able to see the angel in other people. Often we only see in others the things we don't like and miss people's unique gifts. It is with an open heart and deep gratitude that I acknowledge all the angels in my life. The Center was a high point for me, and it provided space for many healers on the cutting edge. I and my house became rather well known in Marin County. To this day people who used it remember it with fondness. The Center was a dream come true and achieved my goal of being a conduit for bringing people together to heal and grow. It laid the groundwork for the emergence of Arundhati.

    Closing the Center left another big void. Although I had

taken yoga a few times, my contact with the healers reminded me of the benefits of this ancient art. I also recognized the need for regular physical exercise to maintain my health in my advancing years. I chose Gold's Gym in Corte Madera during a membership promotion as the place for me to get my body in shape. After using the machines for several months (probably incorrectly), I decided to get a personal trainer. The trainer informed me that there was a world class yoga teacher at the gym. I started timidly in the back of the room, and was soon hooked. As my courage grew, I increased my classes and was surprised and delighted with the excellent teachers and my benefits from their expertise.

Yoga was created by ancient masters to give followers the experience of the Self. Yoga offers potential joy in every posture (asana), joy in the transition from one posture to the next, and joy in every breath. Joy, joy, joy! A good teacher offers the invitation and holds the space for students to ride the magic carpet of the breath, in and out, to very wonderful states of consciousness. Yoga is exercise for some, a spiritual practice for others, an art, a dance; it lends itself to whatever one chooses to make of it. At the end of the class one of my teachers invited us to place our hands in prayer mudra, pausing at the third eye to remember to live in wisdom and clarity, at the throat to live in truth, and at the heart to live in love and compassion. This was how I wanted to live my life. I always appreciated this invitation because it framed my intention for the rest of the day.

In one of my yoga classes, a teacher I hold in the highest regard told the class to find our center and allow all movement to flow from there, following our breath. I did as instructed and became absorbed in the love I found that dwells there. I have had the good fortune of experiencing pure unconditional love on several occasions and have longed to live in that consciousness. The highest and longest experience was my initiation by Baba in 1979. Following yoga class, I was flying high. I went home and I looked myself in the mirror and asked the Spirit for a constant ongoing experience of love. I had no idea what the requirements of my request would be. I realized that I was not going to achieve my goal to become one with love while doing "business as usual." I would have to surrender. In my characteristic style of magical thinking I suppose I thought I would glide right through darkness to light. It did not occur to me that there is a reason enlightenment is the "road less traveled"! I relearned the universal wisdom--be careful what you ask for, you just might get it! However, what appears might not be in the form you desire or expect. (In fact it could lead to your demise.) Thus began my entry into a very protracted "process" of spiritual transformation and my greatest challenge.

PILGRIMAGES TO MY MECCAS

The universe is unlimited in its storehouse of mysterious

experiences uniquely designed for our individual needs. My friend Nancy had invited me to join her in her long-anticipated trip to Zimbabwe. She was fascinated by Shona sculpture, which I liked but it didn't grab me in the same way. However, since the fall of apartheid I had been eager to go to South Africa. I decided that this trip would be the perfect next step on my journey to wholeness.

I remembered that during my trip to West Africa, I had had a conscious experience of being in that country in another lifetime. When I got off the plane in West Africa, I was greeted by an unknown man who said, "Welcome home, sister. You look like you belong to the Sarahuli Tribe." I said I had never heard of that tribe. In response, he asked if I had a husband who disappeared for twenty years without word or contact, would I wait for him?

I said, "That depends."

He said, "On what?"

I said, "Our understanding." He affirmed that I am a Sarahuli woman.

I had been eager to experience Africa and its people. I hired a guide who provided me with a magical tour of Dakar, Senegal. He seemed other worldly, and made connections that were unexplainable. He took me to his home and to the homes of very wise and influential people, including kings and queens of the land. Whenever I would go walking on the road outside my hotel,

I was soon surrounded by young teenaged boys who wanted to practice their English and share their dreams. The doorman at the hotel where I stayed treated me like a queen, referring to me as "My lady." I felt elevated to the status of royalty.

I also had the good fortune to meet the Prime Minister of Germany, who happened to be staying at the same hotel and happened to sit on the same bench with me, in a luscious garden designed by heaven. She explained to me the psycho-social development and present stage of Germany, America, England, and Africa, From her wisdom I was able to instantly understand how the development of individuals and countries are parallel. This was the beginning of a global consciousness and the desire to become a citizen of the world.

Before I left home, I had thought about how nice it would be to see Jahsani, a friend from South Africa whom I met while he was teaching at Fresno State College. I had completely lost contact with him. He since had become a diplomat living in Johannesburg.

By some mysterious move of the universe, our paths crossed in a casino in Abijan, Sierra Leone. We were both struck with disbelief, and began running towards each other, with his two body guards running behind him! All eyes in the casino were on us. I was flabber-gasted by the million in one chance of this occurrence. I experienced again that there was some mysterious energy that connected all things, and we were a part of it.

427

Nancy and I began the planning phase for the trip to Zimbabwe with the help of a San Francisco gallery owner whom my enthusiastic companion had befriended in her many visits to his gallery. He had lived ten years in Zimbabwe while teaching English in the Peace Corps. He fell in love with the people and the land, and has continued to make annual visits to see friends and buy art. He told us many interesting places to go and people to see. He arranged for us to have a private tour guide with a black South African named Virginia. She was one of the few female Shona sculptors. (Rumor had it that she was also his mistress, although she denied it.)

Shortly after we arrived in Zimbabwe we contacted Virginia, who took us to a variety of formal and home galleries. We also perused the art of street vendors ranging from the famous to the least known. We had also been advised to visit Tanganangi, an artists' village developed by a white chief who was described as a very colorful and knowledgeable character, a person not to be missed. A week later we hired a taxi and drove two hundred kilometers to Tanganangi, a full day's ride through towns and villages, on curvy roads, some of which were unpaved. Natural shapes of nature-carved stone animals graced the hills. I was filled with childlike wonder that the same Creator creates both living and stone animals. It is fitting that the country is named Zimbabwe which means Big Stone.

We bumped along in our old London taxi, which was without air conditioning. It was a very dry, hot day, and we made several stops along the way in a desperate attempt to avoid dehydration and heat stroke. We arrived at the village shortly before sundown. We were welcomed by two women who did not speak English. Many of the inhabitants of the village have lived there for their entire lives untainted by the outside world. The chief was away for a few days and the exact day of his return was uncertain. We were not sure that we would get to meet him, and we had so looked forward to experiencing his character (which had earned him notoriety) and hearing his stories.

Since the village was in such a remote area with no stores, my friend and I requested that dinner be postponed so the taxi driver could take us to the next village where we could buy a supply of beer and wine, and some snacks in case we didn't like the food. We were told this was acceptable. We were served a dinner of beef, rice and vegetables prepared with African spices. Throughout the dinner we communicated with gestures, and we all smiled a lot. Afterward the women walked with us in the pitch black through bushes, trees, and shrubs, to where we would stay. They seemed sure footed and very familiar with the path, assisting us as we stumbled along. We were given the royal accommodations which was a very large round hut made of stone with a thatched roof. However, it didn't have electric lights or an indoor bathroom, but it did have mosquitoes. We used flash lights to find our way to the nearby outhouse.

  The next morning we ate breakfast and casually began our explorations. The entire village consisted of about two hundred stone carvers and their families. Zimbabwe is a very economically depressed country, and stone carving is its main industry. We observed fathers teaching theirs sons to sculpt. Women were just beginning to be allowed legitimately to enter the carving world, although some of them had carved secretly. Our hostesses quietly showed us some of their work which they had tucked away in their huts. The stones were huge and varied-- beautiful opal, serpentine, springstone, to name a few. They were efficiently transported with antiquated, simply-constructed wooden carts, and carved with crude chisels and hammers.

  In contrast to the sculpture in the cities where some of the artists had been influenced by Europeans and other traditions, in the village the art is inspired primarily by ancestors. Ancestors appear to the artist during dreams with images which the artists carve the following day. It was fascinating to watch the artists free the statue from the stone. The artists truly became one with the stone, and a sculpture emerged. After watching them work for a while, I became one with their process. The stones came to life with beautiful colors of greens, browns, blacks, and subtle shades which emerged under the flame of a torch, which is how they get the shadings.

As far as one could see in any direction, there were spectacular sculptures nestled against trees and shrubs. Everyone was eager for us to see their work, and we wanted to accommodate the many requests. Our days were spent looking at sculpture and talking with the artists. These interactions were so elevating for me that I felt as if I were walking on sunshine. In the evenings we sat outside, peacefully drinking wine with the mosquitoes by flashlight, looking over a very lovely hillside, marveling on the day's discoveries. I started seeing sculpture in the trees, in shadows, and everyplace I looked. After we had been there three days, the chief returned. He lived up to his reputation as a brilliant storyteller, captivating our interest with exciting stories of his life, the village, and faraway places and people. He also shared some very fine wine from his private collection. This made for another totally entertaining and mesmerizing evening, one of the highlights of my life.

In South Africa, I had the opportunity to meet artists of great achievement and high esteem who validated my eye for art. I also was lucky enough to see not one but two authentic African *nagas,* (a person with the abilities to communicate with ancestors and see the future.) Both acknowledged me as one of them with similar abilities. One said that I would be in contact with people from all four corners of the world.

For a woman who took the trip as an observer, with little intention of buying art, by the time I left, in my altered state of consciousness I had bought forty TONS of sculpture. I had absolutely no idea what I was going to do with it. Shipping this much stone was no easy endeavor, and hugely expensive. It arrived in Oakland after several months, and I had to have it delivered by a special trucking firm with a forklift. I live in Sausalito, California, on a steep hill which the huge truck was not able to navigate. I then had to hire a pickup truck to bring the sculpture from the top of the hill where it was unloaded down to my house. Some of it was so heavy that it could not be lifted by the two men I hired to do the job, and my neighbor volunteered to help. It was almost too much for the three of them, but they were inspired to do the job.

Opening each carefully packed piece was an experience of Christmas in September. My entire house was filled with African sculpture, leaving little room for anything else. These overcrowded conditions became a message that I needed to move some sculpture. I gave some away as gifts to family and friends, and arranged two public viewings in my home. Following the first showing, several people called to tell me how pleased they were with their "living sculpture", and to thank me for being the conduit. I sold several pieces on both occasions, but still had many tons left.

I considered becoming a promoter for sacred art but this was easier said than done. Before I left Zimbabwe, I knew that I would love to promote the artists and their work, but I had no idea how to make that happen. I am not one to sit in a gallery all day, and I did not want the responsibility of hiring and supervising someone else to do it. Besides, I wanted to personally interact with the people who bought my sacred art. In the meantime I was enjoying the companionship of the living sculptures.

Art, like death and loss, is a well-known gateway to self-realization. A talented artist is able to give us glimpses into the realm of timelessness, pulling us right out of ourselves into the present moment. Not only did I have an epiphany in Africa while watching the artists free the spirits from the stone, I have also had a personal experience with the essence of each of the individual sculptures I bought. I therefore know beyond doubt that the unique essential quality embodied in each sculpture is real, offering its essence to anyone who opens to it. Shona artists believe that anyone who owns one of their pieces is connected by ancestors to both the land and the people. I consider it my personal calling and passion to facilitate the interconnections of spirit between the artists, their work, and the recipients of their work. Each piece comes with suggestions on how to develop a personal relationship with the particular quality embedded in the artwork. I am humbled and delighted by the opportunity to share the Spirit of Sacred Art with the world. I am enthusiastically looking forward to promoting the artists, thereby bringing needed resources to a very impoverished community and country.

Years before I went to Zimbabwe, a future seer asked me if I were an artist. I said no because I did not have a particular art form. She seemed surprised at my response and said she saw me surrounded by many artists. The truth of her prediction was manifested in the forty tons of sculpture in my living room. I recognized that I was indeed an artist of sorts and my form was connecting the Spirit of all things. Connecting people with the spirit of Shona sculpture is one way that I could contribute to an underdeveloped country and to world peace.

Julie, the same friend who asked me several years ago if I would be willing to see a shaman, was the catalyst for my recent contact with a healer named Mandaza from Zimbabwe who was visiting in Marin. I immediately felt a strong kinship with him. As I sat down, the healer also acknowledged our connection by referring to me as sister. Before he started he took a large whiff of what looked like snuff. (All of the nagas and healers I saw while I was in Zimbabwe performed this ritual.) He sprinkled and rubbed me with water. He asked numerous questions about my father and paternal grandfather, most of which I was unable to answer. My parents were divorced when I was eight, and I never knew my grandfather--I didn't even know his name. The healer said that my grandfather loved me very much and is one of my guides. He said my grandfather is very concerned that his family are wanderers and don't know who they are. He wants to come to me in dreams, and I was told to prepare for him.

The healer told me that my difficulty started when something penetrated my forehead, and he placed his thumb on my third eye. He said when this happened I was supposed to start foaming at the mouth and go insane. He said that insanity was prevented by my very strong spirit. He connected me to the lineage of my grandfather. I was quite surprised by his inquiry about my relationship with him, because there was little contact with my paternal side of the family. I remember being very affected by the story my mother told me about one of my paternal uncles. She said that he used to ride a horse around the small town they lived in eating pure lard from a can. I also remember that the only paternal uncle I knew spent time in a mental hospital. Stuck in my memory is an image of him sitting silent and without movement. I now recognize that he was probably catatonic. This lineage carries both insanity and priesthood. I resonated with the healer's comments about my predisposition to insanity and remembered that many years earlier when I was finally diagnosed with Cushings Syndrome, I was told by my endocrinologist that people with such an advanced disease are usually found in mental hospitals.

My connection with Zimbabwe and its people is profound.

Mandaza was the first person outside of myself who showed true understanding of my experience. He instructed me to go to the ocean, gather seaweed, come home and boil it in a large pot. Place the pot under a chair, and sit over it, covered from head to toe under a blanket. Breathing in the vapors and the aroma of the sea transported me back to my ancestral roots in Africa. He also encouraged me to move during the treatment, which my body agreed with, whereas all the other "medical" healers advised me to be still while they did what they did. My experience with Mandaza was a confirmation that Zimbabwe is one of my meccas.

In my ongoing floundering search for my unique expression of the spirit through service, I requested a prayer from one of the Religious Science practitioners. I had been looking for a house which would be the locus for my service as well as a better investment of my life savings than the stock market. My prayer was for clarity and direction from the Spirit regarding my interest in a two-million-dollar house which I doubted I could afford. The practitioner asked me to visualize the program and activities I wanted to provide. I was somewhat vague in this department, and she suggested that perhaps I had the cart before the horse.

I received a flier advertising a counseling position at San Quentin. I applied and was later informed that San Quentin did not have an opening at this time. I was told that I could wait for an opening there or accept a position with Vacaville Correctional

Institution. In less than a week, I received a call asking if I could start work at Vacaville on July 11th. After careful consideration of the long commute, I decided that traveling to Vacaville would defeat my purpose; the long drive would be so exhausting that I would have little to offer upon my arrival.

Then one Sunday as I was leaving church, a woman from whom I had requested information about marketing a hospice program excitedly approached me with material from the internet about "becoming the change you want." Since this program works with children, I wondered why she was giving me this information, because I had "been there, done that." A few months later, however, I started thinking about developing an academy to teach boys between the ages of seven and eleven to become ambassadors for peace. This circuitous route took me to training to become a foster parent.

All my life I have wanted to be part of the solution to the plight of children in the world. Julie and I began writing a program called Journey to Peace. Initially the program was written for people making their last transition from this life. We found a magnificent picture of an eighty-year-old woman doing the hula hoop. However, at some point we realized that most of these old folks would not contribute much to world peace as they were making their exit. The next idea was to apply it to church groups, which seemed a good population for carrying the message. After one very successful program with the SPC, it gradually became clear that children are the most receptive to change and are the ideal ambassadors for peace, because they have more hope.

FOSTER CHILDREN AS REFLECTIONS OF MY MATURITY

I explored the idea of getting a license for a group home and again began looking at large homes in Marin. The logistics and red tape became overwhelming, so I contacted Social Services of Marin to inquire about foster care. I realized that I had come full circle and had arrived at the same place where I began my journey at the age of five, vowing to take care of all of the children who did not have parents to take care of them.

I took a required course, and soon one of the social workers from St. Vincent's who taught the course called me. She said she had a young man for whom she thought I would be a good match, and asked if I'd consider helping him prepare for emancipation. I said yes. Justin was described as a seventeen-year-old, bright, college bound African American with one year of high school left. For various reasons foster care had not worked out in the past, and he had spent most of his life at St. Vincent's Home for Boys. He had major issues, but I felt they were nothing that I couldn't handle. Over several months he became less reluctant and more enthusiastic about the possibility of trying foster care again.

Justin and I had our first visit together with his social

worker and therapist, and it went well. He said he enjoyed reading, writing, and playing basketball. We talked about some of his challenges, and some of mine. I said that I wanted to help him become the best person that he could be, and since we both like to write we agreed to keep journals of our experience together which we would share. We also agreed to plan menus, shop, and cook together. He asked if I expected him to do chores around the house without being asked. I said I expected we would take equal responsibility for keeping shared living space neat, and that our home was our sanctuary. We committed to telling the truth and to his learning the necessary skills for his independence. My only request was that if he changed his mind about our mutual goals he would let me know.

Our second visit started in the office with his therapist and we later went to a nearby shopping center for snacks. I discovered that I had changed purses and neglected to put money and credit cards in the one with me. I found three dollars in my car and we went to three different restaurants before we could find one we could afford. I told Justin that he was getting an opportunity to observe my disorgani-zation. He was very understanding and said disorganization was also a problem for him. I think this experience was a valuable lesson in not feeling "less than" because we couldn't afford something we wanted.

The third visit was on Easter Sunday. I took him to church

where he was well received. The minister's daughter took him under her wing and they hid eggs for the younger children. He also met Stephen, an electrical engineer who had volunteered to take Justin on as an apprentice and teach him how to make home repairs. Stephen is also a musician and although I didn't know it, Justin plays the guitar. They seemed to enjoy each other's company throughout the lunch. Later Justin commented that he was very happy about meeting Stephen because he'd always wanted an older man as a mentor. After lunch Justin and I went to my house in Sausalito, and I showed him a bit of the town. Later in the afternoon, we met several members of my family and we all went to see a new house in Novato I was thinking of purchasing, because of its proximity to Justin's school and support system. When I asked Justin if he thought he would be comfortable in the Novato house, he said if I would have him, he would be comfortable in either house. We ended the day with a nice dinner at Maxi's.

As I was taking him home, he asked me if he came to live with me, would he be able to spend the night with friends. I asked if he had anyone in mind. He said that he had several friends who would like for him to spend the night. I asked if he had done it while he living at St. Vincent's. He said no. It crossed my mind that he was testing the limits, and I told him that I was sure it would be okay after I met his friends and their parents and was assured of his safety. I added that he only had one year to learn the many skills he needed to become independent, so this didn't leave much time for distractions or detours down dead-end social paths. He seemed satisfied with my response.

As he was leaving the car, he told me that he had had a good time and enjoyed meeting the family. He also asked for my telephone number and I gave him my card. I had his number from his therapist, but had lost it. Other staff members cannot give out resident's phone numbers. I played phone tag with his therapist for about a week, and in the meantime I also had surgery on my hand. Justin didn't call me, so we had no contact for two weeks.

My friend Stephen had come over to repair a fan for me and suggested that Justin could start learning some skills. Stephen offered to spend a morning mentoring Justin. I called Justin's therapist who said that anyone who spent extended time with Justin would have to be approved. However she was enthusiastic about the plan. I attempted to call Justin and the person who answered the phone told me to wait, then came back and said he couldn't find Justin, that maybe he was taking a shower. I left a message for Justin to call me, and when he didn't, I called again the next day.

After a wait, Justin came to the phone and said he had been very busy with school and SAT tests. We had a brief conversation during which I told him that I decided not to buy the Novato house we had looked at, and that my hand surgery was involved but went well, and about the workday with Stephen. I told Justin that I might need special approval for him to spend the day with Stephen. I informed Justin that I had lost his number, had played phone tag for about a week, and expected that he might have called me. Justin was silent. He simply responded that any time I wanted to schedule a visit with him I only needed to contact his therapist. Then he said he would call me the next day. When he failed to do so, I called him and again was told he was not available.

I became quite concerned about this breakdown in communication and requested a meeting with the therapist and social worker. I began to see Justin's manipulative side and his effectiveness in playing two ends against the middle. In the meeting Justin finally admitted reluctantly that he had lied. After much discussion I decided to proceed with the placement.

Reopening the chapter of motherhood not only had a familiar ring but a tinge of self-assurance. It seems to be in this role that I am most readily willing to surrender my ego and let the power of the spirit come through. It was decided that Justin would move in with me on June 16, which was my seventieth birthday. We had only one year to work together to prepare him for his emancipation.

One of my daughters took me to pick Justin up at St. Vincent's and then took us out to dinner. The following day Justin and I went to purchase his first cell phone which he was ecstatic about. He invited me to lunch at a Mexican restaurant. I told him that when he graduated from high school I would reward him with a trip to Mexico. The next day my other daughter had planned a grand surprise party with most of my friends and family attending. Among the many tributes to me was Justin's expression of appreciation for taking him into my home. We had a delightful honeymoon period. Within a week or two he got a job at Best Buy, and seemed to be very responsible and proud of himself.

    Justin came with a caravan of angels, some with bodies, others invisible. All were committed to "saving him." During the honeymoon period, their job wasn't too difficult, and at times even fun. However, after the romance faded the harder they worked at saving him, the harder he worked at avoiding their net. When school started, the honeymoon came to a screeching halt. He not only rebelled against giving up the freedoms of summer, but he got his first real girlfriend. His testosterone soon captured his brain cells, and many more were destroyed with his ear continuously glued to his cell phone. He performed activities on the outside school benches that are usually considered private or reserved for the bedroom. In spite of his rhetoric about his college ambitions, he did little or no homework, cut class on a regular basis, and often fell asleep in the few classes he did attend. His grades plummeted to all F's and one D.

Much to my surprise he was able to pull the rabbit out of the hat at the last hour and graduate, with the hands-on help of his current and previous foster parents, his therapist, social worker, in-home counselor, several academic tutors and one almost full-time saint in the role of a geometry tutor. Of course he was rewarded at graduation with all the bells and whistles of a tuxedo, a stretch limousine, and dinner at a fancy restaurant, thanks to his doting social worker.

Within a few months he lost his job with his passive aggressive move of refusing to provide a work permit. He was dragging his feet because he wanted to go to a party and didn't want to be scheduled for work on the weekend. His dismissal was a huge surprise to him since he had been acknowledged for his effectiveness with customers and good work habits. He commented several times that he didn't think they would fire him.

Life in an institution is fertile grounds for developing master manipulation skills. He was determined to have his way at any cost. He scanned his environment with laser beam vision but his synthesizer was faulty. He was ingenious at playing both ends against the middle, like pied piper. He had many ingratiating qualities and had developed seduction to a science. He also had many willing participants in the dance.

Justin was very affectionate, gracious, playful, and helpful when the mood hit him. I will always remember the time when we were cleaning the kitchen together and listening to middle-of-the-road music, he invited me to dance. Another sweet memory is when we were having a disagreement, he pulled out his cell phone and called me, even though I was just five feet away. When he wanted to put my picture on his Myspace, I felt honored. He sometimes expressed wisdom beyond his years when we had long philosophical talks at dinner.

On the other hand, his right hand often denied what his left hand was doing. For example, he took my car without permission and smashed the storage boxes in the garage when he brought it back. He used my credit cards on two different occasions without permission, and even took taxis to visit his girlfriend while I was sound asleep. Integrity and respect of personal boundaries are two of the values that I hold most dearly, and Justin repeatedly violated them. His award winning response was that "Nothing happened, nobody saw me, and everything's gonna be okay." He consistently said that he didn't intend not to follow directions or break the rules or be disrespectful, and seemed unmoved by my confusion about how he always managed to do what he was not intending to do.

When Justin and I decided to take another foster child into our family, we had many discussions about the importance for the two of us to be in agreement and consistent about the rules of the house. Since he was the first and oldest, Justin would be the role model for following the rules and helping to assist Lon to feel welcome and safe in our home.

Lon was a tall, heavyset, dark-skinned sixteen-year-old who didn't like black people. He always wore a hooded sweatshirt covering his head. Peeping out from under his hood, he spoke barely above a whisper. Nita called him Darth Vader. He wore his feelings on his sleeve, had a short fuse, and little or no tolerance for frustration. He resisted eating with the family, and he acted as if he was renting a hotel room. Most of the time he was barricaded in his bedroom, and was angry I would not allow him to entertain his friends in there.

In the beginning I was pleased that Justin stepped up to the plate and was supportive of the house rules, even reminding Lon that he needed to be more thorough in cleaning the kitchen. Having another person to tell what to do seemed to help Justin be more responsible for a while. At first Justin commented on the difference in the expectations for him and Lon, but at the time he seemed to understand and accept them. In discussing some of his concerns, I asked him to be patient during the adjustment period, and he agreed. I was delighted to see these signs of growth and progress in Justin.

After a while his behavior began to irritate Justin, because he was an exaggerated version of Justin's issues, especially entitlement. Lon refused to help Justin pay for the high speed internet connection, but he felt it should be available to him

Whenever Lon couldn't have his way, he would call his social worker. Lon changed the dynamics of our family into a triangle, and the daily routine became telling tales and tattling about the chores, rules, privileges, etc. Needless to say, there were major issues in our adjustments to each other. Trying to mediate and keep the peace was for me a déjà vu of the conflicts between Ken and Artem. We struggled with this teetering triangle for several months.

One weekend shortly after Lon moved in, Justin was gone and the Lon and I went shopping together. He had already developed the smoking habit, and had been without cigarettes for the entire weekend. He asked me if I would buy a pack for him. I agreed and told him clearly that it was the only time I would do so because I wasn't going to facilitate a habit I didn't approve of. He gave me the money, and he was more than happy to get the cigarettes. I also bought many of his favorite foods like string cheese, french fries, and pizza. He opened up and was more communicative on this occasion than I had ever experienced before or since. I chose not to relate to the manipulative quality of his behavior, and focused on the fact that the two of us were connecting positively.

Things came to a head when I awoke one morning at five AM and found Justin pacing the hall. I discovered that Lon was entertaining friends in his bedroom without my permission, and had stolen some of my champagne. Justin was ambivalent about telling me because he didn't want to be a snitch. When Lon heard my voice in the hall he hurried his friends out of the house and refused to open the door to talk to me. Coming to my rescue, Justin began threatening Lon. Later that morning Lon secretly called the cops, and told them he was afraid for his life. I heard a loud knock at the front door, and was shocked to see two armed police officers, who took Lon to a shelter.

I realized that no matter how much I wanted to help Lon, it was too little, too late. I came to accept that sometimes the way to be most helpful is to do nothing. The time had come for Lon to move because he blatantly disregarded my house rules and he was not receptive to any help I might have offered him. He was in total denial that he had any problems. Returning with his social worker to get his things, after a perfunctory conference, he left pretty much the way he came, angry, withdrawn, and blaming; he had no idea how he contributed to the unhappy ending.

Along with Justin, I was providing respite periodically for an eleven-year-old severely disturbed boy named Aaron. He is a very good looking, strong, aggressive but appealing child who still has a desire to please. Initially he looked up to Justin but was disappointed about Justin's baggy pants. Aaron thought it was sacrilegious to wear them sagging to church. After a few visits, Justin became very competitive with Aaron. Returning home from a party, the two of them started roughhousing and got into a fist fight in the back of a moving car. Subsequently, I couldn't have them together un-supervised.

Justin's lack of personal boundaries and adamant refusal to take responsibility for his choices was a magnifying glass through which I could see clearly this dynamic of codependency in myself, my family, my clients and my roommates. Reality for Justin was an internal affair with little to do with his surroundings. His truth was based on his feelings of the moment. He became addicted to smoking, despite my strong objections. He continued to smoke even though he had asthma and went to the emergency room several times with difficulty breathing.

He denied that he had changed his mind about being college bound, and adamantly insisted that he was on track to graduate and go to college. Our agreement to cooperate toward achieving our mutual goals was abandoned like an unwanted newborn.

In desperation I invited Justin's previous foster parents with whom he continued to have a good relationship to come over for a "family" meeting. I was hoping that Ray, the father, might have some magical way of reaching Justin, and I didn't want to leave a stone unturned. I was dumbfounded when, in response to Ray's question, about what he would be willing to sacrifice to get what he wanted, with a straight face Justin said that he wasn't willing to sacrifice anything. It's a law of the universe, that those who are unwilling to sacrifice, will be sacrificed.

Ray said that he appreciated Justin's honesty, and he also recognized the futility of trying to help someone by working harder than the person being helped. In this light Ray suggested that Justin try on being a failure because that's the road he was choosing. Justin's body language indicated his discomfort with the image of himself as a failure. With deep sadness I remembered several people who were headstrong in their youth, and who as adults wished that they had made different choices. I knew I was helpless to change the situation. I have learned, with great clarity, that it doesn't work to want more for a person, than he or she wants for themselves.

With deep compassion, I said, "You will live to regret the choice you are making at this very pivotal time in your life." I felt as if I had been struck by lightning and had no choice but to surrender to the spirit. As I did so, I heard the tune of "Que sera, sera, Whatever will be, will be/ The future's not ours to see....Que sera, sera."

I told Justin that I had tried everything, even including bribing him, but nothing seemed to work. He pointed out that I had only bribed him a few days earlier, so how did I know? The truth is that I attempted to bribe him on the first day he came, when I told him I would take him to Mexico when he graduated from high school.   When I had decided to accept Justin, I had vowed to see him with only love. My commitment to my vow required me to give up everything that would prevent me from seeing him lovingly. To keep myself reminded of the commitment I decided to write regular journals and exchange them with Justin. Later I decided to compile the journals into a book called *The Many Faces of my Son.*

In the process of seeing only the love in Justin, I came to know without a doubt, and Justin reassured me, that it was not personal. My illusion that I could change the fate of young black men was completely shattered in this relationship. No matter how creative I became in communicating the consequences of his irresponsible behavior, the timing of the choice to accept this reality was entirely his. Justin had told me on several occasions that he is the kind of person who has to fall on his face before he knows which way is up. This was very hard for me to accept, even when he reminded me that it was "not personal." There were many life-changing challenges but at the end of the year we were both grateful that we had been able to keep our time commitment to each other.

I decided not to make good on my "bribe" to take Justin as a graduation gift, after I discovered he had stolen and used my credit cards. When his friends were helping him move out, my leather jacket grew feet and disappeared. He indignantly told me that his friends didn't steal. I found this very amusing since I knew he himself had stolen from me. Morgan insisted that he repay me for my losses, which he eventually did.

Miraculously at graduation, Justin was awarded a forty-thousand-dollar scholarship to a four-year private college, along with an offer for student employment. This miracle was made possible by one of the trustees of the college who had met Justin when he was younger. Justin attended the High Potential Summer Program designed to prepare him to enter school in the fall. When September rolled around, it was pretty clear that Justin did not have the self-discipline required. However, even then the door was still cracked, with the possibility of returning after junior college. Although Justin was unable to accept this opportunity at the time it was offered, he is a bright young man and I believe he will eventually find his way.

After a period of wandering and homelessness, Justin enrolled in junior college and moved into his own apartment. The foster care system falls short in preparing kids to become responsible adults. Many foster kids hit a wall at eighteen when they are tossed onto the streets not knowing who they are, what to value, or how to set and achieve constructive goals. Justin visited me on several occasions and told me that many things I taught him have come to pass, like turning out the lights now that he is paying the bill.

Unfortunately Justin dropped out of junior college. However he assured me he planned to re-enroll next year. In the meantime he has become the father of a baby girl who looks just like him. I asked if he was planning to support her, and he said, "Yeah, but I still can't support myself." Sadly, Justin seems to be on a fast-moving downward spiral. He lost his job, was evicted from his apartment, and has discontinued all contact. I hope he eventually keeps his promise to pass on to his child some of the wisdom and faith that he has.

Recently while I was in St. Louis I heard that he came by the house hungry and asking for a place to spend a few nights. Keith fed him and sent him on his way. He had been involved in several physical altercations, one resulting in a cracked skull. His bill in the emergency room at Sutter Hospital was $thirty-seven thousand dollars. Creditors of a wide variety call my house on a daily basis looking for him. They refuse to believe he does not live there, and he claims that he does not give them my address.

Justin's involvement in drug use and sales led him to mindlessly try to make a sale to an undercover cop. Of course this landed him in jail. Over a six-month period I accepted several collect calls. He already understood that I have a policy of not visiting jails. He was released early to make room for more serious criminals. Being homeless, he spent some nights with friends and ended up at the apartment of his baby mama. Three days later the three of them appeared at my door, despite my clear requirement that he call before showing up. My door was ajar because I was on my way out, and I had gone back in to get something I'd forgotten.

The image of them standing there in the dripping rain was heartrending. The baby had a cold and runny nose; Justin said he had left her jacket on the bus. They obviously needed rescuing and I could not resist. Justin was very apologetic about not calling but pointed out that my phone wasn't working. Reluctantly I changed my plans and invited them in out of the rain. In short order he let me know he hadn't eaten all day and was starving. As I rummaged through my refri-gerator, I asked if the baby was hungry also. Justin said she eats anything. I suggested he wash his hands and heat the leftovers I had taken out for them. I reminded them several times during the visit that it is not okay to just show up. After they'd eaten and dried out, Deely magically appeared and offered to drive them to San Rafael. I offered my baby car seat but was adamant that it be returned. No matter how well I learn to manage my codependent tendencies, I will never be able to turn away one of my hungry children with a baby in the rain.

Being a full-time foster mom takes more time and energy than I have available at this time of my life. However, my love and compassion for foster children runs very deep in my soul. To continue to honor this calling, I decided to provide temporary and respite care. Respite is relief for foster parents who need a break, usually for the weekend. I like the flexibility.

Aaron's foster mother decided she didn't want to continue taking care of him. The termination was not well handled and was added to Aaron's growing pile of rejections. Because he needed a highly structured environment, the social worker planned to place him in St. Vincent's Home for Boys. Unfortunately St. Vincent's had no beds available at the time, and I didn't want Aaron to go to an unfamiliar foster home to wait for an opening. With the permission of the spirit, I offered to keep Aaron temporarily. This was made possible by a lot of supportive services from St. Vincent's. He seemed to enjoy my acceptance and the time he spent in my home. We played games together, made play dough, and talked about the spirit.

Aware of the trauma of his separation, I wrote Aaron a letter telling him how I thought he must be feeling and my desire to provide a comfortable and safe place for him, and asked him for his cooperation. Aaron believes in God and likes going to church. I suggested that the two of us could pray together and ask God for anything we needed help with. I put a futon at the end of my bed, and not only did I pray with him after I read him stories, I prayed for him throughout the night. He was very responsive, and began to enjoy picking the stories.

He would leave home calm in the morning, but had one crisis after another at school. He was sent home regularly, said to be out of control. I told the social worker that I thought there was something toxic in the school environment. When she investigated, she learned that the school was experiencing financial difficulties which were leading to the dismissal of several staff members, including two of Aaron's favorites. Although the news was not supposed to be known, Aaron (like many abused kids) scanned the situation, picked up the static, but was unable to decode it. My approach with Aaron when he melted down was to remain calm, talk softly, and to distract him by asking for his help with some household chore. He would regain his composure and we would act as if nothing had happened as we watered the plants.

After six weeks Aaron was placed in St. Vincent's. He gradually adapted to group living. He seemed to like the camaraderie of peers and the readily available basketball court. I visited him several times, taking him to lunch or to the video arcade. In the meantime he had reestablished contact with his natural mother, and gradually withdrew from me.

Subsequently I was asked to give a temporary home to a sixteen-year-old named James who had just been evicted from the same foster home Aaron had been in. When I saw James at the top of my steps with all his worldly belongings, I fell in love with the innocence in his eyes, despite the stories I had been told about his acting out behavior. Although he was only supposed to be with me a few days, he said he didn't want to move again, so we prayed together for the spirit's guidance. At the end of a week, the agency had not found him a home, and I didn't have the heart to put him out. I began to put more energy into relating to him, cooking him nice meals when he came home from school, and being available to listen to him.

After a month the honeymoon ended and his behavior became very inconsistent, with his main focus being to do exactly as he pleased. It became increasingly difficult to communicate with him; he had more camouflages than Osama Bin Laden. He resented expectations that he follow the rules, and he was the personification of "I didn't do anything wrong, it's not my fault, and I'm not responsible." Once when he was on a bus, when the driver took a turn that was unfamiliar to him, he got out of his seat and informed the driver that he had taken the wrong turn. Apparently the driver just looked at him in disbelief. When he told me this story I struggled not to laugh out loud. I reminded him that the bus driver takes the same route every day and probably knew the route better than James did. James refused categorically to do homework, and had a reflexive negative reaction to the suggestion that he read a book. He reacted to my gentle persistence by failing to come home on two occasions. He has a history of running away when things are not to his liking, and is a master at weaving social workers and police into his web of dramatic illusions.

I conceded that he was beyond my reach. After six weeks he was placed in a group home, where he stayed for two months, ran away, and began a series of moves. Apparently he was moved twelve times in one year. After he ran away from the last foster home, he was homeless and I was asked to provide emergency shelter, which I did. At first he was solicitous, bringing me small gifts, explaining his first departure as fear of belonging to a family. I received his gifts with grace and the understanding that they were offered as a smoke screen for his manipulations. We did this dance together for two weeks before he stopped coming home at night at all. His repertoire of excuses became so familiar, even to him, that he stopped offering them. He is currently living with an uncle whom he admires and claims he is willing to follow his directions. I think James has good intentions in the moment but lacks the substance to sustain them.

Both Justin and James are classic examples of projecting all responsibility for their shortcomings to the outside world. I now accept this narcissistic attitude for what it is--a thought disorder established as a survival technique so early that in some children it is beyond repair.

I was presented with a fascinating learning curve when I became a consulting foster grandparent to a white foster mother with a black four-year-old girl named Tazz. The initial request was for a consultation on the care of her hair and skin. Caring for hair is a family joke because it's never been my strong suit. However I knew the spirit was resourceful so I accepted the challenge.

On the first visit we decided to wash Tazz's hair. This turned into a major battle of champions. She is strong and strong-willed, and wanted no part of it. She is adamantly resistant to even the most gentle gestures of external control. After all attempts at consoling and cajoling her failed, I had had enough of her out of control tantrums and told her so. She didn't know what I was going to do, and I didn't know either, but we both knew I was going to take control. The foster mother, new to the game, was talking calmly and sweetly and seemed hesitant to lay on hands. I then took Tazz firmly by both arms and told her to take time out in the living room. She could either walk there or I would take her. She stomped around and then crawled under the table. After five minutes she came out and let us wash her hair. We were all relieved when it was over, and we parted friends.

The next visit was overnight, and we had more time to get to know each other. I learned that she is deceptively bright, mature, and articulate. I believe that much of her dysfunctional behavior is under her control and successful in getting her way. She is the biggest four-year-old I have ever met. Her body is perfectly shaped with curves in the right places, and looks as if she is going to burst into puberty any moment. My first encounter with her precociousness came when she gave me a detailed description of the variations in human nature. She used windows and doors and shapes and sizes of mirrors and other objects as metaphors to explain human relationships and preferences. At first I was only half listening, but she soon captured my undivided attention. When I asked her about her own preferences, she expressed appreciation for the room I had decorated for her. She surveyed the entire room and expressed love for each object, with one exclusion, the chenille bedspread. It was "too hard" for her liking.

I am impressed with her clear sense of self and personal preferences. She likes a bubble bath, but in its absence, she will accept bath crystals but refuse bath salts. She hates soap. She eats almost continuously and drinks gallons of hot chocolate. In the beginning I objected to the quantities and suggested a substitute based on my assumption about the high sugar content. She pointed out to me that it was sugar free and contained calcium and vitamins. When I checked the packet and discovered she was right, she asked, "Did you know it was good for you?" I admitted that I did not. She is aware of healthy foods as distinguished from junk foods, and even knows the ingredients.

The one exception is her love for McDonald's. Beyond the food, she is fascinated by the trinkets and prizes. On one of our trips she was very definite about wanting a princess crown that came with the Happy Meal. When she was given a substitute, she was loudly objected. When the waitress said they were all gone, I supported Tazz by asking the waitress to look again. Tazz and I looked at each other as if we were on the same team, and when our eyes met I felt it was a moment of true bonding. The waitress returned with the crown, and Tazz smiled joyfully. We both felt triumphant.

On a later visit to the playground, Tazz met some new friends, which provided several opportunities for me to teach a few social skills. Tazz was eager to share her crown with her friend. When the child refused to wear it, Tazz insisted. I reminded her that she does not like people forcing things on her, and the girl's preference didn't mean that she didn't like Tazz or want to be her friend.

She became very absorbed in playing and didn't want to stop to go across the street use the bathroom. I suggested that we could go behind the building and use the bushes, but she would have no part of either. I repeated her options, but she continued to play until her bladder gave her no choice, and she wet her pants in front of her friends. This was the least desirable option, and it camouflaged the fact that it was her choice. After changing her clothes at home, she came to me and stated, "I will never do that again." I told her I thought her decision was wise because she ended up making the least desirable choice.

On our second visit to the playground, she met a new group

of children and became enamored with a little boy. Again the time came when she told me she needed to use the bathroom, but didn't want to go across the street. She continued to play, and I continued to observe. She waited until there was no time to find bushes, and very reluctantly agreed to squat behind the car door. I considered this real progress, because I believe she has a tendency towards an obsessive-compulsive disorder around cleanliness. I also believe that the motivation to rise above it was sparked by her desire not to wet her pants in front of her new male friend. I complimented her on her choice, and suggested that she might make a decision sooner next time.

Tazz has a lot going for her--she's bright, strong willed, vivacious, fun, and pretty. From her I have learned with great clarity that the less I am involved in her decisions, the faster she comes to her own truth. This is a strong demonstration of the ineffectiveness of codependency. Going forward, I am committed to confining my interventions to simply outlining options and likely consequences. I am looking forward to the times we will spend together.

I was asked to provide a temporary foster home to a seventeen-year-old who had been living with his teacher for a year. The placement failed when Andre started using the internet inappro-priately, and drinking beer, throwing the bottles in the neighbors' yard. Although the social worker continued to look for a permanent home for him, we all knew it would be his "last chance." I accepted the responsibility to help him prepare to live successfully in a family and in the world.

Andre is a tall, well built, handsome young white man who is more intelligent than he would lead you to believe. He presented himself as a minimalist, doing just enough to get by. He used most of his energy to avoid doing whatever he was asked to do. He is the oldest of several siblings whose mom is alcoholic and abuses drugs. He spent quite a lot of time talking about the past, bemoaning the fact that his mother was totally unavailable to him, gave him alcohol when he asked for water, etc. He threw daily pity parties, inviting any and everyone to attend. Andre isolated himself in his room and ran up several hundred dollars on my phone bill of inappropriate phone porno calls, a carry over and the reason his previous placement failed. Although the social agency had most of the charges removed, I insisted he take responsibility for repaying the debt by doing chores. Initially he resisted, until I pointed out to him that I would not have hired him, due to his poor work ethic, but he gave me no choice. I also would not have loaned him the money because he was not responsible. It was like taking my money without permission, in other words, stealing.

Every morning the two of us sat on the deck overlooking the bay and had long discussions about life. After a few days I acknow-ledged that he had been neglected, that alcohol ruled his mother's life, and his attempts to get her attention by setting fires was ineffective and only resulted in his removal from home. However, all of that was in the past, over which he had no control. He could allow past experiences to control his life, or he could choose to let the past go, get over the hurt, and get on with his life. My nephew Keith also talked to Andre at length about his loss of both parents at an early age and his own deprivation. Andre was surprised by Keith's story, almost as if he thought that he was the only person who'd ever been deprived. During one of our discussions, I shared with Andre a little poem that my mother often recited to me:

> *"If you have a job to do,*
> *Labor great or small*
> *It's wise to do it well*
> *Or do it not at all."*

Although he didn't comment at the time, the following day he did a superb job of yard work and subsequently seemed to take pride in his work of cleaning the kitchen and other duties.

Toward the end of his stay I told Andre that I had repeated the same process with all of the teenagers placed in my home, in order to prepare them for personal independence. I told him that the jury was still out on the effectiveness of the teachings. He responded that I had probably done my best work with him. He told the social worker that he had learned more in the three months with me than he had in the seventeen years he'd been in the world. After three months he was placed in a permanent foster home with a mom and dad. Another fourteen-year-old foster child, Peter, was also placed there at the same time, and they are both doing well. I see them for respite about once a month. Peter is a tall, stocky, baby-faced white youth who is shy and very soft spoken. He is easy going, and appears to defer to Andre. He always shows up for meals, but then quickly retreats back to his room. During the honeymoon period of getting acquainted, I did not push family interactions. However he and Andre have always been well behaved, both at home and in social situations in others' homes.

Most of my life, all of my truly intimate relationships have been with women, female children and animals, and inanimate objects. Observing this phenomenon, when Nita was ready to leave home, she strongly encouraged me to seek male companionship to fill my empty nest, but I was not inspired to do so. Yet interestingly, almost all my foster children have been males. Recently when my house became infested with rodents (which were smarter than the exterminators), I was at my wit's end. In desperation, I asked the spirit what was I to do? The response was, "Get a cat."

A friend and neighbor who is an animal lover offered to help me select the perfect kitty. She along with three of my foster children, Peter, Andre, and Tazz went with me on the expedition to acquire the cat. We ended up at the San Francisco SPCA where we observed and played with lots of kittens and cats. I was most impressed with a short hair Russian Blue feline who appeared very quiet and still, but was very observant, acting almost as a witness to our selection process. He had electric eyes that lured you in. He seemed very shy and reluctant to respond to our attentions. His introduction card described him as "standoffish at first but all love once he gets to know you."

Following the directions from SPCA, I kept him in my room for the first two weeks. I changed his name from Kirbie to Piper. He hid under the bed or in the closet except for meal times. After two weeks he gradually warmed up, moved into my bed, and tried to seduce me into petting his tummy or playing with him with a dancing toy. Soon he became so attached to me that he followed me into the bathroom, and after a while he even ventured upstairs to check on my whereabouts, and then dash back down to the bedroom. Now he puts himself directly in my path so I either have to pet him or walk on him.

He refuses to make friends with anyone else, and seems to want my undivided attention, which he seeks assertively. I thought he was being aggressive, but the children assured me he was only being affectionate. Being used to solitude and liking it, I thought his intrusiveness was "too much too soon." He seems to need more stimulation than I am willing to provide. I have been strongly advised both to keep him indoors and to let him go out. To date I have decided to keep him in since I had his claws clipped and worried about his being able to defend himself.

    Even Tazz commented that he seems different from the way he first appeared. In the shelter he was not only still but silent. At home he turned out to be a Cirque de Soleil acrobat and ad libs like Joe Biden. In his world, playing and being petted takes precedence over eating. I am still in shock with amazement at his shameless requests for almost continuous affection, but I am trying to step up to the plate.

    Needless to say, he pulls me far out of my comfort zone, but I am convinced that the universe selected him for me. I have never been one to play games, but since his arrival, it seems that every other day I select the angel card that advises me to "play." I think the message is that God wants me to play and has sent Piper to teach me. No one says that love is easy, and intimacy can be very hard work. I have decided to surrender, seeing in him only reflections of the divine. I have faith that we will work this relationship out to our mutual satisfaction. In the meantime I continued to reach out for consultation and help wherever I could find it.

    Peter turned out to be a cat specialist. At the SPCA he actively observed and described characteristics of various cats. He seemed comfortable and gentle in his interactions with them. He preferred one of the more active cats, but I wanted one who seemed calm. In the end, we all agreed on the blue gray shorthair.

The next time the boys visited, Piper was still closeted in my bedroom, and refused to venture out. I was very concerned about him. I told the boys about some of his wild behavior and referred to him as aggressive. Both boys corrected me, suggesting that he was just being affectionate.

At dinner I asked Peter's advice. First, he pointed out that the cat was still young and energetic and playful, and that he would mellow out when he was older. When I complained that he had taken over my bedroom, Peter said that cats are very territorial and that is their nature. I said I did not want to deprive the cat of his youth and make him old too soon, but I also needed to feel at peace in my own room. Healthy relationships must meet the needs of all involved.

He suggested that I start to move the cat out gradually to the rest of the house, move his food and water upstairs into the kitchen, and come back and get the cat and show him where it is. I might need to do this two or three times, he said. The next step is to place the cat's bed on top of my bed and encourage him to sleep in his own. Later I could move his bed to another part of the house. The third thing is the cat box. I should find an accessible place and move it there. I was deeply impressed with the practicality and effectiveness of Peter's advice. I told him I had recognized him as a wise man on our first meeting, and he had demonstrated the truth of that observation.

I asked Peter how his life had been since we were last together. Peter responded, "Not so good." On further questioning, he said he had to get rid of a relationship. He seemed conflicted about it, and had difficulty acknowledging that he might have positive feelings about the person, even though the relationship might not have been good for him. It became clear to me that he was uncomfortable talking about it, so we dropped it. I commented that I was surprised that at least one good thing had not happened to him, because he has a loving spirit, and as a rule, good things follow people with loving spirits. The perfect way for me to teach Peter about relationships is to have him teach me, in this case about cats.

Andre had to work the following day, so it gave Peter and me the opportunity to bond. Peter wasn't feeling very well, and only wanted oatmeal for breakfast. I took the opportunity to prepare for him a breakfast setting fit for a king. I used black and green plates and matching placemats and cloth napkins. I got out my best china and silver, and set a gorgeous table. Then I went down to his room, addressed him as "Sir," and announced that breakfast was served. After saying grace, I told Peter that my favorite Bible story was about King Solomon and his wisdom. I asked if he had ever seen "Queen for a Day," and of course he had not; (he's too young.) I told him that inside of each of us is a king or queen. I consider it my job as respite foster mom to help boys and girls discover the kings and queens inside of them. I asked if he would be willing to participate in this exploration, and he said he would. The first thing he needed to know about being a king was that real kings, the divine kings, are very loving. He made no direct comment to this statement, but I felt a sweetness around him, and it lasted throughout the day.

I also provide respite for Rich and DJ, who are foster brothers, one black and one white. DJ is a small slightly built fourteen-year-old who looks much younger. He is said to be hyperactive, but he totally loses himself in his games, during which he can be calm and self-contained. He is pleasant to be around, and anxious to please. He is interested in becoming a mechanic, and proved himself to be handy around the house helping me with various jobs. When I told his foster mother how helpful he had been, he beamed with pride. Although he doesn't like to read, he agreed to listen to books on tape concerning mechanics.

Rich is a tall thin black handsome young man, whose favorite pastime is texting. Like his foster brother, he dislikes reading. However he says he wants to become a nurse. After one of my canned speeches about the necessity to prepare for life, he was willing to listen to talking books. When I questioned what he was learning from his constant texting, he said he was learning to spell and social skills. He said it helped him handle his anger without blowing up. He is also willing to hold the mirror for DJ who tends to distort or deny the truth. I was very complimentary to him for encouraging his brother to be honest, supporting both of their health.

Kevin is an eighteen-year-old biracial Asian/white young man. He is a bit rigid in some of his habits, like counting to twenty when he washes his hands (encouraging everyone else to do the same). His favorite pastime is board games, and he was surprised and delighted when I entered his world of games as a neophyte. He thoroughly enjoyed teaching and beating me in the game of Risk. I also liked venturing into this new world, which turned out to be our place of connection. I am very grateful for the gift of openness and willingness to share the worlds of the children who are sent to me.

Katie is a bright, angelic looking child with straight blond hair and enchanting gray eyes. She can be charming when she wants to be, and she lights up a room with her smile. Although she's only eight, she is also precocious, strong willed, vindictive and malicious. Katie is pathologically controlling and determined to have her way at any cost. She enjoys inflicting pain on others, has sticky fingers, and is a cunning, highly-skilled liar. She has traits of both Mary Poppins and the Bad Seed.

She is the oldest of four children, for whom she had been primary caretaker when her parents were out on methamphetamines. She is angry about the neglect and abuse she has experienced in her short life. Her family was referred to Child Welfare Protective Services thirty-five times since her birth. She has had numerous foster home placements. She has mixed feelings about her siblings, especially her five-year-old sister with whom she shared her last foster home placement. On one hand she was very maternal and protective, and on the other she often felt jealous and resentful of the attention the younger sister received. She has tried to hurt her sister on several occasions, using various weapons she made. When she was observed sharpening several sticks in the presence of an adult, this was considered a cry for help. She was removed from the foster home of thirteen months and placed with me for her own safety and the safety of her sister.

When Katie came to me I greeted her with an open heart and a warm blanket. She loved her beautifully decorated feminine bedroom and started acting at home immediately by putting her things away and asking to go out on the deck. I was playing my usual Hindu chant and she asked me if I went to church. She said her previous foster family had gone to church for a while but stopped because it became boring. I said I found church exciting because I loved God. She said she loves God too. I told her I was happy that we both loved God because it would help us get along together.

The next day she gave me some stickers and asked me to give one to her as a reward for good behavior. I thanked her and told her that I prefer to focus on the positive rather than the negative, and the stickers would provide a positive direction for us. In life I look for the easy passage and hoped that she would join me on that path so we could make our time together enjoyable. We agreed upon an eight o'clock bedtime and created some nightly rituals which included prayers and bedtime stories. Katie told me she had a history of scary nightmares, so the first two weeks I let her sleep in my bed. She resisted transferring to her own bed, and often got up during the night to come into my bed. I reminded her that she had already mastered several important developmental tasks, such as potty training and giving up the bottle, so sleeping in her own bed was just another challenge that she would also conquer. I said I would come into her room if she needed me until she could face the monsters in the nightmares on her own. In the meantime, we could use the dream catcher her grandmother had given her to capture the monsters to ask them what they wanted. Gradually her nightmares faded into the background, and she started coming into my room around six AM to cuddle before we had to get up to start the day.

Every time the telephone rang she would make a mad dash to answer it, in spite of being asked not to. She delighted in telling the caller that she was my adopted daughter. One of Katie's favorite games was playing house with me. She asked to do it every day. I was to be the mother and she was the oldest child. She enjoyed calling me "Mother," which was repeated steadily during the play. She wanted me to discipline the younger children, while she was always the good one. When we played school, I was to drive her to school and pick her up and take her to her after school program, where I would stay and watch her perform and give her many accolades. She became so deeply absorbed in her various roles that I had concern about multiple personalities. This play acting was the perfect avoidance of her own responsibilities, because she always blamed one of the other characters for any wrong doing. I requested she be referred for psychological evaluation.

While I was on vacation Katie had two meltdowns, one following a visit with her parents and grandparents, the other when she locked herself in the bathroom and refused to come out for about an hour. While she was in there she apparently broke the ball in the toilet tank, causing the toilet to overflow which resulted in extensive damage. Although she adamantly denied any responsibility, I intuitively knew by her mixed greeting upon my return of both enthusiasm and apprehension. I was persistent in my pursuit of the truth. I told her that I wanted to talk to that part of her that is determined to have her way at any cost, willing to destroy anything and anybody that she perceives as standing in her way.

After due process, she admitted breaking it, adding that when she becomes angry she wants to hurt someone or break something. We talked about using words to express her feelings, beating a pillow, etc., and she agreed to try it. However, when the in-home counselor decided to teach her the right way to hit a pillow, Katie became enraged and hit her with the pillow. In discussing who would pay for the plumbing damage, the social work director tried to avoid responsibility by questioning whether Katie had actually broken the toilet. This was unfortunate for Katie because she is already very crafty at playing her adult caretakers like a strategic game of poker, one against the other. Subsequently my dryer, fax machine, and stereo were also mysteriously broken. I am in the process of negotiating reimbursement for all.

In the meantime, Katie has started to express her anger more with words. She became extremely upset when her parents did not show up to celebrate her birthday, but they had come for the other three children. The social worker, who by her own admission is over-identified with Katie, seemed compulsively driven to overcompensate for the parents' negligence by arranging at least five birthday parties. I thought this was overkill and cringed at the message Katie was being given.

I told Katie that if I was her, I would be upset and angry too if I was expected to understand adults' immaturity when I was only eight years old. A big smile came on her face and she seemed relieved. I told her it was OK to be angry--it was what she does with those feelings that makes the difference.

When Katie is angry she goes for the jugular. She is astute at identifying a person's weaknesses, and she aims with precision during battle. At times she is extremely defiant, and loves to proclaim what she will and will not do, that nobody can force her, etc. She acts as if she thinks she is the adult, or rather a queen talking to her subjects. She is known to get in your face, hands on hips, head shaking, talking loud and boisterous.

Her parents are self-proclaimed racists, although her mother has been pregnant twice with black babies, which she aborted in Katie's presence. Over time, my blackness has surfaced as problematic for Katie. They have told her that it's not ok to hang out with black folks, and she told me she didn't think race really mattered, that what was important was whether or not you could trust a person. I was surprised by her wisdom. I asked her if she trusted me and she said yes. During a family visit her father apparently commented that she had a suntan and was two colors. Katie said that she is really lots of colors, brown, black and white. She said she likes being a mixture of different colors. On one hand she is conflicted and torn between her loyalties, on the other hand she feels free to use the race card to her own advantage.

When I attended open house at her school, she introduced me to one of her friends as her mother. When the little girl looked surprised and continued to ask where her mother was, Katie became impatient, "I told you, she's right here." When her parents missed three consecutive visits, it was easier to blame it on their objections to her placement with me than to face their irresponsibility. When angry at me, Katie has told me that she needs to be with her "own kind." My response is to assure her that I cannot change my blackness and she will have to deal with it or not. She usually backs down when I suggest she could live with people of her own kind, and becomes overly affectionate, throwing her arms around me and kissing me on the cheek.

Recently she has started to talk to me about problems she experienced living with her parents in a one-room hotel while they were using drugs. These conversations are usually followed by acting out behavior. This kid has been identified as having a serious attachment disorder, a perfect diagnosis for testing my detached giving as a mother. However our relationship ends, I will have received a Ph D in mothering.

Katie has a full complement of social workers, counselors, lawyers, all of whom are very interested in her and visit regularly. Katie's social worker has commented to me several times that the "system" is not serving Katie. She says this with such a straight face that I'm sure she doesn't recognize that she is a major part of the broken system. First, she is over-identified with Katie and readily admits her emotional attachment to her. On several occasions she has commented that what in my opinion was inappropriate behavior was either cute or funny. She went over the top in arranging a variety of birthday celebrations for Katie, to the point I questioned the message she was giving. It seems to me that the idea was if you have enough celebrations, it ensures wellbeing. She also became overly excited when she was able to locate a ballet teacher for Katie and stated she would have paid for it out of her own pocket if necessary.

After Katie's removal from her previous foster home, she visited the family every week for dinner, and always returned loaded down with new clothes and gifts of various kinds. This continued for about six weeks until I suggested that she needed time and space to adjust to her new home. I had a lot of questions about all the gifts. Many people delight in buying Katie things, especially clothes, and she has accumulated an amazing amount of stuff in her short life. She needs a professional organizer to help her downsize. She asked me several times why I didn't buy her clothes. Each time I tell her she has more than she needs and I value relationships more than things.

During my vacation in Florida, one of the in-home counselors stayed at my house to babysit Katie. There were several incidents during this time, one involving one of my nephews who was living in my home and had not yet been legally cleared to be around foster children. Since then, Morgan seemed to have a bee in her bonnet about me although she refused to talk directly about what is wrong. While I was away Katie broke the ball in the toilet tank, causing it to overflow. In discussing the damage and responsibility with Morgan, she interrogated me around whether or not Katie was responsible, and then added that she herself had had to take the top off the toilet tank to flush it on one of her visits to my home. When Morgan picked me up to go to lunch to celebrate Katie's birthday, I caught her putting my wallet back into my pocketbook as I reentered the room. Our eyes met but neither of us spoke. I decided not to bring it up because I was sure she would only deny it.

When I attended a three-day conference, Morgan arranged for Katie to spend Saturday with Sonia, who turned out to be a potential long-term placement. In spite of the fact that I had talked to Morgan and Emma several times and we had spent almost the entire day celebrating her birthday, there was no mention to me of plans to explore the new placement. Nita had planned a birthday party for her godchild, and asked Morgan if it would be OK to invite Katie. In spite of the fact that I had been very clear that any weekend plans for Katie would be contingent on whether or not a visit was scheduled with her parents. Apparently Morgan thought that Nita and I had made plans for Katie without consulting Emma, the social worker. She called me at 9:30pm to inform me that she had arranged for Katie to spend Friday night with Sonia. Morgan said Nita would just have to understand the change in the plans, because Morgan was dealing with time pressure for permanent placement. Something about this scenario didn't ring true for me. Katie, beside me in bed, was listening to the entire conversation and became very excited.

In a subsequent conversation with Emma, I questioned the process of planning for Katie's weekend. In response to my question Emma said that she also preferred Katie to spend the night with Sonia, but then suggested I give Katie the choice. I objected because plans to attend the party were totally contingent on whether or not there was a visit scheduled with her parents. I said the plan did not seem well thought-out to me, and to use Morgan's words, it had a flavor of "ambulance chasing." I said I would not have handled it like that; it was not only overly stimulating to Katie, but gave her the wrong message that once again she was in charge. I asked Emma what her plan was for dealing with Katie's anticipated acting out around her visit with her family, since this seems to be an issue that goes unnoticed by everyone but me.

Emma said she would inform Katie's therapist that the parents failed to confirm their visit, and suggested the therapist handle it with Katie. Katie came home before going to therapy and the first words out of her mouth were, "Marie, they didn't confirm the visit." I told her I knew how disappointing that was for her, and for that I was very sorry. I added that her parents had issues they needed to resolve before they could provide the care that she and her siblings needed. I reminded her that the two of us had been working on her changing some of her behavior, which wasn't easy, and her parents would have to do the same. In the meantime she had a lot of people in her life who loved her and would take good care of her until her parents could. She listened attentively and at the end, I asked her to give me a hug, which she did. Later in the conversation with Emma, I was told that Katie is very protective of her parents and refused to talk about them in her therapy.

About a week later, I telephoned Morgan because Katie refused to go to school. I explained to her very clearly that the incident was one of defiance, and I told her that on another occasion when Katie had refused to go to school, I told her that she would be going to school even if I had to drag her there. Morgan used this to inform me that that was a threat of violence for which I could lose my license. She suggested that I ask Katie to get out of bed, and then I should leave the room. I explained that I had tried that several times before, and I had a doctor appointment and time was of the essence. With this she said she would jump in the shower and then come to my house. When I told Katie of this plan she decided to get up.

Morgan insisted that Katie's change of mind was due to her suggested intervention. I corrected her and told her the change was due to the plan. I suggested further that both she and the social worker seemed to operate like Monday morning quarterbacks -- they don't listen and they seem to prefer a nebulous organic process which enables them to find fault and place blame on the foster parent to disguise the absence of an effective treatment plan. I told her that I had informed the social worker that I had asked Katie to clean up the paint she had spilled, and I went into my room and sat on my bed. Katie followed me into my bedroom, put her hands on her hips, got in my face shaking her head, yelling, "I told you I didn't do it," trying to force me to seeing it her way. The social worker asked me if I had ever thought about just giving the command and leaving the room. I repeated in a louder voice that that was exactly what I had done.

Morgan told me that I had threatened to do bodily harm to Katie and she had it on tape. I said I had no recollection of any threat to do physical harm to her, and asked to hear the tape. She said she was going on vacation and would play it for me upon her return. She added that the social worker on call during her absence wanted me to know that she only accepted calls in the case of an emergency, such as a child running away, but not a power struggle. I told Morgan I was not into a power struggle with anyone and she was passing on the wrong information to her staff. Actually she,

Morgan, is the only person in a power struggle. I consider myself very skilled at effective communication. I draw few lines in the sand, but when I do, I show up and it's important for me to win. It's my opinion that it is not healthy for a child to believe that she is equal to or superior to the adults in her life. My behavior wasn't intended to threaten bodily harm; it was designed to demonstrate that I had more power than an eight-year-old.

Morgan continued to insist that I was in a power struggle in spite of my advice to the contrary. I told Morgan that I didn't want to continue this conversation over the phone, that I wanted to look in her eyes when she was making these claims. I asked for a meeting with everybody involved in Katie's care, then after thinking about it decided I had no desire to convince anybody that I was not in a power struggle. I left messages for Morgan and Emma not to arrange a meeting on my behalf.

Because Katie was so distressed about her parents missing her birthday, I suggested she ask them on her next visit what happened. I thought it also might be helpful for her to write down any questions she had about her parents situation. I said that it helps you to remember when you write things down. Although initially she resisted, she did make a list of questions, with Emma's help. She made two columns of good and bad things. Later I told her that I was very impressed that she given a balance, acknowledging both sides. She responded that she has always loved her parents since before she was born. Asked what she loved about them, she said they cared enough to buy them food and her mother made sure that they ate healthy. For example, she had never had soda until she came into foster care. I told her that sometimes people we love hurt us by their behavior, but we love them in spite of that. She denied that her parents were still using, and I said I didn't know, which is the reason I wanted her to find out for herself. She asked if I thought her grandparents would also come with her parents for a belated birthday celebration. Again I told her that I didn't know them, and asked if they had celebrated her birthdays in the past. She assured me that they had, and I told her that based on her experience it sounded like they would. But again, she knew them, not me. Unfortunately the grandparents didn't show up. Although Katie claimed she had a wonderful visit with her parents and siblings, I noticed she became more distant and defiant in her relationship with me. Later she admitted that her parents were still drinking and smoking and that made her angry.

    When I told Emma that Katie's distress around her parents' situation was showing up in her hygiene and refusal to turn in her homework, Emma suggested that I pin the homework on her back as is done for her younger sister. I told Katie that if she didn't turn her homework in, I would have to pin it on her back, per instructions from Emma. Katie asked me if that meant that she couldn't be like the other children, and I said, "In a way, you would be announcing to the world that you were not able to meet normal expectations or to take responsibility for the things you should." I asked her if she wanted to create this kind of image for herself. That evening she said she had turned in her homework.

Arrangements were made for Katie to spend the Thanksgiving holidays with Sonia and her family in Truckee. Since I was unable to find Katie's school uniforms in Marin, Emma offered to ask Nicole to go shopping with Katie in Santa Rosa. In addition to school uniforms, Nicole decided to buy Katie a jacket, snow pants, a scarf, and a hat. Nicole was very proud of the purchases, and Katie thanked her profusely. She even went to her room and got a dollar and change to give to Nicole for repayment. Nicole was quite willing to take the credit although she expected me to write the check for reimbursement. Katie saw me write it, and the following morning she got in my face, licked out her tongue, shook her head as if to say, "Ha ha," I made you buy me clothes anyway." Katie has an abundance of beautiful clothes, and it is no secret that I have consciously chosen not to contribute to her already overstocked wardrobe.

Later I called Nicole and asked her how she had decided what to buy for Katie. She started to imply that the social worker had told her what to buy, but when I questioned this, she said the social worker had told her to discuss it with me. I asked her if she had done this and she said she had been talking to Sonia who said... I stopped her and repeated my question about her taking it upon herself to decide how to spend my money without consulting me. She said she was busy and she would call me back, but she never did. When she brought Katie home, she asked if she should come as usual to keep Katie on Tuesday evening. Again she said she would call but didn't.

When I was on vacation, Nicole stayed in my house with Katie, and I told her to make herself at home. I never expected her to feel free to help herself to my most expensive foods such as shrimp which she generously prepared for Katie and herself. One morning when she came to pick Katie up, I was surprised to find three packages of oatmeal on the counter. When I inquired about it, she said in a voice of entitlement, "It's OK if I have oatmeal, isn't it?" To add insult to injury, she feels free to leave her and Katie's dirty dishes in the sink and doesn't bother to clean the bathroom after Katie's bath or have Katie pick up her dirty clothes. When Nicole takes a nap in the evenings when she babysits, she leaves the blanket thrown on the sofa. I didn't agree to take on the responsibility of two children, so I decided to give notice on working with Nicole.

When I related the scenario to the social worker, she seemed a bit surprised and commented that Nicole owed me an apology. The next time Nicole dropped off Katie, she told me that

Emma had said I wanted to talk to her. There was no mention of an apology. After several attempts we finally had a telephone conversation. I told Nicole that I felt unsupported and even undermined by her and did not feel that we worked well together on Katie's behalf. I listed all my concerns to her. Regarding not picking up after herself and Katie, Nicole said that Katie was difficult to take care of, required undivided attention, and she supposed she was too stressed out. Regarding cooking and eating my foods without permission, she said that I had told her to make herself at home while I was away, and she supposed she continued to do so even after my return. I didn't mention that she brought both her parents to my home while I was gone and showed them through my house, including my bedroom. I told her that I felt that she showed disdain for my values and expectations.

On one occasion I had suggested that Katie try expressing her anger by hitting a pillow. She did a practice run in my bedroom, but she used my good pillow, and I told her to tell Nicole to give her an old one. Instead Katie took a pillow from her bed without asking. Nicole intervened to show Katie her version of the "right way" to hit the pillow. Katie became angry and hit Nicole with the pillow. Katie feels quite free to physically attack Nicole whenever she feels like it. I explained to Nicole that the expert on expressing feelings is the one experiencing them, and there is no "RIGHT WAY" for self expression. I further stated that I am deliberate in my response and directions to Katie. Nicole might not agree with my values or philosophy, but she had to respect and abide by them in my home.

I pointed out that Katie is very aware of my expectations, and is also aware that Nicole does not follow them. For example, one evening Katie asked for cookies after dinner. Then she took the opportunity to tell me that they were all gone and Nicole had taken the last one without asking. Katie also became angry and hit Nicole when she did not turn out the light after Katie asked her to do so. Katie has reminded Nicole on several occasions that she doesn't live there. She also became angry because Nicole refused to remove her shoes as is the custom in our house. She told me to tell Nicole to do so.

Nicole commented that Katie plays us against each other. I agreed that this is true,--Katie is a very intelligent and shrewd little girl-- but I reminded Nicole that it is her (Nicole's) behavior that I am reacting to. I would find it offensive in whatever context and by whomever it occurred. Nicole said she was surprised to hear that I felt this way, and wished I had told her sooner. I said that I thought it was a question of supervision and I was deciding how I wanted to handle the situation. However, when she felt free to spend my money without asking, I felt totally sabotaged and I had reached my limit. I told her insult was added to injury because she had been advised to ask me before spending any money for which she expected to get reimbursed.

Nicole said she wanted to work out our differences if I were willing. I said I did not want to be closed minded but it seemed to me that we were much too far apart to breach the gap. I was willing to give it a light trial run, leaving the door open for her to bow out gracefully. Our inability to work together did not mean either of us is wrong, we are just different. I know it would be good for Katie to see us work through our differences, but the cost is too high with no guaranteed results. I'm not motivated to invest the amount of energy it would require.

Katie has been unable to resolve her ambivalence around race and her confusion around the multiple and changing caretakers and authority figures in her life. With so many adults hovering around her in almost a competitive heat, she has been overwhelmed. She is also aware that Sonia and her husband are a possibility for a new home, and she for a while started to compare me and my belongings unfavorably with them and their things. Katie continues to need to identify a villain on whom she can project the blame for all the problems and emotional uncertainties in her life. Since I was the one talking most about the problems, I became the problem. The child welfare system, also unable to resolve the real issues, seemed more than willing to follow her lead in identifying a scapegoat. Given this scenario, I felt undermined on all sides and my effectiveness compromised. I also decided to give notice on parenting Katie.

After my return from vacation in Hawaii our relationship moved to a new paradigm, and we got along much better. Her affection for me returned in the tenderness of her voice when she said my name, whether she referred to me as Marie or Mom or Mother. Even during our worst times she refused to leave my bed. I was committed to keeping her until they found a suitable placement. I trusted the universe, and hoped it would be timely.

After much deliberation Sonia decided to take Katie for long term foster care with the possibility of adoption. When Katie knew she would be moving, her acting out behavior increased. I felt she was attempting to take some control and handled the separation in the only way she knew how. I did arrange for her to say good bye to her teacher and the class, which I believe was her first positive good bye.

I talked to her several times by phone and she visited me on two occasions. She seemed very subdued, and I wondered if she was experiencing depression over the court's termination of her parental rights as well as sadness over separation from me. Even so, she apparently had adjusted well to her new home and school. She is almost functioning at grade level, and has made new friends. I feel good about the love I have given Katie without attachment.

I assumed that my extended role as foster mom was

completed with Katie and I had decided to focus exclusively on respite care. After a few months I was asked to provide emergency respite for seventeen-year-old Rich , who had left his foster home following an emotional blowout. About a year ago Rich and his foster brother had spent a weekend in my home. I liked him, found him to be easy going, but assumed our relationship would be limited to weekends.

Rich is a tall, slender, brown-skinned young man, with an engaging smile and pleasant manner most of the time. He has a magnetic presence in the world, much of it due to his handsome face and physique, which he does not hesitate to use to his advantage. He strikes me as having a classic pimp mentality of entitlement and intimidation. He is known to be overly aggressive when angry. He is a devoted student of Tae Kwon Do which is a good thing for him but it also has the potential for abuse. He has an extremely short fuse that sometimes ignites without reason or advance notice. He punched holes in the foster mother's door on two occasions, and he was expelled from school for his uncontrolled anger.

He has been in the foster care system since birth. He has lived in more than thirty foster homes. He was in his last home for two years, entangled in a less than healthy foster family triangle. He hated the foster father, (whose work required extended periods away from home), and even though Rich probably had one of his best relationships with this foster mother, he didn't seem to have any genuine attachment to her. As institutionalized as he is, he does not seem to be as damaged by his experiences as some of the other children I have had, or he has cultivated an almost flawless cover. At other times he shows a gentle spirit and an open heart which he selectively invites people into. He hopes to become a psychiatric nurse or social worker.

Our initial bone of contention was centered around food. Rich seems to have strong emotions connected with eating and drinking, and so do I. He consumes an extreme amount of food, especially sugar, and has a tendency to drink several quarts of juice or other drinks like Gatorade in one evening. His explanation is that he is thirsty. He is very wasteful, and becomes highly upset if I bring up the subject of eating, wasting, expense, etc. He says he doesn't want to discuss it because it reminds him of the past and makes him sad. I told him that I live on a limited budget and cannot afford to throw away my meager resources, and I needed him to step up to the present. These are normal and necessary conversations whenever people live together, especially if they expect to do so in any harmony.

Over the years I have done a lot of work on myself to under-stand and control my emotions, but I was shocked at the depth of my emotional reaction to Rich's wastefulness. I think it was both his attitude of entitlement and seeing my money go down the drain that every cell in my body recoiled with repulsion. I remember my mother's voice saying, "Think of all the starving people in China!" I felt my heart close.

When Rich left for work a few hours later, we did our routine hug but my heart wasn't in it. I was surprised by my inability to fake it, and I knew he felt the difference. On reflection I realized that in the past, whenever I was hurt in an intimate relationship and the other person refused to take responsibility, I rationalized my response. Whenever the same behavior continued, my heart closed a little more. Over time I was no longer available to intimacy in the relationship and took on a perfunctory role. This was a light bulb moment for me, and I also realized that Rich was probably not aware of the effect of his behavior on me. I felt I had a responsibility to let him know. When I told him how his behavior made me feel, I said it was his responsibility to choose how he wanted to respond. But if we were going to have a meaningful relationship, I needed him to be more sensitive to my feelings.

One day I commented on his eating three English muffins when there were only four in the package. He became angry and threw his three in the trash. On another occasion he was cooking six eggs and carelessly dropped one on the stove, missing the skillet. He casually said that that often happens to him. Once I bought three different cereals, and Rich fixed himself a heaping bowl of the one I had bought for myself. After a few bites he decided he didn't like it and went to the sink and poured the whole bowl down the drain.

I was livid and told him I was extremely disturbed by his wastefulness, and later I called the social worker to request that she come and objectively explain to Rich how his behavior affected me. She came and reminded him that these were the same issues he had in his last foster home. Apparently the foster mother had tolerated his behavior, and the social worker pointed out to Rich that I was saying I was not going to tolerate it. She went on to elaborate on behavior that causes me to close my heart. Rich retorted that he didn't know of anything that closed my heart except wasting food, and that he didn't do it anymore. I added "disrespect" to the list, and he made no response.

The social worker confronted him with the reality that if he did not make it with me, he would go back to the institution for his last year. He got mad, and karate chopped my table. I ended the meeting because it seemed to me that Rich was justifying his behavior in each incident, totally losing sight of the main point. I said there was no point in continuing the conversation, that in my opinion we were not talking about rocket science, and Rich's understanding would be evident in his future behavior. After I left he tried to continue the meeting with the social worker, admitting that he got the concept and it was not rocket science. Synchronistically, there was a knock at the door and the delivery man needed help, so it was a perfect opportunity to redirect Rich to some hard physical labor, after which his energy had made a hundred and eighty degree turn and he was again his pleasant self.

Rich's mood swings continued, though not as extreme as before. During one of our "Come to Jesus" talks, I again pointed out to Rich that he had eaten all of the cake and left a dirty pan, and who did he expect to wash it? He told me that before he went to bed he had taken care to see that the kitchen was cleaned. I told him that I knew he was trying, and I saw and appreciated his efforts. Unfortunately however, he does not have seventeen years to learn what he needs to know, and I need him to crank up the speed. I said that I am committed to doing my best to help him be successful in life, and that I have given him my undivided attention, which I don't mind because I signed up for it. However, I am not willing to work harder than he does to resolve his problems, and I need him to take ownership and not project onto me. I explained to him that he made it difficult for me to approach him because I didn't know if his response would be to me or to something in his past.

I also said that I am not in conflict with him, that we are on the same team and he does not have to convince me of anything. He should use these efforts for people who refuse to believe in him or support him. I suggested he should take out his aggression in sports or other physical activities. He said he was not in conflict with me either, but I pointed out to him that he certainly acted like it. Subsequently I have seen increasing evidence of improvement in his awareness and his behavior.

It so happened that this conversation took place on the fifth of July, the anniversary of my marriage to Melvin Saunders. I remember standing at the altar wondering what on earth I was doing and begging somebody, I didn't know who, to rescue me. On this day, July 5, 2011 I recognized the importance of being clear of what I was committing to, and what I needed in return. I now fully accepted my responsibility for setting limits and defining the terms of my giving. Rich is also clear about what I need from him to continue, and his responsibility to decide whether to give it or not. Apparently he silently decided to work toward cultivating our relationship. He has become more pleasant, cooperative, and fun to be around. His laughter is very deep and soulful and fills the house with life.

His social worker, my roommates, and I have all observed a very significant improvement in his behavior. Rich has demonstrated clear signs of bonding with me. He has told me on several occasions how much he likes me. One Sunday afternoon when we were hanging out together, I asked him who had put a blanket on the floor. He responded, "My mother did." I said he should tell his mother to get it up and put it where it belongs. He retorted, "You are my mother." I apologized and said I didn't remember doing it. After this incident he called me Mother twice. When I told this to the social worker, she said it was the first time it had happened in his seventeen years of life, and that it was a huge accomplishment.

Rich has become very physically affectionate to me, putting his arms around me in a tender hug. He took several pictures of us together on his phone and put me on his Facebook wall. When I spent a night away from home, he showed signs of separation anxiety and wanted to be more physically close when I returned. When I ran out of gas and had to walk on the freeway, he became very upset and said, "You could have been killed! And then who would take care of me and where would I live?" I told him I would continue to take care of him from the Other Side, but he didn't go for it. He pointed out to me that I needed to get a cell phone, because somebody could kidnap me and he wouldn't know it. He beat his chest and told me that he really cared about me. I assured him that I care about him also. When I left the following morning I joked that I wouldn't be walking on the freeway today.

One night when I picked Rich up at the bus station after he had missed his bus, on the way home he told me he loved me. I told him I loved him too, but he said, "You're lying. You don't really." I gave him the reassurance he was fishing for, and he smiled. This seemed to be the moment where we both decided that we were committed to a relationship with each other.

Through the normal and not so normal turbulence of adolescence and old age, we have continued to return to our intention to "work it out." I occasionally become motion-sick from riding the highs and lows of Rich's oscillations. In the beginning his abject refusal to take any responsibility for the chaos he created in his life floored me. He seemed to think that the world should change in response to his desires, and anger was his reflexive reaction when it didn't. He often became too aggressive in his martial arts practices, and when some students complained, his teacher confronted him. Rich justified his behavior claiming that others were just as aggressive and should shut up and man up.

During our conversation about the subject, he said he really wanted to be a "fighter." I suggested that he take boxing. Being aggressive in martial arts was like going to a Ford dealer, asking for a Chevrolet, and getting angry because they only had Fords. He didn't quite get the lesson. Eventually he decided to stop martial arts for now. He also decided, against my strong objections, to drop his volunteer job at the Boys and Girls club, claiming that it was interfering with his ambition to become a fighter. I continued to stress the importance of having some venues for personal expression. The form it took was not important.

In time Rich discovered poetry and this encounter was like a fish finding water. His life in foster care was his subject, and his repressed voice took on the razor sharp edge of a sword. He was good at spoken word, and in a short time was invited to be on the Tam High Slam Poetry team. At their first competition Rich and I were the only black faces in the auditorium. He received a perfect score of 10 from all three judges and a standing ovation from the audience including the rival teams. He was asked to do a poem at his St. Vincent's graduation and from this performance received an invitation for a repeat performance at the Timothy Murphy High graduation.

    Rich decided to apply for the Sausalito Rotary Club scholarship award of three thousand dollars. He bought new dress clothes with a tie, pulled up his pants, and said he was black and competing with kids from Tam High. I replied I was glad he realized those facts. I told him several times how good he looked. At his request we did a mock interview in his new clothes, during which he presented himself very well. At the end of the interview he said he felt like a man and was strutting around the house like a peacock. He knocked on my renter's door to show him how good he looked. Edwin was profusive with his accolades, and later treated the family to a celebration with pizza. Rich won the scholarship. He commented to me that this period had been the happiest time in his whole life.

    All this success seemed to go straight to his head. He became arrogant, argumentative, and entitled once again. He was told by his psychologist that he did not have PTSD, so he decided he didn't really need his medications. He became increasingly paranoid and less self-aware. At school Rich tried to become too informal with a male teacher, calling him by his first name and referring to him as "Bro." The teacher didn't go for it, Rich became angry, and thought the teacher was disrespecting him. He shut down, put on his earphones and refused to talk or leave the classroom. As a result the entire class had to be moved to another room. Rich later tried to suck me in to take his side, but I just commented that I didn't care who was right or wrong, I was just sorry it happened. I redirected his attention back to his goal of graduating.

Also during this time I was asked to provide a home for Peter, a 6 ft 4, muscular seventeen year old, who liked to throw his weight around. He had come to my house several times for respite, but Rich was King of the Castle. He was only to stay for three weeks, and I did not anticipate how severely he would impact Rich. When they wrestled, naturally Rich lost, and Peter had a way of owning any space he occupied--they had to share a room. One Saturday after one of Rich's poetry readings, he was irritable and began to argue with me. Overhearing our conversation, Peter offered to assist me, and Rich felt threatened and verbally escalated, bordering on abuse towards me. I suggested he needed respite, which he turned into a rejection, and told me that if I was too old to do the job of a foster mother, I should quit. I felt personally attacked and knew that he had crossed a line. Immediately I arranged for weekend respite, but as time passed it was mutually decided that our work together as mother and son was done.

He stayed on at the respite home where he remained for two months. He decided to experiment with alcohol, blew this placement, and was moved to a very religious home in Oakley. Here he found Jesus and became a born-again Christian. During this time he was still attending Tam; he spent several respite days with me and we enjoyed talking about the Bible. He finally graduated, and his mother and aunt, along with a former counselor now living in LA, and several social workers from St. Vincent's, and his CASA worker, and I, were all proud participants in the audience. Afterwards we all went out to dinner, and Rich seemed to thoroughly enjoy his star status. He now lives in Santa Rosa with another foster family, attends SRJC, and he continues to be swaddled in the protective arms of caring females. He is really trying to apply himself in school and in life.

St. Vincent's also gives a graduation for the boys. I was asked by Morgan to give the blessing at their graduation. In it, I summarized my hopes and dreams for the graduates. A few years earlier, I was invited to give a luncheon speech at a celebration for foster parents. I used it as an opportunity to reflect on and share my experiences as a foster mother, specializing in reacquainting children with their true selves. As a weekend respite mom, I got to provide the icing while others had to beat the batter. I provided relaxation and fun. The kids seemed to want to please me, and were usually on their best behavior. My training as a therapist enables me to do professional assessments which the social workers love, and everyone benefits from. I am provided with transportation for the kids and other amenities which made my job easy. Providing respite care is truly the plum job in foster system. I got to provide only the aspects of mothering that I love.

I have also served as a permanent or long-term foster mom who has jumped in the river with both feet. Although more confining and labor intensive, long term foster care has its own special rewards and personal satisfactions. It is a greater commitment, but yields sweeter fruit. Few things are more rewarding than the opportunity to observe the result of your teaching in action. Here is an excerpt from my speech:

"In the past two years I have provided care including respite for children ranging in age from 4 to 18 from St. Vincent's and Marin County Social Services. Each child has provided me with a unique opportunity to practice being creative in my expressions of love. As all parents know, every child is different and one size doesn't fit all. For the child who is threatened by words, I practice a loving touch, look, or smile. I cook with loving thoughts which are reflected in my food.

I believe that each of my children were especially selected for me by the universe and are my teachers. I try to bring to the table of motherhood unconditional positive regard and acceptance. I practice a faith rooted in the belief that we are all part of the same god, and I am open and willing to share my faith with the children through example, discussion, and prayer.

I have touched and been touched by each child placed in my home. I have learned over and over again that the less my personality is involved, the more assured I am of a positive resolution to whatever the child is dealing with. With this realization I became aware that removing the *I* from any equation improves the outcome exponent-tially.

CHAPTER EIGHT

OLD AGE~~THE HARVEST AND PASSING IT ON

"The best thing about getting older is that you don't lose all the other ages you have been."

Madeleine L'Engle

"One is not old as long as they are seeking something."

Jean Rostand

"Fools don't grow old."

Hattie Ford

Every stage of life has its treats and tricks. The best, that is, the most interesting, is always yet to be discovered. It is my opinion that old age has been given a bad rap. Our culture places a high premium on youth. This results in many people engaging in the futile practice of trying to look young in their hair and face while their neck and body are reflecting the natural process of aging. Some people fail to learn from their life experiences causing their behavior to lag behind their chronological age. I privately hoped that by some mystical process my behavior would always be age-appropriate, without the rigidity and calcification that I have observed in many older people. I did not look forward to getting older because of the unkind images of elders projected by our culture-- unappealing, lifeless and devalued. Ads portrayed old folks as wrinkled, dull-witted, boring, smelly, and preoccupied with their anatomy and all its breakdowns. They had no sense of style or humor. Fortunately, my experiences of growing older have been contrary to this disparaging depiction.

At the other end of the continuum, we do not encourage or support our young people in being themselves because it conflicts with who we decide they are or should be. I have come to believe that being oneself is often confused with negative acting out behavior, because it makes other people uncomfortable. I think we are here to encourage and support each other to live in truth--taking responsibility for our choices and personal growth. Too often we are quick to judge and condemn, thereby losing an opportunity to learn and grow. Our culture expects us to conform at the expense of our personal truth, and our desire to please and belong are strong forces for conformity.

In the past I have attempted to be "helpful" to others at all costs, whether I knew how or not. It was almost a reflex reaction to anyone around me claiming to be in need. My computer was stuck on the "HELP" button. I thought being a nice person meant being helpful in every situation whether I wanted to be or not. Needless to say this was not always gratifying or "helpful." Sometimes people asking for help really needed to be redirected to discover their own internal resources, and I needed to be redirected to discover mine. I came to realize that the opinions of others do not define me, sustain me, nor decide my worth. That is an internal job! Who I am is never determined by anything external to me. Carl Jung said, "Those who look outside, dream. Those who look inside, awaken."

I was so caught in the social web of society that it took me almost sixty-five years to act out of my authentic self on a continuous basis. Surviving so many years gave me the courage and confidence to withstand the intense social pressure and judgments I experienced to conform to so-called "normal" standards and expectations. People told me I *should* be Baptist, be married, not become a single parent to multiple children, and not buy an expensive house in Sausalito that I couldn't afford. The list goes on. Thank God I only listened to them with one ear, and secretly listened to my own heart with the other. Gradually I found the strength to follow my own truth consistently. Authenticity requires consistency.

On my 50th birthday, I commented to a friend that if I had known 50 was going to be so sweet, I would have rushed to get there. Bingo, some pieces of life's puzzle seemed magically to come together and fall in place with grace and ease—life had meaning after all. I had realized along the way that the older I got the less I knew. This awareness freed me to let go of the need to know and live in the mystery. I became less anxious, more patient, and willing to accept life on life's terms. Maturity is allowing each other space to be who we really are. Who we are changes over time as we are or are not given permission to be ourselves. We will eventually wade through the quicksand on our own, but if someone offers a helping hand, it increases the momentum.

In my opinion being wise (a gift of maturity) means accepting what is, and acting in ways that are forgiving, respectful, com-passionate, and responsible, even when one does not like what is happening. This is always a free choice. Some choose it, and some don't. Often one might not feel like forgiving or taking responsibility for one's own thoughts and behavior, but maturity requires rising to the occasion.

It has been said that wisdom is the God-given substitute for youth. While old age offers wisdom, youth offers energy. It's unfortunate that society supports the separation of this powerful synergy. In our fragmented, highly mobile society, many children are separated from grandparents and extended families, and are robbed of the security that comes from the experience of the whole of life. One of the remaining strengths of the black family (and some other minorities) is its valuing of elders and support of the extended family. Our society would be well advised to take a page from these cultures and promote the benefits of intergenerational connections.

Being the youngest of thirteen, I was the heir to lots of information about life. I observed the choices my siblings made and the outcome of those choices. Subsequently I tried to avoid situations that might limit or trap me. However, what I didn't recognize at the time was that what I thought I knew for sure -- my "free" choices-- were merely my reactions to the cookie cuts of their examples. I had not yet learned to discriminate between my truth, my rebellion, and the expectations of others.

As a young woman I accepted that I had responsibility to the family and to the society to which I was born. I always knew that there was something more to life beyond these commitments. I often commented to friends that after I paid my debt to society, then I would be free to live my own life. The first part of my life was responding to "shoulds," and it's only as an old woman in the last part of my life that I have started responding to my own truth and practicing authenticity (being myself).

For years I felt compelled to buy Christmas gifts for my friends and family, and anyone else I might encounter on that holy day. Needless to say, this overly inclusive mindless marathon was overwhelming to me. I did not enjoy the hectic pace of acquiring so many impersonal gifts, which were often not well matched to their receivers who usually preferred something else. The expectations of others, my innate desire to please, and the force of habit deluded me into thinking that compulsive giving was a virtue. This compulsion not only distorted but blocked my expression of authenticity. I secretly longed for a more meaningful exchange at

Christmas time.

Over a period of several years, I gradually stopped giving material gifts. This was not easy and was accompanied by self-accusations of "Scrooge, miser, etc." The blaming gradually subsided as I started substituting writing blessings uniquely tailored to the individual. When people asked me where their material gift was, I explained that my only gift was love. The initial disappointment I saw in their faces was eventually replaced by acceptance and smiles.

Recently my niece and I were discussing her frustration with her ungratifying process of Christmas gift giving. I shared my transition with her, and told her that I had not received any less love in the absence of giving material things; if anything, I received more.

I have always been proud of my cultural and spiritual heritage. The desire to share what I learned from my African roots and Black experience has given me a sense of purpose in life. I am from a lineage of people who for generations have been viciously denied the right of self-recognition and self-determination by society. And yet we have triumphed, riding on the wings of the spirit. At my fiftieth high school reunion we took a Black History tour which was outstanding and one of the highlights of the reunion. The historian was very knowledgeable and engaging, offering us an opportunity to participate in a simulation of being sold as slaves. The experience was informative, disturbing, and sometimes very humorous.

We stopped in front of the City Court House of St. Louis, where slaves had been bought and sold. The tour guide had the group stand on the steps, arm distance apart, while she performed the role of the auctioneer. We had to hop on one foot, turn around and hop on the other, to prove our strength and stamina, and we had to open our mouths wide for teeth inspection. The women were spared the usual requirement of pulling up their dresses over their heads to be inspected for breeding qualities. The men were also not asked to drop their pants for inspection of their stud qualities that was required for slaves. The group made several sounds of groans and snickers, and the tour guide identified the sounds as discomfort and nervousness, which would have been cause for severe beatings. At the end of the experience, she reminded us that we are descendants of the strongest group of people in the world, to endure such inhumanity and yet survive and thrive. I felt a surge of strength and pride rising up inside of me, connecting me with the power in my ancestral roots.

I was also surprised, delighted, and encouraged by her stories of some early black settlers in St. Louis who became extremely wealthy. It seems that much of Black History, especially the positive part, is a secret, even to blacks. On leaving the reunion I felt myself walking more confidently in the world, filled with more pride in my black heritage. I haven't always been able to appreciate the strengths that flowed from my black experience. I was ready to accept my responsibility to be free. I have gradually come to accept that freedom is our birthright. Given the power to choose our thoughts we are free to change ourselves and our world, regardless of our circumstances.

Three people have had a profound impact on my life: first, my mother, who was the epitome of strength and courage. Next is President Obama who knows who he is, and manages to stay centered in his own truth while operating with grace in the lion's den. He is very effective at resisting others' attempts to control or define him. He is rooted in the confidence of his own worth. The third is Oprah, the queen of generosity, and my guru for unattached giving of herself and her wealth. Her friend Gayle says that while Oprah is climbing the ladder, she is reaching back to pull someone else along--she is generous without attachment.

"Our behavior is the truest indication of our thoughts and intentions." We create our experiences by what we think and attend to; that is, whatever we choose to think about, or spend time doing, determines the experience we have. If we dwell on negativity we experience pain. If we place our attention on love, we eventually experience joy. This is a law of the universe and a personal responsi-bility. A child complained to his grandfather that he had two people inside of him—one was mean and hateful, the other was loving and kind. He said that they were fighting with each other, and asked his grandfather which one would win. The old man responded, "It will be the one you feed." Happiness is a choice.

A friend asked me to go for lunch and I chose Fresh Choice restaurant in Corte Madera. We spent several hours grazing at the salad bar and talking and having a very good time. I enjoyed it so much that I promised myself I would soon return. Several months later, after hardly eating for three days, I finally kept my promise and treated myself to lunch there. As I passed through the line, I noticed the beautiful colors of the food and the care put into the presentation. Aware of the abundance, it felt as if a sacred table had been prepared before me. The whole place seemed pristine. The music was soft and calming, and the atmosphere uplifting. One of the waitresses even made me a fresh pot of coffee. As I started to eat my lunch, for the first time in a long time I actually enjoyed the process of eating. I savored the different flavors of freshness in my mouth. I kept telling myself how much I was enjoying it. The more I reminded myself, the more pleasurable the experience became. My heart started to open and I was filled with joy and pleasurable feelings reaching all the way down to my toes.

A few months later I tried to return for an encore only to find the restaurant had been closed. I was covered with a wave of disappointment which led to a deeper appreciation of the Buddhist principle of non-attachment. The impermanent nature of things is they come and they go--appreciate them while you have them, and be willing to let them go when they're gone. I realized in the moment of letting go that I am the one who appreciates, and I can appreciate whatever remains. I don't want to spend time mourning what I don't have; my memories allow me to celebrate what I have.

The older I get, the freer I become. I am less anxious, less fearful, more open, and accepting of life on its own terms. Although I have lost some of the energy and agility of my youth, my charming smile and gracious manners bring me whatever I need and more. Now when I travel I accept all the senior benefits offered: friendly assistance, wheelchair rides, handicapped access, kindly smiles reserved usually for beloved grandmothers, etc. I feel the losses are more than compensated by the gains. I am delighted to say that with the recent advent of "senior power," society has started to reevaluate the image it projects of the elderly. There is a new mythology percolating in the media about seniors having good health, discretionary income, and a willingness to have fun participating in life. I feel blessed to be among the trailblazers of the new older generation.

Generativity, or giving back, is the joy of maturity. To reach this stage, one has to come to grips with what is important to a quality life and denounce the illusionary carrots of the world. One is no longer attached to being right or wrong, higher or lower, better or worse, or trying to change *what is* about oneself or others. The Course in Miracles teaches that giving and receiving are one in truth, and God dances between equal partners.

Learning the art of reciprocity has been a major lesson in my life.

Taking care of my mother was one of the pivotal points in my waking up. I had always thought of my mother as the embodiment of courage and strength. When it was my turn to be the caretaker, I wanted to meet the situation with as much grace and commitment as I could. This experience opened the door for my recognizing that if I could take care of the strong person who took care of me, then I would have to be strong. Subsequently, I have become aware that there is the universal cycle of the cared-for becoming the care-giver and returning to the cared-for. It increases the self-esteem of the care giver and affirms the value of the cared for. I have marveled at the blossoming of my own daughters as they have become my needed caretakers.

Identified as the giver for most of my life, I now find myself on the other end of giving, which is receiving. My mother always told me to leave every place a little better than I found it, and to never take more than I give. One of my most difficult lessons has been learning to receive graciously.

In the past I believed that giving was superior to receiving. The Bible tells us it is more blessed to give than to receive. I thought this meant that the giver was more blessed because he or she had more. The truth is that the giver receives twice--the joy of giving and the joy of receiving appreciation from the other. I had to learn to accept grace as my own self in order to receive graciously. This was a trickery slope to navigate.

Learning to dance on the pinhead of reciprocity, it was necessary for me to spend time getting to know myself. Taking the time to commune on a regular basis with the still small voice within is the only way we can learn to discriminate between who we are and who we are not. I have often confused being with myself with being selfish. It is self-centered to be sure, but it is also impersonal. When one does not take the time to be with the self, in whatever form that takes-- meditation, yoga, music, art, nature, prayer, to name a few of my favorites-- it is impossible to know and accept the Self. When one does not know the self, one lives in a world of illusion which is the bedrock of fear. From this place one confuses receiving with being less than.

A few years ago I fell and broke a finger on my right hand, which rendered me almost helpless and practically dependent. At first I was unhappy about this painful, expensive, poorly timed inconvenience. But what could I do? I surrendered, believing that God would take care of me. It was easy to see God in my caretakers because they were clearly answers to my prayers. In these moments of recognition, I was consumed with gratitude.

Although a part of me would have preferred to avoid the

whole experience, it opened the door to a deeper level of appreciation. I experienced a stronger connection between a giver with an open heart and myself as the receiver with an appreciative heart. I discerned that there is a qualitative difference between receiving as a kind gesture and receiving to meet a basic need. This authentic giving and receiving as are one, just two sides of the same coin.

Monastic life has called to me for a long time. When I lived in the ashram I mentioned to my minister that the experience felt as if I was living in one man's house (Baba) while married to another (Christ.) Although part of me wanted to set up shop permanently in the ashram, I was being called loudly to come back to the world. As I have matured I have come to know that what appeared to be a conflict was simply my desire to live in my cave (internally centered in the Self) while remaining active in the world, and that is exactly what I have done. This is the supreme gift of maturity.

To do this I had to spend quality time on a regular basis getting to know the still small voice within me. It helped me to discern who I am from what I am not. In this process, I was able to separate who I am from what I see, hear, think, feel, or do. In some way I think I have always known that I couldn't really trust the information I receive from my five senses, which are conditioned by human experience and the collective unconscious.

The Truth can only be found in the heart. I believe that most people are motivated by their own desires, perceptions and self-interests, and during interactions their projections are more descriptive of them than the other. (It's nothing personal.)

It is frightening to realize we live in a world of illusions. I suppose this is the reason the peace of God is not of this world. It's impossible to live in illusion without fear and equally impossible to live in peace with fear. As the Course in Miracles says, " Love and fear cannot coexist!" The transition requires surrendering to the Mystery where there are no roads or maps. In this abyss one must let go of the past, in order to accept what has not yet become.

I have spent just enough time with myself to live above fear most of the time, but not enough to live in love all of the time. People who live in illusion are robots of their programming. These people do not listen to their own counsel and frequently can be heard taking opposite positions in the same sentence, and then denying that they have done so.

In order to accept personal responsibility to define ourselves regardless of circumstances, it is vital that at least one other person, somewhere along the way, knows who we are and loves us. We learn about our humanity from other human beings. I now have a new appreciation for the importance of recognition and validation of the authenticity of one's way of being in the world.

On my seventieth birthday, I received the greatest gift of all--a lavish expression of unconditional love. Nita managed to pull off a grand surprise party at His Lordships, an upscale restaurant on the Bay with a panoramic view of San Francisco and the water. (I knew something was in the wind, but I had no idea of the magnitude of her plan.) She had paid close attention to all the details--it was beautifully decorated and uniquely orchestrated for my taste. Nita met me outside with a photographer, and when I was ushered into the room, the DJ was playing "She's a Bad Mamma Jamma." When I saw the faces of my many friends, old and new, I was overcome with love, transported to ecstasy, and the music swept my body into a dance of joy.

My sister Ruby arrived late (I wasn't sure she would be able to make it), and I was so excited to see her that I jetted out of my chair and went to greet her, attracting everyone's attention, and she made a grand entrance like that of Lady Gaga. She looked very beautiful and radiant as she stood smiling and waving for the cameras. Ordinarily she is pretty shy and retiring, but she absolutely rose to this occasion. Sharing the spotlight with Ruby was one of the special gifts of the celebration for me; this was her last public appearance.

We watched a video which covered my life from the time I arrived in California some forty-five years ago to the present.

After Nita gave the welcome speech, my friend Julie gave an overview of my life including many experiences and adventures not included in the video. I was touched by the depth of our sharing over the years, the mutual love and support of our friendship, and Julie's ability to capture my essence. LaWanda spoke quite candidly and humorously, as only she can do, about some of the challenges our relationship endured and love's triumph through it all. Carrie sang "You are the wind beneath my wings," and the feeling with which she delivered the message moved me to tears. Harriet recited a very compassionate poem by Maya Angelou, praising women and speaking to the unconditional love of a mother. Thomas, Nita's husband, sang "You are so beautiful to me" with the voice of an angel. I was truly serenaded with love, and felt beautiful. The mike was passed around and I was overwhelmed with loving accolades from my friends. Nita closed with a statement of her deep love for me and my importance in her life. I had to hold on to my chair to keep from levitating.

The dinner was delicious, and Nita picked up the tab, making the celebration a gift for everyone. This was truly a rite of passage for me. She demonstrated that "love is what I taught and love was what she learned." It was the perfect validation for my passage into the realm of "old age." Even though I hadn't realized the importance of external validation, my soul rejoiced as it had never done before. My wish is that everyone should have the good fortune of being recognized and accepted for who they really are, and have it celebrated.

In addition, I wish everyone could have the privilege of travel. After Julie's miraculous recovery from cancer, we wanted to celebrate with a sacred journey. We invited our families to Cancun for a grand, all-expenses paid Thanksgiving vacation. Although preparing for the trip was high drama with my misplaced passport and missing credit cards and license, I felt assured the trip was blessed. It was indeed, and exceeded my wildest imagination.

We stayed at a very beautiful resort in Cancun overlooking an elegantly manicured golf course. The weather was beyond perfect, with a gentle breeze that felt like the stroke of God's hand. My stereotype of Mexican cuisine was beans and rice, and I had never had the pleasure of meeting gourmet Mexican chefs. These guys and girls did fish right. The service was second to none, with the waiters remembering each of our individual pre-ferences, yet they would always take the care to ask before serving us. Everyone we met was gracious and friendly. Our children, as different as they were in age and lifestyles, all got along beautifully together and referred to each other as brother and sister. They said they felt totally relaxed and rejuvenated.

Although Thanksgiving is not a part of Mexican culture, the resort provided an exquisite dinner with a choice of prime rib, ham, or turkey, all of which were extravagantly displayed and juicy and delicious. The table was set for kings and queens. I looked at the bountiful scene and was reminded of the passage in the Bible where God says, "I will prepare a table before you..." His handiwork was evident. In the spirit of Thanksgiving, my favorite holiday, we decided to share the things in our lives we are grateful for. Each individual spoke from their heart, and the entire room was filled with love and gratitude. The waiters received a bountiful tip and were all caught up in the celebratory atmosphere. I felt joy rising in my heart.

After our families departed, Julie and I decided to go exploring the Yucatan Peninsula. We took a bus down the coast to Playa del Carmen, which was named as one of CNN's top five vacation destinations of choice for 2006. This small, developing town was bursting with life, with many repeat tourists, some of whom had taken up residence. The entire town seemed to be involved in development, with construction everywhere. We enjoyed the expertise of the chefs in the local restaurants including Italian and Argentinian specialties, and the family atmosphere of the small, quaint hotel where we stayed. The blue-sky hovering over the white sands of the beaches was heavenly.

Sitting outside each morning for breakfast, we felt a part of the vibrant high-spirited atmosphere. I was deeply touched by the number of fathers with young children, and older couples who had retained their love and respect for each other's company. They continued to share their joy freely. This observation was an important gift which brought renewed understanding of intimacy's requirement for surrender. I realized that my strong need for independence prevented my having a long term, intimate relationship with a male partner. I accepted that the universe was not being unkind in not providing this for me. It was my life's choice. I am looking forward to many returns to Mexico, a perfect place to experience the whole of life--the greatest opportunity for self-awareness offered by any mecca.

Traveling outside the United States frees me from the cultural and racial indoctrinations that often restricted me from being who I am. The warm reception that I have received as a person of color in nations of color, including such far-flung countries as Bali and Mexico, elevated me to a higher consciousness. Africa in particular is a sanctuary for me, both Sub-Saharan Africa and North Africa, especially Egypt.

In February of 2007, a trip to Egypt was planned by the minister of the Seattle Church of Religious Science, who takes a group on the journey every other year. She loves the land and has excellent connections with the people, who see her as an ambassador for the country. The trip spoke to me, and I signed up.

For several months prior to the trip, my assassins had escalated their attacks, and I had been experiencing many health challenges. Although I had purchased traveler's insurance, I was not inclined to cancel the trip. Also, the day before I was to leave I stubbed my toe, which seemed minor at the time. However, it grew increasingly painful and by the time I arrived at the airport I could hardly walk.

The trip's magic began with the transportation to the airport, which was like a carpet ride with the Marin Airporter coming within a few feet of my front door. A friendly driver navigated smoothly through San Francisco's notorious traffic, and we arrived at the airport without a hitch. After a long plane ride from San Francisco to London to Cairo through many time zones, I was quite exhausted by the time I arrived in Egypt.

I got a surge of energy when I was warmly greeted by the tour guide who said, "Welcome home, brown sugar!" The tour started early the following morning, with breakfast and a trip to the funerary complex of Pharaoh Djoser. We had to blaze a path through uneven terrain and climb up and down huge stepping stones. Acutely aware of the pain in my foot and feeling very helpless, I recognized that I could not continue by myself. At this very moment, I felt the hand of one of my fellow tour members on my arm. Shortly thereafter, I felt a second hand on my other arm. In this way I entered the cave, supported by the hands of God.

While in the cave the minister said a prayer and then the group had about fifteen minutes to meditate in silence. During this time I asked God to heal my foot so I could fully embrace the journey, and I would be willing to learn in another way whatever lesson the experience came to teach me. In retrospect, I realized the gift was the humility brought by the surrender.

One of the travelers offered me an organic ointment which lived up to its promise and gradually relieved my pain. Another traveler noticing my distress gave me some sandals which were perfect. She said she was indecisive about bringing them, and she told me she was sure her decision was divinely inspired. Although I was not aware of it at the time, one of my lessons was to serve others by receiving gracefully. I remembered Ernest Holmes' statement, Love is the willingness to extend oneself for another's spiritual growth. I was willing to love and be loved.

Not only was I totally accommodated by the hands, eyes, and ears of God, He also provided wheels in the form of a chauffeur waiting right outside the hotel door to take me to the dining room. The hotel was several blocks long, so a ride to the dining room was welcomed. After three days I refused the ride, even thinking I was strong enough to carry a bag of dirty laundry. But I soon grew weary and just like magic, a fellow traveler appeared as a genie and convinced me that carrying my bag would be a gift to her because she needed the exercise. The love with which she made the request was so authentic it opened my heart. The tour director and guides extended themselves over and beyond the call of duty to accommodate the my every need and desire. Among the many amenities was a designated personal chauffeur who accompanied me on a private shopping trip for upholstery fabric.

The group went to various temples and museums when they were closed to the public. We were granted entrance to areas of the pyramids where only initiates and high priests were allowed to go. Inside the great pyramid it was quite rugged and the flimsy wooden stairs and ropes leading to the king's chamber at the top were challenging to say the least. By sheer determination I persevered to the top, where I was able to sit and experience one of my deepest meditations to date. Nonetheless, I was intimidated by the descent. At that moment another traveler extended her hand asking to assist me. She was not only gracious but obviously experienced and self-confident. I immediately felt secure when it was suggested we climb down backwards and the helper would be behind me to catch me if I stumbled. At dinner I thanked her again for her help. The helper told me that her prayer in the pyramid had been a request for opportunities to give service.

To get to the Sphinx, the group had to rise before dawn for a bus ride. Then they had to climb up and over huge rocks and uneven terrain. I was still feeling somewhat timid in my steps, when I was instantly joined by a fellow traveler who took my arm and asked if she could walk with me. The woman later shared in the group that this was a privilege for her because she was a newcomer to the church and one of her expectations for the trip was to get to know people.

In a few days my foot felt better but was still quite swollen, and I was still reluctant to do strenuous activities. Even though I had looked forward to riding a camel, I questioned the wisdom of doing so. My walking companion suggested we ride together on a camel. Once I was assisted in mounting the camel, I felt safe and comforted holding on to my friend's warm body during the ride. At first I resisted the camel's jerky stride, but when the friend suggested I go with the flow, all was well. Upon dismounting I thanked the camel for fulfilling one of my long held desires. The blinking of his eyes told me he understood.

The two tour guides were very knowledgeable. The one I was with, Emil, was not only knowledgeable but humorous and deeply spiritual, and we seemed to have a special connection which we both enjoyed. When I first met him, he told me that the Egyptians would love me and welcome me as a family member. His prediction proved to be accurate, because everywhere I went people greeted me with overwhelming warmth and affection. Emil claimed that he was a maverick who took pleasure in breaking the rules. He said that all Egyptians were like this, but he seemed to feel it was his personal mission to jar the culture out of its traditional rut. Despite his rebellious posture, he was well-known and well-liked throughout the country. He grew up in Luxor, where he still lived with his wife; his children were away at school.

He decided to take some of the group on a walk in the neighbor-hood where he grew up, entertaining us with wild stories of his boyhood. We visited several homes of his neighbors, one of whom had just finished making fresh bread which she shared with everyone. He invited his neighbors to tell stories about the neighborhood.

As we strolled around, I observed a small group of men gathered in front of a building; they kept looking at me and I seemed to have been the subject of their conversation. About ten minutes later, a young Nubian man ran up to the group, singled me out like a long lost beloved relative, and told me I looked Nubian and in fact was his sister. He seemed genuinely excited to see me and invited the entire group into his home. He said something about wanting me to meet his mother, but I told him I was leaving soon on my tour. He asked to take pictures with me, during which the group of men gathered around to watch. They all were smiling approvingly. I later found out that the men had seen a striking resemblance between the two of us.

As we continued our walking tour with Emil, he asked the group if we wanted to do something wild and crazy. By this time we were learning that with Emil anything was possible, so no one responded to his question. Hearing no objections, he hailed down a donkey-driven flatbed truck, and for a number of overweight and out-of-shape Americans in our group, getting up onto the flatbed was an Olympic challenge. However the Egyptian men were more than willing to place their hands on the American women's behinds and hoist them up.

We headed off to the market, going the wrong way on a very narrow one-way street. Soon our donkey encountered a horse and carriage coming toward us. The horse reared on its hind legs as if outraged. This image was symbolic to me of the cultural resistance to a group of female American tourists parading through town on a flatbed truck as if it was normal and accepted behavior. The horse was forcefully backed up by his angry carriage driver, and the tourists were given safe passage. A sigh of relief erupted in laughter. Soon the joyfulness of our group became contagious, and people were coming out of their houses and shops to greet us and wave and smile. It looked like a homecoming parade and I felt as if I had been crowned as the queen. We rode along as goodwill ambassadors, giving blessings to everyone in sight. After this experience, the group started to refer to me as "the Nubian Princess."

At the end of the walk through the town, Emil invited the group to come to his home and meet his wife. In more than twenty years as a tour guide, apparently this was a first, and spoke to his affection for the group. He was very proud of his home, which was filled with antiques and cultural relics which he had collected over the years. He enjoyed holding court, talking about himself and explaining the history of his collection to the captive audience.

Emil was also passionate about soccer. There was a champion-ship game going on, and the group prayed for Egypt to win. Some of them even bought and wore soccer shirts to support his team. He promised them a special treat if his team won, and when it did, he personally paid for the group to take individual donkey rides through the town. Riding a donkey was new to me, and riding one through the town with traffic would have been a stretch for even experienced donkey riders. People were honking and the skinny underfed donkeys wanted to race—it was truly scandalous. As I rode through pastures, swamps, and narrow cobblestone trails, I enjoyed the gala exchange with the school children as they walked home from school.

Emil loved the word "activate," which means to bestow life and power. Although he talked a lot, he also appreciated the mystery of silence, and frequently encouraged the group to experience it. He instructed the group to "walk as one," suggesting harmony and union. Although it was not discussed, I thought perhaps I and Emil had the same guru because he regularly chanted "Om namah shivaya," my favorite mantra.

The Egyptian economy relies heavily on tourism, and all the Egyptians seem to understand the importance of a welcoming atmosphere and have developed it to a science. They have learned a number of American idioms, like "Adios amigo!" and "Welcome to Alaska." The name Obama is like a theme song heard everywhere. The Egyptians the group encountered were primarily merchants who are known to relish the entertainment of a good bartering exchange. Any time a traveler steps out of a hotel or into a tourist area, they were surrounded by natives selling wares from book marks to massive replicas of museum statues like King Tut. The men had the most endearing way of commanding women's attentions by calling out in a sweet, singsong tone, "Hey lady! Hey lady!" Because of my dark skin, I constantly had the special distinction of being called "my cousin!" Even in huge crowds, I always knew when I was being addressed. Being preferred for my dark skin was a paradigm shift.

The group had a private yacht which cruised the Nile River for a week. The one day we were unable to disembark from the boat, a caravan of small boats greeted us early one morning with "Hola! Hola!" My roommate and I listened to this greeting for several moments before arising to explore the source of this out-of-context call. Even though I vaguely recalled being told we would be visited by floating merchants, I was totally unprepared for the drama it brought.

Just below my second-story balcony, I spotted a very handsome young man standing in a boat loaded down with

Egyptian goods. Before I could say anything, he began throwing plastic bags up to me containing scarves, galabyas, and colorful pashminas. This process got my adrenaline flowing, since I was never well coordinated in sports and my right hand is compromised. It was clear, however, that he was very experienced with this process, and had a clear intention for me to catch the merchandise. Very excitedly I followed his cues, repeating the mantra "Oh my God, Oh my God," and to my surprise, not a single bag hit the water. In the midst of this intense action, we were also negotiating price and calculating the exchange rates between pounds and dollars. What an exhilarating way to start the day!

Later in one of the group discussions, I shared this experience with the comment that my prayer on the trip was to be new in the moment. In my normal daily routines, I rarely invited this much intensity, but I could certainly see how it forced me to relinquish my old conditioning and be fully awake in the moment. The floating merchants were still pedaling their wares around noon when I and other travelers went up to the top deck to watch the boat move through the locks.

As I gazed from the deck, I looked down and saw another young good looking Egyptian man frantically trying to get my attention. He was waving his hands and calling out to me to get ready to receive his merchandise. He seemed to ignore my protests that I didn't want anything and had spent all my money that morning. He insisted that I look in my pockets and put what I had in a plastic bag and toss it down. When I threw down the few piastres that I had left, less than three dollars, he was obviously very disappointed. He suggested I throw back his merchandise but he would keep the money to buy candy for his baby.

This heated interaction continued for about five minutes, resulting in my borrowing a few pounds from the tour guide to buy an Egyptian 533aître533 from him. When the transaction was completed, he shifted to a proposal for marriage, assuring me that he would keep me satisfied. He offered his boat as our marriage bed and permanent home. He told me he would have me pregnant in five minutes. I told him I was eighty years old so this would have to be an immaculate conception. In a short time my suitor's boat was surrounded by several other floating merchants' boats, who joined in the proposal melee, offering their ideas and enthusiastically instigating the match. My roommate was videotaping this outrageous interlude, which was being witnessed by many of our fellow travelers.

One night we were entertained by a belly dancer and a whirling dervish. I was both surprised and not surprised when the belly dancer came over to get me to join her in the dance. I decided since my foot had almost healed I was free to do anything, so I jumped up and shook my tail feathers. The crowd cheered us on. Later one of the guests named Tina came up to me and said, "You looked pretty good on the dance floor, girlfriend!"

On the Captain's night we were encouraged to dress in traditional Egyptian attire. I wore a beautiful white embroidered 534aître534 which I had caught and bought from my itinerant merchant that afternoon. It seemed ironic that the dress happened to be white and he was proposing marriage. When I entered the dining room wearing my lovely "bridal dress" and a black and white pashmina, the 534aître d' admiringly whispered to me that I looked like an Egyptian queen. When we disembarked and I said good-bye to him, he commented to me that there would always be a room there for me, and to please come back.

During the proposal by my floating merchant, Emil was both interpreting and egging it on. He told me that my suitor wanted to "activate" me. I told him I was already "activated." He said he knew, but that it was only spiritual. I replied that when the Spirit activates you, it's on all levels.

On our bus ride to Abyssinia, I observed the most graphic oxymoron I had ever seen, a garden in the Sahara Desert. The French had built a big dam to re-route the water from the Nile for irrigation. There were palm trees and lush vegetation in a green oasis, surrounded by endless dry sand dunes. I was now convinced that whatever is imaginable is doable.

At Abyssinia we stayed in a beautiful hotel overlooking the Nile. It was truly the grandest of the grand. When I went into the gift shop I was swept off my feet by the warm greeting of the handsome, magnetic store owner, Adel. He acted as if I was his long lost beloved and told me that he thought I was beautiful. Once again I was told I looked as if I was Nubian. As proof he pulled out a ceramic figure of a Nubian woman from his shelf and gave it to me for a souvenir. He said he worked long hours in his shop because he didn't have a family. He had everything he wanted except a wife—a three-bedroom house, a car, and a prosperous business. He felt that his selection of local women was limited. He invited me to return to Egypt to enjoy his personal hospitality and he would take me any place I wanted to go. I was flattered.

    The next time I went into his shop he was busy waiting on a customer and did not see me. When he spotted me he immediately came over and gave me a big hug and apologetically told me he would only be a minute waiting on his customer. He told me to pick out something in the store I wanted. I was reluctant to do so, knowing he was going to give it to me as a gift. Sensing my hesitation, he picked up a black and gold silk scarf and handed it to me. I was deeply touched by the sincerity of his admiration. Several of my traveling companions were in the store at the time, and he insisted on giving them all traditional Egyptian bracelets. After that, they teased me about the bracelets being "a gift from the princess." When we were leaving, I went to say good-bye to Adel. He had a sad look on his face and said he would miss me. I took his name and address and told him I would write to him, and that if it was Allah's will I would accept his invitation to return to Egypt someday perhaps as his guest.

As if all this was not enough, on the bus ride back to Aswan we stopped at a little café in the middle of the desert for drinks. There was a group of men sitting at a large table, and when I walked in all of their eyes followed me. One very good-looking young man, around nineteen, got up from the table to greet me, and announced to his friends, "I like her!" Although we only had five minutes, the tour guide suggested that I sit with them so I joined them at their table. The young man left the table and returned with several cans of soda, and asked me to choose one. When I attempted to pay, he insisted there was no charge, although everybody else was paying. We chatted a few minutes, and when I left I said that it was my hope that our paths would cross again some day. I felt honored and recognized at a very deep level. Back on the bus, the minister commented that I was the most popular person on the trip.

Although it was announced that the group needed to pay an additional two hundred dollars or more for tips, I didn't hear the announcement and thought the fifty dollars I had already paid was adequate. By the time I got the message, the hotel had stopped cashing traveler's checks and I had to jump through hoops to cash my check. Finally succeeding, I attempted to pay my share of the tip and was told another guest had already taken care of it so I would not have to worry. The tour assistant refused to tell me who it was, stating it was not a secret but the person had not given permission for her to tell. I asked several times, but she continued to be evasive. I finally accepted the anonymous gift as being from the universe.

As the group parted in the London airport, several fellow travelers thanked me for personally making their trip more meaningful. Having only an hour to make my connecting flight to San Francisco, I expressed some concern about missing the plane. I was reassured by a fellow traveler that I was dearly loved and the call had already been made informing the airlines that the Nubian Princess was enroute and they should hold the plane. I made it with time to spare. As the plane mounted to the heavens, I reflected on my experiences, and accepted the truth of my divine essence. This gift from Egypt was my most highly treasured souvenir.

RANDOM REFLECTIONS

My attendance at my fiftieth high school reunion in 2004 was a first for me. Before I went I requested a prayer in church to be a beacon of light, as well as have a good time. A woman that I have seen often in church came up to me and confirmed that I would have a good time, and would be more powerful when I returned. The reunion was well attended--people came from all four corners of the earth. It was a totally black crowd (except for one woman's white husband). I was amazed to realize that we all now had something in common--old age.

We graduated in 1954, the year of school integration. The group had shared several reunions previously and even planned social events between reunions to stay in touch and nurture friendships. One of the leaders pointed out that the Class of '54 had always been close knit. Although this had not been my experience, it was my observation on this occasion. I was amazed and touched by the many people who remembered me and experiences we shared.

I was deeply impressed by the long-term memory of some compared to my blank screen. It made me wonder where I had been. High school was not an easy time in my life. My memory is that I was invisible. I was filled with fear of becoming like my sisters, whom I saw become paralyzed by early motherhood and meager resources. I knew what I didn't want, and at the same time I wasn't sure how I could avoid it. Intuitively I knew that I had incorporated some of the family characteristics that tied me to the reality I was trying desperately to escape. Fortunately there was a strong part of my consciousness which was determined not to get caught in the quicksand. Even in high school and probably before, my internal light could be seen, even though I was not aware of its presence. I now believe that during this period I was invisible only to myself.

It was really good to connect with these friends from my past. They were very loving and accepting and extended themselves to make me feel comfortable. I re-met people with whom I had attended school from grade school to graduate school. This was quite a kick! One of the women of the group with whom I shared a table asked me if I was a psychologist. I confirmed that I am a psychotherapist. She responded that she had guessed because there was something very special about me.

Some of them have aged better than others, as would be expected. A woman who had been very slim and attractive all the way through graduate school had gained weight beyond recognition. I talked with her for two days not daring to ask her name because I knew I should know it. On the third day I got the courage to ask someone to identify her, and was blown out to learn who she is. Another woman who was very attractive, well dressed, and popular, continues to look very much as she did fifty years ago, and is still very sharp. Some of the outfits she wore at the gatherings were head turners. I was impressed by some on the dance floor who had maintained both style and rhythm.

A man that I did not recognize sat down next to me on a tour bus. He introduced himself and I recognized his name. He added that he now looks nothing like he used to since he'd put on so much weight. We talked about many things including our careers and families. At the end of the tour he said he had enjoyed our conversation and thought I was very special. That night I saw his picture in the yearbook, and I could not believe that he had been the very slim, handsome young man who played saxophone in the band. Interacting with so many black men in one room reminded me of their playful, humorous qualities, which I love and had long forgotten.

I have rediscovered my unique form or style of expressing myself as Love--nurturing. The role of nurturing seems to be my destiny. I have decided to embrace it. Lord knows the world offers us too many opportunities to feel helpless and dwell on negativity. Nita and I were engaged in our morning ritual of talking on the telephone. I was expressing my dismay about the current war the United States has declared on Iraq. Over the years I have observed that some white people, especially men, are masters at using "rational arguments" to justify irrational behavior. It pains me deeply that a black woman is the spokesperson for our arrogant, demented, power hungry president.

As much as I have tried, I have been unable to understand any justification for one country to assume it is their God-given right to dominate and control another. The declaration of war seems both arrogant and self-serving. These motives are hidden behind the self-delusion of being humanitarian and knowing what is best for people they neither understand nor respect. No one, neither individuals or countries, likes to be controlled under the disguise of being helped. Control always creates resentment and invites backlash. With the allure of a carrot, in this case in the form of money in foreign aid, the backlash is usually subtle and passive aggressive.

It is heartbreaking to observe the mass-scale destruction our egotistical leaders are willing to inflict on others, putting everyone, even their own families, in danger. They are creating enemies for generations to come. I am amazed that these power seekers have been able to convince a large number if not majority of the people in this country that their intentions are honorable and justified in invading and destroying Iraq.

Listening to the news it seems to me that many of the young men and women on the battlefield are highly motivated as members of the armed forces to serve their country and do the job they were trained for. Those interviewed spoke very highly about their particular unit and the training they had received and the mutual support and fellowship they shared. Some also seemed very intrigued about the advanced technology and equipment they were using. These idealistic young people seem unaware of the larger ramifications of their role in human destruction. One soldier told a newscaster that he simply doesn't think about the bomb once he has released it. He accepted no personal responsibility for his act. "Just following orders."

The decision to declare war against the strong objections

of the United Nations is a statement that the current administration feels that it is more powerful than the rest of the world. The U.S. leaders also seem oblivious to the passionate protests of millions of anti-war demonstrators in this country and around the world. Protesters using their limited powers against the military and police forces choose to disrupt the capitalistic system by blocking traffic, and preventing business as usual. One evening a commuter became so frustrated that he jumped out of his car and started punching demonstrators who were blocking traffic. One man interviewed was angry at the demonstrators believing that they do not have the right to block traffic. He said that if he does not work, he does not get paid, and he has a family to support. He was equally disinterested in the war and wanted it all to just go away so he could go on with his life.

Several people interviewed appeared disinterested or in denial about the implications of this attack, for them and the rest of the world. Others were identified with force and the display of power, justifying it on the basis of retaliation against terrorists. It didn't seem to matter that the people being attacked were not the terrorists who attacked us. There were several very loose associations made between the attacks of 9/11 and "those people" in the Middle East. In a discussion with one of my housemates who was attempting to justify the attack on Iraq, I became very impatient with his rhetoric and told him that I was not willing to participate in a conversation based on his delusion about the right to abuse power.

This administration's rationale for war on Iraq changes depending on the audience, and covers the range of retaliation, prevention, and being the moral gatekeepers for the world. Although they do not state this lofty objective in these terms, they seem to feel responsible for destroying Saddam Hussein because he is described as an "evil man, " which he may be in truth. However the rest of the world, including his own country, are willing to allow him to be, until the US intervened with the humanitarian solution of executing him.

As a therapist, I am aware of the violent effect of the misuse of control in individual relationships, but watching it displayed on the international stage is devastating. In my own life, as a young woman I was subjected to emotional and physical abuse which had major consequences on my health and sanity. I once was even driven to think about murder as a way of freeing myself. Today, as a more mature woman, I have learned to access my power and will not tolerate personal abuse. As members of the human race, we share a common wellspring of emotions. I am sure that developing countries have similar reactions to bullies, and are willing to use the power of terrorism because that is what is available to them. Our leaders seem to have escalated their personal need for dominance and power from an individual level to include millions. President Bush is similar to a petulant child having a tantrum insisting on having his own way, seemingly unaware of the hypocrisy of forcing people with different world views to accept our so-called democratic form of government! It's not even working for its perpetrators at home.

We cannot create peace with war on any level: personal, local, or global. I am feeling inspired to pray for a president and countries that want peace. I thought I would issue an invitation to the prayer group and the whole church to pray for world peace as often as they remember. Focusing on world peace opens us to the awareness and experience of our oneness. I invite you, the reader, to join this movement also.

During one of our phone discussions, I told Nita that Mr. Bush had failed to learn from history. I also said that when one fails to learn the lessons of history........, and Nita completed the sentence with "....... he or she is destined to repeat it." With some humor, I commented that she knew me so well she could complete my sentences. In my old age, I have learned that individuals and countries will develop in their own way at their own pace, and I am not responsible for the outcome. I'm only responsible for my own thoughts, feelings, and actions. I do believe my vote counts. I also realize that if my candidate loses, it's not personal!

I confessed to Nita that my present feeling of accepting my children and my family has been in the making for many years.

The fact that my throat was sore and still scratchy made me suspicious that there was something there that was hidden deeply beneath my awareness. Perhaps I had not completely let go of beliefs that other people should meet my expectations.

HELLO! End of the road. There was no place left to kick the can. Letting go of anger was the price of freedom. God knows I wanted to be free! I was willing to let it go.

A few nights later I was still in bed and I was tossing and turning. Almost unnoticeably, I gradually became aware of my body gliding into a state of stillness and balance. Oh my God, another one of those undeniable moments of being in Your presence. My heart was filled with gratitude and I fell into the nurturing arms of deep sleep.

In the morning I continued to be aware that my throat was scratchy and my body was still weak, but I felt clear. I realized I still had work to do in releasing my anger, but I was also aware that all I had to do was choose to let it go. Not many people get to witness their own deliverance!

I had been given several quizzes by the universe to see how I was doing with my old friend Anger. The real test came when a contractor recommended immediate installation of some hardwood floors. When I inquired about the forty-eight hours required for the wood to acclimate, he minimized this and implied that it was more of a personal choice. I did not have the physical energy to react in my usual angry manner, so I became witness to this response. I was able to anticipate the probable results of expressing anger in this situation based on past experiences. I was hit with a bolt of understanding that anger was not only inappropriate but would have been so, so ineffective. In fact undisciplined anger can be dangerous.

I decided to have a dialogue with Anger. I started with the admission that I had never seen it in the light of truth. The truth is that you hide me. When I choose you I desert myself. Thank you for all the years I thought you protected me. I will see you around and call on you for help when it's appropriate to do so. Sometimes you have to carry a big stick.

Returning to Nita, I told her this: I know for sure that you are a child of God and God talks to you and all of his children and tells us what to do. I know you know right from wrong. God did not appoint me to force his will on you, nor make you in my image. My intention was to help you define your own course but Lord knows I didn't always know how to do it. I apologize for all the mistakes I made, because it is my soul's song to love you. Loving you will always make my heart sing. It took me a long time to see this reality but I know that it is real and I accept it with all my heart.

I now affirm that being a mother in all of its myriad forms is my life's purpose and personal salvation. For some time I had been searching for the avenue of my unique expression of the

Spirit. I looked all over the mountain, under the sea, and into the cave to find *me*. When I emerged I was more than surprised to find that it had been right under my nose the whole time. The fairy tales tell us that after we search the world for our treasure, we find it right at home. My fantasy of how my expression should look prevented me from seeing God's picture.

God's grace allows me to be a living image of aging gracefully. My body looks fit, well-groomed and stylish. My manner is inviting and my spirit alive, engaged, and content. The people I meet along the way usually respond to me with endearing "grandmother smiles," friendly help, and pleasant conversation. Wheelchair service and handicapped access are godsends to seniors.

By a very circuitous route I found the good fortune of a hairstyle that works for me: salt and pepper twisted dreadlocks that hang freely around my face. My association to this is a very primal return to an ancient natural jungle look. It puts me in touch with my own wildness and audacity to be myself. Like the natural hairstyle of the 70's, it declares that Black is Beautiful. Dreads are as natural as it gets. They really announce that Black is Free. It is very low maintenance, requiring little effort on my part. This is it, folks!

Looking back over my life, I remember being the innocent five year old who told my mother that when I grew up I wanted to take care of all the children who didn't have parents to take care of them. My first job as a professional social worker was in child welfare. A foster mother called me and told me tearfully that there was something wrong with one of the foster children in her home. She said he would stand motionless for hours under the porch without talking. Hearing stories like these over and over, I developed a deep yearning to understand these disturbed children. This led me to study and work in the field of child psychiatry. Differences in perceptions with some of my supervisors led me into supervision. Experiencing the discrepancy between policies and practice, I ventured into administration and later research. Learning that an administrator has more responsibilities than authority, I decided to go directly to the source and become a parent. When my children became adults, I decided to become a foster parent.

Having come full circle, I now understand what was wrong with that child in St. Louis under the porch. He was born into a society with misplaced priorities which disenfranchised and emotionally damaged his ancestors and parents; society's band-aid approach to this festering and metastasizing disease was to establish first orphanages and later, group homes and foster care. These systems were grossly inadequate to meet the needs of the children for love, belonging, and socialization. Like prisons, they often exacerbated the wounds, did not address the real problems, and contributed little towards healing.

It is my hope that America can return to its roots and promise of its Founding Fathers, that all men (and women) are created equal and deserve to be free and supported in the pursuit of their individual dreams. This paradigm shift will contribute to the health of society itself. I am amazed by the many red-blooded patriots ready to fight to their death for their freedom, but who act as if they have the God-given right to deny the freedom of another. These so-called patriots see no conflict in bullying or over-powering their competitors into submission. They feel entitled to be first. We are all alike, and all different, and no one has the right to use differences to separate from another and make the other less than. There are no firsts among equals.

I was listening to Senator Murdock explain his "pro-life" position and beliefs that when a woman is impregnated during rape it is "God's will which must be done," and he seemed oblivious to the fact that God talks to all of us and did not give him special permission to decide how everyone else should behave based on his interpretation of this situation. We are all kings and queens of our own castles, and we are out of place when we start trying to dictate to other kings and queens how they should live. Of course there have to be shared agreements for communities to function harmoniously. This requires equal participation in developing and applying the laws of the land. God's laws are universal and religion's laws are personal.

If we as a society can begin to recognize the importance of healthy family life to the wellbeing of everyone, then we can and will know peace in the world. Still responding to the promise of five-year-old Marie, I am committed to doing my part one child at a time and experiencing the joy of doing what I know works.

MARIE SIMMONS' LAST WILL AND TESTAMENT

Marie bequeaths her vast "fortune"--*the wisdom of the ages*-- to her children, family, friends, and to you, the reader. Your inheritance is to be found in a treasure chest full of precious jewels, named in the published book, *Marie's Treasure Chest*. Remember it's nothing personal. Receiving the wisdom of those who've gone before me, along with the lessons I've learned directly from life, there are a few things I know for sure:

There are universal principles which govern life:
Authenticity
Compassion
Education
Love
Truth
Generosity

Rituals

Work

Faith

Commitment

Acceptance

Humility

Forgiveness

Happiness

Gratitude

Acknowledgement

Patience

Sacrifice

Responsibility

Trust

Surrender

Creativity

Solitude

I believe these qualities are the foundation for a meaningful life. The way to insure that you will receive what you want is to give it. This is the reciprocal nature of the universe, sometimes called the Golden Rule, or Karma; as you do unto others it shall be done to you.

Your personal treasure chest is located in your own

backyard. Everybody has one. These qualities are tools to help you find yours. The universe loves a happy learner. Use your inheritance to guide you in rowing your boat gently down life's stream…merrily! for life is but a dream.

Consider the Golden Rule. When we fail to understand that we are here to learn how to express our own greatness, (instead of trying to shape others' expressions,) we miss the essence of life and are doomed to come back and do it again. (karma)."When we express what is within us, it frees us…if we do not express it, it will destroy us."

When we blame ourselves, others, or God, for bad things happening to us, we remain stuck in the problems and lose our inheritance of the riches of life. Travel light, have fun, and don't take life personally. In the end, we discover the truth: that it was never personal!

It has been said that we are only as sick as our secrets. My life is now an open book. In writing it, I have healed myself. With its publication, the doors of the gate have locked behind me; there's no way I can walk back through the gate. It has thrust me into my soul's calling of knowing and experiencing myself as Love. I am now free from illusions (mostly) and accept the truth of who I am (most of the time). I am love, and so are you. With this awareness, row, row, row your boat gently down the stream.

On her death bed, Marie recognized her assassins and their

weapons. They had stripped away all her externals. Naked, in solitude, Marie lost herself. Like the phoenix, Arundhati rose from Marie's ashes and she is now dancing on top of the world.

As it turned out, it was not just one assassin that murdered Marie, but a conspiracy of many. She identified the assassins by name in the following order: at the top of the list was her family! who laid deadly landmines all along her path (some were camouflaged, many were in plain view). Next, she met Melvin, her first romance, who turned out to be a WMD, a weapon of mass destruction. The clouds shifted and a caravan of angels arrived who slowly killed her with their kindness out of this world. She consulted a group of psychics who destroyed her belief in a three-dimensional world. The assassin with the most deadly weapon was Baba, her beloved guru, who killed her with the laser of his unconditional love.

She identified her many relationships, including family, lovers, children, clients, roommates, foster children, handymen, neighbors, and casual acquaintances as co-conspirators in her murder. Superiors and subordinates at work also played a role in her demise. She then identified a series of programs and spiritual practices, including a Course in Miracles, yoga, tai chi, meditation, churches, the Twelve Steps, and many workshops and retreats. The process continued for years at top speeds of grind, chop, shred, and puree. Some of her assassins were not even human--for example, a cabin, and two cats.

The final and fatal blow was delivered by an unlikely character--the President of the United States. Out of nowhere, Barack Obama triumphantly appeared, shocked the world, and gave Marie a cardiac arrest. His election shattered her doubts and beliefs in limitations into a million little pieces, putting Humpty Dumpty's fall to shame. Barack is a king of a man, an embodiment of Marie's knight in shining armor whom she feared existed only in her imagination. He is a tall, lean, tan, handsome man with a smile as magnetic as Pied Piper's flute. Marie was totally captivated by his campaign for president. As a rule, Marie had no love for television, but she became obsessed with the Tube, listening attentively for any new political developments. She witnessed with disbelief his ascension above the fray, skillfully deflecting the time-honored guerrilla war tactics hurled at him by his opponents. He appeared to have mastered his personal demons--like Daniel in the lion's den, he remained self-assured, compassionate, and forgiving, killing his enemies with love and kindness. Throughout the fierce battles he seemed to be armored in the cloak of the spirit. He enchanted the world as he waltzed light-footedly with his lovely brilliant wife and two perfect girls onto the world stage, cool, calm, and collected.

He surprised everyone with his unquestionable victory, and the universe wept and rejoiced. In this miraculous moment, people felt connected to him and each other and freely expressed their love for life.

All around the globe people felt included and shared in the victory as the color barrier was momentarily shattered. The human family seemed to join Dr. King on the mountaintop.

Barack personifies Marie's family values. Being a devoted husband and father is a high priority for him. Michelle Obama, a black "thoroughbred" from Chicago, has had a national impact on obesity and healthy diet. The dominant black gene is apparent in their two beautiful daughters. The White House will never be so white again.

On several occasions Barack has spoken directly to men, particularly black men, about the importance of their responsible presence in the home. He has also advocated for justice and equal sentencing of men and women of color under the law. He is committed to inclusiveness of all people in the human family, rich and poor, and GLBT. He leads by example, and he walks his talk. He even took his mother-in-law to live in the White House. Although he was reared by a white mother and grandparents, he fully embraces black values, is very knowledgeable about black culture, including black folklore and a working command of Ebonics. This he could have only learned from the feet of his "Obama mamas." His family is not matriarchal, but he has refined the skill of knowing when to defer to his wife. He is grounded in universal moral principles.

Obama's election as president of the most powerful country in the world has opened the doors for oppressed people everywhere. Black men no longer have a viable excuse for underachievement. Marie had become very discouraged by the historical castration and disenfranchisement of black men. She was not very hopeful about being able to influence this dynamic on a large scale. Barack did it for her. After his election Marie witnessed a brighter light in the eyes of black boys and men, and they seemed to be walking a tad bit taller. Someone overheard a black mother discipline her son by pointing out to them that they would never meet Sasha or Melia if they didn't shape up. Walt Disney has even produced a feature movie with a black princess. Marie found herself quoting Barack's slogans of yes-we-can to encourage and give hope to the people around her.

Although Barack honors his blackness, he has been adamant in not using race as an excuse or defense. He declared himself president of all the people. He courageously addressed the previously taboo subject of race, using words like an ointment to soothe the deep wounds of this nation. His being embodies, both literally and metaphorically, the unification of diversity. His inclusiveness authenticated Marie's experience of oneness, freeing her to release the individuality of her body and return to the spirit world. She drifted away with a smile on her face, feeling as safe and secure as she did when she arrived in her mother's arms.

Together all these murderers colluded to bring about poor Marie's total demise, and the case was closed. Although Marie is dead and gone, the assassins are still on the loose. Be careful, they might be stalking you.

Remember, the universe is impersonal in its perfection. As Fate would have it, I seemed to have no choice but to accept this reality. In consulting the runes on several occasions when it seemed that I was walking in darkness, one rune kept appearing in my hand--it was #24 Sowelu, which stands for wholeness, that which our nature requires. It embodies the impulse towards self-realization and indicates the path you must follow, not from ulterior motives, but the core of your individuality. This book is my way of yelling from the mountain top, "Hey World, this is me! And Love is Who I Am!" I have learned with great certainty that love is always present, even in our darkest times.

Too often it is the human tendency to relate more to what a person does than who the person is, and to focus on what's missing rather than what's present. Searching for what was missing in my life, I *asked myself* what I really wanted to do. Although two psychics had predicted that I would work with youth, I strongly resisted the idea because I thought I had completed my role as a mother--been there, done that. Also as a five-year-old, my own prophesy was that I would grow up and take care of all the children who didn't have mothers to take care of them.

Over time, I came to realize that Arundhati, my given spiritual name, is a model of family excellence and one who elevates the consciousness of those around her. Arundhati is who I am. When I accepted this as my destiny, I experienced a shift in my own consciousness which triggered a beginning of releasing of my identification with my behavior, fears and doubts. At this time, I recognized being a nurturer is my soul's desire and life's purpose. I am able to imagine creating a family living in peace and love with more clarity and ownership than ever before. It seems that I had looked all over the world for what was right there in my own back yard. With this awareness came the death of my ego and Marie's demise.

WHATEVER YOU GIVE WILL RETURN TO YOU.

LOVE IS NEVER VOID.

WHAT IS YOUR UNIQUE EXRESSON OF GOD'S GRACE?

WHAT ARE YOU PUTTING OUT THERE?

CHAPTER NINE
THE MYSTERY: WHO MURDERED MARIE??

"**The mind's first step to self-awareness must be through the body.**"

George Sheehan

(The following was written by Marie before she died.)

Marie is no longer with us. She has passed away. Her cremated body lies in a state of ashes from which she came. She leaves a large family and a host of friends to mourn her absence.

Actually, Marie was murdered. The assassination was systematically orchestrated over many years. The process was sometimes tortuous, and at times blissful, killing her softly with its love. Marie was not exactly sure when it started. In the beginning it was very disguised and oh so subtle. Marie left us her journal which reveals what happened in her own words:

For the past twenty years, I have known I was dying. Some-thing strange and mysterious was happening to me, and I didn't know whodunnit!! In recent years, I had done a lot of yoga, which for me was an opportunity to be with myself and experience the union of body and mind through the breath. Wanting to go deeper, I took up to ten classes a week and felt in tune with my body.

In one of the classes, the teacher suggested we find our center and allow all movement to flow from it. I did, and it was such an exhilaration that I wanted some way to maintain the feeling. At the end of the class, the teacher did a short meditation focusing on the third eye for living in wisdom, the lips for living in truth, and the heart for living in loving compassion. My mind wrapped around the wisdom of the invitation, my heart rejoiced, and my soul said yes.

After class I was flying high. I went home, looked at myself in the mirror, and asked God to manifest in my body in a way that would ensure my continuous awareness of His loving presence. I had no idea what I was asking for nor in what form it would show up. My soul seemed ready to detach from mundane reality. I wanted to know myself, and I wanted to know God as myself. In the past I had become confused by trying to intellectualize unconditional love. Failing to achieve the desired result, I smelled a rat.

Anger at one time was my coat of arms. I hid my fears of inadequacy of being in the world. It was my mask, my defense against actual and possible personal onslaughts from any and all directions. My weapon was my tongue and the presence of my small truth. Anger was my socially sanctioned reflex reaction to any situation that displeased me. Most of the time it was unconscious, but sometimes not. There were times I made others responsible and acted as if they instead of me needed to change.

Anger had been hanging around me so long it thought it was my best friend and it was not willing to leave peacefully. I, on the other hand, had been working diligently to let it go. It was deeply rooted in the core of my psyche. I sometimes confused it with my true self.

Life finally provided me with the awareness and opportunity to do so. The fight was on, and I was ready. Each time I chose not to act with my anger the power I gave to it diminished. With daily practice of choosing to love instead of being angry or afraid, I became more identified with what I wanted to become.

In this light I realized my throat felt scratchy. In retrospect I think this was the unshackling of all the anger I had repressed over the years. The heat rose as my body remembered experiences of not getting what I thought I wanted, feeling betrayed when someone did something I thought they shouldn't, or feeling disappointed when life didn't flow according to my plan. Anger was my reflexive response, as automatic as addictive behavior. It was my coat of arms to hide my fears. Anger had been with me for so long it thought it was my best friend, and it was not going to leave peacefully. The "war was on!"

My throat, as are all throats, is the seat of anger. It became more enflamed every time I tried to cough up a thick clingy phlegm from my lungs. My energy was gradually drained away like a thief in the night draining gasoline from a vacant car. I was pulled into bed with the force of gravity.

It gradually dawned on me that anger is not only inappropriate but so very ineffective in getting me what I wanted in any situation. I had never been willing to look at anger in this light. A friend who overshadows me is not one I choose. Thank you, Anger, for protecting me over the years. I will probably see you around and call upon you when it serves me to do so. In letting go of my anger I remembered the Twelve Step Program, first acknowledging that my anger had power over me. I prayed for the willingness to let it go. The more I practiced taking control of my automatic fear reflex, the stronger I became in my resolve to see love all the time everywhere and in everybody.

I intuitively realized that my mind was not to be trusted and my body would probably be my best teacher. I take my body everywhere with me-- it's hard to forget. The body demands to be accepted on its own terms. It speaks without words, and says things nothing else can. You can't argue with a teacher who doesn't talk. My fantasy was that God's moving in my body would feel like my experience of yoga. Was I in for a surprise!

One day soon after the pivotal class, I started feeling unfamiliar movements in my body. My little finger on my right hand seemed to disconnect internally from my hand, and then my right arm disconnected from my shoulder. The only visible symptom was a distortion of my right little finger. In a subsequent class my yoga teacher pointed out to me that I was lifting up my right shoulder. I was not aware of this. For several months I struggled to reconnect my finger and shoulder to my arm. Much to my dismay, I gradually became aware that the core of my body seemed to dissolve into a fluid-like substance and I felt as if it was being pulled down by gravity. I had internal sensations that the right side of my body was disconnected from the left, the top from the bottom, and the internal linings were crisscrossed. At times my entire body seemed to move around with the front exchanging places with the back. This reminded me of the Exorcist movie, and I was afraid to think how crazy I might be. I thought perhaps my body had been taken over by aliens.

In desperation I started blowing in an attempt to keep the internal contents of my body from falling to my feet. I discovered through trial and error a deep breathing process accompanied by a rather loud and weird sound which seemed to keep the fluid-like substance afloat. I also discovered that I could move body parts around with my tongue from a meridian in my jaw. Without a doubt I moved things in places where they seemed to fit but did not belong, and this is really when the trouble began. It was totally frightening to realize that what I had previously perceived as stable body parts on some level did not exist. Sometimes my rectum was displaced by misguided tissue, or some other substance, causing diarrhea or constipation. I experienced urinary frequency with an alarming urgency over which I had no control. Using the meridian in my jaw, I accidentally tangled my spinal tissue with my stomach tissue. I realize that this sounds totally crazy and defies reason, but it's a precise description of my experience. I wondered who or what was trying to kill me.

I felt as if body parts were moving around with great fluidity without direction from me. It was as if my internal veins, arteries, and organs had a mind of their own and a destination unknown to me. Imagine this if you can: my internal body parts move around my skeleton like a car traveling on a racetrack at very high speeds with no driver at the wheel. Or this: a deaf, dumb, and blind person is trying to assemble a very complex, intricate puzzle without being familiar with either its parts, texture, or pattern.

The process (which is the name I've given to my experience) continued 24/7, leaving me little or no discretionary time to do anything else. It consumed both my days and nights. When the process started, it was as if my consciousness went on holiday, and time ceased to exist. I was subject to forget any and every thing, particularly any changes in routines. CPT time (Colored People's Time) has always been an issue for me in my relationships with more punctual friends, even before the process started. Subsequently it has become more problematic.

For example, I scheduled a writing appointment with my friend Julie and called to say I was "running late" (as usual), but she was not at home when I called. It occurred to me that maybe she had forgotten our appointment since I had changed the day we usually meet. I left a message asking her to call and confirm our appointment when she arrived home.

She called back and sounded disappointed that I had not yet left home, a half an hour after the time we were supposed to meet. She said of course she hadn't forgotten the appointment, and asked me why I thought she had, when she had not done so in the past. I immediately recognized my assumption as a projection and felt very ashamed that my behavior reflected disregard for her in our long-time, highly respected and valued friendship. I realized that being late is a form of control, which shows insensitivity to the feelings of other people. Malcolm X once said that a person who does not respect time cannot be trusted. It is contrary to my self-image to be seen as untrustworthy, and I genuinely would like to be on time for appointments! However, despite my most concerted efforts, I was unable to manage it. On several occasions I had plans to attend a yoga class which was one of my few remaining scheduled activities, but the appointed time often came and went without my awareness.

Sometimes I was awakened in the wee hours of the

morning. Hovering between being asleep and awake, I struggled to assist my body in its attempt to come into balance, although I had no idea what I was doing. It was impossible for me to connect the dots and solve the puzzle, because I was unfamiliar with the dots and had no idea where to look for them, or where to put them if I found them. I felt as if I was being systematically demolished, and already brain-dead.

Many times, I left home for overdue visits to the supermarket or other errands, only a short distance away, and ended up spending 4 or 5 hours sitting in my car in the parking lot. When I turned off the engine, my body automatically went deep into the process of trying to balance itself. Taking flight in my swirling orbit, I attempted to ground myself by planting the tip of my right little finger on anything solid. Subsequently I developed a thick callus and deformed nail on my right little finger which eventually required surgery.

The process was like a constant kria, which is an involuntary movement or sound resulting from a spiritual experience. During group meditations with an enlightened teacher, I witnessed involuntary palsy-like movements from some of the meditators. Strange sounds emanated from others, some of which seemed to imitate wild animals. I remembered wondering what kind of experience they were having. I think I found out.

Needless to say, my odd behavior in my car attracted the

attention of passersby, several of whom approached my car to ask if I was all right. Once someone even called the police who came to see if I was in distress. I assured them I was okay. In the beginning I was somewhat surprised at the degree of observers' concern, because I thought I was being inconspicuous. However, I was not seeing myself through their eyes. I've been told it looks like I'm having some kind of epileptic seizure. My head bobs up and down and my body twists and turns, doing an unusual set of internal somersaults. Fortunately, it is mostly without pain.

While all this was going on, I was trying to look and act "normal." I gradually learned to accept the odd sounds and movements, but this was harder for the people around me to get comfortable with, so I retreated to the privacy of my bathroom. Sometimes I felt as if I had been abducted by wild animals and carried off into the jungle. Although I had to make peace and sometimes friends with the animals to survive, it was still hard for me to identify with them because they were so primitive and I wanted to see myself as civilized. The animals, having unique personalities, were unfamiliar to me and unpredictable. They were related to each other by the dynamic conditioning of my past. Sometimes they felt gentle and caressing, as the familiar does. Other times they felt very active, quick, and frightening. It was difficult for me to discern their identity because they were so shadowy.

I believe that the animals in the jungle represented different aspects of my primal fears. In observing myself wanting to be right, wanting to be in control, being arrogant, angry, dependent, self-important, self-righteous, and a well spring of other negative emotions shared by humans, I realized that I don't like these traits in myself or anyone else. So why all the difficulty in letting them go? Letting go of the ego is the ultimate fear. Because of the unconscious nature of the ego and its tendency to project negativity, it is a very subtle, crafty, tenacious force in our lives. Denial is one of my ego's favorite ways of protecting itself.

I'm becoming increasingly aware of the hamster wheel part of my own personality. I have observed my compulsive attraction to behavior that does not work. Although I do not know the cellular memories of my body nor how they are connected to each other, I have persisted for several years in compulsive, repetitive, ineffective behaviors, attempting to bring my body into balance. My mind was completely blown when I discovered how my behavior actually prevented my body from balancing itself. Humbled by this discovery, I was open to recognizing other self-defeating behaviors. This was not a pleasant realization. I became truly amazed that I have been able to accomplish anything, given my overactive saboteur.

Our body is our best friend. It does not deceive us. We may have misperceptions about it because it always follows the path of least resistance. Our body has its own truth which patiently awaits our recognition. It has taught me things about my ego that I couldn't learn otherwise. It is the hardest task master, unavailable for negotiation! Despite the magnitude of the challenge, I was determined to become the captain of my own ship and the master of my fate.

The all-consuming nature of the process required letting go of almost everything external to it. I was unable to do simple daily routines such as clean my room or make myself food. I also had to let go of many of the social graces that helped me feel good about myself. Routinely, I was totally absorbed in the process from eight to fifteen hours a day. Often, I would go on for five or six hours without stop and when I looked at the clock, I was surprised at how much time had passed. I hadn't eaten or showered. I couldn't believe what my body was doing. I was afraid that I would either lose my mind or die, or both.

I struggled to create a pattern or form to make sense out of the experience, so that I could understand it and explain it to other people, but rational explanations continued to elude me. This was such a visceral, non-intellectual experience, that it was impossible to apply familiar concepts. Not only were the assassins not talking to me, I had no words to describe their behavior nor my experience to anyone else. It was mind-boggling.

Sometimes I felt the gentle touch of a hand guiding my

movements, and on occasions I actually got glimpses of shadowy internal images flashing as if on MTV. Although many people encouraged me to seek external help, I was not personally motivated to do so. It annoyed me when even well-meaning people continued to probe about the nature of the process beyond my initial albeit vague descriptions.

A friend whom I don't see very often because she lives in another state called me and said she'd been thinking about me a lot and wanted to know if I was all right. I made some vague response that I was going through a transition that was difficult to talk about. She said, "Oh, you can tell me anything. We've known each other for 35 years." A few words into my tentative explanation, she asked me what I had been smoking! We talked for a while longer and after I hung up, I remembered someone telling me that the difference between a psychic and a psychotic is that the psychic doesn't share her personal experience with other people.

In the first year, I lost 40 pounds, had no body fat, and my skin dangled from my bones like a weeping willow tree. I accepted all this as part of the mystery, but the people around me didn't buy it. Everyone who knew me was alarmed. One day after coming home from a party, much to my surprise my three closest friends were standing in my driveway to greet me. Since they are not people who would normally come together on their own, many thoughts raced through my mind as to why they were there. It was not my birthday, and I wasn't aware of any plans for a celebration. I was highly suspicious, and demanded to know what was going on, but their responses were limited to greetings and pleasantries. I knew something was up when we went inside and I found my daughter there who was also unexpected.

The four of them had apparently been discussing my weight loss and had decided to do a group intervention to stop what they saw as my death process. Each of their individual efforts had failed to get me to go to a doctor. They were trying to respect my efforts to handle the situation myself, but they were also seriously concerned about my health. One said her husband was waiting in the car in case I threw her out of the house. My daughter was fearful that I would be angry and defensive, because we'd already discussed my decision not to consult the traditional medical system, and she knew I was not open to further discussion.

I was touched by the combination of their intimidation and concern. I told them that I believed that they had better things to do on a Sunday afternoon than drive from the Oakland hills, Berkeley, and Concord to present me with some trivialities and flaky requests. Then I lightened up and chose to relate to their love and friendship rather than their interference-- I agreed to go to the doctor the next day. As if I couldn't be trusted, my daughter and two friends showed up in the doctor's little two-by-four examining room, to again express their individual concerns to the doctor, just in case I omitted any significant information. Many tests and many dollars later, my demise still did not have another name, and certainly no recommended cure. Of course, some tentative diagnoses were offered: possible neurological tumor, chemical imbalance, carpal tunnel for my hand, some of everything, none of which really addressed what was going on.

Doctors often believe, and some people agree, that they are the medical authorities and "know the body best." I am not of this school, and believe that the best authority on a body is the person who occupies it. It was extremely difficult to pay homage as well as big bucks to listen to information about myself from the "authorities," when I didn't think they knew what they were talking about. I felt as if I were a stranger in a foreign land, listening to people talk to and about me in words that I understood but did not agree with and could not refute. I had no language or framework to describe what was really going on. It was impossible to describe a mystery to someone who thinks only "the known" is real. I was gradually getting the message loud and clear that "help" would not come from outside of myself, and it would indeed be a solitary journey.

My doctor was so concerned about both my condition and my attitude that she wrote me a certified letter reiterating the seriousness of my situation, and outlining all the possible diagnoses, and reviewing her referral to several specialists.

Reading her dire assessment of my condition, I almost fainted in the post office.

After the first two years my body seemed to settle down and I regained most of my weight and looked normal from the outside. On a subsequent visit to my doctor, she said she was overwhelmed by what she referred to as "a complete neurological change" in my body. She said again she wasn't sure she believed in mysteries. On the other hand, she said she had no explanation for what I had experienced other than "a miracle." She offered to write a supporting statement for this book, so my readers wouldn't think I was "full of shit." Soon thereafter, she received an international accolade, became rich and famous, and terminated her Mill Valley practice to write a book of her own.

Meanwhile, inside, the deathly process continued. Instead of seeking medical help, I decided to hire a private yoga teacher who is excellent at what she does. Her body beautifully reflects the yoga experience. She describes yoga as the marriage between breath and movement. One of the few things that I know for sure is that *breath is life.* Wherever the breath flows, the body responds. In addition to weekly private yoga lessons, I attended several yoga classes a week. For a while I even went to yoga instead of church on Sunday mornings, enhanced by a sauna and steam bath. This combination was great and it occurred to me that I might choose to replace church with yoga. Before long, however, I started missing the fellowship of the church community, and realized I needed both. It is not my purpose to espouse the virtues of yoga in this book, as that has already been done many times and many places. During my dark night of the soul, however, yoga became one of my primary lifelines and I highly recommend it for anyone looking for an anchor.

As time went on, my friend Julie suggested that I see a psychiatrist or shaman. It was her opinion that the process was psychosomatic. She said that she was sure that I thought my body was doing the things I said, but since the process did not show up on tests she thought it was all in my head. She told me about her mother-in-law who insisted that her (dead) sister was outside calling her and throwing rocks at her window every night. She added that schizophrenics are also sure that their experiences are real. She suggested that perhaps a psychiatrist could give me psychotherapy or medication.

I told her that I had no intention of seeking the services of a traditional psychiatrist or taking any psychotropic drugs, and that I was not out of touch with what she calls the rational world as schizo-phrenics are. My attitude was hopeful, my objectives clear, and my intentions steadfast. It is true that I experienced different realities but they were not isolated from each other. I have always prided myself on my ability to think on different levels and from a variety of frameworks, including psychological, cultural, spiritual, and streetwise. This has enabled me to negotiate life with a variety of people and environments. Self-definition is something I had to learn rather early living in a white world as a black woman. It became very clear to me that I could not accept White America's definition of who I am. Depending on others to tell us who we are is a no-win situation. Self-definition is the primary responsibility of everyone seeking self acceptance.

It has been my practice for a long time to try to understand other people's thoughts and behavior from their point of view without thinking it means anything about me. This helps me to choose my responses accordingly with no obligation for agreement or need to disagree. Sometimes my objective responses to my friends' and family's efforts to be helpful were unsettling because some people think that if you don't agree with them, you haven't been listening, or they haven't been heard. If I had bought into the perceptions of others, I would have been in the crazy house or in the ground.

When the same friend told me that she thought I was a little crazy, I asked myself could this be true? I examined what she described as my eccentric behavior, but we didn't see it in the same way, and I did not think her description qualified me as insane. However, when I thought about my daily repetitive attempts to balance my body, I realized that her comment had great merit. For years I had persisted in doing pretty much the same thing every day all day with the same results. I understand that the classic definition of insanity is -- doing the same thing over and over and expecting different results. My behavior certainly fits this description. I also realized that I share this "insanity" with many others; it's only a matter of degree.

I shudder to think how often I and perhaps others engage tenaciously in behaviors which do not bring the desired results. Although I observed myself going through this ritualistic movement, I felt out of control as if at the effect of some very primal process. I suppose one reason I continued to return to the same behavior is that I didn't know what else to do, and neither did anybody else. Attempting to change my behavior would have been an admission that what I was doing was wrong. Even though I have known from the beginning that I was out of control, the fear of facing this reality head-on was more than I was ready for. Denial is a coin with two sides--it can protect or destroy.

Another friend who was not satisfied with my "spiritual" explanation of the process wrote me a three page typed letter reviewing her observations and concerns, ending with her opinion that she did not think God wanted me to lose all that weight! There have been many other expressions of concern ranging from shocked looks and raised eyebrows to gentle but probing questions. My reaction to all of this was to try to see the love in everyone's concern but remain true to my own convictions.

My friends and family were very anxious for the process to be completed. They sometimes acted as if I was in control of it and could stop if I wanted to do so. On my sister Ruby's birthday, I thought that the process was completed and offered its completion to her as her birthday gift. She thanked me profusely and said it was the best gift she could have received. The next day, however, the process was again strong and intense. I called her and confessed its continuation, and she responded, "…but you promised!!" I reminded her that I could not have promised to do something outside of my control, but I sincerely thought that the gift was legitimate. I offered to send her a material birthday gift instead, and I sent her some cash.

One of my friends asked me if the process killed me, would I be willing to die. My response was Yes. The truth was that I had no choice, and aspects of me were dying daily anyway. Another person asked if I would be willing to live with the process to the end of my life. While I considered the possibility that the process may be permanent, in my heart of hearts I hoped and believed it would have an ending point short of my physical death.

I feel I have no choice but to see the process through to its completion. It is the most intense and vivid confrontation with my belief system that I have encountered to date. The meaning and authenticity of my life and death depends on following it through to the end. Follow it I must. I don't know where it's going, but it does. Will I die? And if so, when? It seems predestined, but is it personal choice?

Happiness, like death, is a choice which only requires permission from oneself. Once while listening to classical music, I decided to surrender to the process and enjoy it. When I gave myself permission to become one with the silent witness, I experienced feelings of deep peace and joy. I felt more awake and aware of the beauty of the blooming trees and flowers outside of my window. The trees seemed to be offering a balance of sunlight and shade under the protective eye of the soft clouds. Aware of the connectedness of all life, I felt happy. Later, I wondered why giving myself permission is such a battle. Letting go of desires, fears, grief, guilt, worries, hurts, and other life experiences which sometimes separate us from God is a moment-by-moment second-by-second daily choice made with grace until we let go permanently.

On my way to my book writing appointment, which is usually the time I think about what I'm going to write, I heard an internal voice singing, "Wake up, little Susie, wake up,....it's time to go home." Waking up's so very hard to do. Although it's my soul's desire, I share the human condition of wanting to hold on to my familiar worries. In one moment I let them go, I feel at peace, and a few minutes later I'm trying to recapture my familiar worries. Once we start to entertain fearful thoughts of any kind, they immediately feel familiar and comfortable, and thus are difficult to release.

When I started to mourn my losses, I learned to remind myself of my friend Celeste who lost many body parts to a disease and with each loss she said to herself, "I am not my arms, I am not my legs, I am not my hair, etc....so who am I?" This convinced me like nothing else that we are spirits who have bodies and not bodies who have spirits. The answer was obvious to me--"just surrender all," but heaven knows it is oh so hard to do. I was slowly learning the graceful dance of surrendering my effort to the effortless. Ultimately this would require totally letting go of who I was, or who I thought I was. This was my greatest fear.

My obsession with the process has continued for eighteen long arduous years, with varying degrees of suffering and joy, but always constant. The process has insisted on my undivided attention, and forced me to question my beliefs, values, choices, and everything I held dear. It was very scary and humbling to walk in the world without strong personal beliefs which acted as shields and defenses for me. They either identified me with or apart from other people. The problem with my strong beliefs was that they separated me in some way from people who did not share them and prevented the connection I was seeking. These differences were often viewed from the tainted lens of thinking I knew how I and others ought to be in the world. Without attachment to personal beliefs, I became freer to see people and things as they were, and not the way I thought they should be, rerunning my stale thoughts from the past, and missing the magic of the present. All my lessons seemed to be saying, in a variety of ways, "Let go of who you think you are, have the courage to choose who you want to be, and don't take anything personally."

The conflict between my body and my mind is a microcosm of all the conflicts I've experienced in the world. Truth confronts illusion when what I want is different from what is. In past relationships I have wanted to believe what a person said, in spite of how loudly his or her behavior spoke to the contrary. Wanting to place trust outside of oneself is a tempting seduction. My practice of self delusion often ended in hurt with a quick descent into feelings of being a victim or martyr. In instances when I have wanted some thing or a certain outcome, I have chosen to rationalize signs and indications contrary to my wishes, only to delay the inevitable feelings of disappointment. What we want to believe is sometimes so strong that it overshadows the truth. Strong desires are famous for killing truth in its tracks. During these times I recalled the advice of a guru to her disciples to "trust no one." She said that personalities are fallible and prone to error. Trust is misplaced if it is not in your Self (the Spirit.)

I became more aware of an arrogance in myself which implied that I thought I was somehow above the laws of the land. When I explored this attitude it seemed related to growing up black in a white dominated society. As a young child I realized that the laws and their enforcers were not there to protect me and in some situations were out to get me, especially the black males in my family. This experience continued into my adulthood as I witnessed myself and other blacks as being perceived as second class citizens by many whites in positions of authority. For example, as a new young professional in a state hospital, when I requested the keys from a staff member, he demanded to know if I was the maid. Looking for apartments, I was told there were no openings, although vacancies had been advertised. In professional meetings, I became used to the statements I made being credited to someone else. Consequently I accepted "external authority" with a grain of salt, and I tended to look for ways around the requirements of the laws. I now have come to accept that I, like everyone else, have to respect the laws of the land, and insist that they respect me. The laws of the universe are impersonal and protect everyone equally.

Sometimes I am sure that this process is the final assassination of my ego. Needless to say my ego is loudly protesting. My soul yearns to become one with the Beloved, while I struggle to stay alive and in control. I am suspended between two realities. I am not identified with things and people around me in the way I once was, and I feel estranged from my old feelings and emotions. This feels like being suspended in midair having let go of one trapeze without having caught the other. The Buddhists practice nonattachment, teaching that desires are the root of all suffering.

Whenever a conflict arises between my mind and my body, I have decided to follow the wisdom of the body. My mind is totally blown by my body's intelligence. It forces me to think "outside of the box". I know the impossible must be possible because it's happening within my body. The body responds to mental direction and takes the path of least resistance. Many times it has deluded me into thinking I was "doing it right," and in this way it was the master trickster.

Believing in God outside of myself and experiencing God as myself are qualitatively different experiences. Believing in a God outside of myself allows me to feel a measure of protection and security. The experience of God as myself requires a great deal of hard work, pain, struggle, and death of the ego. Sometimes I feel very grateful to have the privilege of doing this work, and other times I wonder, "WHY ME?" In my ego's absence the light of the Spirit shines. The Spirit knows no preference of person and bridges the gap between self and other. When I let my "little light shine," it seems to enable other people to recognize the light in themselves. In this way I recognize I am a servant of the Spirit, which is my soul's desire, but my ego continues to actively resist the role. It is still yearning to do, in spite of clear evidence that what I want is found not in the doing, but in the being.

I've been stripped of many of my traditional roles and my doing has decreased. As a young woman, realizing that something was missing in my life, I used to joke with my friends about first paying my debt to society (whatever that was) and then finding myself. I used to think I was a mover and a shaker in the world, one who thought she was making things happen, or at least facilitating the action. I now know the truth, that of myself I can do nothing.

Years before the process began, I remember telling a healer that my next spiritual path was going to be my body. At the time I made this comment I was slightly overweight, spent a great deal of time outside of my body, and felt little connection with it. Watching my children dance reminded me of how disconnected I felt and left me yearning to feel more at home in my body.

Shortly after, I started weekly meditations with a ninety-year-old man whom I called my spiritual playmate. He strongly believed that our body is our best friend and repeated this to me often. We focused on affirmations, mine being that my body was healthy, strong, agile, shapely, and youthful. We recited them out loud, over and over for several months. This was the mental preparation that led to my lifestyle changes. I joined the gym and rediscovered yoga. After several months my yoga teacher commented that my body had changed its shape and was more lively and youthful. Even this did not forewarn me of what was to come.

When I became aware that my body was in a process of constant internal motion, it occurred to me that all of our bodies are in constant motion, traveling at the speed of light in the service of internal balance. The motion is so subtle it is almost imperceptible, and most of us are not even aware of it. Many of us take flight from our bodies, some to avoid too much pleasure, others to avoid too much pain. Still others may be too distracted with the challenges of life to be aware of the constant internal pulsations of our bodies. We imagine that our bodies are made up of some solid mass and believe that "we're it," or "it's us."

I became obsessed with this motion in my own body. As much as I thought I wanted to or should want to do other things, it seemed what I really wanted to do was to lose myself in this motion. I could space out any time or anywhere. I have been looking forward with great anticipation to the process completing itself (so I could get on with my life.) However, I am beginning to believe that the process will be completed when I become one with the Whole and no longer need reminders. In the meantime, I will have to learn to live in the world with the awareness of motion in my body as the loving reminder of God's constant presence. (Be careful what you ask for.)

In retrospect, I realize that my body, like everybody else's, has always been my primary teacher. It has never lied to me. I have come to accept it as my best friend. Not only have I learned to listen but I now give it my undivided attention. My body has tried to inform me about my destructive patterns in the past; when I refused to listen to a gentle tap, I was hit with a two-by-four. I ended up in the hospital several times, with multiple ailments, including a rare Cushings Syndrome, which is hypersecretion of the adrenalin gland. As a result of several surgeries I developed gangrene of my small intestines and had to have a large portion removed. There is no question in my mind that my emotional conflict was the subject of the message; unfortunately it took me a long time to hear it. I did not have the inner strength to terminate an abusive relationship, but the time came when it was "less painful for the flower to open than for the bud to remain closed."

In my fifties, I was diagnosed with narcolepsy. If I drank a glass of wine, I would fall asleep in my plate at dinner. I fell asleep driving on more than one occasion, and even went to sleep once while exercising in the gym. I'm sure I had this condition in college, but did not know what it was. In my customary style I attempted to take it all in stride. My hysterectomy, appendectomy, tonsillectomy, adrena-lectomy, etc.--all these "extractions" were an indication of my feeble attempts to externalize the internal emotional conflicts expressed in my body.

Too often my mind speaks with the loudest voice. Although it is my deepest desire to become a more loving and accepting person, I find myself easily frustrated and frequently annoyed at the end of the day when working on the process is all that I've accomplished. I can only hope that this stage is temporary and the path will eventually lead me to my goal, to become patient, long-suffering, and unconditionally loving.

In the beginning it was hard for me to discern my fear thoughts, they felt so natural and gave me the illusion that they were maintaining some weird balance in my psyche. Outside of my awareness, my fear thoughts would storm around wreaking havoc, interfering with the natural flow of love. The ego has many hiding places, very deep in our cells and DNA. When I thought I was being loving, my saboteur was wide awake and fear was only pretending to be asleep. When I was sure I was surrendered, I would discover my feeble efforts to control were running rampant. When I was certain I had let go, I would suddenly notice the frantic holding on by my fingernails to some imaginary security. I came to realize that I had to identify my fears by name in order to recognize them. You can only claim what you can name, and you can only heal what you can feel!

The universe provided me with an objective, graphic, concrete example of how the ego works against itself. Every month I feed the homeless at one of the local churches. The station is a well stocked store-like pantry, (as could only exist in Sausalito). Food is sometimes donated in large quantities. Since most of the homeless are single or living with one other person, we divide up the large quantities to serve more people. The woman working with me went through a process of doing, then undoing, the bagging. I stood and observed her, amazed and totally fascinated by her systematic blocking of her own progress. While I was able to observe her self-defeating behavior with perfect clarity, I was still struggling to identify the many ways in which I block my own progress and continue to make things more difficult for myself.

I am convinced that I have made my journey a lot harder for myself than it needed to be, but I didn't know any other way to do it. My mother always told me that I had to work hard to succeed, and because I am black, I would have to work twice as hard as others just to be noticed. This belief is sanctioned, encouraged, and even rewarded by society. I bought it, hook, line and sinker. The journey can be easier for you. Remember love is what you're after. The universe loves a happy learner.

Although I have always felt protected by guardian angels, my patience is not long enough and my faith is not yet strong enough to look the unknown in the face without wavering. After years of daily disappointments, I am flabbergasted by my continued faith, hope, and optimism, which can only be grace. I sometimes achieve a moment of optimism where I am sure I am about to complete the puzzle. I think I've finally got it, got the map, know the terrain, know the direction, the parts and the pattern. But then the pattern completely changes, or so it seems. Everything becomes new and unfamiliar again, and I am back at square one. Occasionally I plunge into despair and hopelessness. However, I do not indulge in these feelings for long, because I know I have no choice but to continue. With each new day I repeat the routine with childlike expectancy for healing and balance. When I surrender to it, it is very enchanting. When I resist it, it becomes a tyrant.

After much struggle, experience has taught me the art of "effortless effort," which is surrendering to the natural rhythmic flow of breath moving in and out. It is the breath within the breath. Life is a mysterious dance of the breath between movement and stillness. The best dance partner is one who understands the dance and knows how to follow! It *can* be easy!

According to Rumi: "There is a way of breathing that is a suffocation and a shame. There is another way of breathing that is a love breath. It connects us to infinity." The breath flows through our body as life. The movement is so subtle that most of us are unaware of this natural ongoing miracle. The world sweeps us away from our breath and body with its many distractions. Those of us who have taken leave would be well advised to reinhabit our bodies and pay attention to our breath. Wherever we direct the breath in the body, it changes. The breath has the power to calm and restore us faster than anything we can put in our bodies. The breath is the chariot to our innermost being and infinity. The body is the road the chariot must travel.

At church last Sunday I heard a song called "Waking Up is Hard to Do." I accepted this as a personal message of condolence from the universe, and I was reassured that I am not alone in my struggles. The song was so "right on" that I wanted to include it here:

"You tell me to keep breathing,
that your love will guide my way
Then why does my little ego want to say:

Don't take my pain away from me
Don't leave me here without my misery
Cause if I let go, then what would I do?
This waking up is hard to do.

Remember when I loved to fight
Got so much pleasure just from being right
Now pointing fingers just makes me blue

This waking up is hard to do.

They say that waking up is hard to do
So many lifetimes of sleeping through
Don't say maybe I could
Instead of waking up I think I'll hang on to my victimhood.

My guru says only love can heal
My therapist tells me to feel feel feel
Seems every year there's more issues
This waking up is hard to do.

They say that waking up is hard to do
It's hard enough to turn off the tube
Don't say maybe I can
Instead of waking up I think I'll stay in couch potato land.

My challenges, they make me wiser
They help me grow just like some fertilizer
Wish I could grow up without doo-doo
This waking up is hard to do,
Waking up is hard to do."

When the process became extremely difficult and required

ten or more hours a day, sapping my energy and keeping me from doing the simplest household tasks, I have had to remind myself often of what I really believe, that God will provide. Since love and fear cannot coexist, I have periodically witnessed the faltering of my faith. My fears about possible bankruptcy didn't hold a candle to the terror I felt at the beginning of the process, which threatened both my physical form and personal identity. I chose not to allow fear's visits to become too frequent or too protracted. When I asked fear to leave, it did, so I know whenever I become really ready to let it go, it will.

"Darkness and light cannot coexist." It is possible to be aware of one in the presence of the other. For example, it is human nature to forget that light exists when we are in darkness. When we are in pain or sadness, we sometimes think that this state is all there is and ever will be. Remembering experiences of joy and success will not only help us through the hard times, but will shorten their duration. Over time I experienced encouraging signs of letting go of one trapeze without having the other in hand. Trust is the major factor in being able to fly when you have been conditioned to crawl.

Several years into the "process," it seems out of nowhere I recaptured the memory of a psychic's prediction of thirty years ago. She told me that something very miraculous was going to happen in September. For some reason, the year didn't come through clearly and the two of us speculated about it. She asked me if I had any idea what year it might be. I certainly had no vision of anything on the horizon. Many Septembers have come and gone with nothing way out of the ordinary, and the process continues. However, her prediction is a beacon of light, and every fall I am hopeful about the promise of transformation. The lesson is that everything is always new in the Spirit, and every moment is a moment of transformation. I am learning to live comfortably in the mystery.

Human experiences are universal, differing only in the details. I am sharing my tale with you in the hope that it will help you to be more light hearted and self-accepting. Have fun! and remember that the universe is impersonal in its perfection!

Reflections of friends and family

Daughter, La Wanda Marrero

Marie was filled with creative talent, and she was ingenious in overcoming obstacles in pursuit of finding herself and helping others. She loved children and was very giving of herself and made generous sacrifices to take in both relatives and foster children. I was the first and I am La Wanda. I came to live with Marie by train at age 10. We celebrated at least 45 years of our February 9, anniversaries. My Rebe was the first real sense of stability and protectiveness. She cradled me and made me feel safe. I can remember being a child that was anxious, living on edge because I didn't know from day to day what would happen to me in the care of my grandma Ruby in St. Louis. But with Marie she moved heaven and earth to show me love, allow me to explore, music, dance, drama, and all the bicentennial, American flags songs I could sing. She never complained, and believe me, those tap shoes, drums, and clarinet sounds are loud. I became so attached to her I would get emotional and upset when she would leave the house.

I once came into the living room, and she was counseling a male client. I did not understand the meaning of client nor counseling. His close proximity to her triggered an emotional spinout for me, and she made her apologies to him and asked him to leave. She explained to me her role as a social worker and assured me she was safe. Marie had a way with making herself and thoughts clear with compassion, patience, and sternness when necessary. She had this special way of speaking with and to me that others may not have understood. But remember she raised me from a very troublesome child, (Alice) and she found impactful ways to communicate with me tailored for me. She informed me of my backwards thinking over the years as an assistance to give me some relief, because I struggled in my thoughts. I remember her being healthy and having a social life with awesome friends. She was a trouble shooter for me, and she brought in her social work team of friends to help. But even as a team I was like a walnut almost uncrackable. Marie brought out my strengths and became quite familiar with my barriers. She encouraged me to use coping skills that were preventative in nature or at best deescalating. My emotional outbursts brought her home on several occasions. Marie the wise one came up with the idea of everyone bringing their kids and putting them all in one room while the adults engaged in their fun. The story is in my published book, *Alice N Crackland* extensively for you, the reader's enlightenment.

  Thinking of her and gathering stories from her friends and family has been somewhat emotionally unleashing. It's a test of balance of stability in my growth as a matriarch. I have seen her in me as I face unsettling challenges and rise to the occasion. It's a daily battle of giving myself Love and appreciation since her passing. She shared her spiritual wisdom around peace and self-acceptance. Often my mind may want to react, but my heart leads me to create. I see Marie in my expectation of myself and actions, as her wisdom evolves in my life. I'm bound to look past and beyond and with empathy rather than my own hurtfulness. I'm coming to know freedom from separateness and the bondage of how I feel, practicing knowing and walking in who I have been called to be, without doubt and disbelief. My very being has been enlightened and resurrected with the peace of God and his plan for my life.

Marie liked control versus being vulnerable; she was always there with the simplicity of her words and the endurance of her love although I knew she held a huge space for me in her very being. I didn't understand the significance of that at the time. I was a traumatized kid viewing myself as a troublesome child and there were other disturbed children and adults that followed after me into her care. Looking back as an adult I commend her creative brilliance at its finest. Marie was captured by her journey and the responsibilities she faced, growing into a young matriarch's role of caring for her kin. She had a generous nature and learned over the years with much struggle how to become supportive in exchange for codependency. It reminds me of a slogan I learned during my own rite of passage with Cecil Williams and Glide Memorial Days. "You can feed me fish for a day, and I will be full for a day or you can teach me to fish and I will be filled for a life time." She opened her home, heart, and her wallet. She had a ride-or- die attitude through the duration of changes for herself, for me, and others. She believed in people and supported their struggles, and their willingness to create and make changes in their lives.

The End of life

How I knew it was the end? She was ready, she had made peace with her exit from this world and her transition into the Universe as she would have put it. Appearances and decency were core values and pet Peeves of Mommie dearest, as I lovingly referred to her. She often stated, "Presentation is everything, La Wanda." Over the years we often disagreed with my wardrobe choices and other ideas. She would engage me with her social worker pleasantness, benefit of the doubt terms, and then sneak in a statement of persuasion. She became really good at that social work trick and later she was joined by her team of task force social workers friends, Harriet, Dollie, Carrie, and Delo.

My response was to work on listening tentatively while they lectured, questioned, and tried to solve me the twisted puzzle to no avail. Like most of the women in my family secrecy runs deep, ramped, and often to the grave. You might catch a glimpse of the truth if somebody develops dementia and starts rambling. I would not tell them about my traumatizing incest incidents with my uncle while living in St. Louis. It was unspoken, bottled and sealed, even though he followed me to California. No more incest encounters though. I was never left alone with him or any other men while in Marie's care except for Jim and he was like a daddy always teaching me stuff like driving. I felt safe with him.

    I loved my private team of social workers for their efforts and devoted attention to me. They were all so supportive and would show up to all the little dinners and drama shows I surprisingly scheduled without Marie's knowledge. I can honestly say these ladies encouraged me in drama performances, instrument playing, singing, dancing, and whatever my little heart desired without hesitation or complaint. I know it is the reason that I have become the expressive woman of God I am with creativity and openness to compassion for others, because this was what I was shown, and it is engraved into my DNA. These ladies had a positive impact on my life that showed up years later. Perhaps as time passed Marie and I both understood my style of dressing and backwards thinking (her words), assured my sense of independence and control of something in my life and the emotional baggage I carried.

    I tried to wrap a shawl around Marie's shoulders; She had

on a white and powder blue pinstriped gown while she received company, but she declined taking the shawl. Although I was rattled, I threw it around myself as I avoided anxiety and having a panic attack. This was not like her--she would have asked for a shawl to cover her gown. I watched as she put her arms around people with prolonged hugs wishing them wellness and showing her appreciation for them as no one else could do. I was astonished at her strength to choose her goodbyes! Passive aggressiveness is another strong female and male family trait in our family. It often shadows manipulation through its innuendos and silence. But hey! Like grandma Hattie told me during an ancestral visit, "It didn't begin with you, La Wanda, and it won't end with you, La Wanda." I've decided to accept grandma's wisdom and just do my part. Her last words to me on the phone were, "Take care of the children and do what's next." So, I am taking care of the children and what's next is to publish her story.

Friend, Julie Whitten

I met Marie Simmons in the Sausalito Public Schools in the early 70's when she came to speak to my eighth graders about careers. At the time she had a daughter attending the school, and I was blessed eventually to teach five of her girls. She wore an elegant business suit with Birkenstock sandals, a quirky combination which intrigued me; it suggested a few of her qualities I would come to know: powerful, no nonsense, and down to earth, yet glamorous and unique.

After several years of these excellent and inspiring presentations, Marie and I became close friends. She liked to dress me up in her fine clothes for my Back to School nights, lucky me! We worked together on her CARE program for UCSF and co-led workshops called Journey to Peace. We eventually bought a cabin together in the Russian River redwoods for weekend getaways. When we went places together in her sports car, people asked us if we were the FBI, or drug dealers, or gay. (No.) We were FFL, friends for life, navigating our landmines and celebrating our milestones. We shared many happy hours talking, laughing, praying, meditating, exploring, soaking, shopping, eating, and generally supporting each other's well-being. She convinced me that she heard the voice of the Spirit speaking directly to her. (Her deep faith deepened mine.)

When Marie decided to write a book for her legacy, she asked me if I would help her. This involved meeting every Saturday for over 20 years, with her slowly dictating, and me typing every word. Together we composed, revised, edited, researched, and made the many creative decisions that shaped this remarkable book. Then we would have lunch. I felt it was a great honor to work with her and help preserve her brilliance and wisdom for posterity.

Like Marie, the book is true, honest, inspiring, funny, and profound. It is the account of her experiences and evolving beliefs, from very humble beginnings in St. Louis to the scenic top of the world in the Sausalito hills. She offers profound insights into the psychology of many of her family members, kids, therapy clients, roommates, foster kids, and most importantly, her insights into herself. Besides her many strengths, she fearlessly confronts her own weaknesses and openly shares them with us, and for us.

Remember, it's not personal—it is just her journey to wholeness, and lasting peace. She encourages everyone to find theirs.

Niece, Earlene Weathersby

Marie was a light in the darkness for the family. There was a great need of this light. Marie was a mentor for me providing encouragement in pursuing education, providing wisdom for current and future times. Attempts in continuing this wisdom have been profitable in my life. She was a very generous person. Marie and I had many good times of laughter and enjoyment.

Friend, Dollie Brown

When my family and I moved to Fresno, CA in 1970? Delo Washington, who had been instrumental in recruiting my husband, James Walter Whitehead to the faculty of the School of Social Work at CSUF, came from Stockton, CA to Fresno every weekend to insure I met people and made friends. Delo introduced me to Marie and we became close friends. When Marie became mother to several children in her family, those children became friends of my children. When Marie moved to Sausalito, my family and I paid many visits. I recall how Marie took outstanding care of her mother at home when others may have institutionalized her because of her disabilities. We paid visits of support during that time.

Our friendship was so strong that over 20 years later when my current husband, Jimmy M. Brown and I wanted to take our 9-year-old granddaughter and our 6-year-old grandsons to tour the Bay Area, Marie invited the 5 of us to stay at her home. In spite of the fact that she had housemates, she accommodated us. I will never forget what a fantastic time we had, looking from her home to see the Sausalito Bay and visiting all of the Bay Area sights. Much later, Jim and I shared the wonderful surprise birthday party her children gave her.

Then, there was the time Marie joined us for a week

vacation at a timeshare. I will always treasure the friendship that intervening years of no contact did not diminish. We always picked up as though we had been together the day before rather than years earlier. I was proud of Marie's many trailblazing accomplishments professionally and personally. She was some special, talented, Leader, Administrator, Philanthropist, and Caregiver. She loved her family and always backed them up. God Bless You and Yours and keep you safe from the Virus.

Her niece Evelyn

Marie was my mother's younger sister, the youngest of 13 children. In our early ages, we all played together. We set on the steps, Marie, Earlene, and myself eating candy and talking. Grandmother had us washing out five steps with soap and water for ants. Marie was as close as a sister. We played, bought candy together, but Marie always saved her money. After leaving St. Louis she kept in touch calling, visiting me, I also visited her. I learned to draw closer to God. She paid for Daily Word books for me over 50 years ago. I lost my youngest son in an automobile accident. I never stopped reading it after her order ran out; I've been ordering ever since. I now read the Daily Word daily, bread and breakfast with Jesus.

She laid hands on me when my knees were "hurting so

bad!" I believed she was pleased with me for raising five children, at a very early age. She complimented me on my taking care of them, enjoyed my soul food cooking, and I traveled with her on cruises. She paid for them; Earlene was with us. We had so much fun! I will never forget when Bernice her sister passed away. Marie was one year younger than me, Bernice was one year older than me, and we were all close. At Bernice's funeral, when service were over, when it was time to close the top of the casket, Marie jumped up screaming, "No! don't close it," crying so hard! The church was filled with so many uncontrolled family and friends, it just broke my heart. It hasn't been easy remembering the past. Thank you for allowing me to have a say. I love you, La Wanda.

Friend, Harriet Karis

I first met Marie in the early 1970s when she came to apply for the assistant chief, social work position at UCSF medical Center. I had been hired some two years earlier; and as the department's first Black master's degree social worker, I was overjoyed at the prospect of having a Black woman fill a top administrative position.

When I met Marie, I knew immediately that she was perfect for the job in every way. I prayed with all my heart that she would be selected. Of course, thank God my prayers were answered, and she got the job. So began Marie's illustrious career at UCSF where she was ultimately appointed to Chief of the Department. So too began my friendship with her that spanned over 35 years, a friendship forged by prayer and sustained with devotion and love.

The spiritual connection that Marie and I shared was indeed the cornerstone of our friendship. We would talk for hours on end about matters of the Spirit. She was indeed my spiritual mentor, and she gave me so much. What was so noteworthy about the giving was that it was always a two-way street. Marie was just as open to receiving as she was to giving--of being mentored, if you will, as to mentoring.

There was nothing about Marie that reeked of spiritual pride or arrogance – so that the exchange of support between us was free-flowing and even. I could be transparent with her, and she with me. Because of this, Marie and I were able to serve as whetstones for each other to sharpen our refinement in Spirit. It was this dynamic that made our friendship so special, and for me so irreplaceable.

Marie had a favorite saying that she used quite often; if fact she even ended her voicemail greeting with it – "See God everywhere and in everybody." She indeed put this directive into action in every area of her life. It was the basis of the love that flowed so freely from her. Our friendship was made so much the richer, so much the fuller because of this perspective that Marie brought to it.

The friendship that began in the halls of UC Medical Center and ended up (on the physical plane at least) in a Sausalito bedroom was indeed a magnificent Spiritual journey. The late Ram Dass once wrote," We are all just walking each other home." As I reflect on my friendship with Marie, I see just that--two souls firmly connected in Spirit, walking each other home. Our walk was filled with twists and turns, ups and downs, laughter, tears, joy, and pain; but the one constant was LOVE. All that we shared was in the consciousness of knowing that we were homeward bound. Marie made it first! Heaven rejoices.

Friend, Carrie Frazier

I met Marie in the early 70's when I was a medical social worker at the University of California Medical Center in San Francisco. She was hired as the Assistant Chief of the Social Work department. When I met her, I was totally impressed! She was poised, assertive, gracious, articulate, intelligent and a very classy dresser. Marie was also a very kind and compassionate person and an image of "Black excellence"! Although she was my boss, we became very good friends. She became a role model for me. Marie helped me deal with some of the painful circumstances of my life.

Because of her faith in my abilities and coaching, my self-esteem and confidence increased, and I grew professionally.

What kept the friendship going was her kindness and compassion for her family that extended to mine. My family and hers interacted socially on a regular basis, holidays, birthdays, etc. I learned not to doubt myself as a woman or professionally, think outside the box, and to always seek guidance from the Spirit of the Universe. I gave her my love and respect. We went to lunch often, garage sale shopping, mud bath in Calistoga, CA, and family gatherings. I will never forget her Smile and eyes of compassion, and her gleeful excitement when she found a bargain, or decorated another room in her house.

Friend, Delo Washington

Marie and I were friends. My early memories of her were when she was a psychoanalytical social worker in Stockton and Modesto, California. Marie was a close friend. What kept our friendship going was our mutual interest in the field of social work. We also shared an interest in fashionable clothing. I learned from Marie about applying makeup. I was just a country girl and she taught me all about me all about makeup. Marie was a city urban girl and I was a southern rural girl and we learned from one another, and we blended well. We liked to party and ran up and down the California coast in Marie's car. We loved to dance to the "Shotgun." I will never forget her sensitivity, caring, and thoughtful ways. She was very competent; she was a supervisor at the University of California in San Francisco. I can still see her sitting at her desk sharing her views. She was very courageous.

Sausalito Presbyterian Church, Reverend George Mclaird,

I first met Marie Simmons as "Arundhati" when she began attending weekday classes as well as Sunday services at the Sausalito Presbyterian Church, where at the time, I was the pastor. She became a member of the congregation on September 1, 1997. I don't recall a time when she used her given name around the church or us.

She and I hit it off immediately because of our mutual conservative Christian church upbringing, our love for Black Gospel services and music, our love for Mindfulness/Meditation/Chanting with an Eastern religious practice, as well as an uncharted adventure into speculative theologies such as A Course in Miracles and Swami Muktananda, etc. To these classes she brought a skillful weaving of her education, work experience, religious and spiritual curiosity. She was a Master in the Art of knowing how to live in and dance with a cultural interface between Black, White, and Eastern traditions. A part of every Sunday sermon included an immediate dialogue with the congregation. She often participated by giving a perspective on the subject of the day from all of the above.

She came to our home many times for her or someone else's birthday celebration, or, for lunch or dinner where we gathered without agenda there by letting our hair down. She had a great sense of humor and was a delight to be around. Once at a wedding, we danced. She kept saying, "George, move your hips." Afterward I told her that she had her hands full trying to teach an old White guy how to dance like a Black man. She replied, "If I gave you a few more lessons, you'd be dancing my way." About this we laughed and laughed and laughed.

At memorial service it is often said of the deceased, "He/She will be greatly missed." With Arundhati, that is 100% true. I was blessed to know and love her.

Home is where I know and am known just as I am.
When I am home, I belong. You belong to me. I belong to you.
We belong to one another. In an era of homelessness
A voice deep within us is calling us home
To ourselves, to our bodies, to one another, to
Our planet, to kinship with the whole Universe.
Remember Love is who you are.
See Love everywhere and in everybody.

Arundhati Simmons

Made in the USA
Las Vegas, NV
01 September 2022